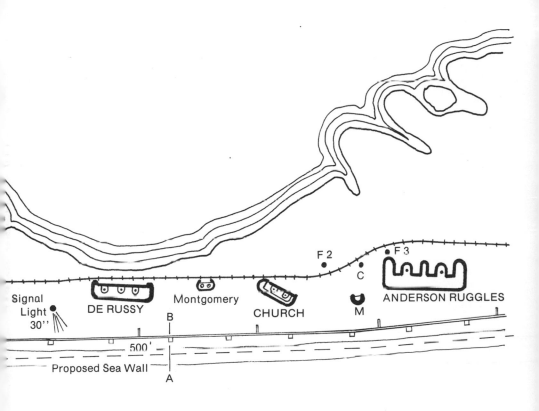

Signal
Light
30''

DE RUSSY

Montgomery

CHURCH

F 2

C

M

F 3

ANDERSON RUGGLES

B

500'

Proposed Sea Wall

A

**Location of Coast Artillery Batteries
Fort Monroe, Virginia in 1910**

Defender of the Chesapeake: The Story of Fort Monroe

by

RICHARD P. WEINERT, JR.

and

COLONEL ROBERT ARTHUR

LEEWARD PUBLICATIONS, INC.   ANNAPOLIS, MD.

DEDICATED TO—

The Soldiers Who Served at Fort Monroe

Foreword to the First Edition

Three hundred and twenty years ago the first fort to be erected in the English-speaking colonies of America was constructed at Point Comfort, on the site later occupied by Fort Monroe. The history of this fort and of its successors is a lesson in preparedness. The first inhabitants of the country, without experience and without precedent to guide them, understood better than did the Virginians of a later date the value of adequate defenses. Through all the early years fortifications sufficient for the needs of the colonists were maintained at Point Comfort, but later, lulled into a false sense of security by their continued immunity from attack, the inhabitants came to the conclusion that defensive measures were an unwarranted burden upon the taxpayers and permitted the fortifications to decay. Their weakness invited attack, and they paid—even as others have paid—for their lack of defense.

Fort Monroe itself, through more than a century of existence, has symbolized preparedness. Born of a need which was only too clearly demonstrated in the second war with Great Britain, it grew slowly and reached its full power at a time when that of the Nation was at its lowest point. With war brought to its very doors, its strength discouraged all thought of attack, and throughout the contest between the North and the South it stood a monument to the foresight of its founders and a guardian of the Nation. In the part it played in the preservation of the Union, in its school now more than a century old, in the development of the science of artillery, and in its ideals and standards, Fort Monroe has established a record in which the Nation and the Army may well take pride.

January 1, 1930

Robert E. Callan
Brigadier General, U.S. Army

Preface to the First Edition

Some fifteen years ago I had occasion to look up some of the details of the history of Fort Monroe and I found, to my surprise, that extremely little of the record of the fort or the Coast Artillery School had ever been put into narrative form. More recently, opportunity has been afforded me to make a more detailed investigation of the available records and literature bearing upon Fort Monroe and the earlier structures of the colonial period, and I have been encouraged to prepare the results of the study for publication. For the colonial period it has been necessary to rely in large part upon secondary authorities, although much has been taken from primary sources, but the record of Fort Monroe itself has come almost entirely from official records, correspondence, and reports. Many interesting, but apocryphal, anecdotes and many legends which may, perhaps, have been founded in fact have been omitted in the interests of accuracy. The imperfections which exist in the book are therefore to be charged to the author, not to the sources from which the material was derived.

The task of completing the manuscript could never have been completed without the assistance received in many places and for which indebtedness must be acknowledged. In particular, I must express my obligations to Brigadier General Robert E. Callan for his encouragement and his suggestions and helpful criticisms; to Mr. Beck and Mr. Sweet, of the Adjutant General's Department, for assistance in searching through old records; to Dr. Randolph G. Adams and his assistants, of the William L. Clements Library of the University of Michigan, for access to many old and rare books; to Mrs. James H. Cunningham for numerous photographs, of which several have been reproduced; to various offices and departments of the Coast Artillery School and the Harbor Defenses of Chesapeake Bay for free access to records, correspondence, and reports; to the Office of the Chief of Coast Artillery for assistance in the preparation of notes; and to Mr. Oliver Friedburger for many details and identifications of the period immediately following the Civil War.

January 1, 1930   Robert Arthur

Foreword to Second Edition

It is in many ways fitting that this history of Fort Monroe should have been published at just this time, at the very beginning of the Nation's third century. The hundredth anniversary of the Civil War not too long ago spurred a major revival of interest in that, as well as other American wars. A decade later, we celebrated for a year or more the bicentennial of the United States itself. Thus, the American people, characteristically turned toward the future, have now paused twice in recent times to look thoughtfully upon their past, upon a nation unique in the world's history, a nation whose idealized abhorrence of war was constantly tempered by an awareness of its own existence within a very real world.

Because of its traditions, its values, and its geography, the United States was in many respects unique in its social, cultural, and technological development. These same factors led as well to a somewhat singular philosophy of defense, at the core of which lay an unusual emphasis upon the protection of the nation's coasts and, particularly, its harbor and river entrances. Until rather late, coast-defense orientation constituted the basic justification for maintaining a sizable navy, and it also led, until the mid-twentieth century, to the construction of seacoast forts in numbers, and of strengths, unsurpassed by those of any country.

Of the hundreds of coastal forts and batteries erected by the United States between the 1790's and World War II, none so well typified this sort of defensive focus as did Fort Monroe. In the 1820's it became the core of the Army's artillery activities in terms of both the training of personnel and the development of doctrine. With the establishment of a separate Coast Artillery Corps shortly after the turn of the twentieth century, Fort Monroe became, as well, the focal point of new developments in the materiel of seacoast defense, and was, as such, the site of the first highly organized and sophisticated efforts in what is today so widely practiced under the heading "Research and Development."

Finally, Fort Monroe was the post to which all regular Coast Artillerymen sooner or later returned; it was here that the spirit of the Corps lived.

When Colonel Robert Arthur wrote the first comprehensive history of Fort Monroe, in 1930, he was for several reasons precluded from presenting a complete account. He could not, for example, deal in detail with the post's then current armament. Nor have subsequent military developments —including those which made Fort Monroe during World War II the headquarters of the most powerful single harbor defense command in the world —been described prior to now.

We are indeed fortunate, finally, to have for the first time a complete history of this post. In extending and, in other ways, improving upon Arthur's original work, Mr. Weinert has given us a first-class account of this outstanding monument to the American defense heritage.

Washington, D.C.   Emanuel Raymond Lewis
March 1, 1978

Preface to the Second Edition

Over forty years ago Colonel Robert Arthur's *History of Fort Monroe* was published by the Coast Artillery School. This book has long been considered a classic history of a military installation. Colonel Arthur not only wrote an excellent history of Fort Monroe, but also contributed a significant study of the development of the Army. He traced the evolution of the colonial fortifications from the founding of the Virginia colony, the development of the massive coastal fortifications resulting from the work of General Simon Bernard, and the evolution of the Artillery School. The school founded at Fort Monroe in 1824 was the first advanced service school in the Army—the beginning of a system which now embraces over twenty schools.

Colonel Arthur's book was published in a very limited edition and has long been out of print. The rapid changes which have taken place since 1930 have also tended to make the book out of date. The approach of the 150th anniversary of the occupation of Fort Monroe—one of the oldest continuously garrisoned posts in the Army—resulted in a proposal to bring Colonel Arthur's book up to date and to republish it. Colonel Arthur, who at the time was living in New Orleans, was approached and generously agreed to a complete revision of his work for publication. Until his death on October 26, 1970, Colonel Arthur contributed valuable help and encouragement to the present work.

In preparing the new edition of this history, considerable rearrangement of the original book was necessary. The part of the present book covering the period before 1930 is for the most part as originally written by Colonel Arthur. The extensive history of colonial Virginia appearing in the original book has been cut approximately in half. Most of the material originally contained in this portion is today readily available in many other works, and only the portion dealing with the colonial defenses has been retained. All but two of the appendices in the original book have been deleted. Because of the peculiar command arrangement which existed at Fort Monroe at the time Colonel Arthur wrote his book, he dealt with the history of the post and of the school separately. The necessity for a separate history of the school no longer exists and that portion has therefore been consolidated with the history of the post to give a chronological presentation. Colonel Arthur relied almost exclusively on the official post records. In the present edition, use has been made of many other sources to round out the history of Fort Monroe.

The last three chapters of this book were prepared by the undersigned to bring Colonel Arthur's history up to the present. For the period to the end of World War II, the *Coast Artillery Journal* has been a major source of information. Much information contained in the chapter dealing with the 1930's comes from diaries kept by Major Harrington W. Cochran, the post adjutant. These diaries are now in the Casemate Museum at Fort Monroe. A basic source for the World War II history is the memoirs of Brigadier General Rollin L. Tilton, the commanding general at Fort Monroe throughout the war. Material in the Historical Office of the U.S. Army Training and Doctrine Command was used in preparing the chapter on the post-war period.

The help and encouragement of many people contributed to the preparation of this new edition. Foremost, of course, was Colonel Robert Arthur himself. Dr. Chester D. Bradley, at the time curator of the Casemate Museum, first urged me to undertake the project and has been a constant source of encouragement, help, and information. Dr. Bradley reviewed the completed manuscript and corrected many errors made by both Colonel Arthur and myself. Brigadier General Rollin L. Tilton has also provided invaluable assistance and encouragement. Besides his World War II memoirs, General Tilton has spent hours recounting his experiences at Fort Monroe from 1909 to 1948, has furnished copies of various documents, and has reviewed the manuscript and provided many helpful suggestions and corrections. Brigadier General Frank S. Clark, Commandant of the Coast Artillery School from 1940 to 1942, has answered many questions covering his service at the post from 1909 to 1942 and provided what is probably the only complete set of *Liaison*. General Clark's memoirs of his wife also contained much interesting material on Army life during this period. Thanks are also due to Brigadier General W. G. Skelton for information about the Chesapeake Bay Sector Mobile Force during World War II. Colonel Manning M. Kimmel, Jr., has provided information on his association with the post from 1913 to the beginning of World War II. Mr. William R. Rodgers, former post information officer, has provided invaluable assistance with research and photographs. Mrs. Martha M. Thomas of the TRADOC Library has been a great help in finding material. Dr. Emanuel Raymond Lewis, Librarian of the United States House of Representatives and an expert on coastal fortifications, has provided encouragement, valuable information, and suggestions. The staff of the National Archives, especially Mr. Elmer O. Parker and his associates, have cheerfully run down many obscure points and contributed their vast knowledge of the records of the old Army. Special thanks are due Mrs. Jo Ann Gauthier, Mrs. Judy H. Alexander, and Mrs. Kathryn C. Vines who typed the manuscript. Without the help and encouragement of the following individuals and organizations this book would not have been possible: Casemate Museum and Casemate Museum Fund Council, Virginia Peninsula Chapter of the Association of the United States Army, Phoebus Civic Association, Old Point National Bank, Fort Monroe Credit Union, Fort Monroe Officers' Wives' Club, Major Marvin E. Stutts, Mr. George Hicks, Lieutenant Colonel Kingston M. Winget, Mr. Jim Peach, Mr. Sam Hayward, Major Robert Hopper, and Captain Michael L. Vice. My wife, Janet, also gave a hand with the proofreading and has patiently endured my explorations of old forts and coast artillery batteries.

The foreword prepared by General Callan in 1930 for the original edition of this history is still valid. This fact is perhaps an indication of the importance of military history. After over forty years the Army has changed and the mission of Fort Monroe is completely different, but the basic importance of national defense remains the same. The threat is different, and Fort Monroe's role in the Army has changed, but the historic old post on Chesapeake Bay is today, as it was in 1930, still a vital link in the national defense of the republic.

Fort Monroe, Va.   Richard P. Weinert, Jr.
March 1, 1978

Table of Contents

Chapter I

Old Point Comfort

NO POST NOW GARRISONED by troops of the United States Army has had a longer record of service to the nation than Old Point Comfort. This point of land on the western shore of Chesapeake Bay has been regarded as a militarily important spot for almost three and three quarters centuries, and it has been occupied more or less continuously by defensive works for most of that period. Other posts—particularly some of those which were established on the western plains—may have been of greater importance in local development and in the expansion of the United States, but none has been more important to the Army itself or has played a greater part in the development of the military efficiency of the nation.

Recognition of the military value of the site of Fort Monroe dates from its earliest exploration. Soon after the colonists established their new homes they began erection of the defensive works at the mouth of the James River. In itself, the construction of seaward defenses for the protection of the colony of Virginia was not singular. It is notable that in practically every colony established in America the two first steps taken by the colonists—Spanish, French, and English alike—were the same. They first erected shelter for themselves and their families, and they then built a fort to face the ocean. With the thousands of miles of seashore from which to choose their new homes and with the hundreds of miles which separated each community from its nearest European neighbor, they all considered seaward defense to be a matter of necessity.

Old Point Comfort is a narrow sand spit forming the extreme tip of the peninsula between the James and York Rivers. It is joined to the peninsula at the northern end by a low strip of sand which has been frequently cut by the waters of Chesapeake Bay. The main portion of Old Point Comfort is separated from the mainland by a small inlet known as Mill Creek. On the east is Chesapeake Bay and on the south Hampton Roads. The mouth of Hampton Roads lies some twenty miles almost due west of the mouth of Chesapeake Bay.

England had made her first attempt to establish a colony in America with the unsuccessful Roanoke Island settlement in the late Sixteenth Century. The mysterious disappearance of this colony resulted in a decline in interest in establishing a colony, but in 1606 two companies were chartered by King James I to make another attempt. The expedition fitted out by the London Company was in readiness before the end of 1606. Three ships were assembled under the command of Captain Christopher Newport: the *Susan Constant,* Captain Newport; the *Godspeed,* Captain Bartholomew Gosnold; and the *Discovery,* Captain John Ratcliffe. These vessels carried 105 colonists. Shortly after Christmas the little fleet set sail down the Thames on its long, tiresome, and uncomfortable trip to the New World. Four months elapsed before the company sighted the American coast. Reaching Cape Henry on April 26, 1607, a part of the company landed and was promptly attacked by Indians, two of the colonists being seriously wounded.

On the following day the company began the construction of a shallop in which a party set forth on April 28 to make a detailed examination of the southern shores of the bay. For a number of hours the exploring party met only with discouragement, for from Lynnhaven Bay to Willoughby Spit they found nothing but shoal water. As the day drew to a close they turned northward and rowed over to a point of land where they found a channel "and sounded six, eight, ten, or twelve fathom," which put them in such "good comfort" that they named the point "Cape Comfort."[1] The "Cape" very shortly became "Point," and when, later, a similar strip of land at the mouth of Mobjack Bay received the name of New Point Comfort, the first point became, logically enough, Old Point Comfort. It is as Old Point Comfort that the site is known to the surrounding communities today, although the present-day exaggeration of the value of time, which leads to haste in action and abbreviation in speech, has shortened the name to "Old Point."

Having named Point Comfort, the party returned to their ships. On April 29 Cape Henry was named, and on April 30 the ships were taken to Point Comfort. Here the colonists saw five Indians running along the shore, so the shallop was manned and a party landed. At first the savages were very timid; but when the captain placed his hand over his heart in token of friendship they laid down their bows and arrows and made signs inviting the colonists to their village, called Kecoughtan. For several days the village remained a base for further exploration along the banks of the James River (then called the Powhatan) and among the neighboring natives.[2]

On May 12, the colonists visited a point of land called Archer's Hope. It was defensible, the soil was good and fruitful, and there was plenty of timber. "If it had not been disliked because the ship could not ride neere the shoare, we had settled there-to all the Collonies contentment," says Percy in his *Discourse*. The following day they decided to make their settlement on a point of land which they named Jamestown—a choice which turned out to be poor but which was made because "our shippes doe lie so neere the shoare that they are moored to the Trees in six fathom[s of] water."[3]

For the first year or two a fort at Jamestown seemed to be sufficient for the needs of the English, but as soon as the colony began to expand beyond the immediate environs of Jamestown, additional fortifications appeared to be necessary for the protection of the lower James. Point Comfort was the logical site, for here, notwithstanding the great width of the James at its mouth, the channel was so narrow that vessels were compelled to approach very close to the shore. John Smith, trading with the Kecoughtan Indians in 1608, had studied Point Comfort and considered this "little Ile fit for a Castle," and the colonists believed that guns mounted there could prevent the passage of hostile ships up the river. A suitable fort thus located would dominate the lower James and would afford complete protection to the settlements above it.[4]

Captain James Davis arrived from England with sixteen men on October 3, 1609. To the company under Davis was added a detachment from Jamestown, and the whole, under Captain John Ratcliffe, was sent to Point Comfort to build the new fort. This work was named "Algernourne Fort" by George Percy, president of the colonial council, in honor of William de Percy, a distant ancestor and first Lord Algernon, who had come to England with William the Conqueror. The use of the name does not appear to have survived Percy's departure for England in 1612. At first, Fort Algernon was nothing more than a simple earthwork, but by 1611 it was well stockaded and contained seven heavy guns and a number of smaller weapons. Its garrison consisted of a company of forty men under the command of Captain Davis, Captain Ratcliffe having been betrayed and killed by the Indians while on a trading expedition up the York during the "Starving Times."[5]

The Jamestown colony, short of provisions and decimated by disease, nearly failed during the dreadful winter of 1609–1610. The colonists had actually started to return to England when the arrival of Lord Delaware in the spring of 1610 with desperately needed provisions saved the colony.

On July 16, 1610, the Kecoughtan Indians killed Humphrey Blunt, one of the colonists, near the point of land on the James River which bears his name. To punish the Indians, Lord Delaware sent out a detachment which destroyed the Kecoughtan village four miles from Fort Algernon on July 19. The governor then ordered the construction below Kecoughtan (Hampton), on the Southampton River, of two forts which were named Forts Henry and Charles.[6] In these two forts, "all those that come out of *England,* shall be at their first landing quartered, that the wearisomeness of the Sea, may be refreshed on this pleasing part of the Countrie."

The location of Forts Henry and Charles was so delightful and the natural resources of the vicinity were so great that the garrison received but one-half of the usual allowances from the public stores. "They stand upon a pleasant plaine, and neare a little Revilet they called Southampton River; in a wholesome aire, hauing plentie of Springs of sweet water, they command a great circuit of ground containing Wood, Pasture and Marsh, with apt places for Vines, Corne and Gardens." Captains Yeardley and Holcroft were placed in command of the two forts, of which Fort Henry stood on the site of the Kecoughtan village and Fort Charles was about a mile or somewhat less further east.[7]

A little later the troops at Forts Henry and Charles were ordered to Jamestown to participate in the ill-advised and fruitless expedition of November 1610, to the Falls of the James to search for gold and silver. After the failure of this enterprise, the two garrisons were retained at Jamestown, and Forts Henry and Charles for a time remained unoccupied. The death rate among the colonists had been so high during the preceding months that the governor considered it expedient to concentrate the colony at Jamestown and Point Comfort only.

After a period of illness, Lord Delaware returned to England to recuperate. His successor, Sir Thomas Dale, arrived at Point Comfort on May 22, 1611, to assume control of the affairs of the colony. As almost his first official act, he inspected Forts Henry and Charles and ordered their repair and reoccupation. Captain Davis, still in the military service of the colony, was appointed "taskmaster" for the three forts—Algernon, Henry, and Charles, our first harbor defense command.

A month after Dale's arrival, the colony received its long-expected visit from the Spaniards. In the latter part of June a Spanish caravel appeared off Point Comfort to spy out conditions among the English in Virginia. After beating to and fro, it landed Don Diego de Molina, Ensign Marco Antonio Perez, and Pilot Francisco Lymbrye to demand a pilot to guide their vessel up the river. Captain Davis, looking upon them as spies, imprisoned all three and sent John Clark aboard the ship to make an effort to bring it closer to the fort. The sailing master, becoming suspicious, made Clark a prisoner and began a parley with the English. Finally, the Spaniard notified the garrison that unless the prisoners were released he would open fire upon the fort. Captain Davis, indifferent to the unfortunate situation of Clark, promptly told the sailing master to "Go to the Devil," whereupon the ship withdrew, carrying Clark with it to Havana.[8]

Antonio Perez died before long, but the other two were ultimately released. Diego de Molina, upon reaching Europe, gave in a letter a description of the Virginia defenses as they were at that time. "At the entrance [into James River] is a fort (*fuerte*) or, to speak more exactly, a weak structure of boards ten hands high with twenty-five soldiers and four iron pieces. Half a league off is another [Fort Charles] smaller with fifteen soldiers, without artillery. There is another [Fort Henry] smaller than either, half a league inland from here for a defense against the Indians. This has fifteen more soldiers."[9]

Worried by the threat of a Spanish invasion to follow this preliminary reconnaissance by a single vessel, Dale wrote to the Prime Minister in August 1611, and requested a "standing army" of two thousand men to enable him to improve his defenses. He proposed to fortify: first, Point Comfort; second, Kiskiack (Chiskiack); third, Jamestown; fourth, Henrico; and fifth, at the Falls of the James. There are no indications that his request received approval, or even serious consideration. It was too manifestly absurd to maintain an army which exceeded in number the colony it was to protect.

In February or March 1612, Fort Algernon was accidentally burned to the ground. At that time the fort consisted of a stockaded earthwork, containing a storehouse, a magazine, and the quarters of the garrison. The armament comprised two pieces of 35 quintales, five of 30, 20, and 18 quintales, and a number of smaller weapons, served by a garrison of forty men. Captain Davis and his men set at once to work to rebuild the fort, and in May some of Captain Argall's men were engaged in "fortifying at the point."

At about this time Captain George Webb was placed in command of Forts Henry and Charles, but a little later the three forts at the mouth of the James were dismantled and placed in the hands of caretaker detachments. Captain Webb was again in command of the forts at Kecoughtan in 1614. In 1616 he had a command of twenty men, of whom one was a minister and eleven were farmers. In 1619, William Tucker was in command.

Captain Argall was appointed governor in 1617, and he arrived in May. He found the fortifications in a poor state of repair and attempted some improvements. Not a great deal was accomplished and when Governor Yeardley returned to the colony in 1619 he found practically no fortifications capable of resisting attack. The climate of Virginia was conducive to rapid decay, and this, combined with the lack of engineering skill among the men of the colony, prevented the erection of enduring works. As a result, from this time to the end of the colonial period the forts quickly fell

into dilapidation and ruin. The London authorities were continually exercised over the defenseless condition of the colony and frequently urged
the construction or reconstruction of defensive works, but the burden of
taxation lay so heavily upon the colonists that they were unable to maintain satisfactorily the desired forts. Combined with a growing sense of
security induced by their continued immunity from attack, there became
an ever increasing tendency to permit the fortifications to fall into complete
ruin.

For several years the colony remained in a state of unpreparedness.
Cannon, many privately owned, were mounted at various places, but
the carriages were made of wood which rotted so quickly that we hear
more of the dismounted guns lying half buried in the sand than we do of
serviceable batteries. The London Company viewed with alarm this evident disregard of the threat to be found in the constantly passing Spanish
vessels, and in 1621, the Company directed Governor Sir Francis Wyatt to
erect fortifications on the larger rivers of the colony. The following year
the Company sent out Captain Samuel Each, of the *Abigail,* to build a fort
in the James River above Blunt Point in modern Newport News. Captain
Each proposed to build a fort, or blockhouse, upon the immense oyster
banks near this point in order to command the passage. This proposal was
considered, but was found to be unfeasible.[10]

Captain Roger Smith reported that a fort upon the shore would command
the channel as well as one in the stream, so he was detailed to supervise
the construction of such work. One man from every twenty in the colony
was drafted for this labor, but, as had happened so often before and was to
happen again, sickness and lack of provisions and supplies caused a suspension of the work. The fort was never completed, and that portion of the
plan which contemplated the erection on Tyndall's Shoals of a platform
large enough to accommodate five or six pieces of ordnance was never
undertaken.

Captain Nathanial Butler, former governor of the Bermuda Islands,
spent some eight months in Virginia in 1622–1623, and upon his return to
England he made public a caustic and somewhat unjust report which he
called "The Unmasked face of our Colony in Virginia as it was in the Winter
of the yeare 1622."[11] Concerning the defenses of the colony, he said: "I
found not the least peec of Fortification. Three peeces of Ordinance onely
mounted at James City and one at Flower-due Hundred, but never a one of
them serviceable Soe itt is most certaine that a smale Barke of one hundred
Tunns may take its time to pass up the River in spite of them and comminge
to an Anchor before the Towne may beate all their houses downe aboute
their eares and so forceinge them to retreat into the woods, may land under
the favour of their Ordinance and rifle the Towne at pleasure."

The governor and the Council, in a general denial of Butler's charges, admitted that "We have, as yet, no Fortifications against a foreign enemy," and pleaded poverty and lack of provisions as their excuse. Taking Butler to task, they went on to say: "His envy would not let him number truly the Ordnance at *James* City: four Demi-Culverin being there mounted, and all serviceable. At *Flower de Hundred* he makes but one of six; neither was he ever there, but, according to his custom, reporteth the unseen as seen. The same envy would not let him see the three pieces at *Newport-News,* and those two at *Elizabeth City.* Two great Pieces there are at *Charles Hundred,* and seven at *Henrico.* Besides which, several private Planters have since furnished themselves with ordinance."[12]

The London Company attempted to settle the discussion in August 1623, by directing the governor to "Proceed with the fort," but the governor and the Council, in the following February, were forced to report that, because of the general sickness of the colonists, they had been obliged to discontinue the work. At about this time a number of Commissioners arrived to inquire into the conditions in the colony. One of their questions was: "What places in the country are best or most proper to bee fortefied or maintayned against Indians, or other enimies that may come by Sea?" To this the Council replied: "Point Comfort is the most use but of great charge and difficulties. Wariscoyake where the fortification was intended [is] more effectual to secure the places above it. From Wyanoke marich upwardes there are divers places which may peremptorily command Shippinge or Boates."

When Captain John Harvey, a member of the Commission, left the colony in 1625, he reported that "of all *the publique stock* which within the past six yeares hath been disbursed there remains no publique work, as guest house, bridge, a store-house, munition-house, publique granary, fortification, church, or the like." The same year the London Company reported to the Board of Trade and Plantations: "As for fortificacon agaynst a forraigne enemy there was none at all, onely four pieces mounted, but altogether unserviceable." These criticisms were reasonably accurate, but nothing further in the matter of fortifications seems to have been done until about 1629. Governor Wyatt, in 1626, asked assistance in the construction of defenses at the mouths of the James and York rivers, and in 1629 the Council declared the colony too poor to undertake unaided the erection of forts. William Pierce stated shortly afterwards that there was "no manner of fortifications" in the colony.

The colonists did not consider forts unnecessary, nor had they lost sight of the military value of Point Comfort. On the contrary, they were fully aware of their exposed situation and they looked upon the occupation of the tip of the peninsula as vital to the safety of the colony. They felt, however, that the expense should be borne by the London authorities rather than by themselves. That they remained defenseless throughout this decade or more resulted from the fact that the authorities would not and the colony could not provide funds for erecting and maintaining forts.

By 1630 the resources of the colony had improved and it was no longer as helpless as it had previously been. The General Assembly, considering that the financial condition of the colony warranted an improvement in its defenses, adopted measures for the construction of an elaborate work at Point Comfort. This new fort was to be more solidly constructed and more permanent in character than any of the preceeding works and the preliminary arrangements were very carefully made. A committee from the Assembly inspected the proposed site, drew up plans, and turned the work over to Captain Samuel Matthews, afterwards governor. Proceeding with expedition, Matthews was able to report in February 1632 that the fort was completed.

In the past, all the forts built in the colony had deteriorated rapidly because there had been no provisions made for their upkeep. In an endeavor to provide for the maintenance of the new work at Point Comfort and four other forts that were built in the next three years, the Council established a system of taxation which was called the "castle duties" or "fort duties." All incoming ships were taxed one-quarter of a pound of powder and a proportionate quantity of shot for each ton of burden, and all immigrants were taxed sixty-four pounds of tobacco to be paid from the first crop.

These taxes varied from time to time. From the very first the ship owners, the traders, the merchants—in fact, all who were directly affected by the taxes—complained loudly and bitterly but to no avail. Despite surreptitious trading, evasions of payment, and petitions, and regardless of the fact that the duties failed in their purpose, the tax remained on the books and tended to increase, rather than diminish, with the passing of years.

Captain Francis Pott, brother of Governor John Pott, was placed in command of the new fort at Point Comfort, but in 1635 he was charged by Governor Harvey with misbehavior and was replaced by Captain Francis Hooke, of the Royal Navy, "an old servant of King Charles." This officer died at Point Comfort in 1637, but during his brief administration his management of the fort was so poor that at his death "there was not soe much powder left in the Fort as would Lode one piece of Ordinance to discharge att his Funerall. But there was due by his Booke fifty pounds of powder to the Fort being Lent by the sayd Capt. Hooke the Summer before to one Lieutenant Upton in case of Distresse and Danger Doubted from the Neighbouring Indians to the Inhabitants of the Isle of Wight County where the sayd Upton is the present commander."

Following Hooke, Captain Christopher Wormeley, one-time governor of Tortugas, was appointed to take charge of the fort. His first care was the replenishment of the powder supply, but this he found a matter of extreme difficulty. All the arriving ship masters objected to making payment to him, claiming that they had paid the proper tax upon their previous departure. What little powder he did secure "was soe bad that it onely served to give every ship a salute at her departure according to the custom of the place."

From the very first, the affairs of the fort seem to have been badly handled and the tax for its upkeep to have been misapplied or wasted. When Captain Richard Morrison, son of Sir Richard Morrison, arrived in March 1639, to relieve Wormeley, there were practically no stores on hand and the fort was in decay. In fact, the General Assembly found it necessary in 1640 to levy a poll tax of two pounds of tobacco on the inhabitants of the colony to effect repairs which practically amounted to a complete reconstruction of the fort, and of three pounds of tobacco to pay a muster master, the captain of the fort, and ten men. Captain Morrison obtained leave of absence in 1641, with permission to visit England, and turned the fort over to his brother, Lieutenant Robert Morrison.

At this time the pay of the garrison, according to the schedule of 1633, was:[13]

	Lbs. Tobacco	Bbls. Corn
To the captain of the fort	2,000	10
To the gunner	1,000	6
To the drummer and porter	1,000	6
For four other men, each of them 500 pounds of tobacco, 4 barrels of corn	2,000	16
Total	6,000	38

Until 1642 tobacco was the sole medium of exchange in the Virginia colony, but with the increase in population came over-production and a consequent depreciation in value. Hence, in 1645, it was ordered that the commanding officer at the fort at Point Comfort should be paid out of the "quit rent by leases" due the Commonwealth from Northampton County.

In 1650 Governor Berkeley received authority to build forts of "lime and stone and other materials," but he made no attempt for some time to avail himself of this privilege. In 1649, Major Francis Morrison, another brother, was appointed by Governor Berkeley to the command, and in about 1664 Colonel Charles Morrison, son of Richard Morrison, succeeded to the command of the fort, which had again fallen into a sad state of disrepair.

For many years the traders and ship owners had protested against the fort duties, but now they made a determined effort to have this tax abolished on the grounds that the fort had become entirely useless and offered no protection. The duties had been too long established to yield to such pressure as the shipping interests could bring to bear. The receipts, however, were not being applied to their proper purposes. The outbreak of war between England and Holland in 1665 caught the colony unprepared, and the uselessness of the fort at Point Comfort was tacitly admitted by the withdrawal of Colonel Miles Cary (then in command), with the garrison and the ordnance, to Jamestown.

Following the outbreak of war, the king directed that fortifications be erected on the several rivers of the colony to serve as a protection to the shipping in case of attack. The Virginia authorities did not take the instructions very seriously. They constructed nothing more than a few breastworks, save at Jamestown, where a somewhat more pretentious work was erected by Captain William Bassett.

From the day of its first examination until the advent of Governor Berkeley, the value of Point Comfort as a site for defensive works was fully and generally recognized. The point had, at times, been undefended, but this had resulted more from necessity than from choice. Whenever the state of colonial finances had permitted, a fort had been maintained at Point Comfort and had been garrisoned. During the Berkeley regime, however, there became apparent a very manifest desire on the part of the governor to locate the James River fort at Jamestown—possibly because he, as senior officer present, would receive the fort duties. He therefore made no effort to keep the fort at Point Comfort in repair, and it soon became entirely useless.

The merchants and traders, having failed to have the fort duties abated, now professed themselves to believe that they were entitled to the protection for which they paid. Although a fort at Jamestown would protect the inhabitants further up the river, a fort at Point Comfort would afford the same protection and would also cover both shores of the lower James and its tributaries—a point which could not be claimed for defenses higher up. Presenting these representations very forcibly, they induced the English authorities to direct that Point Comfort be reoccupied and the fortifications restored.

In protest, Secretary Ludwell wrote Colonial Secretary Lord Arlington on July 8, 1666, that the Assembly had ordered the construction of a large fort at Jamestown—to mount fourteen pieces of ordnance—where the inhabitants would be a sufficient guard to man it, without any charge to the country, but that this could not be done in the face of the king's command to build the fort at Point Comfort. He pointed out the evils attending the erection of the latter fort and trusted that the order might be countermanded. He trusted unavailingly, and the order stood as issued.

In view of his positive instructions, the governor gave his very reluctant consent to the new project, and the guns were returned to Point Comfort. An entirely new work seems to have been planned; but considerable difficulty was encountered in erecting a fort on the loose subsoil of sand, expenses mounted beyond the estimates, and the work progressed slowly. Finally, all construction stopped, and the Council requested the governor to petition the king for authority to discontinue the project.[14]

It is not clear just why the Assembly at this time should have been so heartily in accord with the views of the governor concerning the fort at Point Comfort, except as a matter of political expediency. A complaisant committee from the Assembly recommended against the fortification of Point Comfort on the grounds that the channel was of greater width than had been generally supposed, that the cost would be prohibitive, that the population of the vicinity was unduly sparse, that there was a lack of fresh water, and that the surrounding country was not sufficiently fertile to be of assistance in supporting the garrison.

As a counter-project, the committee proposed the erection of five forts: one at Yeocomoco, on the Potomac River; one at Chorotoman, on the Rappahannock River; one at Tyndall's Point, on the York River; one at Jamestown, on the James River; and one at some suitable point on the Nansemond River. Despite considerable opposition, the recommendations of the committee were approved by the House of Burgesses, and by the end of 1667 the project was fairly under way.[15]

Point Comfort was added to the program of fort building in 1667 after a painful demonstration of the necessity of keeping the mouth of the James blocked. While the point was entirely deserted, the Dutch suddenly entered the river and captured or burned a number of vessels laden with tobacco. In consequence, Colonel Leonard Yeo was, in June 1667, authorized to impress men and material for mounting eight guns at Point Comfort, and Dunbar Gowing was appointed chief gunner.

This project also went awry, for "on the 27th of August followed the most Dreadful Hurry Cane that ever the colony groaned under. It lasted 24 hours, began at North East and went around northerly till it came to west and soe on till it came to South East where it ceased. It was accompanied with a most violent raine, but no Thunder. The night of it was the most Dismall tyme that ever I knew or heard of, for the wind and rain raised soe Confused a noise, mixt with the continuall Cracks of falling houses and the murmur of the waves impetuously beaten against the Shoares and by that violence forced and as it were crowded up into all Creekes, Rivers and Bayes to that prodigious height that it hazarded the drowning [of] many people who lived in sight of the Rivers, yet were forced to climbe to the topp of their houses to keep themselves above water. [The waves] carryed all the foundation of the fort at Point Comfort into the River and most of our Timber which was very chargeably brought thither to perfect it. Had it been finished and a garison in it, they had been Stormed by such an enemy as noe power but Gods can restrain and in all likelyhood drowned."

The very foundations of the fortifications at Point Comfort having been destroyed, nothing further was done on that site for a number of years, despite the desires of the merchants. Even the upkeep of the other forts was found burdensome and they were allowed to fall into decay, so that within three years after their construction they were practically in ruins.

On September 30, 1668, the king, in an autograph letter to "his well-beloved Governor of Virginia," recommended Thomas Beale, Esquire, "of whose abilities the King had had long experience, to be Commandant of His Majesty's fort or castle called 'Castel Comfort,' near York river, which has been for some time void, or if that has been disposed of, to any other fort or castle." The "castle" being, as we have seen, more formidable in name than in fact, the superior abilities of Captain Beale were insufficient to increase its importance in a military sense.

Until about 1670 the fort at Point Comfort appears to have been the most important military work within the colony, but it is difficult to determine its strength or the precise character of the fortifications at any particular time. A statute of 1657 prescribed that "each ffort shall be capable of eight greate guns at the least, the walls tenn foote thick at least." It appears probable that the works at Point Comfort were generally of greater strength and armament than this prescribed minimum, but they were seldom of a value which should have been expected from their size and armament. The cause was, of course, lack of funds for maintenance and lack of skill in the construction. Sir William Berkeley, writing to the Lords Commissioners of Plantations in 1671 regarding the military condition of the colony, enumerated the forts and added:

> But God knows we have neither skill nor ability to make or maintain them; for there is not, nor, as far as my inquiry can reach, ever was, one inginier in the country, so that we are at continual charge to repair unskillful and inartificial works of that nature. There is not above thirty great and serviceable guns; this we yearly supply with powder and shot, as far as our utmost abilities will permit us.

In 1672, the Assembly ordered that thereafter all repairs to forts, unless of a minor character, should be of brick; but only the fort at Jamestown benefited at the time. As a consequence, the colony once again suffered from its lack of fortifications, for in 1673, a Dutch man-of-war destroyed a number of vessels lying in James River. The merchants had continued to urge fortifications at Point Comfort, but none of the other colonists were interested except in Isle of Wight and Lower Norfolk counties. Here, the inhabitants, conscious of their need for protection obtained authority from the General Assembly in 1673 to build a fort on Warrsquoick Bay and another on Elizabeth River; but they felt that more was required than this. In 1676, they petitioned the governor that a fort "be erected att *point Comfort* as being the most conuenient place (as wee humbly conceaue)."[16]

The growing disinclination of the colonists, as a whole, to the maintenance of fortifications seems to have reached its climax at about this time. For the remainder of the century there were no more signs of interest in defensive works. The existing forts were allowed to fall gradually into decay, and one by one they were abandoned. In 1681, shortly after his arrival, Lord Culpeper inspected all the forts and declared that none could withstand attack, either by land or by sea. In 1685, Fort James, on the York River, and Jamestown, on the James River, still had some serviceable guns in commission; but the other forts had almost entirely fallen to pieces, with their cannon lying, for the most part, half buried in the sand. Governor Nicholson, in 1690, reported the fortifications in ruins.[17] Some slight effort to effect repairs was made shortly after this; but in 1695 the fort at Jamestown was demolished, and in 1699 the governor and the Council recommended that all forts be allowed to sink into complete ruin.

The general outbreak of war in Europe in the opening days of the eighteenth century again turned the attention of the governor of the colony of Virginia toward the question of colonial defense. Among the inhabitants of the colony little or no interest was evinced. They had suffered so little from foreign aggression during the preceding century that they no longer felt alarm whenever the countries of Europe went to war. Nevertheless, Governor Spottswood reported that he "was of the opinion that a small fort built upon Point Comfort would be of good use." When, later, rumors of the approach of a French fleet reached Virginia, the governor was stirred to immediate activity. Without waiting to call together the General Assembly, he contracted numerous debts by erecting fortifications. By the latter part of 1711, he had about seventy cannon mounted at Old Point Comfort (which had become "Old" by this time), at Tyndall's Point, at Yorktown, and at Jamestown.[18]

In 1712, Governor Gooch assembled the legislature and, in his opening message, called attention to the unprotected state of the coast and the frontier. He advised the repair of forts and the appointment of annual salaries for the officers and the gunners required for the garrisons and he recommended that the fort at Old Point Comfort be kept in a state of constant readiness. However, forts had so long been objects of aversion that the people were extremely frugal whenever appropriations for defensive works were under consideration. Right though he was, the governor was disinclined to argue the question and not a great deal was accomplished.

For a number of years after this, little is recorded concerning the fort at Old Point Comfort. It was not altogether abandoned, and we learn that George Walker, grandfather of George Wythe, was in charge of the battery at that point in 1722 as "gunner and storekeeper."

At the meeting of the Assembly in 1728, the question of repairs to the works at Old Point Comfort was again recommended for special consideration. Being more responsive than the legislature of sixteen years earlier, the House of Burgesses appointed a committee to "inquire into the present condition of the Battery at Point Comfort, and the fittest place for erecting a battery there."[19] The committee made its examination and reported, early in March, that it had found twenty large cannon, constructed of iron, some of them badly honey-combed, and that it had located a suitable site for a battery. It considered that a round dozen guns would be sufficient for the safety of the colony, and it recommended that twelve of the best guns be again mounted. The House, upon consideration of the report, expressed itself as favoring the project.[20]

Funds having been appropriated, work was started at once upon the most substantial and most elaborate fortification that the colony had ever undertaken. The new fort was built of brick and shell lime in two lines of walls about sixteen feet apart near the present site of the lighthouse. The bricks, homemade, were nine inches long by four inches wide by three inches thick. The exterior wall was twenty-seven inches thick, while the interior was but sixteen inches thick. The two walls were connected by a series of counter-ports ten or twelve feet apart, forming a system of cribs, which were filled with sand. With this wall of brick and sand sixteen feet in thickness, the fort had a substantiality that was more apparent than real, for the brick retaining walls were woefully thin. A breach in the outer wall would endanger the whole structure.[21]

Since the weakness of the work would not be apparent under a casual inspection, the colonists were satisfied. Governor Gooch reported, in 1736, that "no ship could pass it without running great risk." In honor of the reigning king, the work was named Fort George, and it was the original of that name, although the name is now sometimes applied to earlier works. Upon completion, it was placed under the command of Captain Samuel Barron, the ancestor of a distinguished line of naval officers.

When the General Assembly met in 1742 the war with Spain was still going on, but the Virginians displayed little interest. Fort George had been built in preparation for the war, but since its erection it had received little or no care. Governor Gooch, in his message to the Assembly, suggested that money be appropriated for the repair of the batteries at Yorktown and Gloucester Point and for keeping these batteries and Fort George in a constant state of defense. To this the Assembly replied that, although these desirable objects ought by all means to be attended to, the expense should be defrayed from the duties appropriated by Act of Assembly for that purpose and that those duties should suffice. With the Assembly in such a temper, there was little that the governor could hope to accomplish.[22]

During the same session of the Assembly, the question of title to the land at Old Point Comfort came up for settlement, Colonel William Beverly presenting a claim that his father, Robert Beverly, had advanced at an earlier date. There had long been a contest over this matter of ownership. Colonel Beverly claimed that the land, consisting of 120 acres, had been granted to his father by patent on May 2, 1706, and that he was therefore entitled to 120 pounds sterling as reimbursement.

As early as 1628, "Elizabeth Jones, wife of Giles Jones, gent.," was granted 100 acres "as her own personal dividend, being an ancient planter, said land being in the 'Island of Point Comfort,' abuting easterly upon the bay of 'Chesapeiache' and westerly upon the creek which divided said island from the main land." This seems to cover the identical land to which Colonel Beverly laid claim, but it is probable that the original title had been escheated long before 1706 and that it had been repatented after being abandoned as a fort prior to 1700. At any rate, the Beverly claim was referred to the Attorney General for investigation and report.

The outcome was favorable to Beverly, and in 1744 "the said William Beverly for and in Consideration of the Sum of One hundred and five Pounds Current Money to him in hand paid at or before Ensealing and Delivery of these Presents the Receipt whereof he doth acknowledge Hath Granted bargained sold aliened released Enfoeffed and confirmed unto the said William Gooch his Heirs and Assigns for ever All that Neck or Point of Land Sand and Marsh on the South West End of Point Comfort containing about one hundred and twenty acres . . ." William Gooch was lieutenant governor of Virginia at the time and was apparently acting for the Dominion, as the deed was endorsed: "Beverly to the Governor, Deed, Re'd E'd 1744."

In his address to the session of the Assembly which met in 1744, Governor Gooch again raised the question of the provision of adequate defense for the colony. He particularly recommended the repair of the batteries at Yorktown and Gloucester Point and asked for an appropriation to provide for the maintenance of a garrison at Fort George.[23] After the usual prolonged deliberation, the Assembly voted a small sum of money for repairs to the fort at Old Point Comfort.

In 1745, because of the relations then existing between England and France, the colony was advised to put itself in readiness against the dangers which threatened. The governor accordingly convened the Assembly. During considerations of a bill for the repair and maintenance of the colonial forts, it was discovered that nothing adequate to the supposed contingencies could be accomplished because of the determined economy of the Assembly. The proponents of preparedness asked for too much and received nothing, for the bill, after a long and lively debate, was decisively defeated.

It was perhaps, fortunate for the colony that the Assembly kept such a close grip upon the colonial purse strings, for the expenditures, in so far as Fort George was concerned, would have availed nothing. In 1749, that fort fell a victim to another terrific and disastrous hurricane. Captain Barron and the garrison lived in a row of wooden buildings with brick chimneys running up through the center of the roofs. These buildings were somewhat protected by the walls of the fort, but when Captain Barron noticed the approach of the storm and saw that it was to be unusual, he caused his family and the officers and men of the garrison to assemble on the second floor with all the weighty articles they could carry. The protection afforded by the fort and the anchorage provided by the chimneys and the heavy articles carried into the houses kept the buildings firm on their foundations and saved the lives of the garrison, but the fort itself was completely demolished.

With the destruction of Fort George, colonial coastline fortifications in Virginia practically came to an end, for none of the other forts or batteries received any further attention. Early in 1756, Governor Dinwiddie reported to the Lords Commissioners for Trade and Plantation that "we have no forts in y's Dom'n. There was one erected at the mouth of Jas. River, but as it was built on a Sandy Foundat'n, the Sea and Weather destroy'd it [so] y't the Guns lie dismounted, and [are] of no Use. There are two small Batteries on York River, [which] are only of Service to protect the Merch't Ships in y't River, and of no Defence ag'st an Enemy y't have Force sufficient to attack them [by] Land, or a Ship [with] Force to run up the River, may demolish them both."

A year later, Dinwiddie made a more detailed report, in which he said: "I beg Leave to inform y'r L'd'ps y't there are three Fort in y's Dom'n, one called F't George, at the Mouth of James River, where I went to view it. It was built on a Sandy Bank; no care [was taken] to drive piles to make a Foundat'n; the Sea and Wind beating ag'st it has quite undermin'd it and dismantled all the guns, w'ch now lie buried in the Sand. There was mounted on y's Fort ten twenty-four Pounders, six twelve-Pounders and four nine-Pounders, all Honey-comb and fit for no Service. They were sent in here by Queen Elizabeth and King Charles. They have always been expos'd to the Weather so y't they are fit for no Service. The other two forts are on York River, one at the Town of York, had mounted 4 Guns of 18 and 9-P'rs, 10 Small G[uns] of ½ shot, but the large Guns are all Honey-Comb and not fit for Service. The other Fort at Gloucester, on the same River, had 15 Guns of 18, 12 and 6-pounders, mounted, but like the others, not fit for Service. These three Places are very proper for Forts as they are at the Entrance of [the] two greatest Rivers, or most Conseq'ce in y's Colony. The Batteries are in most ruinous Condit'n, tho' considerable Sums have been laid out upon them, yet for want of a skilled Ingineer to direct the Construct'n, particularly in making a good Foundat'n, the Tide and Weather have undermined the walls."[24] In connection with this report, the governor also recommended the location of a fort at Cape Henry, the first time that this point had been considered as a site suitable for fortifications. It was thought that twenty 24-pounders would be sufficient armament for the fort to be located at the entrance to Chesapeake Bay.

There is no evidence to indicate that the governor received either forts or guns. Troops being unnecessary at a demolished fort which was apparently not to be restored in the immediate future, the garrison at Fort George was reduced to a single man. In 1774 one John Dames was charged with the care of the ruins remaining at Old Point Comfort.[25] Time hanging heavily on his hands, he began exhibiting a light at night for the benefit of passing vessels. In the course of time the advantages of a light at the point came to be recognized by the authorities, and in 1775, as a reward to Dames, the House of Burgesses voted him a salary of twenty pounds per annum, to continue until the Cape Henry Light, which was then being built, should be completed.

The early years of the Revolutionary War naturally brought about a revival of interest in coast defense. By 1777, several points in the colony had been ineffectively fortified, the most important work being Fort Nelson, on the western side of Elizabeth River, some distance below Portsmouth. These works failed to prevent invasion at will by the British, who sent a number of expeditions into Virginia. The situation was concisely reported in 1781 by Silas King, who, writing to the governor on March 27 to announce that a fleet of thirty ships had entered Hampton Roads, said: "Must not our situation be deplorable. Our only protection is a Guard of six men below Old Point Comfort, and a guard of twelve men at Newport News, which suffered 17 Boats full of Troops to land and make about fifty Fires, and let them go off without their discovering them. How sorry I am that we should have only such men to trust to."

At the time Lord Cornwallis withdrew from Richmond to Portsmouth in 1781, Fort George had not been restored. Sir Henry Clinton, commanding the King's forces in America, urged the establishment of a defensive position and a naval rendezvous at Old Point Comfort, with occupation of Yorktown, if necessary, to strengthen the situation at the tip of the peninsula. Cornwallis had the site of Fort George examined by a board of officers, and after their report made an inspection himself. All being unanimous in the rejection of the proposed location, the British army seized and fortified Yorktown and Gloucester Point, on the York River. The principal objections to a station at Old Point Comfort were that no drinking water was to be found in the vicinity, that material for construction of the defenses would have to be brought from a distance, that the site was so low that attacking ships would have the advantage of plunging fire, and that the armament present with the British forces could not effectually close the channel so as to provide a safe anchorage for ships in Hampton Roads. These disadvantages were not present at Yorktown, but that point had a greater disadvantage in that it was particularly vulnerable to land attack. In consequence, the fortifications at Yorktown and Gloucester Point were surrendered to General Washington in October, after the siege which followed the most notable concentration of troops taking place during the war.

While the siege of Yorktown was in progress, Admiral de Grasse, commading the French West Indian fleet, assisted by taking station in Chesapeake Bay and preventing the British fleet from entering and relieving Lord Cornwallis. Although de Grasse had secured temporary command of the sea by his junction with Admiral de Barras, commanding the French Atlantic fleet, from Newport, he had no assurance that the British could not unite in sufficient strength to force him out of the bay before the siege could be brought to a successful conclusion. For the purpose of strengthening his position, he landed cannon and mortars from his ships, manned by both soldiers and sailors, and threw up a battery among the ruins of Fort George. The French soldiers at Old Point Comfort standing on the beach at Buckroe could hear the cannonading at Yorktown. With the successful completion of the siege, the fleet returned to Old Point Comfort in November and re-embarked the ordnance and its crews. With cannon firing a salute and the soldiers and sailors cheering, the fleet sailed out through the Capes.[26]

With the withdrawal of the French fleet after the siege of Yorktown, Old Point Comfort was again abandoned. De Grasse's battery was not replaced by any sort of defense work until after the second war with England.

From the arrival of the first English colonists, the military importance of Old Point Comfort had been recognized. But recognition of this fact and doing something about it had proven to be two different things. What meager fortifications that were erected on the site were soon allowed to fall into ruin. Lack of interest on the part of the colonists and the failure to develop and promote a defense policy on the part of both the British and colonial governments prevented any lasting fortifications from being erected on Old Point Comfort. With the American victory at Yorktown, the British were gone. Now the new nation would first have to recognize the importance of the site and then finally erect a permanent fort.

Footnotes Chapter I

1 George Percy, "A Discourse of the Plantation of the Southerne Colonie in Virginia by the English, 1606," in Edward Arber, *Travels and Works of Captain John Smith* (Edinburgh: John Grant, 1910), Vol. I, p. lxiii.

2 *Ibid.*, pp. lxiii–lxiv.

3 *Ibid.*, p. lxvi.

4 Charles Campbell, *History of the Colony and Ancient Dominion of Virginia* (Philadelphia: J. B. Lippincott and Co., 1860), pp. 59, 75.

5 Lyon G. Tyler, (ed.), *Narratives of Early Virginia, 1606–1625* (New York: Barnes and Noble, Inc., 1966), p. 200.

6 *Ibid.*, p. 202; William Stith, *History of the First Discovery and Settlement of Virginia* (Williamsburg, 1747), p. 120.

7 Stith, *loc. cit.*

8 *Ibid.*, p. 138.

9 Tyler, *op. cit.*, pp. 223–224.

10 Campbell, *op. cit.*, pp. 169–170.

11 *The Records of the Virginia Company* (Washington: Government Printing Office, 1906), Vol. II, pp. 11–13, 23, 383–387.

12 *Journals of the House of Burgesses, 1619–1658/59* (Richmond, 1905–1915), p. 24.

13 Campbell, *op. cit.*, p. 188.

14 *Journals of the House of Burgesses, 1659/60–1693*, p. 42.

15 *Ibid.*, pp. 46–47.

16 *Ibid.*, p. 109.

17 *Executive Journals of the Council of Colonial Virginia* (Richmond: Virginia State Library, 1925) Vol. I, pp. 132, 433.

18 *Journals of the House of Burgesses, 1702/3–1705, 1705–1706, 1710–1712*, p. lxi.

19 *Journals of the House of Burgesses, 1727–34, 1736–40*, p. 24.

20 *Ibid.*, p. 26.

21 Letter, R. Archer to Wm. Maxwell, March 22, 1847, in Virginia Historical Society.

22 *Journals of the House of Burgesses, 1742–1747, 1748–1749*, p. xv.

23 *Ibid.*, p. 76.

24 *Collections of the Virginia Historical Society* (Richmond, 1882–1892), Vol. IV, p. 342.

25 *Journals of the House of Burgesses 1773–1776*. Letter, Dr. Edward M. Riley, Director of Research, Colonial Williamsburg, to Dr. Chester D. Bradley, December 2, 1965, in Casemate Museum.

26 "History of Fort Monroe, 1607–1884," ms. in National Archives, Records of the Chief of Ordnance, Record Group 156, Entry 1231. Hereafter records in the National Archives are indicated by the symbol NA, followed by the record group (RG) number.

Chapter II

Forging the Shield

EXCEPT FOR A PITIFULLY SMALL force to police the frontier, the new United States did not possess a permanent military capability. In the early years of the republic reliance was placed almost exclusively on the state militias. As early as 1791, however, President George Washington urged the construction of coastal fortifications. Despite the war in Europe which on occasion appeared to threaten the American coast, the refusal of Congress to devise a national defense policy thwarted the construction of coastal forts by the national government.

As international tensions increased, several of the individual seaboard states began to be concerned with their own defense. In 1793, Governor Henry Lee of Virginia detailed Thomas Newton, Jr. to make an inspection of the shores of Virginia. In a report to the governor, Newton recommended: "The most proper places on our river for defense are Old Point Comfort & Point Nelson—the places where the old Fort stood, nearly opposite to us & half a mile out of Portsmouth."[1]

Pressure for a coastal defense system continued, and Congress finally on February 28, 1794, submitted a statement of estimates and recommendations as to the kinds of works that should be erected and their locations. Secretary of War Henry Knox selected the engineers to direct the erection of the fortifications. As had been the case during the Revolutionary War, he relied for the most part on French engineers. Major John Jacob Ulrich Rivardi received the assignment to Baltimore and Norfolk. He reached Norfolk early in May 1794. The sandy soil at the site on the east side of the Elizabeth River just north of Norfolk made the erection of the parapet of the fort difficult and expensive, but Governor Lee enthusiastically assisted, and a great deal of labor was donated by the citizens. Directly across the Elizabeth River, on the site of the present Portsmouth Naval Hospital, Fort Nelson was built at the same time. Tiny Fort Norfolk still stands in downtown Norfolk, one of the few remnants of the first fortification system surviving, but Fort Nelson has long since disappeared. Dissatisfaction arose almost immediately because the fortifications were too far removed from Portsmouth and Norfolk to afford the protection which the citizens expected, but Rivardi was able to report on December 9, 1794, that the works were almost completed.[2]

The fortification program ran into many difficulties and on April 9, 1798, Secretary of War James McHenry requested $30,000 for establishing new fortifications at Old Point Comfort and at Fort Nelson. After an acrimonious debate, Congress appropriated $250,000 for fortifications without specifying places or amounts for any particular ports. As a result, nothing was done to fortify Old Point Comfort. President Thomas Jefferson on December 1, 1801, declared that coast fortifications cost too much and required too many men to maintain. As a result of this attitude, no further appropriations were made for six years. Increasing tension between the United States and England resulted in the inauguration of a second series of coastal forts in 1807. In the Hampton Roads area, Fort Nelson, which had been begun on the western side of the Elizabeth River in 1794 and extensively repaired and improved in 1802–1804, was again repaired in 1808. Fort Nelson was an irregular work, defended by whole and half bastions, built of brick and sods,inclosed in the rear by a brick parapet, and mounting thirty-seven guns. Fort Norfolk, on the north-eastern side of the Elizabeth River and about 1,000 yards from Fort Nelson, was also rebuilt in 1808–1809. It was an irregular inclosed work of masonry, comprehending a semi-elliptical battery, defended on the flanks and rear by irregular bastions, and mounting thirty heavy guns. A final work, Fort Powhatan at Hood's Point far up the James River, was begun in 1808, but never completed. This was a strong battery of masonry, intended for thirteen guns. Still no action was taken in regard to Old Point Comfort.[3]

The forts erected under the first system of 1794 were crude by European standards. Some of them had revetments of timber, or in rare instances stone, but most were of unsupported earth. The American engineers who designed the second system of 1807 used open batteries, masonry-faced earth works, or masonry forts. The rapidity with which the forts of these two defense projects fell into decay showed that true economy lay in the erection of fortifications of a more enduring character and that even the most substantial defenses deteriorated quickly when not under the care of a permanent garrison. The experiences of the War of 1812 had also exposed the vulnerability of the entire maritime frontier, despite the completion of the forts of the 1807 project.

The British gave a convincing demonstration of the exposure of the American coast during the War of 1812. In June 1813, a British fleet entered the unprotected mouth of Hampton Roads. An attempt to capture Norfolk was thwarted by temporary American defenses at Craney Island. Fort Norfolk, far up the Elizabeth River near the city, never had a chance to get into the fight. The frustrated invaders turned their attention to the other side of Hampton Roads and easily dispersed the militia and captured Hampton. The sacking of Hampton was one of the darker episodes of the war. The following year, in August 1814, the British sailed up Chesapeake Bay unopposed and landed an army behind Washington. At the same time, a naval force pushed up the Potomac River. Fort Warburton, guarding the nation's capital, was blown up by its garrison without a fight and the Royal Navy occupied Alexandria while the army burned Washington. An attempt to capture Baltimore the next month was frustrated by the gallant defense of Fort McHenry. This fort had been erected at the same time as Fort Norfolk, but happily a better site had been selected. During the final year of the war, the British occupied the Maine coast from Penobscot Bay to Passamaquoddy Bay and generally terrorized the coastal areas of Massachusetts and Connecticut.[4]

The indiscriminate and uncoordinated erection of fortifications along the Atlantic seaboard between 1807 and 1812 had induced a false sense of security. The result was disillusionment, the expenditure of great sums of money, and the employment of large numbers of men in ineffectual attempts to provide coastal fortifications. Two lessons the country learned: That forts in themselves provide no protection, and that forts improperly sited are worse than no forts at all.

Dismayed by the incredible expenses which had resulted from want of proper preparation and the demonstrated vulnerability of the extensive coast line, the government took measures designed to provide an effective coast defense. The first step was taken by Acting Secretary of War George Graham, who, on November 16, 1816, ordered a board of officers consisting of Brevet Brigadier General Simon Bernard, Major (Brevet Colonel) William McRee, Major (Brevet Lieutenant Colonel) Joseph G. Totten, Captain J. D. Elliott, of the Navy, and the local Engineer Officer, to make reconnaissance of the various sections of the coast line and to recommend the fortifications considered necessary for an adequate coast defense.

Bernard, who in effect became the father of the coastal fortification system, was born on April 22, 1779, in Dole (Jura) in that section of France formerly known as Franche-Comte. His father was a poor workman without education. Young Bernard had a natural brilliance of intellect which aroused the interest of a kindly priest who gave him lessons. The boy showed a special aptitude for the physical sciences and won honors at the college of Dole. He went to Paris in 1794 to continue his studies at the

Ecole Polytechnique. Bernard graduated second in his class and entered the Engineers Corps of the French Army with the rank of lieutenant in 1797.

Bernard took part in the siege of Philipsburg in Germany, in 1799. He was wounded in the left arm at Mannheim. During Napoleon's second Italian campaign, Bernard, now a captain, distinguished himself at the capture of Ivrea on May 22, 1800. He was in the Battle of Montebello on June 9, and during the passage of the River Mincio on December 26, he was wounded in the knee. The young officer first attracted the attention of Napoleon in 1805 by his successful conduct of a secret intelligence mission in southern Germany and in Austria. He collected information for use in the campaign which was to climax with the defeat of the Austrians at Austerlitz. Bernard reported to the Emperor in person, who was strongly impressed by his personality. The next year Bernard was sent to Dalmatia to fortify Trieste and Ragusa. He returned to France in July 1809, and was sent to Antwerp to design and construct fortifications. In 1811, Bernard was promoted to the rank of major. Bernard was promoted to colonel and made an aide-de-camp to Napoleon on January 21, 1813. He was present at the victories of Lutzen and Bautzen in May 1813. Shortly before the Battle of Dresden in August he broke his leg in a fall from his horse. Despite his still disabled leg, Bernard took an active part in the defense of the Fortress of Torgau following the Battle of Leipzig. Torgau fell on January 8, 1814, after a siege of three months. Bernard was made a Baron of the Empire and promoted to brigadier general on March 23, 1814.

Following the downfall of the Empire, Bernard remained in the French Army under the restored monarchy. King Louis XVIII permitted him to retain the rank of brigadier general. During the Hundred Days, Bernard again served as Napoleon's aide-de-camp. He was with Napoleon at the Battle of Waterloo. This time Louis XVIII was not so generous. Bernard was banished from public life, but was able to get permission to migrate to the United States. He arrived in Washington in the fall of 1816 with a letter of recommendation from the Marquis de Lafayette.[5]

President Madison appointed Bernard assistant engineer with the pay and emoluments of a brigadier general on November 16, 1816. Although his exact legal position in the Army was not clear, a situation which would cause many problems, Bernard was known by the courtesy title of brevet brigadier general during his service to the United States.

On January 18, 1817, the Secretary of the Navy transmitted to the Senate the opinions of Commodores John Rodgers, Stephen Decatur, and David Porter respecting a site for a naval depot and the erection of defenses in Chesapeake Bay. The officers recommended the fortifying of Old Point Comfort. By resolution of February 13, 1817, the Senate directed the President to have surveys made of all the harbors and ports of the

United States to establish a comprehensive system of fortification.

The Bernard board, operating in conjunction with local boards, worked with deliberation and developed the entire project little by little as the examination of the seaboard progressed. Sites were selected and works were begun upon a scale which was intended to be commensurate with the probable growth and future importance of the points to be defended. The board annually reported its progress to Congress, showing the successive stages of its operations.

Brevet Brigadier General Joseph G. Swift, the first graduate of West Point and the Chief of Engineers, had been assigned to the Board of Engineers for the Atlantic Coast of the United States on April 21, 1817. When Bernard assumed direction of the fortification board, Swift had been ordered to assume the Superintendency of the Military Academy. Swift was humiliated by the assignment of a foreign engineer to the important fortification project. He protested what he considered an insult to himself and the Corps of Engineers and reminded the government of the unfortunate results which had been obtained from foreign engineers on previous occasions. Swift argued that it was impolitic to trust the nation's defenses to any foreigner, whatever his ability, whose interest was that of his own country and who, in the event of war, might become a dangerous enemy. Swift protested and sulked for two years and finally, on November 12, 1818, resigned from the Army. Lieutenant Colonel William McRee worked industriously for the board, but sharing the views of the former Chief of Engineers, he too resigned on March 31, 1819. Major Joseph G. Totten, who did not have the personal financial resources of his fellow board members, swallowed his dignity and remained on duty with the board, eventually becoming Chief of Engineers in 1838.[6]

The report of 1821, rendered as the board neared the conclusion of its labors, covered the operations of the three preceding years and constituted an exhaustive discussion of the question of a system of coast defense. Among other things, it said:[7]

> The commission charged with reconnoitering the frontiers of the United States has completed the three most important sections of the maritime boundaries, viz: the coast of the gulf of Mexico, the coast between Cape Hatteras and Cape Cod, and the coast between Cape Cod and the river St. Croix. The coast between Cape Hatteras and Cape Fear has likewise been surveyed; and the only section which remains to be examined, to complete the reconnaissance of the coast, is South Carolina and Georgia.

> *   *   *   *   *   *

> A defensive system for the frontiers of the United States is therefore yet to be created; its bases are: first, a navy; second, fortifications; third, interior communication by land and water; and fourth, a regular army and well organized militia; these means must all be combined, so as to form a complete system.

The navy must, in the first place, be provided with proper establishments for construction and repair, harbors of rendezvous, stations, and ports of refuge. It is only by taking into view the general character, as well as the details of the whole frontier, that we can fix on the most advantageous points for receiving these naval depots, harbors of rendezvous, and ports of refuge.

On these considerations, Burwell's Bay, in James River, and Charlestown, near Boston, have been especially recommended by the commission as the most proper sites for the great naval arsenals of the south and of the north. Hampton roads and Boston roads as the chief rendezvous, and Narragansett Bay as an indispensable accessory to Boston roads. . . .

     *   *   *   *   *   *

After determining the general and connected system of naval depots, harbors of rendezvous, stations, and ports of refuge, the commission in the next place traced the scheme of fortifications necessary to protect this system, and at the same time to guard the whole frontier against invasion. The forts projected by the commission for this purpose satisfy one or more of the following conditions:

1. To close important harbors to an enemy, and secure them to the navy of the country.

2. To deprive an enemy of strong positions, where, protected by his naval superiority, he might fix permanent quarters in our territory, maintain himself during the war, and keep the whole frontier in perpetual alarm.

3. To cover our great cities against attack.

4. To prevent as much as possible the great avenues of interior navigation from being blocked by a naval force, at their entrance into the ocean.

5. To cover the coastwise and interior navigation, and to give to our navy the means necessary for protecting this navigation.

6. To cover the great naval establishments.

     *   *   *   *   *   *

In the Chesapeake, the projected works at the entrance of Hampton Roads have the object to close this road against an enemy, and to secure it to the United States; to secure the interior navigation between the Chesapeake and the more southern States; to make sure of a naval place of arms, where the navy of the United States may protect the Chesapeake and the coasting trade; to cover the public docks, etc., at Norfolk, and those which may be established in James River; and to prevent an enemy force from making a permanent establishment at Norfolk.

While on this subject we will observe, that an enemy might land in Lynnhaven bay, and, in one day's march, reach the narrow position which lies to the east of Suffolk, bounded on one side by the Dismal Swamp, and on the other by Bennett's creek, near the mouth of the Nansemond; this position cannot be turned, and may easily be fortified. An enemy might there defy all the forces of Virginia and North Carolina. Secure of a retreat as long as his fleet occupied Hampton road, he would compel the United States to make the greatest possible sacrifices, both in men and money, before he could be driven out. But if Hampton road is fortified, he will only be able to anchor in the open road of Lynnhaven bay; his march thence upon Suffolk may be turned by our forces crossing at Hampton road, and he will, therefore, find it impossible to take permanent quarters in the country. The expense at which these results will be obtained is one million eight hundred thousand dollars—a trifling sum if compared with the magnitude of the advantages which will be procured and the evils which will be averted.

*   *   *   *   *   *

Some prominent military writers have opposed the principle of fortifying an extensive land frontier; but no military or political writer has ever disputed the necessity of fortifying a maritime frontier. The practice of every nation, ancient and modern, has been the same in this respect. On a land frontier, a good, experienced, and numerous infantry may dispense with permanent fortifications, although they would prove excellent auxiliaries and supports when properly disposed and organized; but though disciplined troops can, rigorously speaking, without their aid, cover and protect a frontier, undisciplined troops never can. On a maritime frontier the case is totally different. Troops cannot supply the place of the strong batteries which are disposed along the important places. The uncertainty of the point on which an enemy may direct his attack, the suddenness with which he may reach it, and the powerful masses which he can concentrate at a distance out of our reach, and knowledge, or suddenly, and at the very moment of attack, are reasons for erecting defenses on every exposed point, which may repel his attack, or retard it until reinforcements can arrive, or the means of resistance be properly organized. By land we are acquainted with the motions of an enemy, with the movements and directions of his columns; we know the roads by which he must pass. But the ocean is a vast plain without obstacles; there his movements are performed out of our sight and knowledge, and we can receive no intelligence of his approach until he has already arrived within the range of the eye. In a word, the vulnerable points of a seacoast frontier are left to their fate, if they are not covered by permanent fortifications; and their only chance of safety must depend upon the issue of a battle, always uncertain, even when regular and well-disciplined troops, inured to danger, have been assembled before hand, and have made all possible preparaions for the combat.

The Board of Commissioners for Chesapeake Bay appointed under the Resolution of February 13, 1817, consisted of Swift, Bernard, Lieutenant Colonel Walker K. Armistead,[8] and Major William McRee, of the Engineers, and Captain Lewis Warrington and Captain Jesse D. Elliott, of the Navy. The board met in December 1817, made a preliminary survey of Chesapeake Bay, Hampton Roads, and York River, and reported on January 24, 1818:[9]

The result of this examination is a conviction, on the part of the commissioners, that the passage into those roads can be so fortified as to prevent the entrance of any hostile fleet. The extent and efficiency of such fortifications will depend upon the decision of the Government as to the length of time which the works should be enabled to withstand the attack of a combined naval and land force, of a given magnitude.

If the amount of resistance to be made at this pass be merely an obstruction of the entrance into Hampton Roads, without any reference to a land attack, the commissioners believe that competent water defenses may be constructed to such an effect. As, however, the object of forcing an entrance into Hampton Roads might be deemed by an enemy worth the expense of a regular siege, the commissioners deem it their duty to recommend a system of defence equal to such an exigency. Such a system should embrace the occupation of the

Rip Rap Shoal with a castellated fort; the channel between that shoal and Old Point Comfort with a boom raft; and Old Point Comfort itself with an enclosed work; the whole to be so located as to afford a mutual protection, and to embrace in the total, the power to resist any force which may be brought against the pass into Hampton Roads. The commissioners have not, as yet, been able to collect sufficient data to authorize them to offer you a complete plan.

On April 21, 1817—before any final decisions had been made, and even before the Commissioners for Chesapeake Bay had assembled—Colonel Armistead was ordered to Old Point Comfort for the purpose of collecting materials for the construction of a fort. During 1817 and 1818, while preparatory operations were under way at Old Point Comfort, he investigated the purchase of materials, while First Lieutenant Theodore W. Maurice,[10] detailed as an assistant, examined quarries, etc. On July 25, 1818, a contract for 150,000 perch of stone from the banks of the York River was awarded to Elijah Mix at a price of three dollars a perch. Deliveries of stone were to commence on September 15, 1818, and continue at a rate of 3,000 perches per month. Actual delivery did not begin until November, and after a few cargoes of stone arrived it developed that the York River variety was not satisfactory and Mix was required to get his stone elsewhere or give up the contract. The stone subsequently delivered under his contract came from quarries on the Potomac River near Georgetown. A reduction in shipping rates and labor costs about that time saved the contractor from complete ruin.[11]

On August 1, 1818, James Maurice, of Norfolk, was appointed by the Secretary of War as agent of fortifications for Norfolk, Hampton Roads, and the lower part of Chesapeake Bay. He was directed on August 17 by the Chief Engineer "to employ a good wharf builder to extend and complete the wharf at Old Point Comfort, sufficiently large and substantial to allow three vessels to come alongside and unload at the same time." Fort Monroe was fairly started, with Lieutenant Maurice as superintending engineer, under the general supervision of Colonel Armistead. On August 11, 1818, Second Lieutenant George Blaney[12] was ordered by the Chief of Engineers to proceed to Hampton Roads and superintend the planting of a number of anchors and the mooring of buoys to be used by vessels discharging stone upon the three fathom shoal opposite Old Point Comfort.

Collection of materials and completion of preliminary arrangements continued throughout 1818. The actual work of construction was begun in March 1819 by Bolitha Laws, contractor, under the superintendence of Major Charles Gratiot. Captain Frederick Lewis and Lieutenants Delafield,[13] Maurice, and Blaney were also employed in the preparations for the work, the two former continuing on duty as assistants to Major Gratiot after construction started. The estimated cost of Fort Monroe was $816,814.96, and of Fort Calhoun, on the Rip Raps, $904,355.40; but both estimates, especially that of Fort Calhoun, were later materially exceeded. It is a tradition of the Corps of Engineers that General Bernard designed the plans of the fortifications, and that Captain William T. Poussin, acting aide to General Bernard, made the drawings.

As designed, Fort Monroe was a regular work, with seven fronts, covering about sixty-three acres of ground and surrounded by an eight foot deep moat. The moat varies in width from sixty feet at the East Gate to 150 feet at the Main Gate. The interior crest measured 2,304 yards. Fort Monroe was one of the first of the third series forts and was typical of its period in its impressive size, irregular plan, and large bastions. The bastion was simply a projecting point of the fortification. When properly designed, there were neither dead angles or sectors and all ground within range was protected by direct, flank, or cross fire. The later forts of the series were on the whole smaller, had a more regular plan, with additional tiers of casemates. Though many still had bastions, most of the armament was concentrated in the major fronts and the bastions were reduced in size. Many of the forts begun after the mid-1820's, such as Fort Pulaski and Fort Sumter, were hexagonal in form and completely devoid of bastions.

Fort Monroe was designed to concentrate the greatest fire possible in the first, second, third, and fourth fronts. The first, second, and third fronts were casemated, providing with the barbette tier a doubling of the fire power. The second and third fronts are in fact the main front directly across the channel at its narrowest point, yet sufficiently seaward of the Rip Raps to keep the fort erected there out of the direct field of fire. These two fronts combined are just about the length of the sixth and seventh fronts, but by breaking the face into two fronts the bastions were reduced and flattened. This increased the direct fire available while retaining their protection in the close defense of the limited land area to seaward.

The first and fourth fronts, of identical length, flanked the main front and extended the seaward fields of fire. The first front, oriented 75 degrees to the right, covered the inner part of the channel and the anchorage and protected the right of the main fronts from the inner harbor area. The fourth front was oriented 45 degrees left of the main fronts and covered the channel entrance. Because of its exposed position seaward and the necessity for considering the land defense of this flank, the fourth front was solid and only had a barbette tier of armament. Seaward of this front was the Water Battery of forty casemated guns, outside the moat and actually part of the outworks. The remaining fronts were not related to the seaward defense. They completed the closure of the main work and protected it from land attack. Of these three fronts, the fifth front directly covered the only land approach down the beach and supported the outworks. The front was solid except for casemates in the flank of the Northeast Bastion designed for the protection of the ditch and the left flank of the Water Battery. The sixth and seventh fronts were both solid. The scarp wall of the main work was twenty-one feet high, and the distance around it, exterior to the ditches of the main work and the redoubt, was one and six-tenths mile.

The outworks beyond the fifth front were typical of the outworks of fortifications of this period. They were designed purely for the protection of the land front of the fort. The outworks consisted of a covered way and a redan, raised above the general level of the ground for the greater protection of the scarp wall and to provide a better field of fire, and a redoubt lower than the others and advanced on the left flank. In front of these outworks was a deep ditch dredged out of the swamp on the Mill Creek side and directly connected with one of the tide gates of the moat and with Mill Creek just north of the redoubt. The sixth front faced directly on Mill Creek and had a covered way only. The glacis of this covered way sloped directly onto the shore of Mill Creek and was reveted. This covered way was primarily to protect movement from the North Gate to the outworks of the fifth front. The seventh front had no outworks but a glacis.[14]

The full armament of Fort Monroe was originally designed to be 380 guns. These eventually ranged in size from the small 24-pounder howitzers mounted in the bastions for flank protection to 42-pounder guns, principally in the Water Battery. The total number of guns was subsequently increased to 412, but these were never all mounted. The fort required a peacetime garrison of 600 men and a wartime garrison of 2,625 men. No other fort in the United States was of comparable size, and it was generally believed at the time that no fort in Europe not inclosing a town was larger. The only fortification in North America comparable was the French fort at Louisbourg in Canada, which did inclose a small town.

About a mile distant from Old Point Comfort, lying directly across the main ship channel leading from Chesapeake Bay into Hampton Roads and James River, was a shoal which was commonly known as the Rip Raps, or Rip-rap Shoal. Had the shoal been an island, it would have made a splendid site for fortifications with which to supplement the works at Old Point Comfort. The two places were within mutually supporting distance and their guns could cross their fire in the channel against ships advancing to an attack. The more the question was studied, the more it appeared that proper defense of Fort Monroe against attack demanded the occupation of the Rip Raps.

The Engineers solved the difficulty by proposing the construction of an artificial island of stone. They held that stones could be piled on the shoal until they appeared above high water and that such a foundation, properly made, would support a fort such as was desired. No flaw appearing in the scheme, it was adopted, and the fort to be erected on the Rip Raps was designed. Since the work at Old Point Comfort was to be named after the President, it was logical to name after the Secretary of War the work which was to be so closely associated with it. So it is as Fort Calhoun (sometimes Castle Calhoun) that the fortifications at the Rip Raps were known until the Civil War.

Fort Calhoun was planned as a tower battery, with three tiers of casemates, built upon a foundation, *a'pierre perdu,* in a depth of water varying from one and a half to three fathoms. Its interior crest measured 381 yards, and it was designed to mount 216 guns—a number which was later raised to 232 guns. The peacetime garrison was fixed at 200 men and the wartime garrison at 1,130 men.

Although work on Fort Monroe was begun in 1819, the property continued to belong to the State of Virginia for a number of years. Two acres had been ceded to the United States some twenty years before for the purpose of erecting a light-house, but it was not until March 1821, that the General Assembly passed an act authorizing the Governor to convey by deed to the United States "the right of property and title, as well as all the jurisdiction which this Commonwealth possesses over the lands and shoal at Old Point Comfort and the Rip-Raps." The area to be ceded at the former locality was limited to 250 acres, and at the latter to 15 acres. The deed also contained the provision "that if the said United States should at any time abandon the said lands and shoals or appropriate them to any other purpose than fortification and national defenses, then, and in that case, the said lands and shoal shall revert to and revest in the said Commonwealth." For some reason which does not appear, the deed was not executed until 1838.

Work at Fort Monroe progressed steadily, and except for some delays on the part of the contractors progress seems to have been as rapid as could have been expected. Work at the Rip Raps was begun at about the same time but progress was much less satisfactory. By the end of 1819, some forty or fifty thousand perch of stone had been applied to the formation of the foundation and, of these, two or three thousand perch showed above high tides. At Old Point Comfort, wharves, roads, machinery, workshops, barracks, and quarters were built and large quantities of materials were collected during 1818 and 1819. By the spring of 1821, the work was reported as two-fifths completed, although its appearance failed to indicate that state of advancement. This was because so much of the labor consisted in collecting and depositing the materials at the points where they were to be used. For this purpose, a canal, following the line of the ditch, was built around the fort, with locks, to facilitate the transportation of the material. The initial operations indicated that the fort would be completed during 1826.

The masonry construction was begun in the summer of 1820, the first efforts being largely confined to the construction of a casemated work to cover the channel with a battery of forty 24-pounders. By the spring of 1822 the fort was considered to be three-quarters finished, and by the fall of 1823 it began to present a formidable appearance. At that time the Chief of Engineers reported: ". . . the exterior wall, ten feet thick at its base, is carried on an average all around the place to a height of twelve feet, and a wet ditch surrounds the whole work. A battery on the covert-way is constructed, capable of receiving forty-two pieces, and in the three fronts of the fortress on the sea side embrasures are partly constructed for eighty-four guns; so that, in case of necessity, a battery of one hundred and twenty-six heavy guns might readily be mounted for the protection of Hampton Roads." At Fort Calhoun, the foundation was completed in 1822, and it was carried to six feet above high water in 1823.

At the beginning the work at Fort Monroe was performed under contract with black laborers, and throughout the period of construction the provision of labor was a serious question. The idea of employing military convicts as laborers on the public works was conceived in 1820, and on October 13 of that year a general order from the Adjutant and Inspector's Office transferred to Old Point Comfort all able-bodied men of the Second Department and those at New York under sentence of court-martial with more than three months to serve. The initial experiment proved to be so successful that in December 1821, it was ordered that "all able-bodied soldiers attached to the different sea coast commands, who may in future be sentenced by courts martial to hard labor for periods exceeding six months," should, if sentenced at any of the Atlantic posts, "be sent to the Engineer superintending the construction of the work at Old Point Comfort, Chesapeake bay." These prisoners soon formed a considerable portion of the garrison—the number reaching an ultimate strength of around 200—and the guard of twelve men provided by the Engineers became insufficient to keep the prisoners under proper supervision.

On July 12, 1823, the Engineer Department reported to the Secretary of War that the number of military convicts employed at Old Point Comfort had increased to seventy-two and recommended that a company of troops be stationed there as a guard. In accordance with this recommendation, and pursuant to instructions from the Commanding General of the Eastern Department, Captain Mann P. Lomax, with his Company G, 3d Artillery, was directed to proceed "forthwith" from Fort Nelson to "Fortress Monroe, Old Point Comfort (Virga.)" and report to Lieutenant Colonel Gratiot, who was still in charge of the construction. Company G embarked on the Hampton steamboat on the morning of July 25 and crossed Hampton Roads to Old Point Comfort, thus becoming the first garrison of Fort Monroe.[15]

The arrival of ten other artillery companies during the spring of 1824 to form the Artillery School of Practice caused the formation of two separate and distinct commands. The Engineer Corps remained in charge of the construction, and its personnel was kept entirely distinct from the artillery garrison, even to the extent of having a separate commissariat and a commissary officer who had nothing to do with the supplies for the artillery. Lomax's company, acting as guard for prisoners, was, however, carried on the school morning report, and prisoners were frequently released and assigned to companies at the post.

After the completion of the foundation at Fort Calhoun in 1823 it was proposed that this artificial island be allowed a year or so in which to settle before the superstructure was erected, and for a time all activity ceased. Because of the lack of an available officer to supervise the work, operations were not resumed as promptly as had been anticipated, and it was 1826 before the actual construction was undertaken. The laying of the cornerstone took place on September 17, 1826, with an elaborate ceremony, of which a full and flamboyant account was published in Nile's *Weekly Register* of September 30.

The date of the ceremony was the anniversary of the fierce sortie from Fort Erie during the second war with Great Britain and was selected as a compliment to Major General Jacob Brown, the Commanding General of the Army, who was then on a visit of inspection at Fort Monroe. After a prayer by the Rev. Mr. Westwood and music by the band of the Artillery School of Practice, Colonel Gratiot advanced to General Brown and said:

> General: On this anniversary of the sortie from Fort Erie, and to commemorate that eventful day, permit me to request of you, as the leader on that occasion, to officiate on this, and to lay the first corner stone of this great national work of defense. I now present you with the tools necessary to perform the operation.

The General replied that he felt flattered by the honor that had been conferred on him and that he received with pleasure the presented tools. He then handed them to Mr. Keatinge, the master mason, and addressed to him and to Mr. Smith, the master carpenter, a few appropriate remarks on the magnitude and importance of the duty confided to them. Turning to the military personnel, he observed: "In thus assisting my brother officers in laying a corner stone of this great work, in honor of the seventeenth of September 1814, I must be permitted, in gratitude to our Common Parent, piously to remember those exalted spirits, who, on the seventeenth of September, the fifteenth of August, and on every day during the siege of Erie, endeavored to sustain the moral power of their country."

The master stone was laid in due form, and when the last stroke from the General's hammer announced the consummation of the act, the colors were raised and a salute was fired from Fort Calhoun. The salute was answered by the guns of Fort Monroe, and the company then withdrew to the strains of Yankee Doodle to partake of a collation prepared by order of Colonel Gratiot.

Progress in construction of Fort Monroe continued to be satisfactory, but the fort was still far from complete in 1826. In August 1832, malignant cholera made its appearance among the workmen and caused a suspension of all operations for a time. This suspension was followed by a period during which work was considerably retarded by the difficulty of securing workmen, the system of using military convicts having been discontinued some years before. Work was finally resumed, and no further interruptions of a serious nature arose. By the spring of 1834 the work was nearly finished, and Fort Monroe, pursuant to General Orders No. 54, A.G.O., was turned over to the Artillery for completion. Concerning the status of the fort, the Chief of Engineers reported under date of November 1, 1834:[16]

All the permanent parts of this work were completed last year. The ramparts of fronts 5, 6, and 7, together with the glacis and road in advance of these fronts, were, with the exception of a small portion of front 5, formed and covered with earth. The rampart of covertway and place of arms, in advance of front 5, was in a state of forwardness along its whole extent, and fifteen thousand cubic yards of sand were deposited towards, the construction of the redoubt; five hundred tons of stone were collected and put in place for the protection of the beach in front of the casemated battery and the glacis of front 6; conduit pipes for conducting water from the roof of casemated battery laid; the piazzas of curtains 2 and 3 completed, and all materials for the draws to bridges and gates procured; the draws and gates to main entrance finished, and the timber for the others partly prepared; the earth for the parapets on all fronts, except 1, 2, and 3, was collected at the foot of the scarp-wall; the ditches of all the fronts were excavated to their proper depth, and the glacis and road in advance formed, except those on front 1; the casemated covertway on front 4 was completed, and the funds available, with the force then organized, amply sufficient for the completion of the fort, with the exception of putting parapets on the main and outworks, which was not deemed advisable for the present, when the operations of the Engineer department were arrested by general order No. 54. This order directed that the work with its funds, be placed under the immediate orders of the officer commanding the troops at that station. The main work was, therefore, entirely completed, except the gates, the raising of the half parapets on fronts 1, 2, and 3, and the whole parapets on the other fronts—the earth required for these last being placed at the foot of the scarp. Four thousand three hundred and ten cubic yards of earth were required to complete the rampart of covertway on front 5; twenty-one thousand three hundred and eighty to finish the rampart of redoubt; twenty thousand two hundred and ninety-seven yards for the construction of the parapet on covertway; and eight thousand eight hundred and ninety for the parapet of the redoubt.

It has already been stated that the funds available for this work were, at the time they were transferred, deemed amply sufficient for its completion according to the terms of the estimate upon which the appropriation of the last session of Congress was requested; and but for the circumstance above referred to, I should likely have had the gratification of reporting it finished. . . .

By this time, $1,731,284.14 had been expended in the construction of Fort Monroe, and the revised estimates of the engineers, made in 1834, placed the total amount to be expended at $1,889,840.

The armament at Fort Monroe at this time, exclusive of guns stored in the arsenal, was, according to a report made by Brevet Brigadier General John E. Wool on June 15, 1835, one 42-pounder and twenty-two 32-pounders mounted in casemates and one 24-pounder in casemate and one in barbette, which, together with ten to be mounted that month, would form a battery of thirty-five heavy guns. Under date of February 27, 1836, the War Department estimated that completion of the armament at Fort Monroe would require sixteen 24-pounders, thirty-two 32-pounders, ninety 42-pounders, all casemate guns; thirty 24-pounders, fifty 32-pounders, fifty 42-pounders, all barbette guns; fifteen 10-inch heavy mortars; eight 10-inch light mortars; and ten howitzers, making a grand total of three hundred and one guns. This armament would cost about $500,000, an item which was not included in the Engineer estimates for the completion of the fort.

Th Artillery did little in the way of construction, and General Orders No. 86, A.G.O., 1835, placed the work again in the hands of the Engineer Department. Lack of available officers, difficulty of obtaining labor, and, at times, lack of funds, prevented the Engineers from prosecuting the work vigorously. In 1836, Colonel Gratiot reported to the Secretary of War that the work could be considered as completed according to the design of the Board of Engineers, but that considerable additional work was required. He stated that the entire counterscarp of the ditch required a permanent revetment, instead of the earth slope which had been planned; that the dimensions given the scarp wall were insufficient to bear the weight of the ramparts; that the land front was without means of resisting a land attack; that the casemated battery in advance of the adjacent water front, containing the most powerful water battery of the fort, was exposed to flank attack; that furnaces for heating shot were required; and that quarters for the garrison, other than the casemates, should be provided.

In 1837, an "especial board" of Engineers was appointed, principally as a result of General Gratiot's recommendations, to examine the works at Fort Monroe. This board recommended extensive repairs and modifications, which were undertaken as soon as funds were available. These repairs, the completion of the modified plan, the mounting of the guns continued for several years, until, in 1845, the work was practically complete. In his report for that year, dated November 1, the Chief of Engineers stated:

The work yet to be done, in order to give this fort its entire efficiency, comprises the following objects: The construction of the stone revetment of the counterscarp; completing furnaces and bridges; building a detached magazine; modifying the principal magazine; paving the ditch and removing the surplus sand thereform; embanking and grading portions of the glacis, finishing the redoubt and the caponniére leading thereto; constructing the batterdeau, and painting the various walls of the fort.

The mounting expense of the fortification program resulted in much grumbling in Congress. In response to a resolution of the House of Representatives in 1840, Colonel Totten submitted a report of a board in which the whole subject of the military defense of the country was reviewed. The feelings of the Corps of Engineers regarding General Bernard are reflected in the following comments on the fortifications in Hampton Roads:[17]

The same criticism complains of the unreasonable magnitude of one of these works, (Fort Monroe) and we concede that there is justice in the criticism. But it has long been too late to remedy the evil. It may not, however, be improper to avail of this opportunity to remove from the country the professional reproach attached to this error. When the system of coast defense was about to be taken up, it was thought best by the government and Congress, to call from abroad a portion of that skill and science which a long course of active warfare was supposed to have supplied. Fort Monroe is one of the results of this determination. It was not easy, probably, to come down from the exaggerated scale of warfare to which Europe was then accustomed; nor for those who had been brought where wars were often produced and always magnified by juxtaposition or proximity, to realize to what degree remoteness from belligerent nations would diminish military means and qualify military objects. Certain it is, that this experiment, costly as it was in the case of Fort Monroe, would have been much more so but for the opposition of some whose more moderate opinions had been moulded by no other circumstances than those peculiar to our own country.

The mistake is one relating to magnitude, however, not to strength. Magnitude in fortifications is often a measure of strength; but not always, nor in this instance. Fort Monroe might have been as strong as it is now against a water attack, or an assault, or a siege, with one-third its present capacity, and perhaps at no more than half its cost. We do not think this work too strong for its position, nor too heavily armed; and as the force of the garrison will depend mainly on the extent of the armament, the error has caused an excess in the first outlay chiefly, but will not involve much useless expense after completion.

The final work and minor repairs occupied the Engineers during the following years, and the Civil War found the fort in a reasonable state of defense.

The auspicious beginning of Fort Calhoun did not presage the rapid completion of the fort. When the walls and piers had been carried up to the level of the second story, it was found that the additional weight caused a subsidence of the foundations. Operations were suspended and the material for the completion of the fort, which was still being received, was distributed about the fort by the Engineers so as to equalize the pressure on the bottom as much as possible and thus produce a uniform settling. As the subsidence continued for several years—amounting to six inches in 1831—the weight was constantly increased until the foundations were carrying fully 20,000 tons more than the estimated weight of the completed fort. By the end of 1835 no further progress had been made, except that all the stone required to complete the fort had been assembled. Up to this time $1,380,333.68 had been expended on Fort Calhoun, and the Engineers estimated that the total cost would amount to $2,014,816.08.

Operations were resumed in 1858, but the Civil War found this fort still in an incomplete state. Fifty-two casemates of the lower tier, with iron-throated embrasures, had been finished and were ready for guns. On the second tier, the scarp walls and piers of those portions of the work bearing on the channel had reached nearly to the height of the embrasure lintels, the embrasure irons had been set, and the floors of most of the casemates had been paved. On the gorge face very little work had been accomplished. Fort Calhoun was never completed as contemplated.

Since the Civil War, Fort Monroe has changed but little in appearance. On the east, the Water Battery, and on the north, the redoubt, have been removed. From the casemates and from the parapet, the armament with which the fort was provided has been removed. For a time rifled weapons of a postwar period were mounted on the ramparts of the eastern front, but these, too, have been removed. These changes are all comparatively slight, and in its general appearance the work remains as it was during the Civil War.

The faltering coast defense policy of the young United States had led to disaster in the War of 1812. The smoking ruins of Hampton and Washington were monuments to a policy that prepared to repel foreign aggression only after the war had begun. The system of forts which arose along the coast in the years prior to the Civil War were a direct reaction to the experience of 1813 and 1814. The largest of these forts—Fort Monroe— was to become the most famous. Why Simon Bernard decided to build a fort on such a massive scale is as much a mystery today as it was to the American military engineers of the time. Fort Monroe dwarfs even the largest of the other third system forts. Work on Fort Monroe proceeded slowly and in many ways was never finished. Nevertheless, by the middle of the 1830's, Fort Monroe was in most essentials completed and was the strongest element in the coast defense system. The vast size of the fortification made it ideal for other missions in addition to the basic defensive one. The Army was quick to recognize this fact. The sprawling fort on Chesapeake Bay immediately became the artillery center of the Army.

Footnotes Chapter II

[1] The governor was "Light Horse Harry" Lee, the famous Revolutionary War officer and the father of Robert E. Lee.

[2] Edgar B. Wesley, "The Beginnings of Coast Fortifications," *Coast Artillery Journal*, 67 (October 1927), pp. 281–290; Emmanuel Raymond Lewis, *Seacoast Fortifications of the United States: An Introductory History* (Washington: Smithsonian Institution Press, 1970), pp. 21–22, 28. Rivardi was one of the French engineers and was appointed a major in the American service on February 26, 1795. He was honorably discharged on June 1, 1802, and died in 1808. Francis B. Heitman, *Historical Register and Dictionary of the United States Army* (Washington: Government Printing Office, 1903), Vol. I, p. 833 (hereafter cited as *Heitman*).

[3] Wesley, *op. cit.;* Lewis, *Seacoast Fortifications*, pp. 25, 28; "Early Coast Fortifications," *Coast Artillery Journal*, 70 (February 1929), pp. 134–144.

[4] For details of the capture of Hampton see J. Mackay Hitsman and Alice Sorby, "Independent Foreigners or Canadian Chasseurs," *Military Affairs*, XXV (Spring 1961), pp. 11–17; and Parke Rouse, Jr., "Low Tide at Hampton Roads," *U.S. Naval Institute Proceedings*, 95 (July 1969), pp. 77–86. The expedition which led to the destruction of Fort Warburton is described in Charles G. Muller, "Fabulous Potomac Passage," *U.S. Naval Institute Proceedings*, 90 (May 1964), pp. 84–91. Fort Warburton was also known as Fort Washington and was located on the site of the post-War of 1812 fort of that name which still stands.

[5] Maj. Gen. William H. Carter, "Bvt. Maj. Gen. [sic] Simon Bernard," *Journal of the Military Service Institution*, LI (1912), pp. 147–155; Georges Six, *Dictionnaire Biographique des Generaux & Amiraux Francais de la Revolution et de l'Empire (1792–1814)* (Paris; Georges Saffroy, 1934), pp. 83–84.

[6] George W. Cullum, *Biographical Register of the Officers and Graduates of the U.S. Military Academy* (Boston and New York: Houghton, Mifflin and Company, 1891), Vol. I, pp. 51–52, 60–61, 63–65 (hereafter cited as *Cullum*).

[7] House Executive Document No. 153, 19th Congress, 1st Session.

[8] Armistead succeeded Swift as Chief of Engineers in 1818 and held that position until 1821, when he became the colonel of the 3d Artillery. *Heitman*, p. 169.

[9] House Executive Document No. 153, 19th Congress, 1st Session.

[10] Maurice had entered the Corps of Engineers in 1813. He was promoted to captain in 1818 and died in 1832. *Heitman*, p. 697.

[11] William E. Beard, "The Castle of Rip Raps," *Coast Artillery Journal*, 78 (January-February 1935), p. 44.

[12] Blaney was an 1815 West Point graduate who was promoted to captain in 1824 and died in 1835. *Heitman*, p. 224.

[13] Gratiot, an 1806 graduate of West Point, became a brevet brigadier general and Chief of Engineers in 1828. He was dismissed from the service in 1838 and died in 1855. Lewis was commissioned in the Corps of Engineers in 1812 and resigned in 1824. Delafield graduated first in the Class of 1818 at West Point. During a long and distinguished career, he was superintendent at the United States Military Academy from 1856 to 1861 and became brigadier general and Chief of Engineers from 1864 to 1866. General Delafield died in 1873. *Heitman*, pp. 365, 470, 630.

[14] Brig. Gen. Rollin L. Tilton, "Some Technical Aspects of Fort Monroe," ms. in Casemate Museum. Lewis, *Seacoast Fortifications*, pp. 48, 52.

[15] General Orders No. 43, 6th Military Department, July 18, 1823; Orders, Fort Nelson, July 24, 1823; NA, RG 393.

[16] *Annual Report of the Chief of Engineers, 1834.*

[17] Quoted in "History of Fort Monroe, 1607–1884," NA, RG 156.

Chapter III

Establishment of the Garrison

THE WORK OF SIMON BERNARD and the Corps of Engineers had created the greatest fort in America. While work still continued on this massive monument to military engineering skill, Fort Monroe emerged as one of the key elements in the national defense. It was not the great fort alone, impressive as its stone walls were, but the part the garrison was to play in the intellectual development of the Army which was to place this post apart from the other historic forts of the country. At first glance, life at Fort Monroe appears to be dull and routine. But here, only a year after the arrival of the first garrison, was planted the seed which eventually grew into the far flung Army school system. Through much of the period prior to the Civil War, Fort Monroe was the most important post in the Army and its garrison included men who would lead the troops in Florida, in Mexico, and on both sides during the great internecine struggle. The first decade as an active post established the pattern which was to characterize Fort Monroe throughout its entire existence.

Captain Mann P. Lomax, commanding Company G, 3d Artillery, was the first commanding officer of Fort Monroe. A native of Virginia and a representative of one of its oldest families, it was fitting that his name should be associated with the inauguration of a Virginia fort. Joining the Army as a second lieutenant of artillery on June 10, 1807, he served during the War of 1812 as a major and assistant adjutant general. He reached his captaincy in 1814 and joined the 3d Artillery in 1821, receiving his brevet of major three years later for ten years' faithful service in one grade. In 1838 he was appointed a major of ordnance, which rank he held until his death in 1842. "He was among the most fearless and courageous of men, a thorough tactician, and a favorite with his associates no less than among the soldiers of his battery," wrote one who knew him well.[1]

Captain Lomax found the post in all the disorder attending the construction. The fort was scarcely a third completed and was provided with few of the living comforts. There was, had he cared to make use of it (and he probably did), an eating house, or hotel, called the Hygeia, which had been erected primarily for the convenience of the workmen on the post. In 1821, Colonel Gratiot had granted permission to William Armistead—who had been appointed superintending engineer two years earlier—to build the Hygeia. The approval of the Secretary of War was obtained, the agreement was signed on January 17, 1822, and the hotel continued to operate through the succeeding years, expanding as the demands upon it increased.

The need had existed since the Revolutionary War for a method of training young officers. Cadets upon graduation from West Point were found to be prepared only to begin their professional duties. Additional instruction in the details of their arms of service was still necessary and could be secured only by special instruction in their regiments. This problem was particularly acute in the technical branches, such as the artillery.[2]

Congress in 1818 called upon Secretary of War Calhoun for his opinion concerning the expediency of establishing one or more military academies similar in character to that at West Point. The Secretary apppointed a board of officers, consisting of General Bernard and Major McRee, to study and report upon the "considerations on the course of instruction necessary for the officers of the different arms of the army." Replying to the question submitted by Congress, Calhoun, on January 29, 1819, advocated the establishment of one additional military academy and took advantage of the opportunity to submit to Congress the report of the Bernard board.

The board divided the theoretical and practical knowledge necessary in the conduct and operations of an army into two distinct parts. The first part embraced everything that was common to all arms; the other included all subjects, peculiar to the separate arms. For instruction in the first class of subjects, the members of the board felt that West Point, although not then up to the desired standard, could be made entirely adequate. The board, however, did not believe that the Military Academy could be satisfactorily expanded to teach branch peculiar subjects. They considered that no special school was then required for officers of infantry, but they strongly recommended that a school of application be established for the younger officers of the engineer, artillery, and topographic corps. At the same time, they recommended that no such school be incorporated as a part of the Military Academy.

The subject, having been opened, received considerable discussion and much modification in the ensuing years. Generally speaking, the Army received the proposal with approval, and Quartermaster General Thomas S. Jesup, in 1823, went so far as to outline a suggested organization and curriculum. The transition from a school of practice to an artillery school of practice was gradual, but when the decision was finally made it was determined to organize a school of instruction for artillery officers alone. Taking the name perhaps from the precedent set in organizing a "Corps of Engineers" for duty at the Military Academy at West Point, the Artillery School was at first named the "Artillery Corps for Instruction."

The selection of a site for the school presented no difficulty. Fort Monroe had progressed some three-quarters toward completion and was nearly ready to receive a garrison; it was the largest of the forts then under construction; and it afforded the advantages of location, climate, and transportation facilities. So, on April 5, 1824, the Adjutant General ordered the organization of the institution and directed the troops and the officers to report to Fort Monroe.[3]

Ten companies of artillery were ordered to Fort Monroe to form the instruction troops of the school: Two companies each from the 1st and 3d Regiments of Artillery, and three companies each from the 2d and 4th Regiments of Artillery. Company G of the 3d Artillery was already at the post and was not at first considered a part of the school troops. Later, the duty of guarding the prisoners was distributed among the companies, and all eleven companies participated in the instruction.

Although there should have been no conflict of authority, it was foreseen that the activities of the school might hamper the construction of the fort and that there might be friction in the administration of two branches. The two commands were entirely separate, but the War Department drew a clear line:[4]

> In establishing a school of practice at Fortress Monroe it is not intended that any interference is to take place with the Engineer Department, or the operations carrying on at that place under its direction. The command of the Troops will be entirely distinct from the fortifications or works until the latter are turned over to the commanding officer.
>
> The commanding Engineer will select the quarters for himself and officers, and the workmen and others attached to his Department, and will also designate the quarters to be occupied by the troops, after which no change will take place unless the circumstances of the work require it. As the convicts are to labor on the public works, they will, during the continuance of them, be exclusively under the direction of the commanding Engineer.
>
> A sufficient guard will be detailed from the troops to take charge of the convicts, the officer commanding the guard to receive his orders from the commanding Engineer.
>
> The officer commanding the troops will give out the parole and countersign, and furnish the commanding Engineer with a copy thereof.

In disposing of the guards and sentinels, care will be taken not to interfere with the operations of the Engineer Department, leaving the wharves, roads and other avenues open and free to the passage of the officers and workmen thereof.

A separate commissariat will be established at Old Point Comfort for the Engineer Department, which will supply the workmen and convicts with their subsistence, under such regulations as shall hereafter be established.

Companies C, D, and I, 4th Artillery, arrived in February 1824, and Captain Benjamin K. Pierce, commanding Company D, assumed command of the post.[5] Company F, 1st Artillery, Companies D, G, and H, 2d Artillery, and Companies D and F, 3d Artillery, joined in March; and the garrison was completed by the arrival of Company E, 1st Artillery, in May.

It will be noted that the organizations making up the garrison were designated "companies," whereas today they would be called "batteries." At that time a clear distinction existed between the two terms. A "battery" referred to the weapons with which the company was armed. Since field artillery materiel and personnel were practically inseparable, the term "battery" gradually came into general use as comprehending both, and the term "company" was gradually discontinued in the years following the Civil War. In harbor defenses, however, the batteries were fixed in position and the personnel and materiel were distinctly separable. The distinction between companies and batteries persisted in the coast artillery until the addition of heavy mobile guns during World War I and the adoption of a regimental organization after the war made it advisable to conform to field artillery practice in terming its organizations "batteries."

The companies were all brought up to their full quota of commissioned officers, and these company officers constituted the student personnel of the school. The school board consisted of the field officers, the director of artillery, and the instructor of mathematics, over whom the senior officer present presided. The school itself came directly under the orders of the War Department, through general headquarters.

Colonel and Brevet Brigadier General John Rogers Fenwick, of the 4th Artillery, was selected to serve as the first commandant of the Artillery Corps for Instruction—which became the Artillery School of Practice nine months after its organization—but various duties prevented him from joining until several months had passed. General Fenwick had had an excellent education and had served with distinction in the Marine Corps and the Army, so that his selection by Secretary of War Calhoun, with whom General Fenwick had enjoyed for many years close social relations, was perhaps as good as any that could have been made from among the colonels of artillery at the time. However, in his absence the labor of organizing the school fell upon Lieutenant Colonel and Brevet Colonel Abraham Eustis, 4th Artillery, detailed as second in command.[6]

Colonel Eustis was well educated and had seen distinguished service. He brought to his task a discipline and a zeal that carried the school over many obstacles and brought it to real success. Austere in manner and in appearance, he was a strict disciplinarian—hard and severe, but just. His subordinates, while either liking him intensely or disliking him with equal intensity, were all glad to serve under him. The story is told of one officer who served under Colonel Eustis so long as quartermaster that he became known throughout the service as "Eustis's quartermaster" but who would never have any social relations with his commanding officer. Each of them respected the other for his ability, but they were too much alike in disposition and character to be able to get along personally.

Colonel Eustis arrived at Fort Monroe on March 31, 1824, and proceeded energetically with the organization of his command. The first order of the school—Orders No. 1, Artillery Corps for Instruction— were issued on April 11, at which time but half of the troops ordered to the school had joined. With the arrival of Company E, 1st Artillery, in May, Colonel Eustis found himself in command of one of the largest and most important posts in the Army, his garrison approximating 600 officers and men, or almost one-third of all the artillery in the Army. Only three other stations at that time possessed garrisons exceeding 300 officers and men.

Under the date of June 30, 1824, Colonel Eustis was informed by John McLean of the Post Office Department: "Your letter of June 23rd is before me. If I can have the mail delivered at Fortress Monroe for a reasonable consideration, I shall, agreeably to your request, establish a post office at that place and appoint Lieut. McIntire Postmaster."

The nucleus of a library was formed in July by a shipment of books (for which Colonel Fenwick signed the receipt) forwarded by Christopher van de Venter, with his best wishes for the success of the Artillery School.

With First Lieutenant John R. Vinton, 3d Artillery, as Adjutant (succeeding Second Lieutenant Samuel B. Dusenberry, 4th Artillery, who acted for a short time), Captain Rufus L. Baker, 3d Artillery, as Ordnance Officer, First Lieutenant Andrew McIntire, 1st Artillery, as Commissary (succeeding Second Lieutenant Clifton Wharton, 3d Artillery, in June), Captain Henry Whiting, 1st Artillery, (joining in June) as Quartermaster, and Assistant Surgeon Robert Archer as post surgeon (succeeding Assistant Surgeon George W. Maupin), the post got underway.[7] The object to be attained by the command was announced by Colonel Eustis on April 12 as the establishment of a perfect uniformity, not only in the system of police, routine of duty, and general aspect of organization, but also in the more minute details of dress, equipment, and personal appearance of all the individual members of the garrison. This was, in fact, one of the basic ideas in the assembly of so large a part of the artillery in a single garrison. Fort Monroe even without its school features was a station of great value to the artillery because of its large garrison.

At the start there appeared to be a threat of some confusion in the fact that companies of the garrison from different regiments had the same lettered designation. Such a matter would not be given a second thought today, but at that time artillery organizations were unaccustomed to serving together and it seldom happened that two companies with the same letter met in garrison or in the field. On the rare occasions when such an event did occur, there was a bit of awkwardness in distinguishing between the organizations because it was unusual to refer to a company by both its letter and its regimental number.

To avoid this difficulty—foreseen, rather than encountered—Colonel Eustis went back to the practice which had been usual before 1816. In the first order issued after the establishment of the artillery school, he directed that the companies should be known and designated in all reports (except those made to regimental commanders) by the names of their respective captains. It was usual for captains of the line to be associated with their companies for many years—perhaps for their entire service in the grade. A detail to detached service or to a staff department did not necessarily create a vacancy to be filled by promotion or by transfer. A captain might be absent from his company for years but the company would still be his. Many organizations were better known by the names of their captains than by their correct designations.[8]

Expecting General Fenwick to join at any time, Colonel Eustis hesitated to proceed far with the organization of the school, and the many details of the establishment of a garrison kept him busy for some months. The troops required uniforms and equipment; staff departments had to be created and stocked; barracks, quarters, and a hospital were necessary; and text and reference books were required. The school staff was engaged in preparing a system of regulations and a detailed schedule of instruction.

The regulations were duly received at the War Department, approved, and issued. In them it was prescribed that the course of instruction should embrace:[9]

a. The duties usually performed by a regiment in garrison under the head of police: Roll calls, guard duty, cooking, messing, washing, cleaning quarters, and grounds, mustering, etc.

b. Infantry and cavalry exercises, parades, reviews, and inspections.

c. Artillery exercises (including the manual and service of the pieces of field, garrison and seacoast guns, mortars and howitzers), mechanical maneuvers, maneuvers and exercises of field artillery, horse and foot, and evolutions of batteries.

   d. Practical gunnery and target practice—point blank, random, and richochet, with hot shot, grape, canister, and shells.

   e. Duties of the laboratory: Preparation of ammunition of every description; making fuzes and loading shells, portfires, rockets, and other military fireworks; packing caissons, ammunition boxes, and wagons; proof and inspection of gunpowder, shot, shells, etc.

   f. Arsenal construction: The nomenclature and graphical delineation and construction of all parts of gun carriages and of the implements of every description of mortar beds, caissons, traveling forges, pontoons, and artillery equipages of all sorts—their dimensions, weights, expense of construction, materials, time required by any number of workmen to complete a given number, etc.

   g. Castramentation and the service of artillery in the field, in garrison and in sieges; crossing rivers and marshes, passing, attacking, and defending defiles; convoys, reconnoitering, topographical surveys, construction of field works, and the attack and defense of fortified places.

   h. An encampment for two months between April 1 and June 30 in each year for the purpose of instruction in field duties and exercises.

   As laid out, this program seemed to be ambitious. In practice there were four periods of daily instruction. From sunrise to 8:30 the troops, in fatigue clothing, were instructed as a battalion of infantry, with selected officers present to receive instruction in infantry exercises. Officers not required to be present at infantry drill were instructed in the nomenclature and manual of artillery and in mechanical maneuvers. One would suspect that by the end of the battalion drill the men would have become hungry, but breakfast was not served until 9:00.

   From 9:30 to 11:30 the troops were formed by company, with three officers present with each company, and were exercised on alternate days in the school of the company as infantry or in the mechanical maneuvers and manual of artillery. Officers not present with the companies received artillery instruction.

   At noon a selected class of officers reported to the Ordnance Officer to receive instruction in the duties of the laboratory. Whenever an Instructor of Mathematics was present, a class of selected noncommissioned officers reported to him at the same hour for instruction in mathematics. Dinner was served at 3 p.m.

   Dress parade, in gray woolen overalls, was held at 4:00, and the troops were then held in ranks and exercised as infantry until retreat. Tattoo at 9:00 p.m. closed the day, but it is probable that few of the men were awake to hear this call. Guard mount was at 11:30 a.m. A review and inspection of the troops in ranks and an inspection of barracks was held every Sunday morning, weather permitting. Officers belonging to the company on guard were excused from parade but were required to attend all other instruction.

This schedule did not materially change until after the Civil War. Breakfast was moved to 8:00, but the infantry instruction continued to predominate in the schedule probably from force of habit, for the artillery had seldom been equipped other than as infantry from the close of the Revolution.

It was contemplated that in a two-year course of instruction the personnel at the school could be taught all the subjects the school had to offer. In addition, both the officers and the men were subject to all the routine of ordinary garrison duty—guard, fatigue, courts-martial, ceremonies, administration, boards, etc.—the drills being a part of the instruction. In this way it was hoped that all—commissioned and enlisted alike—would be perfected in their duties, both theoretical and practical, and would be given an understanding of the functioning of a regiment in all its parts. Guard duty proceeded strictly according to the roster; leaves of absence were frequent; and transfers to and from the garrison were far from unusual. Perhaps the greatest trouble lay in the requirements of detached service. Details to the Military Academy, to the Ordnance Department, to the Topographical Engineers, to the Recruiting Service, to court-martial duty, and elsewhere kept a considerable part of the commissioned personnel absent at all times. Not until November 11, 1824, were all eleven captains present at the same time. On one occasion near the close of the school the garrison of eight companies had but four officers present for duty out of a total of forty carried on the rolls.

The staff of the school consisted of one colonel, one lieutenant colonel, and one major, a director of artillery and an assistant, a professor of chemistry, an instructor of mathematics and an assistant, an instructor of military drawing, an instructor of engineering, and the normal number of post staff officers. With such a corps of instructors, it would have been possible to have taught artillery in all its detail. At no time during the first period in the life of the school, however, was the staff more than half complete. One or more of the field officers remained absent or not detailed, and it was not unusual for the school to be temporarily under the command of one of the captains. The director of artillery was, in fact, the post ordnance officer, and was so called after January 1825, although laboratory instruction remained in his charge. The professor of chemistry and the instructors of military drawing and of engineering were never detailed. The instructor of mathematics, when present, was engaged principally in the instruction of noncommissioned officers. Thus, the instruction of the personnel and conduct of the school devolved almost altogether upon the field officers and the ordnance officer and his assistant.

Much of the petty history of the post may be read from its orders if we can but read between the lines. The orders tell us, for example, that men were as fond of pets a hundred and fifty years ago as they are today. No doubt the laborers in their camps at Old Point Comfort, the soldiers in their barracks, and even the officers in their quarters brought dogs with them when they came to Fort Monroe. Three or four dogs around a company might not be an inconvenience when the company was serving by itself, but when to these three or four are added the dogs of ten other companies in a compact garrison, they become noticeable, to say the least. At any rate, Colonel Eustis, as early as May 20, 1824, was led to make a declaration in orders which his successors in command have been repeating at various times and in varying phraseology for a hundred and fifty years:[10]

> The number of dogs at this place has increased until they have become a decided nuisance. Henceforth, no dogs will be permitted to go at large on the public grounds at Old Point Comfort. Three days will be allowed for their owners to secure or dispose of them and on Monday the 24th inst. the police guard will be directed to destroy all the dogs, male or female, which may be found running at large, whether the property of citizens or soldiers.

Still, care must be used in reading the orders, for they do not always mean what they appear to say. An example is found in orders in June 1824, which tells us: "The practice of bathing during the day having been represented by the Surgeon as prejudicial to the health of the troops, all soldiers are therefore forbidden to bathe while the sun is above the horizon." Shocked to learn that any such belief could have been prevalent but a hundred and fifty years ago, we turn to the sick report only to find that the Surgeon has been correctly quoted. It is not until we look into the bathing facilities at Fort Monroe that we find that the dangers feared by the authorities were sunburn and sunstroke, rather than some of the hazards attendant upon indoor bathing.

There was in 1824—and for many years thereafter—no water supply at Fort Monroe. Numerous attempts to obtain water locally from wells failed, but at the time the first garrison moved in the first wells had not yet been attempted. Rain water was caught and saved and a steady water supply was brought from the mainland under contract, the first contractor being Robert Lively, of Hampton. The supply of water was a duty of the Quartermaster. Each of the barracks, quarters, and other occupied buildings was furnished, according to the number of occupants, with one or more barrels, which were filled at regular intervals. Consumption was necessarily limited to the capacity of the barrels, and one suspects that bathing in the home was reduced to a carefully scheduled minimum.

It was not until 1830 that the system of water supply was changed. In the spring of that year a reservoir, or tank, was built on the post, and it was put in operation in May. Water call—added to the list of calls—was sounded daily at reveille, at 12:00 noon, and immediately before retreat.

General Simon Bernard, the designer of Fort Monroe.

Brevet Brig. Gen. Abraham Eustis, founder of the Artillery School.

Maj. Gen. Benjamin F. Butler, commander of Fort Monroe twice during the Civil War.

Maj. Gen. John A. Dix

*Maj. Gen. John E. Wool,
commander at Fort Monroe
during 1862 operations.*

Fort Monroe and the lighthouse, sketched about 1850.

Old Point Comfort and Fort Monroe as they appeared at the beginning of the Civil War. The first Hygeia Hotel is in foreground.

The Lower Chesapeake

Maj. Gen. Nelson A. Miles.

Col. William F. Barry reestablished the Artillery School in 1868.

The rifled 12-inch Union gun and the 15-inch Lincoln gun at Old Point Comfort in March 1862.

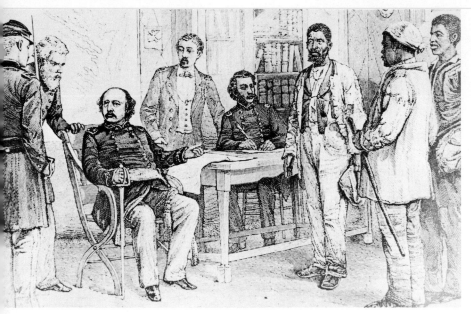

Maj. Gen. Benjamin Butler making his "Contraband" decision, 1861.

The battle between the USS Monitor and CSS Virginia, March 9, 1862.

Details from all organizations proceeded to the tank with suitable receptacles and received from a sergeant of the Quartermaster Department the proper amount of water, which they then carted to their barracks. This was undoubtedly an improvement over the previous system of providing water, but it did not materially improve the situation as to bathing.

This matter of bathing was, for the enlisted man, made a formation. Bathing while the sun was above the horizon being forbidden, the best hour seemed to be at sunset. Each day, therefore, before the organizations were dismissed from the formation for retreat, each first sergeant gave some such command as "All men desiring to bathe will fall in on the left." The detail forming in accordance with this command was then turned over to one of the duty sergeants, who marched it to a selected—and secluded—section of the beach and there permitted the men to gratify their desire for cleanliness. We are not informed of the extent to which the men made use of their small hand basins for bathing purposes—the only barracks facilities—during the winter, but the situation was undoubtedly no better than fifty years later, when the post surgeon reported his belief that most of the men omitted baths from November to May.

In 1824 there was, of course, the same need that there is today of enabling both officers and men to obtain supplies additional to the limited list of articles carried in the commissary. The equivalent of the Post Exchange of today was the sutler's store or shop, which carried in stock many of the items demanded by soldiers. One of these items was whiskey, which was authorized for sale but which was the subject of many restrictive orders. As early as May 25, 1824, it was necessary to order the sutler not to "sell or give to any enlisted soldier even the smallest quantity of distilled, vinous, or fermented liquor without the express sanction in writing of the man's company commander." Men on guard were forbidden to enter the sutler's store at any hour, and the hours during which the store might remain open were carefully regulated.

Whiskey was at that time also a part of the ration—so well considered that an extra gill was always ordered issued on the Fourth of July as a part of the day's celebration. It was issued directly until 1830, when instead the money value was paid to the men in commutation of the issue. Not until 1832 was it entirely discontinued as a component of the ration and coffee substituted, but even then it was obtainable from the sutler. One wonders why the sutler should have been permitted to carry whiskey in stock, particularly when it was an issue article, but the court martial records indicate that the local supply was always inadequate and that there was a great deal of smuggling during the early days.

Another convenience for the garrison was the "market." In July 1824, a shed was built near the boat wharf for a market for the "purchase and sale of provisions and eatables of every description." Peddling or huckstering on the post was forbidden, but dealers could meet in the market in open competition for the business of the members of the garrison.

All the early commanding officers—save only Colonel House—left behind them reputations as disciplinarians. It was probably necessary for them to be severe, for the court martial orders alone of those early days cover more paper than all the other orders combined. Most of the infractions of discipline came under one of four general heads, each, however, with many variants: unsoldierlike conduct, drunkenness, absence without leave, and neglect of duty. The men were ordinarily tried by garrison court martial, and many and varied were both the charges and the sentences. The sentence, in case of conviction, almost always carried a forfeiture of whiskey ration, and usually carried a forfeiture of pay. Confinement was not so common, for the court had only to draw upon its ingenuity and its imagination for a substitute penalty suitable and appropriate to the offense.

Private John Lewis was found guilty, in May 1824, of stealing another man's shirt. He was sentenced to forfeit his whiskey and his pay for one month, to walk daily for the term of four days under the charge of sentry No. 1 from 10:00 a.m. to 2:00 p.m., carrying his full equipment, and to wear "a flannel shirt outside his clothing with the word 'Thief' conspicuously written on it." John Rowland, appearing before the same court, was convicted of stealing a pair of shoes. The flannel shirt idea being inapplicable, he carried "2 12-lb balls or their equivalent in weight" in his knapsack, which was labeled "Thief."[11]

A somewhat different form of punishment accompanied a conviction for smuggling. Private Henry McMurry was found guilty of "attempting to bring into the barracks a quantity of ardent spirits, contrary to the standing rules and regulations of the garrison." In addition to his whiskey forfeiture, he was sentenced to "be placed in the stocks two hours each day for ten days" and during the remainder of his month serve at hard labor.[12]

The case of Private James Kelly offers a curious contrast in punishment. In 1827 he was found guilty of forgery and sentenced to forfeit four-fifths of his pay and all his whiskey for one month and to be confined at hard labor for twenty days. Forgery would appear to have been a somewhat less hazardous occupation than bootlegging.

Life at Fort Monroe was far from comfortable at first, but in one respect the women of the post enjoyed an advantage over the women of today. There were plenty of capable servants, both slave and free. Many, if not most, of them lived off the post—or at least outside of the fort—and their comings and goings were made the subject of a number of restrictive orders. Servants could pass the chain of sentinels only between certain hours and at certain points; those not living on the post had to leave the fort before a specified hour; all—resident and non-resident—were forbidden to appear on the grounds after a stated hour. The orders embraced both male and female employees and both free and slave. It is not at this time quite clear just why the servants were so excluded from post grounds at night. They were not so numerous that an uprising of slaves need have been feared, but one may infer from the orders that the commanding officer was giving some thought to the morals of the enlisted men.

It is quite probable that the caliber of servants was unappreciated by their employers. Comments on their capabilities sounded much like those of today. There are some very familiar remarks in the following letter which Mrs. John A. Dix wrote her parents on December 21, 1826, shortly after her arrival at Fort Monroe:[13]

> We are expecting our furniture very anxiously, and the moment it comes we shall take possession of our two rooms, without waiting for a carpet. We should build a kitchen, if we considered ourselves established here for any length of time. We have two very handsome rooms, with marble mantlepieces and folding-doors; but not a store-room, nor a closet, nor a pantry to be found on our premises. We are going to have pine cupboards made, and our dinner-table can be supplied with meat from the mess-room. I have seen nothing here that deserves the name of a vegetable. It is the poorest place, I believe, on the whole face of the earth. The worst part of Sweden is a garden compared with it. I give you my word there is not a eatable thing to be procured here but oysters and fish. They send to Norfolk, and Washington even, for the commonest articles of food, and have to pay high for them; and then such servants—all black; and so careless and improvident! . . .

One gathers that Mrs. Dix did not think highly of Fort Monroe. Captain Dix, completing his wife's letter gives this interesting insight into the life of a company officer during that time:

> Since the first moment of my arrival here I have been incessantly occupied—on drill, on parade, on guard, on court martial, on inspection, on review; and busied with a thousand other modes of duty, which scarcely give me time to think. . . . One is no sooner in the midst of a reverie on some interesting or important matter, than a fellow comes in to break off the chain of thought with—"Captain, the sergeant won't let me have my rations of whiskey;" or, "Captain, Private Such-a-one has got drunk and lost his musket."

There being no steam laundries in the 'Twenties, the washing was cared for by laundresses, hired for the purpose. Many of these were wives of enlisted men, and others lived with the families of enlisted men. From this fact is derived the name "Soapsud's Row," given to the line of non-commissioned officers' quarters throughout the Army for so many years. The scenic effect of "Soapsud's Row" was ever one of a group of small houses entirely surrounded by lines of underclothing and overhung with the persistent odor of soapsuds and lye.

Laundresses were "retainers of the camp" and subject to restrictive orders, so here again one must not jump to conclusions when women are mentioned in post orders. For example, when the troops returned to Fort

Monroe from Camp Experiment, at Buckroe, at the conclusion of their field training in June 1826, it was ordered that "Three women per company and *no more* will be permitted to reside in the barracks, and no black or colored women are to be harbored or employed in or about the barracks." These three women were, of course, the laundresses, the authorized allowance being three per company, and all three were probably the wives of members of the company.

In 1827, three of the laundresses were tried by regimental court martial —the only case, so far as discoverable, in which women were tried by a military court at Fort Monroe. For that reason the record of the case is quoted in full.[14]

> By a Regimental Court Martial convened at this post on the 12th inst. in obedience to Orders No. 4, of which Captn. Ripley is President, was tried:
>
> *   *   *   *   *   *
>
> 15th. Were arraigned and tried Alice, wife of Corpl. Loring Butterfield, Elizabeth, wife of Private Aaron Voorhies, both of Gardner's Compy, 4th Artillery, and Patsy, alias Martha Ann Buchanan, a woman residing with Musician Murphy, of Taylor's Compny, 3d Artillery, all laundresses, followers and retainers of the Camp, who were severally charged with "Disorderly conduct tending to the subversion of good order and military discipline." Specn. For that the aforesaid Alice Butterfield, Elizabeth Voorhies, and Patsy alias Martha Ann Buchanan did jointly and severally on the evening of the 11th of February 1827 obtain and secrete in the woods and land near Fortress Monroe, a large quantity of spiritous liquors, viz: Eight gallons, more or less, with intent to introduce the same, clandestinely without the chain of sentinels.
>
> Sigd. Abm. Eustis
Lieut. Col. Commandt.
>
> To which Charge and Specification, they severally pleaded Not Guilty. The Court find Alice Butterfield, Elizabeth Voorhies, and Patsy alias Martha Ann Buchanan each and severally "guilty" of the Charge and Specification alledged (sic) against them and do sentence Alice Butterfield, Elizabeth Voorhies and Patsy alias Martha Ann Buchanan to be deprived of their rations and other privileges as laundresses, followers and retainers of the Camp, to have their heads shaved and a bladder drawn over them, and then to be drummed out to the tune of the Whore's March;[15] to be prohibited for the future from entering within the line of sentinels and to be excluded from all barracks, encampments, or grounds within the military jurisdiction of the Post.

Colonel Eustis, probably feeling that a woman without her hair was indeed a woman unfrocked, remitted that portion of the sentence which required the heads to be shaved, but the remainder of the sentence he ordered executed.

In contrast with this sentence, one more case, appearing before the same court, must be introduced. It may be taken as an example of the old adage that the woman always pays, or it may be considered merely an indication that soldiers were harder to secure than laundresses. Of three almost identical cases, the case of a corporal is selected because he was a noncommissioned officer. He was tried and found guilty of selling whiskey to enlisted men. The offense would seem to us to be more serious than that of the women, who did not even get their liquor into the post, but he was sentenced "to be reduced to the station of a private sentinel, to have the chevrons stripped off in front of a dress parade, to forfeit his pay for one month and his rations of whiskey for six months. The Court recommend that a pole be erected on the parade ground of a suitable height with a cross piece near the top bearing the label 'I am a whiskey dealer,' with a barrel standing beside it on which they further sentence the prisoner to stand with his arms extended along the cross piece from guard mounting until 11 o'clock A.M. and from 3 o'clock P.M. until after Retreat when the weather will permit for seven successive days, and to be kept in close confinement during the intervals."[16]

The sentence might not withstand the scrutiny of a grammarian, but it was approved, although that part requiring the prisoner to stand on the barrel, etc., was remitted. Perhaps Colonel Eustis had a prejudice against laundresses.

At sunrise on August 1, 1824, the garrison entered upon a period of strenuous labor. The operations of the Engineer Department had left piles of sand, uneven mounds of dirt, and rubbish all over their zones of activity. The troops had nowhere to drill—and drill and parade formed the major part of their instruction for some time. So with hand carts, wheelbarrows, and intrenching tools, the entire garrison turned out to make a level parade ground. All other duty, except the necessary guard and police, was suspended until October 6, when the parade ground was considered completed.[17]

Hardly had the daily schedule become routine when it was interrupted. General Lafayette, "the only surviving Major General of the war of the revolution," was at that time in America as a guest of the nation. To participate in the reception which was to be given in his honor at Yorktown on October 19, 1824, the battalion at Fort Monroe (except Lomax's company) left on October 15 and marched to Yorktown. Here it established camp, and took part in the review and the celebration held for the famous Frenchman.[18] General Lafayette expressed to Colonel Eustis his "delight" at the fine appearance of the battalion, and the Secretary of War added his approbation.

The troops started back to Fort Monroe on the twentieth and hastened to clean up the post in anticipation of a visit by Lafayette. The General arrived on the twenty-fourth, and in the evening he received all the officers of the post at the quarters of Colonel Eustis. The following morning he inspected and reviewed the troops, and after his departure the garrison returned to its routine.

The troops had now been at Fort Monroe for six months and had so far developed the post that they could settle down to a regular schedule of instruction, but it must not be imagined that it had been an easy task. Many were the adjustments to be made. Colonel Eustis in particular must have required a great store of patience. Vexatious incidents were continually arising, of which the case of Private John Brown may be taken as an example.

Brown, in August, complained that he was beaten, kicked, and abused by Lieutenant Dusenberry and demanded a court of inquiry. He must have been what was in later days known as a "guardhouse lawyer," intent upon his own rights but oblivious to those of others. At any rate, the court found that Lieutenant Dusenberry "did strike and kick the complainant, but from the insolent and seditious spirit manifested in the complainant's conduct and from other very aggravating circumstances tending to the subversion of subordination and discipline, together with Lieut. Dusenberry's want of means to confine him; the Court are of the opinion, that the punishment inflicted by Lieut. Dusenberry upon the complainant, cannot be viewed as an unnecessary and wanton exertion on his part, to correct him,—on the contrary the Court are fully convinced that the chastisement was merited. . . ."[19]

Conscientious, upright, and orthodox though he was, justice and mercy under Colonel Eustis always leaned toward the side of law and regulations, and this court reflects the attitude of courts held at Fort Monroe during his regime. A complainant certainly had to come into court with clean hands and to present a good case or he received scant consideration.

In November, a band was organized as a "Detachment, 4th Artillery," by the transfer of eleven men from the several companies to the detachment;[20] and in December the receipt of regulations for the conduct of the Artillery School enabled the garrison to close its period of preliminary instruction and to take up the progressive scheme of a two-year course.

The year 1825 passed without particular incident. The Inspector General, John E. Wool, inspected and reviewed the troops and inspected the station and the records in November; and Brigadier General Edmund P. Gaines reviewed the troops a few days later. These facts are important only in that they mark the first official inspections of the post.[21]

As the first two-year period of instruction drew to a close, the consensus of opinion throughout the Army was that the school, despite obvious difficulties, had been a success. So impressed were the authorities with the value of the institution to the Army that an Infantry School of Practice was established at Jefferson Barracks, Missouri, in 1826. According to Major General Jacob Brown, the Commanding General of the Army, the benefits derived from the school were, "in general terms, habits of uniformity and accuracy in the practical routine of service, fresh incitement to the cultivation of miltary knowledge, emulation and *espirit de corps* among the troops, and mutual conformity and general elevation of individual character among the officers."

The tour of duty of the original garrison having come to an end, eight companies arrived at Fort Monroe in the early spring of 1826, followed by three others in the autumn. The new garrison entered at once upon its duties under the guidance of Colonel Eustis. General Fenwick had joined in the early part of 1825 but had been transferred before the end of the year, whereupon Colonel Eustis resumed command.

In May 1826, the garrison moved to "Buck Roe Farm" for a period of training in field duties and in practical gunnery. Pursuant to instructions, Colonel Eustis had, the preceding September, leased for three years from Nathaniel B. Carey and Gill A. Carey, of Lynchburg, the eight hundred acres adjacent to Mill Creek, known as Buckroe Farm, at a rental of $350 a year. The lease provided that not more than one-third of the arable land should be cultivated, and advantage was taken of the opportunity of providing the organizations at the post with gardens from which they might amplify the issue ration. On the portion of the land not under cultivation, the exercises were held. At the conclusion of the camp, which had been named "Camp Experiment," it was felt that the experiment had been a decided success, and the camp therefore became an annual affair.

Many of the young company grade officers who passed through Fort Monroe in the first two-year course of the Artillery School were later to hold important military positions. First Lieutenant Lewis G. DeRussy eventually became a major and paymaster before being dropped from the service in 1842, apparently for a technicality. He was the brother of Rene DeRussy who served for many years as superintending engineer at Fort Monroe. Lewis DeRussy became colonel of the 1st Louisiana Volunteers in the Mexican War and subsequently served as colonel of the 2d Louisiana Infantry and of Engineers in the Confederate Army. Second Lieutenant Walter Gwynn resigned in 1832, but served as a Brigadier General of Virginia Militia during the Civil War and was in charge of the defenses of Norfolk.

First Lieutenant William W. Morris, after a distinguished career in the Seminole and Mexican Wars, rose to Colonel of the 2d Artillery and was brevetted major general for meritorious services in the Civil War. First Lieutenant Samuel Ringgold was brevetted for gallantry in the Seminole War and mortally wounded in the Battle of Palo Alto in the Mexican War while commanding his company. First Lieutenant James W. Ripley subsequently transferred to the Ordnance Department and rose to Brigadier General and Chief of Ordnance from 1861 to 1863. First Lieutenant Daniel Tyler resigned in 1834, but was appointed a brigadier general and commanded a brigade at the first Battle of Bull Run.

Second Lieutenant Robert Anderson was the defender of Fort Sumter at the beginning of the Civil War, was promoted to brigadier general, and brevetted major general. First Lieutenant Samuel Cooper eventually became Colonel and The Adjutant General of the United States Army. He joined the Confederacy and became General and Adjutant and Inspector General of the Confederate Army. First Lieutenant Richard B. Lee, the uncle of Robert E. Lee, became a Major and Commissary of Subsistence and then served in the Confederate Army as Lieutenant Colonel and Commissary. First Lieutenant James Monroe, the nephew of President James Monroe, resigned in 1832. His subsequent distinguished civilian career included a term in the House of Representatives. Second Lieutenant George Nauman eventually became Lieutenant Colonel of the 1st Artillery and commanded the artillery at Newport News in 1861 and 1862.[22]

The long hours of drill and instruction were broken on occasion by social events. On July 17, 1827, about 200 persons, including citizens of Norfolk, Portsmouth, and Hampton and Navy and Marine officers attended a ball at Fort Monroe in honor of the officers of the U.S.S. *Natchez*. Part of the officers quarters were converted into a ballroom decorated with naval and military devices, including Perry's famous "We have met the enemy, and they are ours." One of the guests commented, "But what gave the entertainment its most captivating attraction, was the rich display of female beauty that circled so gracefully in the mazes of the dance, to the thrilling music of the elegant and scientific band—which . . . feasted every eye and delighted every ear. These, with the graceful and refined attentions of the officers of the Garrison, the splendid array of rich uniforms, and the elegant and bountiful refreshments, served in the neatest and most alluring style, rendered the *tout ensemble* delightful beyond description, and kept the company together until after 2 o'clock in the morning."[23]

The officers of the garrison made a good impression on the parade ground as well as in the ballroom. Captain Basil Hall of the Royal Navy witnessed the evening parade on February 7, 1828, and commented, "for the first time in the United States [I] saw a regular body of troops under arms. About 200 men were drawn up, amongst whom were no fewer than twenty-four officers, principally cadets sent from the Military Academy at West Point, to acquire a more thorough and practical knowledge of their business. The appearance of these troops was very soldier-like, and in every way creditable to the superintendence of the experienced officer in command of the station."[24]

The normal tour of duty for organizations at Fort Monroe was two years, and in 1826 and again in 1828 the entire garrison, with the exception of the faculty and staff of the Artillery School, was changed. Colonel

Eustis, after having been stationed at Fort Monroe for four and a half years, left in November 1828. Three classes had come under his instruction at the Artillery School, and most of the subaltern officers of the artillery had passed under his observation. In relinquishing the command, he stated: "During the past five years, nearly all of the company officers of the four Regiments of Artillery have passed under his immediate notice and command; he takes pride in recording his firm conviction, that for gentlemanlike accomplishments, honorable pride, professional acquirements, unimpeachable integrity and undoubted gallantry, the whole world cannot produce a corps of officers equal to the American artillery."[25] Colonel Eustis may have been severe and a great stickler for discipline, but he cannot be accused of being ungenerous.

Fort Monroe had become the home of the first Army service school. Problems abounded—the unfinished facilities at the post and difficulties in providing the school units being predominant—but under Colonel Eustis' able direction a professional program of instruction began to take shape. Although one of the newest posts, Fort Monroe had one of the largest garrisons in the Army. The ability to keep such a large proportion of such a small Army in one place was to prove to be the deciding factor in the success of the school.

Footnotes Chapter III

[1] He was the father of Maj. Gen. Lunsford L. Lomax, a cavalry officer in the Confederate Army. Ezra J. Warner, *Generals in Gray* (Baton Rouge: Louisiana State University Press, 1959), p. 190.

[2] William E. Birkhimer, *Historical Sketch of the Organization, Administration, Materiel and Tactics of the Artillery, United States Army* (New York: Greenwood Press, 1968), pp. 120–122.

[3] General Orders No. 18, Adjutant General's Office, April 5, 1824.

[4] General Orders No. 10, Adjutant General's Office, February 13, 1824.

[5] Pierce had entered the Army in 1812 and was promoted to captain in 1813, thus being senior to Lomax. He was brevetted for distinguished service in the Seminole War and became lieutenant colonel of the 1st Artillery in 1842. He died in 1850. *Heitman*, p. 791.

[6] Heitman and several other sources give Eustis' name as Abram. His tombstone and many contemporary documents, however, show the name as Abraham. The confusion apparently comes from the fact that he usually signed his name as "Abrm." Letter, Richard Ivey to Dr. Chester D. Bradley, June 15, 1971, in Casemate Museum.

[7] Vinton was an 1817 graduate of West Point and served at Fort Monroe from April 5, 1824, to March 1, 1825. Promoted to captain, 3d Artillery, he was brevetted for gallantry at the Battle of Monterrey and killed in action during the siege of Vera Cruz in 1847. Dusenberry was an 1820 West Point graduate who eventually became a Quartermaster major and died in 1855. Baker had entered the Army in 1813 and rose to the rank of lieutenant colonel before resigning in 1854. McIntire had entered the Army in 1814 as an enlisted man and had been commissioned in 1818. He resigned in 1826 and died in 1836. Wharton had been commissioned in 1818, transferred to the infantry in 1826, and became lieutenant colonel of the 1st Dragoons before his death in 1848. Whiting had been commissioned in the Light Dragoons in 1808, transferred to the infantry after the War of 1812, transferred to the artillery in the reorganization of 1821, was

brevetted brigadier general for gallantry at the Battle of Buena Vista, and became colonel and Assistant Quartermaster General before his death in 1851. Maupin served as a medical officer with the Army from 1802 until his death in 1825. Archer had entered the medical service in 1814 and served, with a brief break in 1826, until his resignation in 1840. Following his resignation, he established the Sherwood Inn at Fort Monroe. He sold the hotel in 1850 and died in 1877, *Cullum,* Vol. I, pp. 159–160, 253–254; *Heitman,* pp. 168, 184–185, 668, 697, 1022, 1030.

[8] Orders No. 1, Artillery Corps for Instruction, April 11, 1824. NA, Fort Monroe records, Records of United States Army Continental Commands, 1821–1920, RG 393.

[9] *General regulations of the Army; or Military Institutes* (Washington, 1825).

[10] Orders No. 24, Artillery Corps for Instruction, May 20, 1824, NA, RG 393.

[11] Artillery School, U.S.A., Court Martial Proceedings, April 8, 1824 to August 15, 1825, pp. 25–26, NA, RG 393.

[12] *Ibid.,* p. 67.

[13] Morgan Dix, *Memoirs of John Adams Dix* (New York: Harper & Brothers, 1883), Vol. I, pp. 79–80. Dix had been commissioned in 1813 at the age of fourteen. He became a captain in the 1st Artillery in 1825 and resigned in 1828. Dix then launched a brilliant political career. He served as Secretary of State of New York, United States senator from New York, Postmaster of New York City, and Secretary of the Treasury of the United States. At the beginning of the Civil War he was commissioned major general of volunteers. Following the war, he was Minister to France and Governor of New York.

[14] Special Orders No. 8, Artillery School of Practice, February 12, 1827, NA, RG 393.

[15] Careful research has failed to identify further this apparently standard military musical composition.

[16] Special Orders No. 8, Artillery School of Practice, February 12, 1827, NA, RG 393.

[17] Orders No. 60, Artillery Corps for Instruction, NA, RG, 393.

[18] Orders No. 90, Artillery Corps for Instruction, NA, RG 393.

[19] Artillery School, U.S.A. Court Martial Proceedings, April 18, 1824, to August 15, 1825, pp. 78–87, NA, RG 393.

[20] Orders No. 99, Artillery Corps for Instruction, November 2, 1824, NA, RG 393.

[21] Orders No. 125, Artillery School of Practice, November 18, 1825; Orders No. 126, Artillery School of Practice, November 21, 1825; NA, RG 393.

[22] *Cullum,* Vol. I, pp. 114–115, 119–123, 133–137, 150–151, 160–161, 222–223, 261–262, 280–281, 304–305, 347–352.

[23] John C. Emmerson, Jr., *Steam Navigation in Virginia and North Carolina Waters* (Portsmouth, Va.: privately printed, 1949), pp. 46–47.

[24] Capt. Basil Hall, *Travels in North America in the Years 1827 and 1828,* quoted in Col. Earl W. Thomson, "The Army of the United States from 1830 to 1840," *Coast Artillery Journal,* 79 (November-December 1936), p. 442.

[25] Orders No. 134, Artillery School of Practice, November 13, 1828, NA, RG 393.

Chapter IV

Alarms and Excursions

THE GREAT EXPECTATIONS that Fort Monroe would become the center of artillery development in America were soon doomed to disappointment. As the Artillery School of Practice steadily declined, the role of the post changed. War in far off Florida eventually reduced the garrison to its lowest level in the long history of the post. With peace, or at least a diminishment of hostilities, in Florida, Fort Monroe resumed normal operations. The Mexican War caused a brief flurry of activity, but it was not until the 1850's the artillery branch was finally able to again consider the question of better professional training.

A significant change in the attitude of the War Department toward the Artillery School of Practice had begun in 1828. The death of General Brown in February of that year deprived the school of a staunch friend. Major General Alexander Macomb, the new Commanding General of the Army, though an artillery officer, was of the opinion that the school should give up some of its companies for duty at ordinary artillery posts. The numerous fortifications completed or under construction along the Atlantic seaboard required garrisons which could only be provided by reducing the garrison of the Artillery School. There was no idea at this time of discontinuing any of the activities of the school, but the two-year system of rotation was broken up and the garrison was reduced to six companies of the 1st Artillery through transfer and reassignment during 1828 and 1829.[1]

During 1828, the school suffered another blow with the transfer of Colonel Eustis. Colonel James House, of the 1st Artillery, arrived in the latter part of the year to relieve Colonel Eustis as commandant and within a short time after his arrival he practically turned the school over to the second in command, subordinating the school to the post. House was at this time already an old man. During the Revolutionary War he had acquired a fair reputation as a portrait painter, and when he entered the service (in 1799) at the age of thirty-nine as a lieutenant in the 1st Artillerists he had no particular adaptation to military life and no special military training. Never a strict disciplinarian, his reputation was that of an "old fogy," and he was inclined to be of a morose, unsociable disposition, due perhaps to the fact that many of the younger officers delighted in worrying and annoying him. He was a man of strict honor, probity, and morality, of artistic tastes, unobtrusive and diffident in manner, but always courteous. House enjoyed the particular confidence of General Macomb and was highly respected at the War Department.

An incident occurred on December 20, 1828, without remark at the time but which has more than passing interest to us now. On that day, pursuant to Special Orders No. 91, Private E. A. Perry, of Company H, 1st Artillery, reported for duty in the Adjutant's office. Private Perry is better known to us as Edgar Allan Poe. Following increasing difficulties with his foster father, Poe had enlisted in the 1st Artillery at Boston in 1827. Company H was transferred to Fort Moultrie, South Carolina, in November 1827 and then to Fort Monroe on December 15, 1828. Poe was promoted to regimental sergeant major on January 1, 1829, only a few days before his twentieth birthday.

Poe had risen to the highest noncommissioned grade in a surprisingly short time, but he had no ambition for a military career. Intent on pursuing his literary ambitions, Poe had revealed his real name and the reasons for leaving home to First Lieutenant Joshua Howard, who commanded Company H.[2] Taking an interest in the young man, Howard discussed his case with other officers and they agreed that Sergeant Major Perry could be discharged if he was reconciled with his foster father. At first ignored by John Allan, his foster father, Poe tried again:

> Lieut. Howard . . . promised me my discharge solely upon a re-conciliation with yourself—In vain I told him that your wishes for me . . . were, and have always been those of a father & that you were ready to forgive even the worst offences—He insisted upon my writing to you. . . . He has always been kind to me, and, in many respects, reminds me forcibly of yourself—The period of an Enlistment is five years—the prime of my life would be wasted—I shall be driven to more decided measures if you refuse to assist me. You need not fear for my future prosperity. . . . I feel that within me which will make me fulfill your highest wishes. . . .

Still receiving no reply, Poe wrote on December 22, 1829: "All that is necessary to obtain my discharge from the army was your consent in a letter to Lieut. J. Howard . . . Lieut. Howard has given me an introduction to Col. James House. . . . He spoke kindly to me, told me he was personally acquainted with my Grandfather Gen Poe[3] . . . & reassured me of my immediate discharge upon your consent."

The continued refusal of John Allan to respond to his foster son's pleas finally resulted in Sergeant Major Perry being taken to the post hospital with a fever. Upon his recovery, Poe set about to obtain a cadet's appointment to the Military Academy. With this tempting offer, Poe finally obtained John Allan's consent to a discharge. Colonel House wrote to the Eastern Department on March 30, 1829, giving a fanciful account of the sergeant major's early life and recommending that he be discharged on procuring a substitute. A substitute was found—Sergeant Samuel Graves. Unfortunately, at the time that Graves offered his services, neither Colonel House nor Lieutenant Howard was present to make the negotiation. Ordinarily, the bounty for a new recruit who offered himself as a substitute was $12. Graves, however, was a sergeant and probably had a good idea how badly the sergeant major wanted out. His price was $75. Poe was forced to give Sergeant Graves $25 in cash and a note for the remaining $50. He was discharged on April 15, 1829, and left Fort Monroe a week later, fortified by three letters of recommendation from his superior officers. Poe entered the Military Academy finally on July 1, 1830, where he served only until his dismissal on March 6, 1831.[4]

During 1829, the Commanding Officer encountered a new period of tribulation because of animals—cows, this time. Many of the members of the garrison kept cows that they might have fresh milk. Theoretically, the cows were brought into the fort only during milking periods. Practically, they ran at large. The ramparts of the fort provided them with more luscious grass than was to be found elsewhere and there they were usually to be found. Their sharp hoofs damaged the embankments, causing great annoyance to the authorities over this injury to the fortifications. Orders were issued. Cows were not to be permitted to run at large, they were to be removed from the fort before nightfall, gates were to be erected at the main gate, etc.; but the damage continued. Finally, orders were issued directing that all cows found loose be impounded by the guard and held until identified by the owners. These, disclosing their own identity in claiming their stock, were then to be forbidden to keep cows on the post. This apparently had the desired effect, and cows ceased to be a feature in post orders.[5]

President Andrew Jackson arrived at Fort Monroe by boat on the afternoon of July 9, 1829. He was accompanied by Secretary of War John H. Eaton, Secretary of the Navy John Branch, Postmaster General William T. Barry, Generals Macomb and Bernard, and a number of naval officers and friends. As the boat hove in sight, the south bastion of the fort was manned by a detachment of artillery and a guard was paraded on the beach to escort the President to his quarters. When the steamer docked, Colonel House, with his staff and the officers of the post, went on board to meet the President. They then proceeded to Colonel House's quarters as the artillery boomed a salute.

The next day, the President and his party went by boat to Norfolk and Portsmouth to inspect the navy yard. On their way back to Fort Monroe that evening, Jackson stopped at the Rip Raps to see the progress of the fortifications. Apparently he was favorably impressed by the rocky little artificial island. On Sunday, President Jackson attended divine services at Fort Monroe performed by the Reverend Chevers and then returned to Washington on Monday.[6]

At this time, Jackson was embroiled in the controversy over Peggy Eaton, the wife of the Secretary of War, and was in poor health. The visit to Fort Monroe in July had supposedly been for his health, but it was obvious that the number of official functions during that visit gave him no opportunity to rest. He returned in late August, accompanied by Eaton and General Gratiot. This time the President chose to stay at the Rip Raps rather than at Fort Monroe. He spent his time bathing in the sea and refused to take part in any official functions, although any visitors appear to have been welcome. After ten days of relaxation, Jackson departed for Washington on August 31.[7]

Jackson found the Rip Raps to be a good place to get away from the many problems in Washington. He returned in late June 1831 for a few days with Nicholas Tryst and two or three friends. He returned again in July 1833, this time bringing along the entire White House family, including all the children and five servants. During this vacation, the President enjoyed an excursion to the Virginia Capes and witnessed a target firing by the Artillery School. A contemporary newspaper described the President's retreat in the following terms: "His *hotel* at the Rip-Raps is a delightful summer residence, freely inviting the breeze over the waters from every point of the compass, and with the polite and attentive host of the Hygeia, Mr. Marshall Parks, to cater for his table, he cannot be otherwise than 'comfortable.' "[8]

The last visit by Andrew Jackson to the Rip Raps was in July, 1835. Again accompanied by a large party of friends and relatives, he combined a vacation with official functions. During his stay he visited the navy yard and on July 14 went to Fort Monroe to review the troops and witness a target firing by the 32-pounder guns. Nearly a hundred persons from Norfolk came to witness the spectacle, but, as one of the newspapers reported, "they were cruelly disappointed; the review was over two hours before they arrived, and the target could not be adjusted in the desired position . . . in consequence of a strong breeze and high swell. But they saw the President . . . partook of the good cheer of the Hygeia, and came home tolerably reconciled." After a stay of about a month, Andrew Jackson departed Fort Monroe and the Rip Raps for the last time.[9]

After a year at Fort Monroe, Colonel House had turned the command over to Major and Brevet Colonel John de Barth Walbach, 1st Artillery, under whom the course of instruction was pursued during the year 1829–1830. A native of Germany and a graduate of Bonn University, Colonel Walbach had entered the American army in 1799 as a lieutenant of light dragoons. His service had been distinguished and he was noted as a soldierly officer. His rule was marked by a firm discipline, but he possessed the confidence of his associates to a remarkable degree and his administration of the Artillery School during the brief time he was in command was highly appreciated in the War Department.

In November 1829, a fire company was organized under the direction of the Quartermaster and the Commissary. On alternate Thursdays, the fire company formed, brought out the fire engine, and held a fire drill.[10]

An order of December 13, 1829, provides another idea in hygiene and sanitation.[11] "In consequence of a representation of the Surgeon of the Post that the continued practice of washing the floors of the Company Barracks Rooms is 'detrimental to the health of the troops' the Commandant calls the particular attention of Company officers to a paragraph in Order No. 4, dated January 13th, 1827, *expressly forbidding the same.*" The original prohibition was contained in an inconspicuous paragraph of general post orders, and was probably occasioned by the excessive moisture within the fort in those days of no drainage.

By 1830, life at Fort Monroe had become much more comfortable than in the earlier years. The fort was nearing completion and much of the rubbish incidental to construction had been removed. The physical well-being of the garrison was provided for by the hospital, which had been completed in the latter part of 1827; by the new system of water supply, installed in May 1830; and by the "public hotel," of which Mr. Parks was then the "keeper." We even find a "soda shop" conducted by Stephen Allen. The quarters of the artillery garrison (with the exception of one or two officers living outside who were moved into the fort in 1831) were within the fort (the casemates of fronts 1 and 2 caring for many of the officers), and the quarters of the Engineer garrison were outside. To make room for officers moving into the fort in 1831, noncommissioned officers were moved from Carroll Hall into casemates.

Colonel House had returned to command in December 1830, and had but four companies remaining under him—the number of companies at Fort Monroe marking at all times the strength of the commissioned student body. When the War Department decided in 1831 that the school should be sustained, Colonel Eustis was recalled from the command of New York Harbor and instructed to present plans for the re-establishment of the school. With him came enough troops to rebuild the garrison to ten companies. By the end of October 1831, the total strength of the school had reached twenty-seven officers and 565 enlisted men. "The School reopens," writes Colonel Eustis, "under the most gratifying conditions, and we may expect from it with reason, a season of profitable work."

The garrison now began to look to its recreational and spiritual welfare. There was communication with the mainland by a toll bridge over Mill Creek, but no good road was built to the bridge until March 1831. A theater was erected at this time, or a little earlier, the first reference to it being under date of August 19, 1831, when orders were issued directing that the theater not be used without special permission.

The religious interests of the garrison were in the charge of the Reverend Mark L. Chevers, of Hampton, who was later appointed post chaplain and joined the garrison on December 1, 1838. At first, church call was ordered whenever Dr. Chever's boat from Hampton landed at the wharf, but in February 1831, it was prescribed that church call should be sounded at 11:00 and 4:00 on alternate Sundays. After Chaplain Chevers joined at Fort Monroe he continued on duty there until his death on September 13, 1875.

In March 1831, Mr. Baker, of the Quartermaster Department, assisted by several women of the post, established a Sunday School for the benefit of the children at Fort Monroe. One gathers that the children were reluctant to attend. At any rate, post orders "enjoined on the commanding officers of companies and detachments to cause the children of the men under their command to attend" the Sunday School. The children themselves were required to be "cleanly in their persons and decently clad."[12]

There is little information about the climatic conditions at Fort Monroe. The very few brief references to the climate scarcely justify the formation of an opinion, but the little information available seems to indicate that the winters used to be longer and more severe than they are at the present time. Going all the way back to the days of the Jamestown Colony, we find that really severe winters were frequent, rather than otherwise. Captain John Smith tells us: "The sommer is hot as in Spain; the winter cold as in Fraunce or England. The heat of sommer is in June, Julie, and August, but commonly the cool Breeses asswage the vehemencie of the heat. The chiefe of winter is halfe December, January, February, and halfe March. The cold is extreme sharpe, but here the proverbe is true that no extreme long continueth."

"In the year 1607, was an extraordinary frost in most of Europe, and this frost was found as extreame in Virginia. But the next year for 8. or 10. daies of ill weather, other 14. daies would be as Sommer." In this connection, Percy says that on September 18, 1607, there "died one Ellis Kinistone which was starved to death with cold."

In 1824, the Surgeon noted on the sick report of September 21—six to ten weeks before cold weather may now be looked for: "Several of the sick are suffering materially for want of winter clothing." Fifty years later the weather statistics show a mean annual temperature of about 53°F. and a minimum winter temperature of about 12°F., with cold spells seldom lasting for more than a day or so—figures which approximate those of the present.

Fort Monroe received its official name on February 1, 1832, when Orders No. 11, A.G.O., prescribed: "It is the order of the Secretary of War that all the military posts, designated as Cantonments, be hereafter called Forts, and that the work at Old Point Comfort, be called Fort Monroe, and not Fortress Monroe."

So far as can be ascertained, the fort had never been formally named, although it had been known as Fortress Monroe from the very beginning. The name was natural enough. Since the fort was the largest to be constructed under the 1818 project, it was reasonable to name it after the President. The "Fortress" was also logical. At the time, it was generally believed that Fort Monroe was larger than any fort in Europe not inclosing a town or city, and thus, although it was not, strictly speaking, a fortress, we get the name "Fortress Monroe." That the name was not officially announced was probably from a sense of delicacy in naming an important military work after the President while he was living and in office.

With the close of the third decade of the century, the demands made upon the artillery for duty in the field and in the many fortifications along the coast became so numerous that the garrison at Fort Monroe was constantly shifting. Companies continually departed for some hazardous duty or rejoined after a period of absence. Routine instruction was almost entirely broken up, for the organizations were spending barely sufficient time at Fort Monroe to recuperate, recruit, and re-equip.

On December 19, 1830, Companies A (William J. Worth) and G (Reynold M. Kirby),[13] of the 1st Artillery, left Fort Monroe for Wilmington, North Carolina, in order "to be prepared to meet any insurrectionary movement which may take place at Wilmington or its vicinity about the period of the Christmas holidays," and with instructions not to let the reasons for the movement become known. No outbreak took place, and the two companies returned on May 14.[14]

In August 1831, the famous Nat Turner Rebellion in Southampton County, Virginia resulted in the murder of a number of the white inhabitants. Colonel House, commanding at Fort Monroe, responded to an appeal from the civil authorities for assistance by sending three companies. The Negroes were so quickly killed or captured by the militia and the white inhabitants that the troops had no chance to act and returned to the post after an absence of six days.[15]

At New Bern, North Carolina, it was feared that there would be a similar outbreak on the part of the slaves, so on September 10, 1831, Company I (Fabius Whiting),[16] of the 1st Artillery, was sent to assist the civil authorities in maintaining order. The company was relieved in November and sent elsewhere, but the alarm had not yet fully subsided. The women of New Bern sent a petition to the President asking that the company of artillery be sent back. President Andrew Jackson replied:

> Ladies: On the receipt of the memorial of the ladies of Newbern, N.C., I lost no time in referring the same to the secretary of war, with directions if Capt. Whiting's company had been removed from thence to order another company to Newbern for their protection and safety. I herewith inclose the reply of the secretary of war. That will show with what promptness I have met the prayer and wishes of the fair petitioners. Be pleased to communicate this to the memorialists, and believe me, with great respect.
> Your most obedient servant,
> Andrew Jackson

The inclosure was the following assurance from the Secretary of War:

> War Department, Dec. 5, 1831

> The secretary of war has the honor to return to the president the letter of the ladies of Newbern, inclosing their memorial, and to inform the president that Capt. Whiting's company was some time since withdrawn, but that another has this day been ordered from Old Point Comfort to supply its place.

Company H (Henry W. Griswold),[17] of the 1st Artillery, left Fort Monroe in response to this petition on December 16, 1831. In April 1832, the company was moved to Beaufort, North Carolina, where the Negroes were reported to be in a very uneasy state, and, although no uprising took place, the company was not returned to its proper station until June 1833.[18]

Only a few weeks before the Nat Turner Rebellion, a young second lieutenant of the Corps of Engineers and his bride arrived at Fort Monroe. Robert E. Lee was assigned as assistant to Captain Andrew Talcott, the constructing engineer at the post.[19] The arrival of three companies of the 3d Artillery and two of the 4th Artillery soon after to guard against any further rebellions brought Second Lieutenant Joseph E. Johnston, a friend of Lee's from West Point, to the garrison.[20] Lee's first son, George Washington Custis Lee, was born at Fort Monroe.[21]

Lee came to Fort Monroe as an assistant of limited experience. He was to leave fully qualified to direct a large engineering project. Captain Talcott was absent on other duty for part of the building season in 1832, and for virtually all the seasons of 1833 and 1834. The counterscarp wall was finished, the scarp wall pointed, and a considerable part of the casemated covertway was arched by August 1832, when cholera broke out and forced Captain Talcott, who was then on duty, to suspend operations. Slave owners became alarmed for the safety of their servants and would not hire then out in adequate numbers. The arches, however, were finished before the season ended. Labor continued scarce during 1833, despite an increase of 15 percent in wages. Some painting and a good deal of carpenter work was done, but progress was not so rapid as had been hoped. It was nearly December before enough workers were at hand to resume labor on the ramparts, and only a short time later they had to be laid off because of the damage done by a heavy storm.[22]

Lee went to work as soon as he could assemble his force of laborers at the beginning of the 1834 season and, undeterred by another storm that wrecked several vessels in Hampton Roads, he got an extensive season's programme under way. When the project was nearing completion, uncertainty concerning further appropriations threatened to force the discharge of the laborers, but this was averted for the time. Very little work was undertaken at Fort Calhoun, despite President Jackson's desire to have it completed before the expiration of his term. The foundations continued to sink at the rate of three inches a year. All that could be done was to continue to pile up stone in the hope that the substratum would be so compressed that it would carry the weight of the walls.

Lee did some designing of buildings, wharves, and fortifications; he supervised the preparation of accounts and of monthly and annual reports; he faced some of the problems of sanitation, with which the science of his day was unable to cope; he had a large experience in estimating construction costs; he was inducted into the mysteries of banking and departmental finance. The art of dealing with labor he acquired so successfully that after an emergency in April 1834, when all hands had been called out to build a barricade in a blinding blow of sand, hail, and rain, he had been able to say with pride, "I never saw men work better." Lee bargained closely for schooner hire, and was uneasy when he thought the vessels did not carry so much as they should. When additional stone was needed at Fort Monroe he figured he could take the rough hewings at Fort Calhoun and dress them for not much more than half what the material would cost elsewhere.

An interesting comment on the effects of garrison life on the officers is given by Lee in a letter to Second Lieutenant John Mackay: ". . . My opinion on these matters has been formed, from the little experience I have had of a Garrison life in time of peace, where I have seen minds formed for use and ornament, degenerate into sluggishness and inactivity, requiring the stimulus of brandy and cards to rouse them to action, and apparently a burden to the possessors and perhaps an injury to their companions." The drinking in which some of the officers indulged in their idleness ceased to be taken as a matter of course and came to puzzle Lee. "He is a fine looking young man," he said of a lieutenant who had been arrested for being drunk on parade. "Graduated very well in 1832 and appears to be intelligent. But his propensity, it is impossible for me to comprehend."

Of more immediate and serious import, however, were the constant jealousies and conflicts of authority between the staff and the line. The line officers disliked the large liberty the engineers had to make contracts and to disburse public funds. Following a clash with Colonel Eustis in 1831 over orders for the exclusion of Negroes from the fort, there had been several squabbles, and in one instance a controversy of some seriousness over the discharge of Lee's principal overseer because of a quarrel with a captain at the post. In this instance, junior officer though he was, Lee did not hesitate to express to headquarters his sympathy with the discharged man, who, he said, had been zealous and faithful in the discharge of his duties. Lee's differences, however, were incidental to a continuing feud between Captain Talcott and the line. This quarrel was over the engineers' use of quarters within the fort,[23] and, more hotly, over the direction by the engineers of the remaining work at Fort Monroe. Talcott thought the engineers should complete the whole enterprise. The officers of the garrison wished it finished by the troops and laborers of the fort. Each side suspected the other of plotting against it.[24]

In May 1832, the Black Hawk War had broken out in Illinois and the Commanding Officer at Fort Monroe was directed to send five companies to Chicago, by way of New York and the Great Lakes. The battalion, commanded by Brevet Lieutenant Colonel Ichabod B. Crane, consisted of Companies G (R. M. Kirby), of the 1st Artillery, B (Upton S. Fraser) and E (Elijah Lyon), of the 3d Artillery, and C (Patrick H. Galt) and G (John Munroe), of the 4th Artillery.[25] These troops left on June 19, and were followed three days later by Company H (Aeneas Mackay), [26] of the 3d Artillery. While the troops under General Winfield Scott were crossing the lakes from Buffalo, cholera made its appearance. The artillery battalion, with a strength of about 220, lost fifty-five men through this dread disease. Lieutenant Ebenezer S. Sibley,[27] commanding Company G, 1st Artillery, fared particularly well, in that he lost but one man. The disease disappeared as suddenly as it had appeared, but the battalion recovered too late to take an active part in the campaign. Relieved from duty in the field, it arrived at Fort Monroe on November 7.[28]

The war having resulted in the defeat and capture of Black Hawk, that chieftain and several of his leading men were sent to St. Louis in the custody of Second Lieutenant Jefferson Davis. The Indians arrived in Washington on April 22, 1833, but they were not permitted to see the President until April 25. They were greatly cast down when he told them that they must go to Fort Monroe, to stay until he decided they could go home. There were several reasons for sending them to Fort Monroe. First, it would be difficult for them to escape and, if by any chance they did, they could be easily apprehended. Secondly, by placing them in a more thickly populated area of the country, the Indians would be impressed with the futility of further resistance to such a numerous and powerful people. Their arrival at Fort Monroe was heralded long in advance by the newspapers of New York, Washington, Richmond, and Norfolk. As far back as February the editor of the *Norfolk Herald* had pointed out that the Indians would be "objects of much curiosity at Old Point Comfort" and had gravely cautioned Marshall Parks, then owner of the Hygeia Hotel, that unless he made some additions to "his already extensive establishment . . . he will very probably be at a loss for room to accommodate the visitors who will crowd upon him to see those 'Lions of the West.' "

The Indians and their escort, commanded by Lieutenant Thomas L. Alexander, left Washington on the same day they saw the President. They arrived in Richmond on April 28 and departed for Fort Monroe on the morning of May 1 on the steamer *Patrick Henry*.

Colonel Eustis had been instructed to deal leniently with the hostages. They were to be given "every proper indulgence" and to be "restricted only to the limits of the garrison." As had been predicted by the editor of the *Norfolk Herald,* Black Hawk and his companions were "the objects of much curiosity." They were daily "beset by visitors who crowded to see them from all quarters." Steamboat excursions to Old Point Comfort were organized for this purpose. Noted artists came to paint their portraits. It is reported that Robert M. Sully spent six weeks at Fort Monroe making portraits of Black Hawk, Whirling Thunder, and the Prophet. Other artists who came to make portraits of the Indians were Samuel M. Brookes, John Wesley Jarvis, and Charles Bird King.

Of his stay at Fort Monroe, Black Hawk said, "The war chief (Colonel Eustis) met us on our arrival, and shook hands, and appeared glad to see me. He treated us with great friendship, and talked to me frequently. Previous to our leaving this fort, he gave us a feast, and made us some presents, which I intend to keep for his sake. He is a very good man, and great brave! I was sorry to leave him, although I was going to return to my people, because he had treated me like a brother, during all the time I remained with him." The Indians left Fort Monroe on the evening of June 4, 1833, with Brevet Major John Garland in charge of them.[29]

The troops returning from the Black Hawk War had but a month before they were again called away. Political disturbances, arising from the unwillingness of the State of South Carolina to permit the collection of duties on certain imports, induced the governmental authorities to assemble additional troops in Charleston harbor. Companies C, of the 1st Artillery, and B (James W. Ripley), of the 4th Artillery, left for Fort Moultrie on November 16, 1832; and Companies G, 1st Artillery, B and

E, 3d Artillery, and C and G, 4th Artillery, followed on December 23. Modification of the tariff allayed the irritation, and five of the companies returned to Fort Monroe in May 1833. It was their fortune to remain this time for six months before their services were again required elsewhere.

In September 1833, the Secretary of War, by direction of the President, instructed the United States marshal for the Southern District of Alabama to remove all white persons from the territory ceded to the United States by the Creek Indians in March 1832. Since the authorities of the State of Alabama seemed disposed to prevent the marshal from obeying his orders, a strong detachment was sent into that region to assist and protect him in carrying out his instructions. A part of this detachment consisted of eight companies ordered from Fort Monroe to Fort Mitchell, Alabama. These companies, which departed in the latter part of November, were A, H, and I, of the 1st Artillery, B and H, of the 3d Artillery, and A, B, and C, of the 4th Artillery. The one company remaining at Fort Monroe— E, 3d Artillery, Captain Elijah Lyon commanding—was reinforced in December by Companies C and I, 3d Artillery. No collision took place in Alabama, and in April Companies I, 1st Artillery, and A, B, and C, 4th Artillery, accompanied by Companies C, 1st Artillery, and F, 2d Artillery, returned to Fort Monroe, bringing the garrison again to nine companies.[30]

The experiences of these few years were most discouraging. The frequent moves of the garrison and the constantly changing personnel had made instruction all but impossible. Since the future showed no encouraging prospect it was decided to give up for a time all attempt to maintain the school. On April 19, 1834, the War Department directed that the garrison at Fort Monroe should no longer be regarded as the School of Practice and that it should assume the status of other military posts.[31] Since Colonel Eustis, the Commandant, Major William Gates, the Major, and Lieutenant William Maynadier, the Secretary—the three remaining members of the staff of the school—had been absent for more than four months, and since the garrison had been reduced to two companies, both of which had been present for only four months, the order closing the school was merely a gesture which made of record that which had already become an accomplished fact.[32]

The engineers regarded the dissolution of the Artillery School of Practice as a victory, though they had no part in bringing it about. Lieutenant Lee rejoiced that "the Cincinnati," as he put it, were called "from their ploughs to their swords." The number of idlers, in the eyes of the busy engineers, was greatly reduced. When some of the artillery officers were ordered from Old Point Comfort they were put aboard the *Alabama,* and there they remained—indefinitely, as it seemed. Having nothing to do, the bored artillerymen arranged a grand party. They did not invite the wives of the officers of the garrison or the young aristocrats of Hampton Roads. Instead, they summoned to the ship the ladies of easy virtue in the neighborhood.

If they had to be caged in that confounded ship, forever rolling and pitching in the wintry sea, the gunners would at least have one great evening, with merriment unrestrained. High preparations were made in galley and in cabin; eagerly the young officers awaited the arrival of the Circes. They came not. At last, when an explanation was had, it was distressful: In order to tune themselves up for the evening the expected guests had indulged themselves in a little spirits and, most deplorably, had become too drunk for the journey. Johnston had no part in this, except perhaps as a spectator aboard the ship, but it was a flat anticlimax to the residence at Old Point of officers who had given gaiety to day and noise to night.[33]

On July 18, 1834, General Macomb came to Fort Monroe with the Secretary of War and examined the work being done at Old Point Comfort and at the Rip Raps. He said little about his findings but went back to Washington and filed a report. Six days later the inspector general of the army, General Wool, arrived at the fort to examine the works. Captain Talcott happened to be absent in Norfolk at the time, so Lieutenant Lee had to do the honors. When he waited on Wool for that purpose, the general asked if it were not a fact that General Macomb had recently made an inspection. As Lee confirmed this without comment, Wool said that he saw no reason for going over details of the work, but that, for his own information, he would like to see Fort Calhoun. Lee took him out to the Rip Raps immediately, despite the fact that it was a blistering hot day. Wool inquired if there were not quarters outside the fort for the engineers, which Lee took as a bad sign. Wool did nothing further that day and on the following morning merely walked on the ramparts with Lee for a time before breakfast.

On July 31, the War Department directed that "on the report of the Major General Commanding the Army" the engineer department in Hampton Roads should be transferred to the Rip Raps and that the commandant at Fort Monroe should be charged with the completion of the works at Old Point Comfort, "under directions and instructions from General Head Quarters." Only one officer of engineers was to be left at Hampton Roads and he was to take up his quarters at the Rip Raps, with all his force, by August 31, "or earlier if convenient."[34] The engineers were allowed to get their water from the cisterns at Fort Monroe. The order concluded with a statement that it was understood no further appropriations were to be asked for Fort Monroe. It was hoped by a judicious application of unexpended balances, and funds made available through the sale of surplus engineering property, "that Fort Monroe may be placed in a respectable condition both as to defence and appearance."

The engineer's workmen were to go to the Rip Raps, with Lee in charge, and Talcott was sent to the Hudson River. The frustrated engineers could not foresee that in a little more than a year the offending order would be revoked and the authority of the engineers restored. For the time the work was ended. Lee moved over to the poorly equipped Rip Raps. He went there so much in advance of the designated August 31 date that he wrote Talcott on that day he might "be considered an old inhabitant." At the Rip Raps, Lee's task was simply that of supervising the piling up of stone on the foundations, which still continued to sink just enough to make construction of the fort impossible. It was no work for a young and active man whose ability his chief in Washington had already discovered. About October 25, 1834, when he had been at Rip Raps only two months, Lee received an invitation from General Gratiot to come to Washington. Gratiot offered Lee the job of an assistant in his office. In November, Lee was relieved at Fort Calhoun by Captain W. A. Eliason and was ordered to report for service as assistant to the Chief of Engineers.[35]

Colonel Eustis had been relieved of command of Fort Monroe in June 1834 by Major Alexander C. W. Fanning, 4th Artillery, who remained in command for two months. After him, the fort was commanded successively by Colonel and Brevet Brigadier General Walker K. Armistead, 3d Artillery, to July 1835; Lieutenant Colonel James Bankhead, 3d Artillery, to October 1835; and General Armistead again to July 1836.[36]

The outbreak of the war with the Seminole Indians in Florida over their reluctance to emigrate to the West again took the garrison from Fort Monroe. Two companies were sent to northern stations in 1835, and four companies were dispatched to Fort King, Florida, in February, as a precautionary measure. Two companies joined during the winter and spring of 1835–1836, bringing the garrison to five companies. Four of these were sent to Fort Mitchell in May 1836, and the final company left for Garey's Ferry, Florida, on June 30, three days before General Armistead himself departed.

The post, reduced to a garrison consisting of some recruit detachments, now came under the command of a subaltern—First Lieutenant Timothy Green, 1st Artillery—whose record is worth repeating. Lieutenant Green had been Commissary at Fort Monroe from the early days of its occupation. In 1832, when he became due for promotion, he weighed the relative advantages of duty at Fort Monroe as brevet captain, first lieutenant, and commissary with the advantages of duty elsewhere as captain. Deciding in favor of Fort Monroe, he declined the promotion and was humored with a vengeance. Apparently he was never again offered promotion, and he remained at Fort Monroe, the senior lieutenant in the 1st Artillery, until his death in 1847.

During the five years that the Army remained in the South, Fort

Monroe served as a base for the troops in Florida. Here recruits were assembled and prepared for service before proceeding south, and here troops from Florida were recuperated. In August 1837, there were at Fort Monroe, ten companies of recruits (numbered from 1 to 10) with an average strength of 100 men each. In January 1839, the garrison had been reduced to three officers (including the surgeon and the chaplain) and nine enlisted men present.[37]

There was, however, considerable activity at Fort Monroe, other than that of the artillery. The Engineer Department, a separate command, was continuing its efforts towards the completion of the fort; and the Fort Monroe Arsenal, another separate command, had grown to be one of the large arsenals of the country.

This arsenal was a growth, probably accidental, from the instructional courses of the Artillery School. In 1824, Captain Rufus L. Baker had joined the School as Director of Artillery, but within six months he became the local Ordnance Officer, and his assistant, Lieutenant John Symington,[38] was called the Assistant Ordnance Officer. These two officers were charged with the laboratory instruction, at which classes of officers were taught the manufacture, care, and handling of powders. The laboratory—as such things do—tended to expand under Captain Baker, who was relieved in 1828.

First Lieutenant William H. Bell, 4th Artillery,[39] and Second Lieutenant William Maynadier, 1st Artillery, took over the ordnance duties and further expanded that department. In October 1829, they were taken up on the morning report as a detachment of Ordnance, and in February 1830, they were joined by four enlisted men of the Ordnance Department. In 1833, the organization became a depot, and by 1836 it had become an arsenal. In 1834, the arsenal employed thirty-nine workmen, a number which was exceeded only by the arsenals at Watervliet, Washington, Detroit, and Pittsburgh.

Probably because the arsenal at Fort Monroe was not general in its operations, it did not appear on the list of arsenals given in the Army Register until 1852, when Brevet Major George D. Ramsay, Ordnance Department, was in charge.[40] It specialized in seacoast armament, manufacturing seacoast gun carriages, and in 1841 it was one of the four manufacturing arsenals in the United States.

In 1837, under a reorganization of the forces of the United States, the country was divided into military departments, of which Department No. 4 embraced the States of South Carolina, North Carolina, and Virginia.[41] General Orders No. 57, issued shortly thereafter, assigned Brevet Brigadier General Eustis, Colonel, 1st Artillery, to the command of the Department, with headquarters at Fort Monroe. General Eustis arrived in September, but he remained a scant six weeks, his services then being required elsewhere. Exigencies of the service not only prevented building up of the garrison at Fort Monroe, but withdrew such garrison as was then present. Except for very brief periods of time when troops en route to the South stopped at the post, Fort Monroe was garrisoned only by detachments of recruits until 1841.

In 1838 practically all of the recruits at Fort Monroe were ordered to Sacket's Harbor, New York, or to Swanton, on the Vermont frontier. This move was a precaution resulting from the Mackenzie Rebellion in Canada. Company K, 3d Artillery, arrived in July to garrison the post but was withdrawn in November, following receipt of General Orders No. 49, which directed that all troops be withdrawn from Fort Monroe in order that the Engineer Department might proceed with repairs to the fort. Troops of the Ordnance Department were excepted from the requirements of these orders, and that department continued its operations at the arsenal.[42]

In 1841 the Artillery regarrisoned Fort Monroe, Companies C, H, and K, 2d Artillery, joining in September, with Lieutenant Colonel Alexander C. W. Fanning in command. Fanning was a highly respected one-armed veteran of the War of 1812 and the Seminole War. Eight companies of the 4th Artillery joined in July 1842, the three companies of the 2d Artillery leaving. Once more the garrison had reached a respectable size, and Lieutenant Colonel Ichabod B. Crane, 4th Artillery, assumed command, only to be relieved in August by the recently promoted regimental commander, Colonel John de Barth Walbach, returning to command after an interval of twelve years.[43]

Andrew Jackson was not the only President who sought the solitude of Fort Calhoun. On September 10, 1842, Letitia Christian Tyler, the first wife of President John Tyler, died at the White House after a long illness. On the ensuing Monday after a funeral service in Washington, the remains were brought to New Kent County, where they were interred. The President then boarded a steamer above Jamestown for Old Point Comfort. Accompanied by Henry A. Wise and Caleb Cushing, the President retired to Fort Calhoun. While the party was at Fort Calhoun, a delegation from Norfolk tendered the President the hospitalities of the borough. Tyler excused himself, expressing a wish to avoid all public attentions.[44]

In 1844, President Tyler married Julia Gardiner. The honeymooners left Washington by boat on July 3 and arrived at Old Point Comfort early the next morning. They were met at the dock by Lieutenant Colonel Rene E. De Russy, the chief engineer at Fort Monroe, who conducted them to their cottage. De Russy had acted as the President's agent and had made all the arrangements for the couple's stay at Fort Monroe.[45] The next two days were filled with social activities. All the officers of the garrison marched in a body to pay their respects to the Commander-in-Chief and his bride. The Tylers remained at Old Point Comfort until early August, taking time to visit the President's plantation, Sherwood Forest, above Jamestown.

In late June 1845, ex-President and Mrs. Tyler returned to Old Point Comfort to celebrate their first anniversary. This time they joined the glittering social set gathered for the season at the Hygeia Hotel. This visit had an added bit of excitement when a hurricane struck in late June. The storm ripped the roof and shingles off the hotel, but Mrs. Tyler calmly rescued her canary amidst the confusion.[46]

In the latter part of 1842 another reorganization of the geographical departments of the United States had made Fort Monroe the headquarters of Military Department No. 7, embracing the States of Delaware, Maryland, and Virginia, and including the stations of Fort McHenry, Fort Severn, Fort Monroe, and Fort Washington.[47] The first three of these forts were garrisoned by the 4th Artillery, but Fort Washington was without a garrison. Late in 1848, by a contraction of the military departments, Department No. 4 was formed to embrace the States of Virginia, North Carolina, South Carolina, Georgia, and that part of Florida included in the Eastern Division. Department headquarters was temporarily established at Baltimore, but by General Orders No. 1, A.G.O., 1849, the headquarters was moved to Fort Monroe and its command was assigned the Brevet Brigadier General James Bankhead. The existing arrangement of geographical departments was abolished in October 1853, and Department No. 4 was merged with others in the Department of the East, which had its headquarters at Baltimore.[48]

The outbreak of the war with Mexico again called the troops into the field and left Fort Monroe once more with but a small garrison. Again the post was made a rendezvous for recruits, and for a large part of the period from November 1845 to July 1848, the only garrison was in the form of recruit detachments or organizations awaiting transportation to Mexico. Five companies of the First Virginia Volunteers, temporarily under the command of Captain Robert G. Scott, Jr., reached Fort Monroe after dark on January 3, 1847, arriving unexpected by Colonel Walbach. Nothing had been done to provide the "comforts necessary *even* for a soldier," Captain Scott complained. There was barely sufficient quarters for the battalion, and Scott suggested that no more companies be sent to the post until after the battalion had sailed, or at least until there were better accommodations. Another company arrived on January 8, and on the following day Major Jubal A. Early assumed command of the battalion.[49]

Colonel Walbach wanted to send off the companies in the first available transports, but upon learning that the troops lacked proper clothing, the War Department directed Walbach to wait until the clothing had arrived from Richmond. Colonel John F. Hamtramck and the clothing both arrived toward the end of the month. Four companies sailed on January 26 and two more companies left for Mexico on January 28. The remainder of the regiment had closed at Fort Monroe by February 10.[50]

The regiment had taken much longer to get off than the War Department had anticipated. The delay had one outstanding social result. On February 11, Governor William Smith arrived at Fort Monroe to present the regiment a flag that had been voted by the General Assembly. Captain James L. Kemper, the regimental quartermaster, recorded the ensuing festivities:[51]

> Today was a great day, a day to be remembered & recorded. The Flag prepared by order of the Legislature and presented by the Gov.—a studied speech, no big thing at that. Hamtramck accepted it in a *great speech* of a few words. The officers next went to the house of Col. Walborough Walback (or whatever his name may be) and we all got gloriously merry over cold meats and champagne—a profusion of wit, puns, toasts and all that. Came back to my quarters considerably elevated—*Vidi Elephantum.*

Three more companies of the First Virginia sailed from Fort Monroe on February 22, followed by the remaining companies under the command of Major Early on March 1. Company B, 13th Infantry, Company A, 11th Infantry, Callwell's Company of Voltigeurs, and Company M, 4th Artillery, were organized at Fort Monroe during the spring and early summer of 1847 and were sent to Texas or to Mexico without delay.[52]

In the summer of 1848, four companies of North Carolina volunteers and the First Virginia Volunteers returned to Fort Monroe, where they were mustered out of Federal service, and nine companies of the 3d Artillery joined and were transferred to other stations along the coast from Boston to New Orleans.[53] Companies C and G, 3d Artillery, joined in October to form the permanent garrison until the latter part of 1853, when they were replaced by Companies B and E, 1st Artillery.

Fort Monroe was again host to the chief executive when President Millard Fillmore visited the post on June 21, 1851. The President arrived early in the morning on board the Baltimore steamer and was greeted by a twenty-one gun salute. The officers of the garrison assembled at 5 a.m. at Colonel Bankhead's quarters to accompany him to meet the President at the landing.[54]

Colonel Bankhead was relieved in November 1853, upon the arrival of Colonel Ichabod B. Crane, 1st Artillery, with the field and staff of his regiment; but Colonel Crane remained only until July 1854, being succeeded by Captain Bennett H. Hill, of the same regiment.[55] Early in 1854, Companies L and M, 1st Artillery, which had become greatly reduced in strength from a long tour of duty on the Pacific coast, rendezvoused at Fort Monroe, were then reorganized by the assignment of a full complement of men, and were, in December, ordered to duty in Florida.

In 1855 occurred the organization of the new 9th and 10th Regiments of Infantry, the headquarters of the 9th being established at Fort Monroe, where its colonel, George Wright,[56] had been directed to repair to superintend its organization. Lieutenant Colonel Silas Casey was the first to join and by virtue of his rank assumed command of the post on April 14,[57] being relieved by Colonel Wright on July 3. Companies A, F, and G were organized in May, Companies B, H, and I in June, Companies C, D, and E in August, and Company K in September. In December, the whole regiment left the post, Major Francis Taylor, 1st Artillery, suceeding to the command of the remaining garrison—Companies B and E of his regiment.[58]

For a number of years following the Mexican War the artillery was actively employed in service in Florida, Oregon, California, and other parts of the United States. Gradually the demands on the artillery decreased, and by 1856 it had become possible to plan for the reopening of the Artillery School.

On October 30, 1856, the War department directed "Companies M, 2d Artillery; C, 3d Artillery; and G, 4th Artillery, to be discontinued as light artillery companies, and, together with Company I, 1st Artillery, to be hereafter designated as garrison, sea-coast and siege artillery" and to be concentrated at Fort Monroe to "form a school of practice for service with heavy guns."[59] Beyond transferring the headquarters and band of the 2d Artillery to Fort Monroe in May 1857, nothing more seems to have been done towards establishing the school until the end of the year. On December 29, 1857, orders directed: "In pursuance of the authority granted the General-in-Chief by the War Department, on the 8th instant, Brevet Lieutenant Colonel Harvey Brown, 2d Artillery, will, with the Companies and Officers now under his orders, immediately proceed to the organization of an artillery school of practice at Fort Monroe, Va., of which he is appointed Commandant."[60]

Major and Brevet Colonel Harvey Brown, 2d Artillery, who joined in May 1857 to assume command and to reopen the school, was much interested in the post and was industrious in promoting its welfare and its appearance. During the winter and spring of 1857–1858 he set out some five hundred trees around the reservation. About two hundred and fifty of these were planted inside the fort and the rest were set along the water front and on both sides of the road and causeway leading from the main gate to the bridge over Mill Creek.

In 1858, the chapel inside the fort was erected under Colonel Brown's supervision for religious purposes and Protestant worship, open to all sects. The funds were derived from private subscription, the principal contributor being Lieutenant Julian McAllister, of the Ordnance Department. On June 22, 1855, an explosion had occurred in the mixing room of the laboratory of the Fort Monroe Arsenal. Lieutenant McAllister was in the room with Artificer Francis M. McKnight and Artificer Henry Sheffis at the time. One of the men was mixing pyrotechnics which caused the explosion, completely destroying the building and damaging an adjoining building. McKnight was instantly killed and Sheffis died of his injuries on June 25. Although badly burned, Lieutenant McAllister miraculously survived. The chapel was his recognition of the Divine mercy shown him in preserving his life. Captain Alexander B. Dyer, commanding the Fort Monroe Arsenal,[61] acted as agent and superintendent of construction at the request of Lieutenant McAllister. The chapel—which is known as the Chapel of the Centurion—was consecrated on May 3, 1858, with due formality, by Assistant Bishop John Johns, of the Diocese of the Protestant Episcopal Church of Virginia.[62]

For many years, Roman Catholic priests had visited Fort Monroe to look after the spiritual welfare of the members of that faith. On June 8, 1860, Colonel De Russy and the Right Rev. John McGill, bishop of Richmond, signed articles of agreement providing for the erection of a Roman Catholic chapel on Fort Monroe. The agreement was approved by the Secretary of War on June 20, 1860, and the chapel—which was called St. Mary Star of the Sea—was immediately built. St. Mary was unique in that it was owned by the church, which provided the priests, and was not an Army chapel.[63]

In January 1858, a board of officers, consisting of Captains Augustus A. Gibson, John F. Reynolds, and Albion P. Howe, with Lieutenant John Bennett as recorder, had been convened to arrange a two-year schedule of instruction based on regulations furnished by the commandant.[64] The board prepared and arranged the courses of study, practice, and experiments, specifying the particular courses for each year and the time to be devoted to each course. It also prepared lists of such books, fixtures, instruments, etc., as it considered necessary to carry the plan of the school into execution. Colonel Brown's plan for the organization of the school was based on this report.

The regulations of the school provided that "there shall be established, at Fort Monroe, for the theoretical and practical instruction of Artillery, a school, to be termed THE ARTILLERY SCHOOL," The school consisted of the officers and companies of the garrison at Fort Monroe, with the senior officer as commandant. The commandant was to be assisted by a field officer of artillery; and these two officers, the captains of artillery on duty at Fort Monroe, and the commander of the Fort Monroe Arsenal were to form the staff of the school. The garrison was to consist of two companies from each of the four regiments of artillery, and these companies were to be stationed at Fort Monroe for two years, one company from each regiment being relieved each year. All graduates of the Military Academy assigned to the artillery were to be ordered to the school for a year before joining their regiments.[65]

The plan contemplated the selection by the commandant of an adjutant, who would also be secretary to the staff, an instructor of drawing, an instructor of mathematics, an instructor of engineering, an ordnance officer to assist the commanding officer of the arsenal, and such enlisted personnel as might be found necessary to perform the duties of sergeant major, quartermaster sergeant, clerks, etc. The course was to be both theoretical and practical, including the usual duties of guards, police, parades, reviews, and inspections. There was to be an annual encampment of one month, during which the instruction was to be confined to castramentation, camp duties, field fortification, and surveying. Examinations were to be held annually beginning September 12 for the subaltern officers, and semi-annually beginning September 20 and March 20 for the noncommissioned officers.

Pending the approval and publication of the regulations governing the conduct of the school, instruction during the spring and summer of 1858 was limited to the service of the piece and to mechanical maneuvers and the September examinations were restricted to these subjects. The instruction was divided into three departments: Laboratory, Theoretical, and Practical, among which the available captains were distributed and assigned to duty as instructors. In the Noncommissioned Officers' School, the director was assisted by two subalterns detailed from the companies at the post.

During the first year the personnel under instruction consisted of the subaltern officers of two companies from the 1st Artillery, two from the 2d Artillery, and one from the 4th Artillery. The addition of three companies in 1859 brought the garrison up to the contemplated strength. The last of the three had scarcely arrived when the growing national unrest began to indicate the propriety of again suspending operations at the school.

When, in October 1859, John Brown made his raid upon Harper's Ferry, a portion of the command was ordered there, but before its arrival Brown's entire party had been killed or captured. The troops therefore returned to Fort Monroe, but on November 30, 1859, Company A, 1st Artillery, was again ordered to Harper's Ferry, where it remained during the execution of Brown and his followers. On November 26, Colonel Brown was relieved by Lieutenant Colonel Justin Dimick, 2d Artillery, who retained the command after the opening of the Civil War.[66] The routine change of garrison was started in 1860 but was discontinued after three of the companies had been relieved. The school was not closed by a formal order, but there is nothing to indicate that it functioned after the close of the September examinations. The school staff held its last formal meeting on September 19, 1860.

Up to this time, the history of the fort had been comparatively uneventful. The salubrity of the climate had gradually attracted increasing numbers of visitors from abroad, and Old Point Comfort was becoming well known as a resort. The presence of Black Hawk and his chief leaders after the close of the Black Hawk War had induced many people to come to Fort Monroe for the first time. These discovered that the spot was one of unusual attractiveness, possessing an excellent hotel and exceptional bathing facilities. The number of visitors rapidly increased, until it became necessary to enlarge the hotel to a capacity of four hundred guests. The Hygeia Hotel stood on the glacis of the fort south of the main gate, extending from the site of the present Y.M.C.A. building to a point just north of Building 138. The proprietor of the hotel, awake to the opportunity, chartered steamboats and brought excursionists daily from Norfolk, Richmond, Washington, and Baltimore, until, by speedy development, Old Point Comfort became famous throughout the country as a watering place.

To the natural attractive features of Old Point Comfort were added the fort and its military garrison, as well as naval visitors to Chesapeake Bay. It had become somewhat of a custom for English, French, and Spanish war vessels on the Atlantic and West Indian stations to rendezvous in the sheltered waters of Hampton Roads during the period of hurricanes in the West Indies. Their stay was always marked by a round of visits of ceremony, receptions, and balls on shore and on board ship. It was not unusual during these periods for several bands, representing the ships of as many nations, to be playing in the ballroom and on the veranda of the hotel. Afternoon concerts were given by the excellent band belonging to Fort Monroe; and the evening parades were always of particular interest to the visitors.

During the period from 1850 to 1860, Old Point Comfort was the most fashionable resort for the planters and statesmen from the southern States. Many of the wives and daughters of the members of Congress and of government officials spent the season at Fort Monroe, where they were joined by the men of their families during the weekends. To the South, Old Point Comfort was the watering place of fashion and wealth that Saratoga was to the North.

Life at Fort Monroe had come full circle. The preceding three decades had begun with the activities of the post centered on the Artillery School and now the period closed with a second Artillery School in operation. In between there had been the alarms and excursions of Indian wars, slave insurrections, and the war with Mexico to add a little diversion to the dull garrison routine. Once again, however, life at Fort Monroe was about to change dramatically. With the close of this decade at the middle of the century, the political clouds that had been gathering for years heralded the approach of civil war. The hotel, the beaches, and the walks at Fort Monroe were deserted. The Artillery School discontinued its routine of instruction, and the garrison began to prepare to take the field where officers and men were to meet in combat their comrades and friends of other years. Even the fort itself, once deemed impregnable, was seriously menaced.

Footnotes Chapter IV

[1] Birkhimer, *op. cit.*, p. 124.

[2] Howard had been commissioned in 1813 and rose to the rank of captain before resigning in 1835. During the Mexican War he served as lieutenant colonel of the 15th Infantry and was brevetted colonel for gallantry at Chapultepec. He served as an additional paymaster of volunteers in the Civil War and died in 1868. *Heitman*, p. 546.

[3] Edgar Allan Poe's grandfather was David Poe, who served as assistant quartermaster general in the Revolutionary War.

[4] Francis Winwar, *The Haunted Palace: A Life of Edgar Allan Poe* (New York: Harper & Brothers Publishers, 1959), pp. 94, 99, 102–108.

[5] Order No. 51, Fortress Monroe, August 6, 1829, NA, RG 393.

[6] Emmerson, *op cit.*, pp. 108–109, 110, 112–113, 115, 116.

[7] Marquis James, *The Life of Andrew Jackson* (Garden City: Garden City Publishing Co., 1940), p. 517; Emmerson, *op. cit.*, p. 121.

[8] James, *op. cit.*, pp. 577, 646–647; Emmerson, *op. cit.*, pp. 180, 182, 234, 236.

[9] Emmerson, *op. cit.*, pp. 318, 319, 324, 325.

[10] Order No. 88, Artillery School of Practice, November 18, 1829, NA, RG 393.

[11] Order No. 98, Artillery School of Practice, December 13, 1829, NA, RG 393.

[12] Orders No. 22, Fortress Monroe, April 23, 1831, NA, RG 393.

[13] Worth had been commissioned in 1813 and was brevetted for gallantry in the War of 1812. He became a major of Ordnance in 1832 and colonel of the 8th Infantry in 1838. Worth was brevetted brigadier general for gallantry in the Seminole War. For gallantry at the Battle of Monterrey in 1846 he was brevetted major general and presented a sword by Congress. General Worth died in 1849. Kirby had been commissioned in 1813 and brevetted twice in the War of 1812. He died in 1842, still a captain. *Heitman*, pp. 603, 1061.

[14] Fort Monroe Post Return, December 1830 and May 1831, NA, Records of the Office of the Adjutant General, RG 94.

[15] Fort Monroe Post Return, August 1831, NA, RG 94.

[16] Whiting had been commissioned in 1812, became a captain in 1819, and was brevetted major for ten years faithful service in one grade in 1829. He died in 1842. *Heitman*, p. 1030.

[17] Griswold was an 1815 graduate of West Point and at the time was a first lieutenant and brevet captain. He was promoted to captain in 1832 and died in 1834. *Cullum*, Vol. I, p. 133.

[18] Fort Monroe Post Return, December 1831 and June 1833, NA, RG 94.

[19] Talcott graduated from West Point in 1818 and was promoted to captain in 1830. He resigned in 1836 and served during the Civil War as Chief of the Virginia Corps of Engineers with the rank of colonel. Talcott died in 1883. Lee was an 1829 graduate of West Point. *Heitman*, p. 943.

[20] Johnston had graduated from West Point in 1829 and been commissioned in the 4th Artillery. He resigned in 1837 as a first lieutenant, but was appointed with the same rank to the Corps of Topographical Engineers the following year. He served as lieutenant colonel of the

Voltigeurs in the Mexican War, being brevetted three times for gallantry. After the war he reverted to captain, but was promoted to lieutenant colonel of the 1st Cavalry in 1855. In 1860 he became Quartermaster General with the rank of brigadier general. Appointed general in the Confederate Army, Johnston commanded the Army of Northern Virginia and later the Army of Tennessee. He died in 1891. *Heitman*, p. 578.

[21] Custis Lee graduated first in the 1854 class at West Point and resigned his commission as first lieutenant of Engineers in 1861. He rose to the rank of major general in the Confederate Army. He succeeded his father as president of Washington and Lee University and died in 1913. Warner, *op. cit.*, p. 179.

[22] Douglas Southall Freeman, *R. E. Lee* (New York and London: Charles Scribner's Sons, 1934), Vol. I, pp. 111–112, 117, 119–120.

[23] Talcott and Lee shared the west half of Quarters No. 17, part of the twin "Tuileries" built in 1819. The east half of the quarters was occupied by Brevet Major Julius F. Heileman and Brevet Captain Charles Mellon. Lt. C. D. Dimmock, Assistant Quartermaster, to the Quartermaster General, reporting on quarters at Fort Monroe in July 1834, NA, RG 92, Records of the Office of the Quartermaster General, Consolidated Correspondence File.

[24] Freeman, *op. cit.*, pp. 120–123.

[25] Crane had been commissioned in the Marine Corps in 1809 and resigned in 1812 to accept an appointment as captain in the Army. He was major of the 4th Artillery at the time of the Black Hawk War and became a colonel of the 1st Artillery in 1843. Colonel Crane died in 1857. Fraser had been commissioned in 1814 and was killed in action in the Dade Massacre at the beginning of the Second Seminole War in 1835. Lyon had entered the Army as an enlisted man in 1808, been commissioned in 1813, reached the rank of captain in 1827, and died in 1843. Galt had been commissioned in 1814 and rose to major of the 2d Artillery in 1847. He was brevetted for gallantry at the Battles of Contreras and Churubusco in the Mexican War and died in 1851. Munroe was born in Scotland and graduated from West Point in 1814. He was brevetted in the Seminole War and twice for gallantry in the Mexican War. Munroe became lieutenant colonel of the 4th Artillery in 1856 and died in 1861. *Heitman*, pp. 335, 434, 444, 649, 736.

[26] Mackay had entered the Army in 1813. He transferred to the Quartermaster Department in 1838 and became lieutenant colonel and Deputy Quartermaster General in 1846. He died in 1850. *Heitman*, p. 670.

[27] Sibley had graduated first in the West Point class of 1827. He rose to captain in the 1st Artillery and then transferred to the Quartermaster Department. Sibley was promoted to lieutenant colonel and Deputy Quartermaster General in 1861. He resigned from the Army in 1864 and died in 1884. *Cullum*, Vol. I, pp. 386–387.

[28] Fort Monroe Post Return, June 1832 and November 1832. NA, RG 94.

[29] Hudson Strode, *Jefferson Davis, American Patriot* (New York: Harcourt, Brace and Company, 1955), pp. 74–77; Donald Jackson, (ed.), *Black Hawk: An Autobiography* (Urbana: University of Illinois Press, 1955), pp. 4, 6, 8–11, 170–171. An Indian pipe given to Jefferson Davis by Black Hawk in appreciation of the kind treatment he had received is now in the Fort Monroe Casemate Museum.

[30] Fort Monroe Post Return, Nov. 1833 and Apr. 1834, NA, RG 94.

[31] General Orders No. 31, A.G.O., April 19, 1834.

[32] Gates had graduated from West Point in 1806 and became major of the 1st Artillery in 1832. He was dismissed from the service in 1836, but reinstated in 1837 and became colonel of the 3d Artillery in 1845. He retired in 1863, and was brevetted brigadier general for long and faithful service. General Gates died in 1868. Maynadier graduated from West Point in 1827 and transferred to the Ordnance Department in 1838. He rose to the rank of colonel and was brevetted brigadier general for meritorious service during the Civil War. General Maynadier died in 1871. After leaving Fort Monroe, Eustis took a prominent part in the Seminole War, serving briefly as the commander of the army in Florida. he was made a brevet brigadier general in June 1834.

[33] Freemen, *op. cit.*, pp. 123–124.

[34] General Orders No. 54, A.G.O., July 31, 1834.

[35] Freeman, *op. cit.*, pp. 124–129.

[36] Fanning had graduated from West Point in 1812 and became major of the 4th Artillery in 1832. He was brevetted for gallantry in the Seminole War, was promoted to lieutenant colonel in 1838, and died in 1846. Armistead, who had begun the construction of Fort Monroe in 1818, was brevetted brigadier general in 1828 and died in 1845. Bankhead had been commissioned in 1808 and became lieutenant colonel of the 3d Artillery in 1832. He became colonel of the 4th Artillery in 1838, was brevetted brigadier general for gallantry at the siege of Vera Cruz in the Mexican War, and died in 1856. *Heitman,* pp. 169, 189, 412–413.

[37] Fort Monroe Post Return, Aug. 1837 and Nov. 1839, NA, RG 94.

[38] Symington had graduated from West Point in 1815 and had been commissioned in the Ordnance Department. He was transferred to the Artillery in the reorganization of 1821 and returned to the Ordnance in 1832. He eventually became a colonel, retired in 1863, and died in 1864. *Heitman,* p. 942.

[39] Bell had graduated from West Point in 1820. He transferred to the Ordnance Department and reached the rank of major. A North Carolinian, he resigned in 1861 and died in 1865. *Heitman,* p. 208.

[40] Ramsay was an 1820 West Point graduate who became brigadier general and Chief of Ordnance in 1863. He retired in 1864, was brevetted major general for long and faithful service, and died in 1882. *Heitman,* p. 813.

[41] General Orders No. 32, A.G.O., May 19, 1837.

[42] Fort Monroe Post Returns, July and Nov. 1838, NA, RG 94.

[43] Fort Monroe Post Returns, Sept. 1841, July and Aug. 1842, NA, RG 94.

[44] Beard, "The Castle of Rip Raps," p. 45.

[45] Rene E. De Russy had graduated from West Point in 1812 and had been commissioned in the Corps of Engineers. He became a lieutenant colonel in 1838 and was in charge of completing the construction of Fort Monroe, commanding the post from November 1838 to September 1841. Promoted to colonel in 1863, he was in charge of constructing fortifications on the Pacific Coast during the Civil War. He was brevetted brigadier general in 1865 for long and faithful service and died in the same year. *Heitman,* p. 369.

[46] Robert Seager II, *and Tyler too, a Biography of John & Julia Gardiner Tyler* (New York, Toronto, and London: McGraw-Hill Book Co., Inc., 1963), pp. 10–11, 12, 304–305.

[47] General Orders No. 40, A.G.O., July 12, 1842.

[48] General Orders No. 25, A.G.O., Oct. 31, 1853.

[49] Early graduated from West Point in 1837 and after serving in the Seminole War resigned in 1838. He rose to the rank of lieutenant general in the Confederate Army and commanded a corps in the Army of Northern Virginia. He died in 1894. *Heitman,* p. 393; Warner, *op. cit.,* pp. 79–80.

[50] Lee A. Wallace, Jr., "The First Regiment of Virginia Volunteers, 1846–1848," *The Virginia Magazine of History and Biography,* 77 (January 1969), pp. 54–57. Hamtramck had served as a sergeant in Zachary Taylor's expedition up the Mississippi River, and apparently as a result of his gallantry he was appointed to West Point in 1815. He resigned from the Army in 1822, and died in 1858.

[51] Robert R. Jones, (ed.), "The Mexican War Diary of James Lawson Kemper," *The Virginia Magazine of History and Biography,* 74 (October 1966), p. 418. Kemper commanded a brigade in Pickett's Division in the Confederate Army and was severely wounded at Gettysburg. He was promoted to major general and served as governor of Virginia following the war. Kemper died in 1895. Smith also rose to major general in the Confederate Army and then again served as governor until the end of the war. He died in 1887. Warner, *op. cit.,* pp. 169–170, 284–285.

[52] Wallace, *op. cit.,* p. 58.

[53] *Ibid.,* p. 77. The First Virginia arrived on July 23–24. Their large number of tents "whitened the shore for nearly a mile."

[54] Orders No. 70, Fort Monroe, June 20, 1851, NA, RG 393.

[55] Hill graduated from West Point in 1837 and was promoted to captain in 1848. He retired

in 1870 as lieutenant colonel of the 5th Artillery having been brevetted colonel and brigadier general. He died in 1886. *Heitman*, p. 529.

[56] Wright graduated from West Point in 1822 and was brevetted for gallantry in the Seminole War and Mexican War. He had been lieutenant colonel of the 4th Infantry when he was promoted to command the 9th Infantry. He was brevetted brigadier general in 1864 for long and faithful service and drowned in 1865. *Heitman*, p. 1062.

[57] Casey was an 1826 West Point graduate who had been brevetted twice for gallantry in the Mexican War, he was promoted from captain of the 2d Infantry to lieutenant colonel of 9th Infantry. During the Civil War he served as a major general of volunteers and again was brevetted twice. He became colonel of the 4th Infantry in 1861, retired in 1868, and died in 1882. *Heitman*, p. 289.

[58] Taylor graduated from West Point in 1825 and was brevetted twice for gallantry in the Mexican War. He died in 1858. *Heitman*, p. 946.

[59] General Orders No. 9, Headquarters of the Army, October 30, 1856.

[60] General Order No. 15, Headquarters of the Army, December 29, 1857. Brown graduated from West Point in 1818 and had been brevetted once during the Seminole War and twice during the Mexican War for gallantry. He became colonel of the 5th Artillery in 1861 and was brevetted brigadier general for the defense of Fort Pickens and major general for the suppression of the New York draft riots. He retired in 1863 and died in 1874. *Heitman*, p. 251.

[61] Dyer graduated from West Point in 1837. In 1864 he was promoted to brigadier general and Chief of Ordnance and brevetted major general for his services in the Civil War. He died in 1874. *Heitman*, p. 392.

[62] Brevet Major J. G. Martin to Colonel H. K. Craig, June 22, June 25, and June 28, 1855, NA, RG 94. McAllister was an 1847 graduate of West Point and rose to the rank of colonel. He died in 1887. James G. Martin was the assistant quartermaster of the post and wrote the reports of the accident for McAllister who was too badly burned to write himself. Martin graduated from West Point in 1840, and lost an arm at Churubusco in the Mexican War. In the Civil War he was adjutant general of North Carolina and then a brigadier general in the Confederate Army. He died in 1878. *Heitman*, pp. 651, 692. Warner, *op. cit.*, pp. 213–214.

[63] *Centennial Anniversary of St. Mary's Star of the Sea, Fort Monroe, Virginia, 1860–1960.*

[64] Gibson graduated from West Point in 1839 and served as colonel of the 2d Pennsylvania Artillery in the Civil War. He became lieutenant colonel of the 3d Artillery, retired in 1870, and died in 1893. Reynolds was an 1841 graduate of West Point. He was a major general of volunteers and commanding the I Corps of the Army of the Potomac when he was killed in action at Gettysburg. Howe, who also graduated from West Point in 1841, was a brigadier general of volunteers in the Civil War and was brevetted major general. He rose to colonel of the 4th Artillery, retired in 1882, and died in 1897. Bennett graduated from West Point in 1856 and died in 1859. *Heitman*, pp. 211, 453, 547, 825.

[65] General Orders No. 5, War Department, May 18, 1858.

[66] Dimick had graduated from West Point in 1819 and was brevetted for gallantry in the Seminole War and the Mexican War. In 1861 he was promoted to colonel of the 1st Artillery and he retired in 1863. He was brevetted brigadier general for long gallant and faithful service and died in 1871. *Heitman*, p. 374.

Chapter V

Outpost of the Union

THE NEXT FIVE YEARS were to be the most dramatic and, in many ways, the most important in the long history of Fort Monroe. Because of its strategic location and relatively large garrison, the post figured prominently in the plans of the government once the Civil War began. By 1861 the fort, even though not completely armed and far short of its planned wartime garrison, was sufficiently strong to preclude easy capture.

During the year preceding the outbreak of hostilities, many repairs and improvements had been made under the supervision of Colonel DeRussy. Magazines were repaired, quarters and cisterns overhauled and put in good order, port-cullis hung, ovens built, gun platforms repaired, drawbridges put in order, roads repaired, bridges to the sixth front (north gate) rebuilt, gates made and hung in the advanced redoubt, and other work performed to improve the fortification. At Fort Calhoun, attention had been devoted to building third, fourth, and fifth courses of the scarp, piers and foundations, magazine walls, casemate floors, etc., and then to preparations for mounting guns.

On December 31, 1860, Brevet Lieutenant General Winfield Scott, the Commanding General of the Army, ordered Colonel Dimick to embark four companies on the *Brooklyn* (at least 200 men) destined to reinforce Fort Sumter, with a secret admonition, "Manage everything as secretly and confidentially as possible. Look to this."[1] On January 23, 1861, Captain Israel Vogdes, with Company A, 1st Artillery, at full strength, and with six field howitzers, was ordered to reinforce Fort Pickens.[2] This reduction in garrison left Fort Monroe with an altogether insufficient force to fill its wartime needs, but otherwise it was reasonably prepared for war. The Chief of Engineers reported on January 18, 1861, that the works were "in excellent condition; needing minor repairs only," but the same report stated that Fort Sumter was "a very strong work, in good condition for defense, having been greatly strengthened within the last few months."[3] So we are at liberty to question the entire accuracy of the Engineer judgment. Fortunately, Fort Monroe was not put to the test, for if there was any plan to seize the fort by stratagem or to carry it by assault during the early days of the rebellion, it never reached a point of action.

The commanding officer at Fort Monroe, Colonel Dimick, was a veteran officer in whom the War Department placed great confidence. Born August 5, 1800, he had graduated from West Point shortly before his nineteenth birthday and had served for more than forty years with zeal and distinction. Finding himself in command of Fort Monroe at the most critical period in the history of the country, he was fully alive to the necessity of observing every precaution. As early as January 16, 1861, he had submitted a requisition for thirty barbette guns to be added to the forty-one then mounted, and these were promptly forwarded and placed in position. He had already identified those officers of his command whose loyalty was at all doubtful, had redoubled his vigilance concerning the minutest details of administration, and during the intense excitement following the South Carolina convention had maintained constant communication with General Scott.

Among the earliest measures on the part of the Government to protect its property within the insurgent states was the attempt to secure the navy yard at Gosport, below Norfolk. The Virginia Convention adopted the Ordinance of Secession of April 19, and two days later General Scott instructed Captain Horatio G. Wright, of the Corps of Engineers, "as an engineer officer of high science and judgment," to proceed to Gosport to assist in designing and executing a plan of defense. The General suggested that he first call at Fort Monroe and secure from Colonel Dimick a detachment from the garrison to assist in the defense of the navy yard.[4]

Captain Wright proceeded to Fort Monroe, and the 3d Massachusetts, which had just arrived, was detailed to accompany him to Gosport. The time for securing the yard had, however, passed. The expedition, having participated in the destruction of the ships and property which it was impracticable to defend or remove, returned the next morning (April 21) to the fort.[5] On April 28, Colonel Dimick reported to General Scott the arrival of the 3d Massachusetts (Colonel David W. Wardrop) and the 4th Massachusetts (Colonel Abner B. Packard) on the twentieth. He also informed the General of the arrival of over 200,000 complete rations and some ammunition. "I consider I have now on hand," he stated, "a sufficient amount of ammunition for immediate use." The garrison at this time consisted of 24 officers and 345 enlisted men in the 3d Massachusetts; 34 officers and 429 enlisted men in the 4th Massachusetts; 15 officers and 253 men for duty, 94 men on extra and daily duty, 10 men sick, and 3 men in confinement in the Artillery garrison.[6]

The family of ex-President Tyler was one of the first in the South to suffer the loss of their property in the war. Mrs. Tyler was slow to realize that the war was not a game played by "high-toned gentlemen" and was no respecter of private property. Late in April, one of the Massachusetts units ("these scum of the earth," Mrs. Tyler called them) seized Villa Margaret, the Tyler summer home in nearby Hampton, for use as barracks. The home continued to be used as quarters by various regiments during the following months.[7]

There is a legend that Fort Monroe was never attacked by the Confederates because General Robert E. Lee knew from his experience during its construction that the fort was impregnable. Like so many legends, this appears to have little basis in fact. As has been proved from ancient Tyre to Dien Bien Phu, any fortification can be captured if the attacker has the resources and sufficient desire. No record has been found of any Confederate intention to attack the fort. There is an account of a plan to seize the fort early in the war with the help of the treachery of part of its garrison, but this has not been substantiated.[8] From a practical viewpoint, the Confederates never had the opportunity to attempt an attack. The only time the fort would have been weak enough to fall easily was during April and early May 1861, and mobilization of the Virginia militia and volunteers did not begin until May 5. At that time, the Confederates did not have sufficient trained troops in the area or the required siege artillery. Even more important, the Confederates never had the naval strength to dominate Hampton Roads and Chesapeake Bay and thus cut off Fort Monroe from supplies and reinforcements. Because of its location on a narrow spit of land a formal siege would have been extremely difficult at best and probably impossible if the fort was supported by naval forces in the bay.

The War Department made every effort to secure the safety of the lower Chesapeake in order that Fort Monroe might become a base of supplies and operations. On April 30, General Scott, after informing Colonel Dimick that fourteen 10-inch Columbiad barbette carriages, twenty-eight 42-pounder barbette carriages, and twelve 8-inch Columbiad barbette carriages were to be sent to Fort Monroe, wrote: ". . . Fort Monroe is by far the most secure post now in the possession of the U.S., against any attack that can be possibly made upon it, independent of the War Vessels, the *Cumberland* and the *Niagara,* at hand, and approaching you." [9]

On May 13, the forces at Fort Monroe were increased by the arrival of the 1st Vermont (Colonel J. Wolcott Phelps), numbering 778 rank and file, and two additional companies of the 3d Massachusetts, 132 officers and men, so that on the evening of that day the roll call showed an aggregate force of 2,154 present within the fort, which was now considered capable of resisting any possible attack. This having been accomplished, the War Department turned its attention to a series of plans for the recapture of the forts and government property on the Atlantic coast. Fort Monroe was the natural base of operations, so it was determined to mass at that point a considerable force of the volunteer troops. From among these troops were to be formed the various contemplated expeditions and movements.

General Scott selected Major General Benjamin F. Butler, who had been prominent in securing the safety of the capital, to organize and direct these preparations. On May 18, General Butler was ordered to proceed to Fort Monroe and assume command "of that post," Colonel Dimick's command being limited to the regular troops composing a part of the garrison. General Butler was informed that nine regiments of volunteers would soon be ordered to Fort Monroe and that the entire force—save 1,500 men considered necessary to hold the fort against any probable attack—would be available for aggressive purposes. The immediate objects to which the general's attention was to be directed were:

a. Not to let the enemy erect batteries to annoy Fort Monroe;

b. To capture any batteries the enemy might have within a half day's march of the fort, or which might be reached by land;

c. To capture any batteries the enemy might have at or above Craney Island, even though requiring water craft; and

d. To menace and recapture the navy yard at Gosport in order to complete its destruction, with its contents, except what it might be practicable to bring away in safety.

To secure naval cooperation, General Butler was told to put himself into free communication with the commander of the United States naval forces in Hampton Roads and to invite his cooperation in all operations which were in whole or in part by water. "Boldness in execution is nearly always necessary, but in planning and fitting out expeditions or detachments great circumspection is a virtue. In important cases, where time clearly permits, be sure to submit your plans and ask instructions from higher authority."[10]

In this connection, it is a matter of incidental importance that General Butler, who was at the time in command of the Department of Annapolis, protested against his removal from that position and his assignment to a minor command as an undeserved censure upon his actions. Doubtless this, with important coincident questions of policy, determined General Scott to create a department out of Fort Monroe and its vicinity. General Butler's protest was dated May 18, but on the twenty-seventh, by General Orders No. 1, and "In compliance with instructions from the Lieutenant-

General commanding the Army," he assumed command of the Department of Virginia, embracing the area within sixty miles of Fort Monroe, which became department headquarters. Two days later he reported his arrival and that of the 2d New York, numbering 782 officers and men.[11]

This regiment, together with the 1st Vermont, was sent into camp on the Segar farm, at the Hampton end of the bridge across Mill Creek. This camp, called Camp Troy for a time, was afterwards named Camp Hamilton, probably in honor of Schuyler Hamilton, lieutenant colonel and military secretary to General Scott, who had been sent to Fort Monroe to meet General Butler. As is usually the case with an improvised Army, there was considerable difficulty in properly clothing and equipping these newly raised troops. The first clothing issue was "shoddy" and lasted no time at all. Colonel Joseph B. Carr, of the 2d New York said that his men appeared on parade at Fort Monroe wrapped in blankets that they might conceal a lack of proper garments, and "sometimes stood sentinel with naked feet and almost naked bodies."[12]

Major John B. Cary, who had been principal of the Hampton Military Institute, commanded the 130 Confederate volunteers in Hampton. Lieutenant Colonel Benjamin S. Ewell, the president of William and Mary College, had been ordered by General Lee to prepare the defense of the Peninsula and to organize the volunteers in the area. On May 14, Ewell was in Hampton and learning of demonstrations by the troops at Fort Monroe went to see Colonel Dimick. Dimick informed Ewell that he had taken possession of a spring west of Mill Creek to get water for the garrison, but he had no immediate idea of aggressive movements. They agreed to keep their pickets apart and Ewell ordered Cary to keep his men one half mile from the fort. Ewell also ordered Cary to form a camp of instruction for some 820 men. There were, however, only 300 muskets available, half of them obsolete flintlocks.[13]

Cary reported to Ewell on May 21 that Dimick appeared ready to advance. Ewell considered this likely and prohibited Cary from any useless resistance unless the Federals moved beyond the range of the fort's guns. Ewell continued, "It is difficult to manage Hampton. The people are excitable and brave even to rashness and are unwilling to give way. It [Hampton] might, on the approach in force of Federal troops, be evacuated by the military, and the remaining citizens ought to make terms, unless, indeed, it is made a second Saragossa. I doubt if, from the nature of the buildings, this could be done."[14]

At this early date, the war still had an unreal quality. On the afternoon of May 23 most of the 1st Vermont advanced to Hampton. As Phelps' troops neared the town, Major Cary was vainly trying to burn the bridge across Hampton Creek. Cary sent Lieutenant Cutshaw over to Phelps to demand the reason for his approach with so large a force. Phelps replied that he had no hostile purpose, but General Butler had sent him to reconnoiter. Receiving assurances that the people and property of the town would not be molested, Cary, with some citizens and the Vermonters, put out the fire on the bridge. The 1st Vermont then marched into Hampton, remained a short while, and then returned to their camp.

Lieutenant Colonel Ewell hurried forward to find out what was happening. Cary had meanwhile gone to Fort Monroe to learn from General Butler "how far he intended to take possession of Virginia soil, in order that I might act in such a manner as to avoid collision between our scouts." Butler informed Cary that it was "a military necessity" for him to occupy some land for an encampment, but if he was not interfered with he would molest no one. By this time, Ewell had blundered into the Federal pickets and had been unceremoniously captured. After a protest by Cary, Colonel Dimick promptly released Ewell. Ewell immediately ordered Cary to complete the destruction of the Hampton bridge.[15]

The consolidated morning report of May 26 shows the following force, present and absent:

United States Regulars	415 officers and men
3d Massachusetts Volunteers	727 officers and men
4th Massachusetts Volunteers	783 officers and men
1st Vermont Volunteers	779 officers and men
2d New York Volunteers	782 officers and men
7th New York Volunteers	850 officers and men
Unattached Massachusetts Volunteers	101 officers and men
Field and Staff	14 officers
	4,451 officers and men

On May 24, Cary was back to see General Butler. Three Negroes, the property of Colonel Charles Mallory of Hampton, had run away to Fort Monroe. Butler told Cary that he would take possession of anything necessary to meet his own requirements or that might be an aide to the enemy. He refused to give up any Negroes which came to the fort, stating in effect that they were property and "contraband of war." This policy was to have a far reaching impact.[16]

While this force was being built up at Fort Monroe, the Confederates had erected a strong battery at Sewell's Point at the entrance to Elizabeth River, about four miles from Fort Monroe, and about two and a half miles from Fort Calhoun. In the rear of this battery they had massed some three or four thousand men in the belief that General Butler intended to attack Norfolk, and they had erected a battery at Pig Point to command the Nansemond. Information was also received that the enemy was about to occupy and fortify Newport News, about nine miles from the fort.

To seize Newport News with sufficient force to maintain the position, to threaten Craney Island and the approaches to Norfolk, and to hold the approaches to Richmond was regarded of the highest importance by General Butler. Accordingly, an expedition consisting of three regiments of volunteers and a detachment of Regulars with two 6-pounders left the fort on the morning of May 27, landed on the high, open ground south of the present shipyard without opposition, threw up an intrenched camp, which was named Camp Butler, and erected a battery of four 8-inch Columbiads to command the upper channel on the Nansemond side of the James River. As a result of the Federal advance, there was a general exodus of women and children from Hampton and Major Cary fell back beyond Newmarket Bridge on Newmarket Creek.[17]

To reduce the Pig Point defenses, plans were in active preparation when the concentration of Confederate troops in the vicinity of Manassas required the presence of all available forces. In response to this call, the command at Fort Monroe was required to contribute about 4,000 men.

While the Government was thus active in building up the defenses of the lower Chesapeake, the enemy had been no less busy in massing their forces at the upper end of the Peninsula. Colonel John B. Magruder had been appointed to command the Confederate forces in this area on May 21. By the end of May, he had 2,504 poorly equipped troops with almost no transportation and limited ammunition in the vicinity of Yorktown and Gloucester Point. Although the Confederates had withdrawn their forces from the Hampton area, Magruder kept his patrols active around Hampton to protect the citizens loyal to the Confederacy and to keep an eye on the Federal troops near Fort Monroe and Newport News. General Butler had too many troops to permit any more aggressive action.[18] The occupation of Hampton and frequent reconnaissances toward Yorktown sufficed to keep the enemy at a safe distance and secured the lower peninsula during the occupation and defense of Newport News.

On the morning of May 30 a steamer arrived at Old Point Comfort carrying the Naval Brigade. This strange aggregation had been recruited in New York City. Colonel Washington A. Bartlett, a former Navy officer, had formed this unit mostly from sailors with the intention of providing them with light draft gunboats mounted with cannon, the brigade to serve afloat or ashore. They had refused to be mustered into State service and for reasons which are not too clear, the President ordered the unit to report to General Butler. The Naval Brigade arrived without arms, except for two rifled guns and a quantity of James and Sawyer projectiles. General Butler did not know what to do with the troops, but he had an excellent use for their guns.

With the help of the small boats of the frigate *Cumberland,* the men of the Naval Brigade were landed at Fort Monroe. General Butler ordered Colonel Bartlett to mount the Sawyer gun on the Rip Raps. Because of delay by the small boats, it was dark on May 30 before the Sawyer gun could be landed on the Rip Raps. Colonel Bartlett climbed up the rocks of the island and held a lantern to direct his men. The colonel made a misstep in the dark and fell seventeen feet onto the jagged rocks. The injury was believed to be fatal, so Lieutenant Colonel H. D. Whittemore and Major E. M. Dickinson promptly started for Washington to secure their promotions. The colonel regained consciousness after eleven hours, and despite the fact that the surgeon told him any movement would be fatal, Bartlett immediately got out of bed and started for Washington to get his regiment back.

Their inauspicious arrival and the sudden departure of all the field officers completely demoralized the brigade. Since General Butler could not muster the Naval Brigade into service, he offered to enroll them as laborers in the engineer, ordnance, and quartermaster departments at Fort Monroe. Those who wished to do so, were allowed to return to New York on the same steamer which had brought them. Those who remained were still not happy with the idea of becoming laborers. General Butler placed a guard around their camp on the beach and ordered that no rations should be issued to them until they enrolled. This did not particularly bother the former sailors, since Chesapeake Bay offered an abundance of oysters, clams, and crabs. The nebulous status of the regiment finally was satisfactorily resolved and it was mustered into service at Fort Monroe as the Union Coast Guards. Part of the regiment, which was redesignated the 99th New York Infantry in January 1862, formed the garrison at Fort Calhoun until October 1862.[19]

Fort Monroe soon became the base for frequent patrolling operations. On June 4, a report that some of the men of the 1st New York had been captured caused the dispatch of part of the 5th New York to Fox Hill, some five miles from Fort Monroe. After a forced march, the troops reached Fox Hill, but found no sign of the enemy. After a short rest, the troops then proceeded another five miles to Back River, but again were unable to locate the enemy. A courier caught up with them here and reported that the 1st New York was safe. The expedition returned to the fort by way of Hampton. While passing through the village, Lieutenant Burnett, with a flanking party in advance, was struck in the breast by a spent ball, suffering a slight wound. This minor injury was the only casualty of the frustrating expedition.[20]

On June 6, Major E. B. Montague moved to Big Bethel with three companies of Virginia volunteers, two howitzers, and two troops of cavalry. He reported to Magruder that he was about to be turned by a force from Newport News as well as one up the Poquoson River. Magruder ordered Colonel D. H. Hill and the 1st North Carolina Infantry, Major Randolph's battalion of artillery, and Lieutenant Colonel W. D.

Stuart's command of four companies of the 3d Virginia Infantry—in all a force of about 1,458 men—to Big Bethel.

On June 7, Hill made a reconnaissance of the area around Big Bethel and started work on intrenchments which continued the next two days. The same day, Captain Werth of the Chatham Grays made a reconnaissance to Newport News ending in a skirmish with Federal working parties, developing no information of value but alerting the Federals. On the same day, Federal troops from Hampton had been reconnoitering and plundering in the area south of Big Bethel and were met and driven back beyond Newmarket Creek by detachments from Big Bethel and the Halfway House.

On June 9, Butler had learned of the establishment of the Confederate outpost at Little Bethel and that a stronger position was being prepared at Big Bethel. Little Bethel was a small church on the Yorktown road about eight miles from Hampton and an equal distance from Newport News. General Butler determined to send a force to drive them out and destroy their camp. Accordingly, Brigadier General Ebenezer W. Pierce, then in command of Camp Hamilton, was directed to send Duryea's 5th New York Zouaves across Hampton Creek during the night and put them in the rear of the enemy between Little Bethel and Big Bethel. Colonel Frederick Townsend's regiment, the 3d New York, with two howitzers, was to march an hour later. The commanding officer at Newport News, Colonel Phelps, was directed to send out at the same time a battalion of picked men under Lieutenant Colonel Peter T. Washburn to make a demonstration upon Little Bethel in front. This demonstration was to be supported by Colonel John E. Bendix's 7th New York, with two field pieces, Bendix and Townsend to effect a junction about a mile and a half from the Bethel church. The entire force amounted to 2,875 men. The march was so timed that the attack would be made at daybreak on the tenth. To avoid confusion, Townsend's men wore white armbands, and the word "Boston" was to be shouted when unrecognized troops were approached.

Duryea sent out an advance guard under Captain Judson Kilpatrick,[21] which reached Newmarket Bridge at 1:00 a.m. on June 10. Duryea passed the remainder of his command over Hampton Creek in scows and pushed on to Newmarket Bridge. Kilpatrick's detachment proceeding on the road to Little and Big Bethel made contact with the enemy a little before daylight. Some shots were fired and a Confederate officer and two men were captured.

Everything went according to plan until the 7th New York approached the fork in the road where the two columns were to meet. Unable to see the white armbands in the dark, Bendix's troops opened fire on the 3d New York and killed two and wounded sixteen before Townsend's men could identify themselves. The firing caused several of the Federal units to retrace their route and had alerted the Confederates. General Pierce, nevertheless, decided to follow orders and proceed with the attack. The 1st New York and the 2d New York were ordered forward at Pierce's request as quickly as possible.

Magruder had started his Confederates toward Hampton at 3:00 a.m. He had not advanced far when he learned of the Federal force in the area —probably as a result of the firing at the road junction and the loss of the pickets captured by Duryea. He hastily retired to the intrenchments at Big Bethel.

Pierce found Little Bethel abandoned and burned the small church before proceeding toward the Confederate intrenchments at Big Bethel. Meanwhile, Colonel Hill had taken advantage of the delay caused by the Federal collision in the dark to deploy his Confederate troops effectively. A Parrott gun and one howitzer of the Virginia Howitzer Battalion were placed in the main battery on the right of the road, near the front of the church; a howitzer under Captain Brown in the battery on the right, beyond a ravine; a howitzer near the bridge over Brick Kiln Creek, on the right of the road; and a rifled howitzer manned by cadets from the North Carolina Military Institute on the left of the road. To the south of the creek and on the right was the Confederate advanced work. The area was heavily wooded except for some fields in front of and to the left of the Confederate position.

Kilpatrick drove in the advanced Confederate pickets and making a hasty reconnaissance reported to Duryea that the enemy had a strong position on the opposite side of the bridge with earthworks and a masked battery in advance of the creek. When Pierce had advanced to within 800 yards of the Confederate position, enemy artillery fire caused some confusion and the hasty deployment of the Federal force. The 5th New York pushed forward with skirmishers to either side of the road and Greble's small battery opened fire. This advance was quickly checked by three Confederate companies.

The 3d New York moved to the left to reconnoiter and develop the right of the advanced works of the enemy position. The 5th New York and the 2d New York soon joined in the advance and Duryea carried the Confederate position south of the creek. Hill promptly ordered an attack by Company A, 1st North Carolina, which recaptured the position. Townsend, mistaking one of his own units beyond a hedge for an enemy force about to flank him, fell back and called off the attack.

Major Theodore Winthrop, an aide to General Butler, next led Washburn's Vermont and Massachusetts troops in an attack on the Confederate left flank. Crossing the creek, the men charged with a cheer. The Confederates responded with a withering fire and Major Winthrop was

killed as he tried to rally his men. With this repulse, Pierce decided to
break off the action. The retreat was followed by Captain Douthatt's
Confederate dragoons as far as Newmarket Bridge.[22] Magruder left a
cavalry force at Big Bethel and withdrew his infantry and artillery to
protect Yorktown.

The Federal forces lost a total of 76 men—18 killed, 53 wounded, and
5 missing. Confederate casualties were only one killed, seven wounded,
and three missing. Among the Union casualties, the death of First Lieutenant John T. Greble deserves special mention. He commanded the
artillery and was gallantly engaged with the enemy when the order to
retreat was given. Before he could complete arrangements for withdrawal he was struck in the forehead and killed—the first officer of the
Regular Army to give his life for his country in the war. The gun was
abandoned and Greble's body left beside it. Colonel Carr of the 2d New
York ordered one of his companies to retrieve the gun, which was accomplished with Greble's body lying on it.[23]

The effect of this small engagement—besides causing a sensation in
both the North and the South—was to cause a feeling of uncertainty on
the part of both commanders as to the strength and purposes of the
opposing forces, combined with an overestimate of the importance of
the victory or disaster to either party. A policy of caution and timidity
continued until the progress of events in northeastern Virginia had drawn
the attention of both governments to that more important scene of action.
On June 15, Colonel D. H. Hill, commanding the troops at Yorktown,
confided to General Lee his fears of a surprise or siege attack by General
Butler in force.[24] Again, on the nineteenth, Colonel Magruder reported
from Yorktown that he had withdrawn from Bethel after receiving information that the enemy was approaching in force via Warwick Court
House.[25]

General Butler was equally uninformed and mistaken as to the plans
of Magruder. "It is among the possibilities, and perhaps the probabili-
ties," he wrote on the twentieth to General Scott, "that a concentration
of troops may be made at Yorktown via James River, and an advance
movement upon this post ensue. . . . Newport News, perhaps, can hold
out with the three thousand men there against the attack of five thousand
or six thousand men, but we have not, as yet, any field artillery here.
To defend ourselves outside the fort, we have but about three thousand
effective men, and some of them not the best troops. . . . The enemy are
apparently preparing for an advance movement from Yorktown and the
Norfolk troops, should they attack, I should be, to say the least, largely
outnumbered." In the same letter, General Butler reported the mounting
of the Naval Brigade's 24-pounder gun at Fort Calhoun. The gun was
capable of firing a 53-pound elongated Sawyer shell which was able to

strike the enemy's batteries at Sewell's Point with a great degree of accuracy. General Butler was so impressed with the gun that he ordered the ordnance workshop to rifle two 6-pounder cannon to take the shells.[26]

The armament at Fort Monroe received a welcome addition on June 14 with the arrival of the "Union" gun. This mammoth 12-inch rifled gun weighed 52,005 pounds and was sixteen feet long. It fired a shell weighing from 360 to 420 pounds. On its way to Fort Monroe, the massive gun had gone overboard and ended up at the bottom of the river in Baltimore. The gun had been retrieved and now the problem was to move it from the wharf to its emplacement near the lighthouse. On June 18, twenty-five men of the Richardson Light Infantry[27] were detailed to unload the Union gun. After straining all day, the men managed to drag the gun fifty feet from the wharf. General Butler decided on June 23 to mount the gun on the carriage of the 15-inch Rodman gun located near the lighthouse. Tracks were laid from the wharf to the gun emplacement, the 15-inch gun dismounted, and on August 9 the Union gun was finally in position and ready for action.[28]

The 15-inch gun which was dismounted in order to mount the Union gun was the first cannon of this size manufactured by Captain Thomas J. Rodman. At the time, it was the largest gun in the United States. Guns larger than ten inches in bore cast solid had been found wanting in strength. Captain Rodman invented the method of casting large caliber guns hollow and then cooling them from the inside out by introducing a stream of water into the core. The 15-inch gun was the first large cannon cast by this method and had been brought to Fort Monroe for testing in the spring of 1860. The giant gun weighed 49,100 pounds and was 15 feet 10 inches long. The gun had achieved a range of 5,375 yards in its service tests, a tremendous range for a smooth bore weapon. By the end of the Civil War, the 15-inch gun had become a standard seacoast weapon and eventually seven were mounted at Fort Monroe. Captain Rodman cast two 20-inch guns later in the war, but the development of rifled artillery made the 15-inch and 20-inch guns obsolete.[29]

Two expeditions left Fort Monroe on June 24. Five companies of the 9th New York reconnoitered the vicinity of Big Bethel. The next morning they were joined by three more companies from other regiments and drove in the Confederate pickets. Ordered not to bring on an engagement, the expedition then headed back to camp. One of the participants later wrote that there was considerable plundering on the return march. A carpenter shop, which was full of shavings, was wantonly set on fire and everything that could not be carried off was destroyed.[30]

The other expedition consisted of 100 men of the 10th New York. They left Fort Monroe at 8 a.m. on June 24 and marched ten miles to Back River. Here they met the steamers *Fanny* and *Adriatic,* an armed steam launch from the frigate *Roanoke,* and several batteaux, manned by men of the Union Coast Guard, which were to transport them up stream. The object of the expedition was to destroy vessels being used to trade with the Eastern Shore. On the way up the river, eight or ten sailing vessels and numerous small boats were burned. The expedition turned about soon after nightfall, running down the stream and continuing the work of destruction up Harris Creek, where six schooners were destroyed. The burning of each vessel necessitated the landing of part of the force from the flatboats, sometimes through mud and water waist deep. The launch shelled the woods at intervals to cover the operation. The Confederates were aware of the expedition and dispatched forces toward Back River, but failed to arrive in time to make contact. The troops returned to Fort Monroe on the morning of June 25, tired and dirty, but satisfied with their work.[31]

On June 28, Magruder left his works at Yorktown with two regiments of North Carolina troops, one of Louisiana Zouaves, a howitzer battalion, and some 250 cavalry, with the intention of attacking the post at Newport News, but after advancing to within reach of the Federal pickets, he changed his course up the James and camped at Young's Mill, on the Warwick road about twelve miles from Newport News, near Mulberry Point. Magruder reported that, "We found a most respectable man (Captain Smith) and his family still living on their place, but subject to the threats, annoyances, robberies, and abuses of these unprincipled foes, who threatened their lives, as well as to burn their property, on the ground of their being secessionists. After leaving his house I addressed a letter to Col. Phelps, in command at Newport News, calling his attention to this improper and uncivilized conduct, and stating to him that it was not to be expected that the courtesy and humanity that characterized our treatment of those who had fallen into our hands would continue if such conduct on the part of his officers and men was longer tolerated."[32]

General Butler did make some effort to restrain the pillaging of the area by his troops. When the residents complained of some acts of vandalism, Butler was informed that a certain regiment was guilty. Lieutenant Butler, the general's young nephew, was sent to summon the colonel of the regiment. Entering the colonel's tent, the young lieutenant said, "Colonel, Uncle Ben wants you, and is going to give you hell!"

"Who is Uncle Ben?" inquired the bemused colonel.

"Why, General Butler!"

"Very well, I will attend, but not to 'get hell,' young man. I do not come here for that purpose."

"That's right," said the lieutenant, brightening considerably. "I like to see men who are not afraid of Uncle Ben."[33]

Near Young's Mill entrenchments were thrown up and the force strengthened by the 5th Louisiana and the 6th Georgia. On the morning of July 5 a detachment from this body, in an attempt to ambuscade a foraging party, was repulsed with the loss of its commander, Lieutenant Colonel Charles D. Dreux, of the Louisiana troops, and several enlisted men.[34] A second skirmish occurred on the twelfth, near Newport News, between a patrol of twenty-five men of the 7th New York Regiment and a small detachment of Confederate cavalry under Major John B. Hood, in which the Federals lost two officers and ten men captured and four men killed. No demonstration in force, however, was made by either party.[35]

On June 10 the organization and instruction of a corps of signal officers and men had begun at Fort Monroe under the direction of Major and Chief Signal Officer Albert J. Myer, and on the twenty-seventh the fort was in communication with its detached posts at Camps Hamilton and Butler. Communications with the latter camp at Newport News was also kept up by steamers plying daily between the two points, but these facilities were too slow and unsatisfactory to meet the emergencies of the hour. Men and materials for the erection and operation of a telegraph line were sent to Old Point Comfort and, the action at Big Bethel having been followed by a withdrawal of the enemy to Yorktown, a line was speedily erected from the fort, via Hampton, to Newport News and was in operation early in July. James R. Gilmore was the first superintendent of the line, assisted by Richard O'Brien and his younger brother, John, at Fort Monroe, Jesse H. Bunnell and Henry L. Smith at Hampton, and John M. Lock and John B. Stough at Newport News. Thus was Fort Monroe first connected by telegraph with the outer world.[36]

The War Department determined to replace the demoralized troops whom the disaster at Bull Run had thrown back upon the Capital with fresh troops. As a part of this movement, General Scott telegraphed Butler on July 24: "By the first line of steamers running between Fort Monroe and Baltimore, and the railroad from Baltimore, send to this place without fail, in three days, four regiments and a half of long term volunteers, including Baker's regiment and a half."[37]

The 3d and 4th Massachusetts, which had been advanced from Camp Hamilton into Hampton on July 1, with pickets to Newmarket Bridge, were at once recalled to Camp Hamilton, and Hampton was abandoned. The 2d and 3d Massachusetts and the 1st Vermont, being composed of 3-months' men, had been or were soon to be discharged. This detachment of troops weakened the position at Fort Monroe to a dangerous point, but General Butler immediately ordered the troops at Camp Hamilton and vicinity to prepare to march, and on July 26 and 27 the 3d, 4th and 5th New York and Baker's California regiment (71st Pennsylvania) left the post for

Washington. On the same day, Butler pulled his remaining forces back across Hampton Creek, and abandoned the village of Hampton.[38]

General Butler's apprehensions that the withdrawal of so large a portion of his force would be speedily followed by aggressive movements on the part of the enemy were only too well founded. On July 29 the general left the fort and repaired to Washington. Butler informed the General-in-Chief more fully as to his exposed situation than could be done by correspondence and urged upon him the desirability of committing so great a trust as the lower Chesapeake to a Regular officer of experience and rank.

By this time, Old Point Comfort had assumed the appearance of a busy town. The surrounding waters were covered with shipping and the docks filled with small sailing vessels and lighters unloading stores. The Hygeia Hotel had been partially converted into a hospital, and another part was occupied by the provost guard. Besides the various buildings used by the Quartermaster and Commissary Departments, and the Government foundries and work shops, many frame buildings had been erected, which were occupied by sutlers and the workmen employed on the post. Flanking these were numberless shanties and tents erected to house the hundreds of escaped slaves. The highest prices were asked by the sutlers for everything, but there were plenty of buyers, the volunteer soldiers seeming determined to eat of the best while their money lasted. The Regulars were not so free with their pay and generally contrived to live on what the Government furnished, with extras purchased by the company fund.[39]

As soon as Magruder learned of the Confederate victory at Bull Run, he sent 2,000 men under the command of Colonel Robert Johnston to make a reconnaissance of Hampton and Newport News. This force rounded up about 150 Negroes and sent them back to Williamsburg, but when the Confederates arrived in Hampton on July 25 a large balloon suddenly rose from behind the Federal lines. On June 5, General Butler had offered John La Mountain the job of aerial observer with his command. LaMountain eagerly accepted, but it was July 23 before he managed to get his two balloons and equipment to Old Point Comfort. La Mountain made his first ascension on the evening of July 25, but a stiff wind was blowing at the time and he was unable to attain sufficient altitude for effective observation. He rose high enough to see for a radius of ten miles, but the only thing of interest within view was a sloop on Back River.[40]

The Confederates withdrew to Yorktown and Williamsburg on July 29 and 30. While the Confederates rested, La Mountain made two ascensions on July 31. The first one ran into technical problems, but on his second attempt La Mountain rose to 1,400 feet and had an excellent view for a

radius of thirty miles. La Mountain discovered a concealed camp in the
rear of the water battery at Sewell's Point. The camp contained fifty-eight
tents, denoting several hundred men, but not the force of thousands
which had been believed. Another camp, of about forty tents, was also
spotted hidden behind the Pig Point battery. All appeared to be quiet
toward Yorktown. La Mountain went up to about 1,000 feet on August
1 and reported that Hampton was not occupied by the enemy and again
could find no signs of Confederate activity.

On August 3, the first American "aircraft carrier" set sail. La Mountain's balloon was inflated and placed on board the small gunboat *Fanny*
and secured to the stern by mooring ropes and a windlass. Steaming to a
point opposite Sewell's Point, La Mountain ascended to 2,000 feet and
made a careful inspection of the Confederate position. The enemy, concealed by a screen of trees, was busily at work erecting additional fortifications with gun pits and embrasures for pieces evidently intended to
bear on Fort Calhoun, Fort Monroe, and the shipping in the Roads. The
Fanny then proceeded toward Craney Island and Pig Point, but nothing
new appeared to be taking place at these locations.[41]

La Mountain had been of great help to General Butler, but unfortunately he did not see the Confederates when Magruder finally decided
to advance. On the afternoon of August 6, Magruder advanced to within
a mile of Newmarket Bridge with a force consisting of 4,000 infantry,
400 cavalry, and Randolph's howitzer battalion. That night Confederate
scouts penetrated well behind the Federal lines. The next morning
Magruder advanced to within a mile and a half of Newport News and
tried to induce the Federals to come out and fight. Despite the fact that
this large Confederate force was placed squarely between the troops at
Fort Monroe and at Newport News, the Federals remained behind their
entrenchments. The Confederates then marched to within a mile of
Hampton.

Near Hampton occurred one of the more unfortunate incidents of the
war. A copy of the *New York Tribune* fell into Magruder's hands. The
paper, quite incorrectly as it turned out, announced that General Butler
intended to occupy Hampton, dispossess the inhabitants, and use the
town as a camp for runaway slaves. Magruder promptly decided to
destroy the historic old colonial town. He called in Captain Jefferson C.
Phillips, commander of the Old Dominion Dragoons and a native of
Hampton, and gave him the disagreeable assignment. Captain Phillips
took his company, Captain Goode's Mecklenburgh Cavalry, Captain
Curtis' Warwick Beauregards, and Captain Sinclair's York Rangers to
destroy the town. Colonel James G. Hodges and his 14th Virginia Infantry accompanied Phillips to guard the bridge over Hampton River.
Shortly after dark the expedition crossed Newmarket Bridge and rode into

town. The citizens were quickly alerted that the town was to be burned and soon each of the four cavalry companies was busy setting fire to a quarter of the town. A short encounter with the Federal pickets at the bridge was the only opposition encountered. By the next morning the expedition had rejoined Magruder and Hampton was in ruins. "A more wanton and unnecessary act than the burning, as it seems to me, could not have been committed," General Butler reported. "I confess myself so poor a soldier as not to be able to discern the strategical importance of this movement."[42]

In destroying Hampton, the Confederates had cut the telegraph line between Fort Monroe and Newport News. Richard O'Brien, the chief operator at Fort Monroe, accompanied the troops which rushed to Hampton and helped in attempts to save historic St. John's Church. The ex-firemen in the 10th New York had resurrected a couple of ancient fire engines at the fort. The ropes were manned by Companies C and H, aided by a numerous body of runners, and the engines were quickly hauled to Hampton.

This was not the last time that the telegraph line would be cut. Confederate patrols from the camp near Big Bethel frequently cut the line. On one occasion, O'Brien went out to repair such a break with an escort of infantry. He was on horseback and rapidly outdistanced his escort. Finding the break near Newport News, O'Brien quickly repaired it and started back toward Hampton. As he passed the Newmarket road, he received simultaneously a bullet through his coat and an order to halt from a Confederate patrol. O'Brien spurred his horse and succeeded in reaching his escort, which drove off the Confederates with a volley. On another occasion, John O'Brien went out with a four-mule wagon and a lineman and some Negro laborers to repair a break. On nearing Newmarket road they saw a party of cavalry rapidly advancing toward them. The teamster turned the wagon across the road to slow the cavalry and the Negroes took off on the run for Fort Monroe. Young O'Brien hid in the woods, but soon observed the cavalry gathered around the wagon and the teamster gesticulating for him to return. When he cautiously came out of hiding, O'Brien discovered that they had encountered a detachment of the 1st New York Mounted Rifles returning from a scouting expedition.[43]

The authorities acted promptly upon General Butler's suggestion that a Regular officer of rank and experience be sent to Fort Monroe, and on August 8 General Scott telegraphed Major General John E. Wool, at Troy, New York: "It is desirable that you repair to and assume command of the department of which Fort Monroe is the place of headquarters. It is intended to re-enforce that department (recently reduced) for aggressive purposes. Is your health equal to that command? If yes, you will be ordered thither at once. Reply immediately." General Wool signified his readiness to accept the command and he was ordered to Fort Monroe to take command of the Department, which now became that of South-eastern Virginia. Arriving at Fort Monroe on the seventeenth, General Wool assumed command and assigned General Butler to the command of all the volunteer forces within the Department outside the walls of the fort. At that time these troops consisted of the 1st, 2d, 7th, 9th, and 20th New York, a battalion of Massachusetts Volunteers, the Union Coast Guard, and a squadron of the 1st New York Mounted Rifles.[44]

During his tenure of command at Fort Monroe, General Butler had displayed considerable ability in civil organization and administration and had ruled with an autocratic hand. Within his command he had sought a strict discipline, and foraging and depradations were strictly forbidden. His legal training had led him to issue a number of orders concerning the rights and privileges of civilians—particularly their property rights—and this same legal training had enabled him to draw a fine line when escaped slaves sought sanctuary within the Federal line. Claimed by their owners as private property and therefore subject to reclamation under the terms of his own orders, Butler declared that slaves were "contraband of war" and therefore confiscable. The slaves remained and labored mightily in the defensive preparations in and around the fort.

Butler's first care upon arrival had been to fix upon a camp for the arriving troops. Pursuant to instructions, he examined the "pine forest" on the narrow strip of land next to the beach north of the fort. This proved to be an objectionable site because here was the post cemetery—which has long since been abandoned—containing the bodies of all the soldiers and others who had died at Fort Monroe during more than half a century. His choice was therefore fixed upon the open lands across Mill Creek.

The general then inspected the fort itself and found its "ramps and ramparts in good condition. Its only weak spot as far as construction was concerned was in its magazines, which had been made safe only on the sea front. In the rear they had been left in a very unsatisfactory condition, the construction engineer never supposing that the fort could be assaulted or bombarded from the land side. As it was, if it were attacked by the rebels from that side, with mortars throwing a curved fire into the fort and against the walls of the inner ramparts, the magazines were wholly without protection." For these reasons he started to cover the magazines with bags filled with sand, but before the work was completed the war had been removed far enough from the fort to dissipate any fear of attack from the landward side.

Butler also ran a railroad line to the post, proving to his engineers that loose sand can be made to support a locomotive and a train of cars.

Another care was the water supply of the garrison. Wells dug by the troops on the far side of Mill Creek cut off much of the water from the garrison, and it was found necessary to bring water to Fort Monroe from Baltimore at a cost of as much as two cents a gallon. To supplement this, a plant to distill seawater taken from the moat was erected. At the same time, Butler started to sink a well on the reservation and had got down to about 350 feet when the work was suspended at the time he was relieved.

La Mountain's operations as aerial observer ended at about the same time as Butler's command of Fort Monroe. La Mountain made five ascensions on August 10, reaching a maximum elevation of 3,500 feet. He discovered a large Confederate camp about six miles from Hampton. These were Magruder's troops who had constructed new fortifications at Bethel and then had moved back to Young's Mill and were busily fortifying the area. That night, La Mountain had his balloon attached to the tug *Adriatic* and accompanied by General Butler again made successful observations. This exhausted La Mountain's supplies and he left Fort Monroe on August 16. General Wool apparently knew nothing about the aerial observations, and when La Mountain returned the next month the general sent him to Washington, where he eventually found employment with the Army of the Potomac.[45]

Like his predecessor in command, General Wool was at once impressed with the meagerness of his force when compared with the importance of his position and what was expected of him. On August 24 he wrote to General Scott, reciting his great need of experienced officers and men and adding: "To operate on this coast with success . . . we want more troops. . . . If I had 20,000 or 25,000 men, in conjunction with the Navy, we could do much on this coast to bring back from Virginia the troops of North Carolina, South Carolina, and Georgia; but the arrangements should be left to Commodore Stringham and myself. We know better than anyone at Washington attached to the Navy what we required for such expeditions."[46]

On September 14, fifteen political prisoners arrived at Fort Monroe from Baltimore under strong guard. They were immediately confined in the casemates of the fort, a fate which others eventually would share. The following day, General Wool wrote to Secretary of War Cameron, "The crowded state of this fortress which from the great number of stores and supplies within it has obliged me to place these prisoners in very close quarters where they cannot obtain even the necessary conveniences of health and must suffer seriously for the want of air and ventilation, and to detail a strong guard for their safe-keeping which with the reduced force now at my disposal has necessarily interfered with other important duties of the men. . . . At the Rip Raps they could not be accommodated from the great number of prisoners waiting there for conveyance to the Tortugas." Three days later, the War Department ordered the prisoners transferred to Fort Lafayette in New York Harbor.[47]

General Wool was not long in showing that he took an interest in the smaller details of military discipline at the post. Often at reveille, accompanied by an orderly, he would leave his quarters, either for a "constitutional" or to observe how affairs progressed at that early hour. Like soldiers since that time, many of the troops had a tendency to roll over at reveille and go back to sleep or to answer roll call and then head back to bed for another hour or so. One dark morning, after the roll had been called, someone pulled at the flap of one of the tents of the 10th New York, and shouted to the sleepers inside to turn out. The man nearest the door aimed a vigorous kick at the intruder, at the same time telling him to "Leave that flap alone." A pull at the blanket sent the laggard to the door to find himself confronted by General Wool. The soldier stammered an apology and received a quiet admonition from the general not to return to bed after reveille in the future.

The slim, bent form of General Wool became a familiar figure upon the ramparts of the fort, where he would be seen early in the morning or at sunset, with tight-fitting frock coat and either a well-worn silk hat or a glazed cap of Mexican War vintage. The sentinels grew exceedingly alert as the time approached for his grand rounds.[48]

The armament of the fort was continually increased during the early months of the war. Larger and more modern weapons began to replace the more antiquated pieces in the fortification. The 10th New York mounted the new guns and in addition rapidly was trained in heavy artillery drill. The regiment seemed to take to this branch of the service with alacrity, and the readiness of the soldiers to learn, coupled with their efficient discharge of other duties devolving upon them as garrison troops, won the praise of Colonel Dimick and the other Regular officers.

By the middle of September there were 163 guns and 17 mortars mounted in the fort. Of these, 67 guns were in the casemates and 96 were mounted in barbette. Thirty-nine 42-pounders were mounted in the water battery facing the channel. Most of the barbette guns were old 32-pounders, but there were also two 7-inch rifled guns, eleven 8-inch Columbiads, and ten 10-inch Columbiads. In addition to these guns in the fort proper, the 12-inch rifled gun near the lighthouse provided a formidable armament. At Fort Calhoun, in addition to the 24-pounder Sawyer gun mounted on the wharf, there were seven 8-inch Columbiads mounted in the casemates. Two rifled 42-pounders were on hand and ready to be mounted.[49]

On August 26 the first expedition against the coast of the Confederacy had left the fort, bound for Hatteras Inlet, North Carolina. The detachment, which was commanded by General Butler, was composed of 500 men of the 20th New York (Colonel Max Weber), 220 men of the 9th New York (Colonel Hawkins), 100 men of the Union Coast Guard, and 60 men of the 2d United States Artillery. The capture of Hatteras and its forts on August 29 and the desirability of holding them, even at the expense of Fort Monroe, at once complicated the situation already reported by General Wool. General Butler, returning to Fort Monroe on the thirty-first, was sent to Washington to ascertain the wishes and the policy of the War Department. Four days later, General Wool reported Fort Monroe and Hampton Roads as "the most important position on the coast," and on September 13 he wrote: "I am anxiously looking for more troops."[50]

An order, received at about this time, to send four artillery companies to Washington, left General Wool in despair. On the fourteenth he wrote: "I have at this moment received your communication of the 12th instant, directing four artillery companies to Washington—the four companies about 200 strong—leaving one company at Fort Monroe, one at Newport News, and one at Hatteras Inlet, about 50 strong. We are thus, as you perceive, left with only about 130 regular artillery for Fort Monroe and Newport News, the most important post on the coast and the key to all the States south. . . . The force we have is not sufficient to defend both positions if seriously attacked."[51]

To the little command in the vicinity of Fort Monroe this was a season of keenest anxiety, amounting almost to despair. The force of the enemy was being constantly augmented, and fears of a surprise necessitated the utmost vigilance. Throughout the month General Wool continued his appeals for assistance, reaching a climax on October 6: "We want more regiments. I only ask that you will give me sufficient number of troops to defend this place. The enemy have been re-enforcing their troops."[52] As if to confirm Wool's fears, the Old Dominion Dragoons on October 12 captured twelve Federals near Newport News and on October 21 there was a small skirmish near Young's Mill.

The command at Fort Monroe was not alone in demanding recognition of its requirements. The situation at Washington was scarcely less embarrassing to the War Department than was that in the lower Chesapeake to General Wool. General Scott, after a lifetime of devotion to duty, found himself unable, in his declining years, to cope with an enemy of great resources and greater determination. Yet he found time to consider the appeals of General Wool, and on October 8 he wrote that "the Tenth Maine regiment has this day been ordered to Fort Monroe, and that tomorrow about 200 sailors, skilled as artillerists, will be sent down. Several companies of volunteers drilled as artillerists will also be sent you, as soon as they can be made ready. . . ." A proposal of the Navy

Department, in which General Scott concurred, to transfer responsibility for defense of the Rip Raps was also broached.[53]

For some unexplained reason, or reasons, no attempt was made by the enemy to take advantage at this time of the exposed and defenseless situation at Fort Monroe. Magruder's forces at Yorktown, Warwick, and Young's farm (Denbigh) amounted to 9,500 men, and Huger's, at Sewell's Point, Pig Point, and Norfolk, to 7,500 more. Thus a force six times his own might have massed against General Wool during September and early October. Possibly an explanation of this inaction may be found in a report of General Magruder to the Confederate Secretary of War, dated October 7, from which it appears that while General Wool was appealing for enough men to defend his position "an intelligent and reliable deserter" from the fort was confiding to Magruder the surprising intelligence that Wool intended to attack Yorktown immediately, both by land and water; that 5,000 troops had reinforced Fort Monroe and Newport News the day before and 30,000 more were expected immediately; that seventy brass rifled field pieces for field service and 500 horses were at the fort in charge of the regulars; and that troops were arriving in considerable numbers daily at Fort Monroe and Newport News and were being sent to quarters by night to avoid being seen by Huger's troops at Sewell's Point.[54]

On October 19, Lieutenant Colonel Dimick, who had been in command of the fort for several years, left for Fort Warren, Boston Harbor, to which he had been transferred. The 10th New York and the two regular batteries formed in line and escorted the departing commanding officer to the landing, where he bade the soldiers an affecting farewell, to which they responded with many rounds of cheers. Major Joseph Roberts, 4th Artillery, succeeded Colonel Dimick in the command of the fort and its garrison.[55]

The ensuing two months was generally a period of apparent inactivity at Fort Monroe, but in reality was one of preparation for coming operations for which that point was to be the base. The authorities at Washington were considering plans for expeditions against New Bern and Beaufort, in North Carolina; for a movement against Norfolk; and for the more important advance upon Richmond. The first of the activities along these lines was the organization at Annapolis of Brigadier General Thomas W. Sherman's expedition against South Carolina, which rendezvoused at Fort Monroe and sailed on October 29, 1861. This force captured Hilton Head and Port Royal Sound on November 7, giving the Union a toe hold between Savannah and Charleston.

On November 11 and 12 skirmishes occurred between scouting parties near Newmarket Bridge, and during the month reconnaissances from Fort Monroe and Newport News brought out the information that the enemy had evacuated the lower peninsula and had concentrated in force about Yorktown. All the farm houses and barns within ten miles of the fort were found to have been burned or destroyed, the whole country presenting a sad picture of desolation.[56]

Some excitement was generated on November 14 when a flag of truce was sent from Fort Monroe to Craney Island, near Norfolk. The small steamboat *Washington* made the trip, carrying thirty-seven Confederate prisoners captured at Hatteras who had been exchanged. The *Washington* anchored near the enemy batteries on Craney Island and awaited the arrival of the steamboat *William Selden* from Norfolk. The prisoners were delivered to the Confederate vessel along with the mail for the Federal prisoners then held at Richmond. The next day the sloop-of-war *San Jacinto* arrived in port on her way to Fort Warren. On board were James M. Mason and John Slidell, Confederate agents to Europe who had been seized from the British ship *Trent*. The resulting international incident almost involved Great Britain in the Civil War. After this brief flurry of activity, the garrison began to prepare to celebrate the holidays, aided by the newly formed regimental band of the 10th New York.[57]

On November 30, the force under the command of Major Roberts at Fort Monroe consisted of:[58]

Batteries D and L, 4th Artillery	8 officers and 130 men
1st Massachusetts Infantry Battalion	3 officers and 96 men
Troops A and B, 1st New York Mounted Rifles	5 officers and 164 men
10th Regiment, New York Volunteers	35 officers and 887 men
	51 officers and 1,277 men

The year 1861 closed without material change in the composition of the garrison, although the forces at Camp Hamilton and Camp Butler were, during the latter part of December, considerably increased. On the thirty-first of the month, there were under the command of General Wool over thirteen thousand officers and men, distributed as follows:[59]

Fort Monroe	1,453
Camp Butler (Newport News)	4,054
Camp Hamilton and vicinity	5,427
Fort Calhoun (Rip Raps)	187
Hatteras Inlet, N. C.	1,892
Total	13,013

If Fort Monroe ever repaid the vast sums of government money expended in its construction, it did so during the opening months of the Civil War. As the last remaining symbol of Federal authority in the upper South, the key strategic location of Fort Monroe was to have a profound effect on the course of the war in Virginia.

General Butler's reputation is badly tarnished as a result of the bitter controversy over his subsequent command of New Orleans and inept experience as a field commander. The decline in his fortunes is in sharp contrast with his first tour of duty as senior officer at Fort Monroe. Butler's administrative talents were invaluable in helping sort out the confusion that existed at the beginning of the war. His famous contraband decision was to have a major impact throughout the war.

The expedition to the South Carolina coast opened a new phase in the war for Fort Monroe. During the following months the fort was to serve as the base for several expeditions against the southern coast and for a major drive to capture the Confederate capital.

Footnotes Chapter V

¹ Scott to Dimick, December 31, 1860, *War of the Rebellion: A Compilation of the Official Records of the Union and Confederate Armies* (Washington: Government Printing Office, 1880–1901), 130 vols. (hereafter cited as *OR*), Series I, Vol. I, p. 119.

² Orders No. 13, Fort Monroe, January 23, 1861, *ibid.*, p. 353. Vogdes had graduated from West Point in 1837 and became a brigadier general of volunteers during the Civil War. He became colonel of the 1st Artillery in 1863, retired in 1881, and died in 1889. *Heitman*, p. 988.

³ Bvt. Brig. Gen. Jos. G. Totten to Hon. Joseph Holt, January 18, 1861, *OR*, Series III, Vol. I, p. 50.

⁴ Scott to Capt. H. G. Wright, April 19, 1861, *OR*, Series I, Vol. II, p. 23. Wright was an 1841 graduate of West Point and served as a major general of volunteers during the Civil War, being brevetted three times for gallantry. In 1879 he was promoted to brigadier general and Chief of Engineers. He retired in 1884 and died in 1899. *Heitman*, p. 1062.

⁵ Report of Capt. H. G. Wright, April 26, 1861, *OR*, Series I, Vol. II, pp. 21–23.

⁶ Fort Monroe Post Return, April 1861, NA, RG 94.

⁷ Seager, *op. cit.*, p. 467; Alfred Davenport, *Camp and Field Life of the Fifth New York Volunteer Infantry (Duryea Zouaves)* (New York: Dick and Fitzgerald, 1879), p. 39; Henry W. Howe, *Passages from the Life of Henry Warren Howe, consisting of Diary and Letters Written During the Civil War* (Lowell, Mass.: Courier-Citizen Co., 1899), pp. 19–20.

⁸ An account of this episode may be found in the "History of Fort Monroe, 1607–1884," NA, RG 156.

⁹ E. D. Townsend, A.A.G., to Col. J. Dimick, April 30, 1861, *OR*, Series I, Vol. II, p. 612.

¹⁰ Scott to Maj. Gen. B. F. Butler, May 18, 1861, *ibid.*, pp. 640–641.

¹¹ Brig. Gen. Benj. F. Butler to Hon. Simon Cameron, May 18, 1861; General Orders No. 1, Department of Virginia, May 22, 1861; Maj. Gen. Benj. F. Butler to Lt. Gen. Winfield Scott, May 24, 1861; *ibid.*, pp. 641–642, 643, 648–651.

¹² *Heitman*, p. 494; *Battles and Leaders of the Civil War* (New York: The Century Co., 1884–1888), Vol. II, p. 144.

¹³ Benj. S. Ewell to Maj. Gen. R. E. Lee, May 16, 1861, *OR*, Series I, Vol. II, pp. 853–854.

¹⁴ Lt. Col. Benj. S. Ewell to Maj. Gen. Lee, May 21, 1861, *ibid.*, pp. 862–863.

¹⁵ Maj. J. B. Cary to Lt. Col. Benj. S. Ewell, May 23, 1861; Lt. Col. Benj. S. Ewell to Maj. Gen. R. E. Lee, May 24, 1861; Maj. Cary to Col. J. B. Magruder, May 24, 1861; *ibid.*, pp. 35–36, 870–871.

¹⁶ Maj. Gen. Benj. F. Butler to Lt. Gen. Scott, May 24, 1861, *ibid.*, pp. 649–650.

¹⁷ Maj. Gen. Benj. F. Butler to Lt. Gen. Scott, May 27 and May 29, 1861, *ibid.*, pp. 52–54.

¹⁸ Col. J. B. Magruder to Col. R. S. Garnett, May 29 and June 2, 1861, *ibid.*, pp. 893–894, 900–901.

¹⁹ Philip Corell, *History of the Naval Brigade, 99th N.Y. Volunteers, Union Coast Guard* (New York: Regimental Veteran Association, 1905).

²⁰ Davenport, *op. cit.*, pp. 41–48.

²¹ Kilpatrick was an 1861 graduate of West Point. He was the first Regular officer wounded in the war. He rose to the rank of major general of volunteers and had a contro-

versial career as a cavalry commander. He resigned from the Army in 1865 and later served as Minister to Chile. Kilpatrick died in 1881. *Heitman,* p. 597.

[22] The reports of the battle are in *OR,* Series I, Vol. II, pp. 77–104, and Vol. LI, Part 1, pp. 3–5. Davenport, *op. cit.,* pp. 49–73; William J. Kimball, "The Little Battle of Big Bethel," *Civil War Times Illustrated,* VI (June 1967), pp. 28–32; Charles W. Cowtan, *Services of the Tenth New York Volunteers (National Zouaves) in the War of the Rebellion* (New York: Charles H. Ludwig, 1882), p. 34. An excellent analysis of the battle can be found in Brig. Gen. R. L. Tilton, "Military Operations on the Peninsula During the First Year of the Civil War—1861," ms. in Casemate Museum. *Battles and Leaders,* Vol. II, p.148–151.

[23] Greble had graduated from West Point in 1854 and from the Artillery School at Fort Monroe in 1860. *Heitman,* p. 473. *Battles and Leaders,* Vol. II, p. 150.

[24] Col. D. H. Hill to Gen. R. E. Lee, June 15, 1861, *OR,* Series I, Vol. II, p. 927.

[25] Col. J. Bankhead Magruder to Col. George Deas, June 19, 1861, *ibid.,* pp. 940–941.

[26] Maj. Gen. Benj. F. Butler to Lt. Gen. Winfield Scott, June 20, 1861, *ibid.,* pp. 708–709.

[27] The Richardson Light Infantry was an independent Massachusetts company which arrived at Fort Monroe on May 25 and was attached to the Regular Army garrison. The company was redesignated the 7th Massachusetts Light Artillery Battery in March 1862. Frederick H. Dyer, *A Compendium of the War of the Rebellion* (New York and London: Thomas Yoseloff, 1959), Vol. III, p. 1245.

[28] Howe, *Passages from the Life of Henry Warren Howe,* pp. 13–14, 25, 26; *Frank Leslie's Illustrated Newspaper,* August 10, 1861, pp. 193–194; Capt. A. B. Dyer to Brig. Gen. J. W. Ripley, July 23, 1861, Letters Sent, Fort Monroe Arsenal, NA, RG 156.

[29] *Harper's Weekly,* March 30, 1861, pp. 204–205; J. G. Barnard, *Notes on Sea-Coast Defence: Consisting of Sea-Coast Fortifications, the Fifteen-Inch Gun, and Casemate Embrasures* (New York: D. Van Nostrand, 1861); John J. Tidball, *Manual of Heavy Artillery Service for the Use of the Army and Militia of the United States* (Washington: James J. Chapman, 1891), pp. 119–120.

[30] Charles F. Johnson, *The Long Roll* (East Aurora, N.Y.: The Roycrofters, 1911), p. 25.

[31] Cowtan, *op. cit.,* pp. 44–45; Col. Robert Johnston to Maj. G. B. Cosby, July 25, 1861, *OR,* Series I, Vol. II, pp. 576–577.

[32] J. Bankhead Magruder to "Sir," *OR,* Series I, Vol. II, pp. 960–961.

[33] *Battles and Leaders,* Vol. II, p. 146.

[34] *OR,* Series I, Vol. II, pp. 188–192.

[35] *Ibid.,* pp. 293–298.

[36] John Emmet O'Brien, *Telegraphing in Battle* (Scranton, 1910), pp. 18, 35.

[37] Maj. Gen. John A. Dix to Gen. B. F. Butler, July 24, 1861, *OR,* Series I, Vol. II, p. 761.

[38] Special Orders No. 186, Fort Monroe, July 24, 1861; Maj. Gen. Benj. F. Butler to Lt. Gen. Scott, July 26 and July 27, 1861; *ibid.,* pp. 761, 763–764, 765. Davenport, *op. cit.,* pp. 89–90.

[39] Cowtan, *op. cit.,* p. 42; Davenport, *op. cit.,* pp. 75–76; Howe, *Passages from the Life of Henry Warren Howe,* pp. 10–11.

[40] F. Stansbury Haydon, *Aeronautics in the Union and Confederate Armies* (Baltimore: The Johns Hopkins Press, 1941), Vol. I, pp. 85–93.

[41] *Ibid.,* pp. 93–97.

[42] Brig. Gen J. Bankhead Magruder to Col. George Deas, August 2 and August 9, 1861; Maj. Gen. Benj. F. Butler to Lt. Gen. Scott, August 8, 1861; *OR,* Series I, Vol. IV, pp. 567–573. "Smoke Over Hampton, 1861," *Syms-Eaton Museum Horn Book Series,* No. 6; *Battles and Leaders,* Vol. II, p. 151.

[43] O'Brien, *op. cit.,*pp. 36, 37–38, 59–60; Cowtan, *op. cit.,* pp. 42–43, 46.

[44] Winfield Scott to Maj. Gen. Wool, Aug. 8, 1861; General Orders No. 1, Dept. of Southeastern Virginia, Aug. 17, 1861; Special Orders No. 9, Dept. of Virginia, Aug. 21, 1861; *OR,* Series I, Vol. IV, pp. 600–601, 602.

[45] Haydon, *op. cit.,* pp. 101–104, 111–113; Maj. Gen. Benj. F. Butler to Lt. Gen. Scott, Aug. 11, 1861, *OR,* Series I, Vol. IV, pp. 600–601.

[46] Maj. Gen. John E. Wool to Lt. Gen. Winfield Scott, Aug. 24, 1861, *OR,* Series I, Vol. IV, pp. 602–603.

[47] Maj. Gen. John E. Wool to Hon. Simon Cameron, Sept. 15, 1861; E. D. Townsend to

Maj. Gen. John E. Wool, Sept. 18, 1861; *OR,* Series II, Vol. I, pp. 596–597. Cowtan, *op. cit.,* p. 54.

[48] Cowtan, *op. cit.,* pp. 54–56.

[49] Cowtan, *op. cit.,* pp.56–57; Capt. C. S. Stewart to Brevet Brig. Gen. Jos. G. Totten, Sept. 13, 1861, NA, RG 77.

[50] Daniel Ammen, *The Atlantic Coast* (New York: The Blue & Gray Press, n.d.), pp. 165–171; Maj. Gen. John E. Wool to Hon. Simon Cameron, Sept. 4, 1861, and to Lt. Gen. Winfield Scott, Sept. 13, 1861, *OR,* Series I, Vol. IV, pp. 605–606, 607; David Stick, *The Outer Banks of North Carolina* (Chapel Hill: The University of North Carolina Press, 1958), pp. 120–121; Corell, *op. cit.*

[51] Maj. Gen. John E. Wool to Brig. Gen. L. Thomas, Sept. 14, 1861, *OR,* Series I, Vol. IV, pp. 612–613.

[52] Maj. Gen. John E. Wool to Lt. Gen. Winfield Scott, *ibid.,* p. 621.

[53] E. D. Townsend to Maj. Gen. John E. Wool, Oct. 8, 1861, *ibid.,* pp. 621–622.

[54] Brig. Gen. J. Bankhead Magruder to Gen. S. Cooper, Oct. 7, 1861, *ibid.,* pp. 672–674.

[55] Cowtan, *op. cit.,* pp. 58–59. Roberts had graduated from West Point in 1835 and was promoted to major a month before he took command of Fort Monroe. He became colonel of the 3d Pennsylvania Heavy Artillery in 1863 and was brevetted brigadier general for meritorious service during the Civil War. Roberts became colonel of the 4th Artillery in 1877, retired the same year, and died in 1898. *Heitman,* p. 835.

[56] Brig. Gen. J. Bankhead Magruder to Gen. S. Cooper, Nov. 18, 1861, *OR,* Series I, Vol. IV, pp. 598–599.

[57] Cowtan, *op. cit.,* pp. 60–62.

[58] Fort Monroe Post Return, Nov. 1861, NA, RG 94.

[59] Return of the Department of Virginia for Dec. 1861, *OR,* Series I, Vol. IV, p. 632.

Chapter VI

Springboard
for Attack

THE YEAR 1862 OPENED with the armies of the Union thoroughly organized, equipped, and disciplined, so that the War Department was in a position to develop plans of operations which had necessarily been delayed. Among the early propositions of Major General George B. McClellan, the new Commanding General of the Army, was the formation of a corps for service in the bays and inlets of the Chesapeake and the Potomac to cooperate with the Army of the Potomac in a contemplated advance upon the enemy's position about Richmond. To this end he had, as early as September 6, 1861, asked for and received authority to organize a force of ten regiments and a fleet of tugboats.[1] Navy Department interest in the coast of North Carolina induced a change in the objective of this expedition before its organization was completed. The command was given to Brigadier General Ambrose E. Burnside, and he, having assembled three brigades at Annapolis, was ordered to unite at Fort Monroe with the fleet under Flag Officer Louis M. Goldsborough for operations against Roanoke Island and New Bern and ultimately against Beaufort.

Burnside's force embarked on January 8, 1862, and steamed to Fort Monroe with the sailing vessels in tow. Here it was joined by the naval part of the expedition, and the whole force assembled in Hampton Roads. On the evening of January 11 a large part of the convoy put to sea, followed the next night by the remainder of the expedition. The success of the expedition gave the Federals control of the area around Roanoke Island, New Bern, Beaufort, and Fort Macon. Burnside, recalled from other duties, returned on July 7 to Fort Monroe with 8,000 men, leaving Brigadier General John G. Foster in command of the Department of North Carolina, with headquarters at New Bern.

Despite the withdrawal of Hatteras Inlet from his Department and its assignment to the Department of North Carolina, General Wool still had a respectable command. The garrison at Fort Monroe had, by January 31, been rebuilt to a strength of 1,534 officers and men present to man the 223 heavy guns and the 23 field guns at that station. The whole command consisted of:[2]

Fort Monroe	*Camp Hamilton*
Maj. Jos. Roberts, 4th Artillery	Col. Max Weber, 20th New York
10th New York	1st Delaware
1 Co., 99th New York	16th Massachusetts
6th Massachusetts Battery	20th Indiana
Batteries D and L, 4th U.S.	20th New York
Artillery	6 Cos., 99th New York
2d & 4th Batteries Wisconsin	11th Pennsylvania Cavalry
Light Artillery	4 Cos., 1st New York Mounted
2 Cos., 1st New York Mounted	Rifles
Rifles	

Camp Butler	*Fort Calhoun*
Brig. Gen. J. K. F. Mansfield	Lt. Col. G. B. Helleday, 99th N.Y.
1st New York	2 Cos., 99th New York
2d New York	
7th New York	
11th New York	
29th Massachusetts	

The enemy had not been idle during the winter. As Fort Monroe was to the Union cause a strategic position of the highest importance, so the defense of the Peninsula was the key to the security of Richmond. On January 31, Magruder's forces on the Peninsula aggregated nearly 15,000 present for duty, distributed as follows: at Yorktown and vicinity, 5,555; along the James, beyond Newport News, 6,137; at Williamsburg, Gloucester Point, Jamestown, and Lebanon Church, 2,808. With these forces there were 39 pieces of field artillery and 192 of heavy artillery, so that the actual effective force surrounding General Wool at this time exceeded 30,000 men supported by nearly 250 pieces of artillery.[3]

In preparation for military operations on the Peninsula, a telegraph line was run down the eastern shore of Delaware, Maryland, and Virginia to Cape Charles, which it reached on February 5, 1862, giving direct wire connection between Washington and that point. A dispatch boat plied across the bay to Fort Monroe in three hours. Shortly afterward an attempt to lay a cable across the bay from Cape Charles resulted in the wreck of the vessel containing it on Cape Henry, where the con-

Lt. John Greble's guns in action at the Battle of Big Bethel, June 10, 1861.

Officers and their families in front of casemate quarters during the Civil War. Col. Joseph Roberts, the post commander, stands in front of the door.

The 3d Pennsylvania Heavy Artillery formed for inspection on the parade ground during the Civil War.

A 15-inch Rodman mounted in a bastion near the end of the Civil War.

Brevet Lt. Col. John J. Craven attending Jefferson Davis in his casemate cell. Painting by Jack Clifton.

Carroll Hall, the officers' apartment complex in which Jefferson Davis was imprisoned.

Converted Rodman rifles and a 15-inch Rodman in the South Bastion, about 1885.

A 100-pounder Parrott rifle about 1885. The end of the Water Battery to the left, lighthouse in center background, and Hygeia Hotel to the right.

15-inch Rodman guns mounted on the north end of the Water Battery, about 1890.

Fort Monroe, Virginia about 1880

A bird's eye view of Old Point Comfort, Fort Monroe, and the Hygeia Hotel about 1885.

The main barracks as seen from across the parade ground, about 1885.

Quarters No. 1, home of the commanders of Fort Monroe during the Nineteenth Century, about 1890.

Trophy Park on edge of parade ground contained trophies of Yorktown and Saratoga.

Gun No. 40, a 10-inch Rodman, in the Water Battery, about 1890.

The "Maid of the Moat" and the Casemate Club.

Battery formed for inspection just inside main sally port, about 1890.

Fort Monroe from Hygeia Hotel about 1890. Ordnance Yard is at left.

struction party narrowly escaped capture. A second attempt, under Mr. W. H. Heiss, proved successful and opened direct wire communication from Fort Monroe to the War Department, through repeaters at Wilmington, Delaware, though at first messages were transcribed and repeated at Wilmington. This cable was a piece of the first Atlantic cable, none other being available. It was also broken more than once, and Cape Charles being a rather stormy point, the land line on the Eastern Shore was finally run down through Eastville to Cherrystone Inlet, a more sheltered position, and the Fort Monroe cable was relaid over to that point.[4]

About the middle of February, General Wool received information from sources which he considered reliable that the enemy was about to make a combined attack by land and water on the camp and works at Newport News. Believing that he would be able to resist the land forces with the troops at his command, he promptly reported the matter to Washington, urging that one or more war vessels be ordered immediately to Hampton Roads to defend the camp from the apprehended attack. It had been known to the authorities for some time that the Confederates at Norfolk were armoring and equipping the ironclad *Merrimack,* which had fallen into their hands when Norfolk was abandoned. The Washington authorities, therefore, learning of the possible ravages by this rebuilt vessel, responded to the request of General Wool by sending a large frigate to his aid and directing the ironclad *Monitor* to proceed to Hampton Roads.[5]

The *Merrimack* was one of three powerful steam frigates—*Merrimack, Roanoke,* and *Minnesota*—which the United States had built at different navy yards in 1855. They were nearly all alike, of about 3,500 tons burden, carrying from forty to fifty guns. In April 1861, the *Merrimack* was at the Norfolk Navy Yard undergoing repairs. When that place was abandoned she was set on fire and scuttled. Shortly afterwards she was raised by the Confederates, and a committee, ordered to examine her condition, reported that her upper works were so much damaged that she could not be rebuilt without great expense and delay but that the bottom part of the hull, the boilers, and the heavy parts of the engine were almost without injury and could be adapted for a shot-proof steam battery more quickly and for one-third the cost of construction of a new vessel.

The central part of the hull for something more than half its length was cut down to within three or four feet of the waterline to form the gun deck, and the hull was plated with iron to a depth of about six feet below the waterline. Pine beams, a foot square and fifteen feet long, were placed side by side, like rafters, at an inclination of about forty-five degrees. These projected over the sides of the vessel like the eaves of a house, their ends dipping two feet below the water. Upon these beams were placed two layers of oak planks four inches thick—one layer horizontal and the other vertical. These oak layers were first overlaid with ordinary flat bars of iron four and a half inches thick, and then a layer of railroad iron was added. There was a flat space on top, rendered bombproof by plates of wrought iron, from which projected a short smokestack. To this craft, which had a draft of twenty-five feet and a speed of seven and a half knots, was given the name *Virginia*.

The expected attack had been set for February 28, but that date passed without incident. Several days of quiet elapsed, and the danger was believed to be past when the *Merrimack* made its sudden incursion into Hampton Roads. At noon on Saturday, March 8, the *Merrimack* rounded Sewell's Point, standing up towards Newport News, attended by two small steamers, *Raleigh* and *Beaufort*. The *Congress* and *Cumberland* were anchored off Newport News, about a quarter of a mile apart and about the same distance from the shore. The rest of the Federal fleet was lying near Fort Monroe, several miles distant. As soon as the *Merrimack* came within range of the *Congress,* both Federal ships opened fire. Entirely undamaged by the fire of the *Congress,* the *Merrimack* continued straight at the *Cumberland,* opening fire as she approached. Rammed by the *Merrimack* at about three o'clock in the afternoon, the *Cumberland* filled and sank to her tops. The *Merrimack* then again turned to the *Congress,* which had grounded and was helpless. Hot shot were fired into her, and soon she was on fire. Lieutenant Joseph B. Smith, her captain, was killed, the ship full of wounded and on fire, and the colors were hauled down at 4:00 p.m. At 12:30 a.m. the ship blew up, the fire having reached the magazines. The *Merrimack* next turned its attention to the other Federal ships in the area, but returned to Norfolk without causing any more serious damage.

The consternation that followed this assault was intense. At Fort Monroe the alarm gun had sounded when the *Merrimack* appeared and the long roll of drums summoned the garrison. The 10th New York was formed on the parade ground and detailed by companies to man certain points in the fort, but remained under arms on the parade ground until such time as their services were needed. Apparently the guns of the fort did try a few shots, but the range to the naval engagement was far too great. George Cowlam, the telegraph operator at Newport News, sent a running account of the battle to Fort Monroe. Interspersed with his terse messages came occasional remarks such as "There goes a shell through this shanty," and "That one knocked my bunk away." Cowlam managed to come out of the Confederate bombardment with only a few splinters in his clothes.[6]

At Fort Monroe, many feared that the entire fleet in the Roads, and even the fort itself, might prove ineffective against so destructive a vessel. The despair was lifted somewhat when the *Monitor* put in its appearance a little later. The *Monitor* was an ironclad of 900 tons, with a draft of ten feet and with only about one foot of her hull above the waterline. She was protected by five inches of iron armor and five feet of oak. The principal feature was the revolving turret, nine feet high and twenty feet in diameter, with armored sides eight inches in thickness. These sides were constructed of plates of iron one inch thick, three feet wide, and nine feet long, applied in eight layers. Her armament consisted of two 11-inch guns. The *Monitor* had left New York on the afternoon of March 4 and had entered the Virginia Capes in time to hear the firing in Hampton Roads but not in time to arrive before the *Merrimack* returned up the Elizabeth River.

At eight o'clock the next morning the *Merrimack* approached from Norfolk. The two antagonists slowly approached each other and shortly were engaged in their memorable battle. Fighting at such close range that at times their sides touched, neither ship seemed able to injure the other. Hundreds of soldiers watched the maneuvers of the warships from the ramparts at Fort Monroe. General Wool, having seen to the disposition of the forces within the fort, rode out with his staff through Camp Hamilton to a point on the shore nearest the *Minnesota* (which had grounded off Fort Monroe) and there remained during the whole of the combat. For four hours the battle continued, but at last the *Merrimack,* leaking from a hit near the waterline, withdrew from action.[7]

All during the forenoon, the 10th New York stood ready to serve the heavy guns on the ramparts of the fort and in the Water Battery, but no necessity required their action. A view of the conflict was easily had from the ramparts, and the men who manned the barbette guns and those who could be spared from other positions stood during the four hours which the battle lasted watching the combat which marked the inauguration of a new era in warship design. Upon the retirement of the Confederate vessel, the regiment was allowed to disperse.[8]

The guns at Fort Calhoun were the only part of the fortifications actually to take an active part in this battle. When the *Merrimack* steamed out of the Elizabeth River on March 8, the battery at Sewell's Point opened fire on the Federal ships. This quickly brought a reply from Fort Calhoun. The guns at Fort Calhoun apparently fired at both Sewell's Point and the *Merrimack,* but the range to the latter made their efforts ineffective. The garrison at Fort Calhoun at this time consisted of two companies of the 99th New York, commanded by Lieutenant Colonel Gustave B. Helleday.

The appearance of the *Merrimack* in Hampton Roads brought forth the wrath of Secretary of War Edwin M. Stanton in peculiar fashion. On March 18 he informed General Wool, "That in recognition of faith-

ful service by a distinguished and gallant officer, the name of the fort on
the Rip Raps is changed from Fort Calhoun to Fort Wool. . . ."[9] There
were a few who disapproved of this action. Former President James
Buchanan wrote to a friend:[10]

> I am decidedly in favor of prosecuting the war with vigor to a successful
> termination, but I still consider it bad policy unnecessarily to exasperate the
> Southern people. The insult offered to the memory of Mr. Calhoun, by chang-
> ing the name of Fort Calhoun to Fort Wool, will sink deep into the hearts of
> the people of the cotton states—men, women, and children. It was my fortune
> to differ from this great and pure man on many important questions, but his
> character was so elevated that Clay and Webster and others pronounced
> eulogies upon him in the Senate and in the House after his decease. He died
> ten years before the commencement of the troubles, and even before the
> Compromise of 1850. I do not think the administration will derive much honor
> from having attainted his memory. But *de gustibus est disputandum*. Had he
> been living, I do not think we should be involved in our present difficulties.

At 1:00 p.m. on the ninth, General McClellan had telegraphed General Wool to hold his position at all hazard.[11] Before receipt of this
dispatch, however, the *Monitor* had solved the problem which the sudden
appearance of the *Merrimack* had raised, but it could not entirely allay
the anxiety which the mere fact of her existence created. On the twelfth,
General McClellan inquired of the Navy Department: "Can I rely on the
Monitor to keep the *Merrimack* in check, so that I can make Fort
Monroe a base of operations?" Gustavus V. Fox replied: "The *Monitor*
is more than a match for the *Merrimac*, but she might be disabled in the
next encounter. . . . The *Monitor* may, and I think will, destroy the
Merrimac in the next fight; but this is hope, not certainty. . . ." "The
possibility of the *Merrimac* appearing again paralyzes the movements of
this Army, by whatever route is adopted," wrote Brigadier General
John G. Barnard, McClellan's chief engineer, in discussion of the contemplated movement upon Richmond.[12]

The appearance of the *Merrimack* had led to hurried efforts to strengthen
the defenses of Fort Monroe. On March 11, Secretary of War Stanton had
ordered the name of the 15-inch Rodman gun changed from the "Floyd" to
the "Lincoln" gun and suggested that it be mounted on the beach. Work
began immediately to prepare a temporary carriage and gun platform for
the Lincoln Gun next to the 12-inch Union Gun near the lighthouse. The
gun was mounted on March 24 and two test rounds were fired on April 2.
With these two powerful guns mounted, the mouth of Hampton Roads
was effectively closed against the *Merrimack*.[13]

Among the difficulties experienced by General Wool at this time was
one growing out of the magnitude of the operations at Fort Monroe, its
proximity to the front, and the excellent accommodations afforded by

the Hygeia Hotel. A multitude of people crowded the hotel and swarmed over the walls of the fort and along the beaches and roads of the reservation. The congregation of pleasure and curiosity seekers, newspaper correspondents, and other characters that attend upon the movements of an army was a distinct embarrassment to the military authorities. So desirable did the abatement of this nuisance become that on March 14 Secretary Stanton telegraphed General Wool:

"It is represented that a large number of visitors for pleasure, dealers in trade, and other persons not in the public service are now congregating at Fort Monroe, whose presence may embarrass the grave naval and military operations now in progress or in contemplation there. You are authorized, in your discretion, to require the immediate departure of all persons not in the service of the United States, whose presence may incommode operations and to exclude unauthorized persons from stopping or remaining there, until further notice. You will, from and after this date, exercise the most rigid discipline and police within the territory under your command."[14]

Part of the problem was solved later in the year. Since the Hygeia Hotel stood upon the glacis of the fort, it was demolished on December 1, 1862, under the terms of the original agreement and pursuant to orders of the Secretary of War, dated September 1, 1862. A part of the building not connected with the main structure was left standing near the postern gate and was used for a time as a hospital. After December 1 the idlers no longer had a place to stay on the post.

Before the first of April, the whole Army of the Potomac (112,000 men, 14,592 animals, 1,150 wagons, 44 batteries, 74 ambulances, pontoon bridges, telegraph materials, and enormous quantities of stores and equipage) had been transported from Alexandria and Washington to Fort Monroe and Newport News. Brigadier General Samuel P. Heintzelman's division landed at Fort Monroe on March 18 and Brigadier General Fitz John Porter's division on March 23. The garrison at Fort Monroe and its dependencies, which did not (except for a brief time) come under General McClellan's command, had reached an aggregate of 13,900 officers and men. Of the garrison at Fort Monroe, the two batteries of the 4th Artillery and the two companies of the 1st New York Mounted Rifles had been withdrawn, and one of the 99th New York had been added, leaving a total of 1,495 officers and men in the fort. At Camp Hamilton, the 20th Indiana had been moved, but the addition of the 1st Michigan, 58th Pennsylvania, Battery A, 1st Massachusetts Light Artillery, and Battery D, 4th U.S. Artillery, brought the strength of that post to 6,351 officers and men. At Camp Butler, the 5th Maryland, 20th Indiana, and Battery L, 4th U.S. Artillery, had joined to make the strength of the garrison 5,892 officers and men. At Fort Wool, there had been no change in the 181 officers and men of its command.

On April 3 there were in the vicinity of Fort Monroe the 3d Pennsylvania Cavalry, the 2d, 5th, and part of the 1st U.S. Cavalry, a part of the reserve artillery, two divisions each of the III and IV Corps ready to move, one division of the II Corps, and Brigadier General George Sykes' brigade of Regular infantry. Brigadier General Silas Casey's division of the IV Corps was at Newport News, totally unprovided with transportation. Brigadier General Israel B. Richardson's division of the II Corps and Brigadier General Joseph Hooker's division of the III Corps had not yet joined. General McClellan himself arrived on the afternoon of April 2, and the advance of the Army of the Potomac started on the fourth. Fort Monroe had been removed from McClellan's command the day before.[15]

On the morning of April 11 the *Merrimack,* accompanied by the *Jamestown,* the *Yorktown,* two other gunboats, and two tugs, steamed into Hampton Roads. To their surprise, the harbor was empty—the Federal fleet having withdrawn beyond the forts into Chesapeake Bay. The *Monitor* and Fort Monroe each promptly fired an alarm gun. When abreast of Sewell's Point and well out in the channel, the gunboats and tugs stopped while the *Merrimack* continued toward Fort Monroe. At 7:45 a.m. Fort Wool fired two rounds at her, both falling short. While the *Merrimack* held the attention of the Federals, the gunboats *Jamestown* and *Raleigh* slipped across the harbor and captured three transports near Newport News. The *Merrimack* and the Federal ships exchanged fire at long range until late afternoon without inflicting any damage and then the Confederates withdrew to Craney Island.[16]

The last significant engagement on the lower Peninsula took place near Lee's Mill on the Warwick River on April 16. After withdrawing from the Big Bethel area, the Confederates had established a line of fortifications stretching from the Warwick River, in the area now occupied by Fort Eustis, to Yorktown. In an attempt to feel out the Confederate positions, Brigadier General William T. H. Brooks' Vermont brigade began skirmishing with the enemy on the opposite side of the river. In the afternoon, after considerable small arms and artillery fire, four companies of the 3d Vermont pushed across the river. The Confederates countered by rushing up reinforcements and laying down a heavy fire. The Federal forces then broke off the engagement, having lost 35 killed, 121 wounded, and 9 missing. Twenty Confederates were killed, including Colonel Robert M. McKinney of the 15th North Carolina.[17]

The movement upon Norfolk, long contemplated by the War Department and repeatedly urged by General Wool, was now to be attempted. On May 4, Secretary Stanton asked General Wool, by telegraph, the condition of his force. General Wool replied that he was ready to move at any moment, with provisions and ammunition but with a shortage of horses.[18] Upon receipt of this reply President Lincoln, accompanied by Secretaries Salmon P. Chase and Stanton, left Washington for Fort Monroe, where he arrived the following morning and was received with honors. The mission of the President was primarily to visit McClellan's camp before Yorktown; but the movement upon Norfolk was timed to accommodate his presence. A council of war was held at General Wool's quarters with Flag Officer Louis M. Goldsborough. Disturbed by the lack of action, the President ordered the fleet to attack the Sewell's Point battery on May 8. To get a better view of the action, Lincoln journeyed over to Fort Wool and watched the bombardment from its ramparts. The *Merrimack* at the time the bombardment began had been steaming from Norfolk back to her anchorage at Craney Island. She immediately moved to the assistance of the Confederate battery and the Federal squadron withdrew under the guns of Fort Monroe. The *Merrimack* followed almost to the Rip Raps and Fort Wool opened fire —the shot passing over the Confederate ironclad and landing a mile away. The *Merrimack* waited for her challenge to be accepted, but finally Commodore Josiah Tattnall in a tone of deep disgust gave the order, "Mr. Jones, fire a gun to windward, and take the ship back to her buoy."[19]

On May 8, Secretary Stanton telegraphed Assistant Secretary P. H. Watson at the War Department:

"The President is at this moment (2 o'clock P.M.) at Fort Wool witnessing our gunboats—three of then besides the *Monitor* and *Stevens*— shelling the rebel batteries at Sewell's Point. At the same time heavy firing up the James River indicates that Rodgers and Morris are fighting the *Jamestown* and *Yorktown*. . . . The Sawyer gun at Fort Wool has silenced one battery on Sewell's Point. The James rifle mounted on Fort Wool also does good work. . . . The troops will be ready in an hour to move. . . ."[20]

With the departure of the *Merrimack,* the bombardment of Sewell's Point was resumed. This bombardment is important if for no other reason than it marks the first recorded use of a forward artillery observer by the Army. Major Albert J. Myer, who had been conducting a signal school at Fort Monroe, boarded a small steam tug on the day of the bombardment. With him were Lieutenants Evan Thomas, Leonard F. Hepburn, and Theodore S. Dumont, who had been studying the art of signalling. With each shot fired, Myer and his students signalled the battery with flags of the effect and range corrections.[21]

The Confederate fortifications were of no great strength, but the Federal gunnery, despite Myer's spotting, was not of much greater accuracy. The bombardment continued until late on the night of May 9, at which time it was considered that the batteries had been cleared of the enemy. During the afternoon of May 9, the troops embarked from the wharf at Old Point Comfort. The advance force, consisting of the 10th, 20th, and 99th New York, the 16th Massachusetts, a battalion of the 1st New York Mounted Rifles, and three batteries of light artillery, was under the command of Brigadier General Max Weber. Under tow of the steamers, the transports, most of them canal boats, moved out at midnight, followed by the remainder of the force under General Mansfield an hour later. About daylight on the morning of the tenth the troops were disembarked at Ocean View, and the advance immediately pushed forward.

Upon reaching Tanner's Creek, the bridge was discovered to be on fire, necessitating a return to the cross-roads. Here General Wool took direction of the column and pushed forward by the old road to the entrenchments in front of the city, which were reached shortly before 5:00 p.m. Accompanied by Secretary Chase, the General proceeded toward Norfolk and was met at the city limits by the mayor and a select committee of the common council. General Wool took possession, appointed Brigadier General Egbert Viele military governor of the city, and shortly afterward occupied Gosport and Portsmouth.[22]

Meanwhile, back at Fort Monroe, President Lincoln was expressing his displeasure about the way the operation was being conducted. Lincoln summoned Colonel Joseph B. Carr and Brigadier General Joseph K. F. Mansfield from Camp Hamilton to Fort Monroe.

"Colonel Carr, where is your command?"

"At Camp Hamilton, sir," Carr replied uneasily.

"Why are you not on the other side at Norfolk?"

"I am awaiting orders."

Turning to General Mansfield, Lincoln said, "Why are you here? Why not on the other side?"

"I am ordered to the fort by General Wool," replied Mansfield.

Exasperated, President Lincoln dashed his tall hat on the floor, and expressing strongly his disapproval and disappointment, finally said, "Send me some one who can write."

Colonel Legrand B. Cannon of General Wool's staff was called and Lincoln dictated an order to his commander that troops at Camp Hamilton be at once ordered to Norfolk, and that the troops already there be pushed forward rapidly. This order was complied with, but the delays in forwarding and pushing the troops allowed the Confederates time to burn the Navy Yard and shipping at Portsmouth.[23]

The capture of Norfolk caused the destruction of the *Merrimack,* which was blown up by the Confederates early on the morning of May 11. Before evacuating the place, the enemy set fire to all of the buildings at the Navy Yard and partially blew up the dry dock. More than

200 cannon—many of them of large caliber—together with a large amount of ammunition, fell into the hands of the captors. Shortly afterwards, Suffolk, twenty miles further out, was occupied by General Mansfield with some 7,000 troops.[24]

Immediately after the capture of Norfolk, the President tendered his congratulations to General Wool and his troops in the following order:[25]

> The skillful and gallant movements of Maj. Gen. John E. Wool and the forces under his command, which resulted in the surrender of Norfolk and the evacuation of strong batteries erected by the rebels on Sewell's Point and Craney Island and the destruction of the rebel iron-clad steamer *Merrimac,* are regarded by .the President as among the most important successes of the present war. He therefore orders that his thanks, as Commander-in-Chief of the Army and Navy, be communicated by the War Department to Maj. Gen. John E. Wool and the officers and soldiers of his command for their gallantry and good conduct in the brilliant operations mentioned.
>
> By Order of the President, made at the city of Norfolk on the 11th day of May, 1862.
>
> Edwin M. Stanton
> Secretary of War.

The repeated demands from General McClellan, who was about to enter upon the famous seven days before Richmond, at last induced the President to give him sole command of all the forces within his vicinity, which could only be done by transferring General Wool to some other field, an act which Mr. Lincoln had theretofore resisted. On May 31, the Army of the Potomac encountered the enemy on the field of Seven Pines and Fair Oaks, and on the following day the President notified McClellan that General Wool's Department was being merged with his. Major General John A. Dix was assigned to command of the forces at Fort Monroe, Norfolk, Suffolk, and their vicinities, and General Wool took leave of his troops in the following order:[26]

> The Department of Virginia having been assigned to Maj. Gen. George B. McClellan, and Fort Monroe to Maj. Gen. John A. Dix, and the latter having arrived to assume command, Maj. Gen. John E. Wool this day takes leave of the department which he has commanded more than nine months with pleasure and entire satisfaction.
>
> The discipline and good order of the troops render it due to them to say that he has ever, when required, found them prompt, zealous, active, and energetic. In parting with such a command he would do injustice to his feelings were he not to say he does it with extreme regret. He, however, derives consolation from the fact that they are hereafter to be commanded by generals who can appreciate their discipline, good order, and efficiency.

Of all the commanding officers at Fort Monroe during its history of a century and a half, perhaps the most distinguished, and in many respects the ablest, was Major General John Ellis Wool. Born in Newburgh, New York, February 20, 1784, of a family that had contributed five sons to the Revolution, his early education was merely such as the limited advantages of a country school afforded, and this was interrupted at the age of twelve in order that he might contribute to the support of the family. At the outbreak of the second war with Great Britain, he sought and, through the intercession of Govenor Clinton, of New York, received a commission as a captain in the 13th Infantry to date from April 14, 1812. His conduct at Queenstown Heights on October 13, 1812, brought him his promotion to the grade of major, and his gallantry at Plattsburg two years later gained for him the brevet of lieutenant colonel.

Under the Act of April 24, 1816, reorganizing the staff, Wool was appointed Inspector General, with the rank of colonel, a position he retained until he was appointed brigadier general on June 25, 1841. In 1832 he made a professional tour of Europe to examine the various military systems then prevailing abroad. He was present with Louis Phillipe, then on the French throne, at a grand review of 70,000 men; and he was present with the King of Belgium at a more imposing review of 100,000 men. He also witnessed the famous siege of Antwerp. Returning home, he conducted, in 1836, with delicacy and firmness, negotiations for the transfer of the Cherokees to their new home in Arkansas. During the war with Mexico his services with Major General Zachary Taylor at Buena Vista brought him the brevet of major general "for gallant and distinguished conduct." He received the thanks of Congress in 1854 for his services during the Mexican War and was assigned to the command of the Eastern Military Department, and later the Department of the East. He was transferred from Fort Monroe to Fort McHenry and placed on the retired list August 1, 1863. General Wool died at his home in Troy, New York, November 10, 1869, at the age of eighty-five years, having passed more than fifty years in active service in the Army.

At the time of General Wool's departure from Fort Monroe, that station was safely beyond any threat of attack by the Confederates. On the south bank of the James, the Union forces were in comparatively undisturbed possession of all the country to Suffolk, while the Army of the Potomac covered the Peninsula. Fort Monroe thereafter remained a base of operations. Numerous expeditions continued to be outfitted at Fort Monroe or rendezvoused in Hampton Roads before departing upon the last leg of their respective journeys. A division of General Butler's expedition to New Orleans sailed from here in December 1861. A number of smaller expeditions against points on the James and Potomac Rivers and in the vicinity of Chesapeake Bay were also organized at Fort Monroe.

Fort Monroe was also the headquarters of the territorial command which embraced southeastern Virginia. The limits of the command changed frequently; and with each change it was given a new name. With the departure of General Wool, General McClellan assumed command of the department, and the troops under General Dix were given the status of a separate corps on June 15. The forces under General Dix were designated the VII Corps on July 22, with headquarters at Fort Monroe.[27]

General Dix had served at Fort Monroe in the 1820's as an artillery captain. Resigning from the Army, he launched a brilliant political career and served as Secretary of the Treasury in the last days of President Buchanan's administration. While in this position, Dix in January 1861 had sent a telegram to a harried revenue official in New Orleans saying, "If anyone attempts to haul down the American flag, shoot him on the spot." President Lincoln commissioned Dix a major general of volunteers in June 1861.

Upon arrival at Fort Monroe in June 1862, one of General Dix's first acts was to relax the annoying restrictions which then existed upon the trade with Norfolk. The Treasury Department, on August 28, prescribed "Regulations concerning commercial intercourse with insurrectionary States and sections." The Secretaries of War and Navy, by separate orders, called on the officers of the Army and the Navy to respect and carry out these regulations. The Secretary of the Navy, however, instructed Rear Admiral Samuel P. Lee, in command of the naval forces in Hampton Roads, not to allow any traffic whatever. The Secretaries of War and the Treasury had in the meantime jointly granted permits for traffic with Norfolk and Portsmouth. Admiral Lee, acting under his instructions, seized and stopped all vessels from those places with return cargoes, even though they might have permits from another department of the Government. General Dix protested that the inhabitants of Norfolk and Portsmouth, though in the hands of the Federal authorities, were treated as if their cities were under strict blockade. He insisted that the laws of blockade had no application to them as they were under military occupation. He finally received permission for provisions to be sent to Norfolk and Portsmouth by any persons on their exhibiting a manifest and getting a permit from the military authority of the port. The sole condition was that the goods should be sold at their market price in Baltimore. This was a great relief to the local inhabitants, who had been suffering for the necessaries of life.[28]

From this time on, during the war, the record of Fort Monroe is largely one of troops moving about in the vicinity of or supplies going to troops under the command of the Department commander. The troops in the Department were organized in two corps—the IV and VII—garrisoning Suffolk, Portsmouth, Norfolk, Sewell's Point, Gloucester Point, Williamsburg, Yorktown, Camp Hamilton, Fort Wool, and Fort Monroe, with the bulk of the forces at Suffolk under Major General John J. Peck.

In the quiet that followed Major General Ambrose Burnside's abortive "Mud March" after the Battle of Fredericksburg, the Confederates began to worry that part of the idle Army of the Potomac might be used for a raid somewhere along the coast. These fears appeared to be justified in February 1863 when the IX Corps, with which Burnside had occupied the coast of North Carolina the year before, suddenly boarded transports at Aquia Creek in northern Virginia and arrived at Newport News. Major General Henry W. Halleck, the Commanding General of the Army, had ordered the corps to report to Dix. The veteran IX Corps closed at Newport News between February 6 and 21. The Confederates reacted swiftly. At the urging of the War Department, General Robert E. Lee released two divisions from his army and ordered them to Richmond on February 18. To command the divisions from the Army of Northern Virginia and the scattered units in southside Virginia and North Carolina, Lieutenant General James Longstreet was placed in command of the Department of Virginia and North Carolina on February 26.

The arrival of the IX Corps in Hampton Roads had caused Confederate reinforcements to be brought to the area. In turn, the arrival of Longstreet's corps caused the Federals to reinforce their exposed outpost in Suffolk. The IX Corps had hardly got comfortable when it was loaded back onto the transports and shipped to Baltimore on its way west. But the arrival of Longstreet caused Brigadier General George W. Getty's division of the IX Corps to be detached to reinforce Peck's garrison at Suffolk.

Longstreet apparently realized that there was little hope of driving the Federals out of the area or of attacking Norfolk, but he hoped that he could tie the Federal forces down in defending their garrison towns, thus giving him a chance to gather valuable supplies for the Confederates. The most important of these Federal garrisons was Suffolk. Whether Longstreet ever had any hopes of actually capturing that town is not clear, but on April 11 he pushed his corps across the Blackwater River and began the siege of Suffolk.

General Peck had constructed extensive fortifications around the town. The Confederates closed in from three sides, but never attempted a major attack. Peck's line of communications were kept open by the railroad to Norfolk and by Navy gunboats on the Nansemond River. Skirmishing and a few sharp actions took place in the following weeks, but on April 29 Longstreet received word that the Army of the Potomac was finally moving. On the night of May 3 the Confederates pulled back to their original line on the Blackwater and Longstreet's corps rejoined Lee.[29]

The garrisons of the several stations kept changing from time to time, and there was a general tendency to reinforce the department. On May

31, 1863, there were 43,000 troops in the department, distributed as follows:[30]

Department Headquarters, Major General John A. Dix	17
Fort Monroe, Colonel S. M. Alford	663
Camp Hamilton, Major J. A. Darling	623
Norfolk, Brigadier General E. L. Viele	2,692
Suffolk, Major General John J. Peck	26,821
West Point, Brigadier General G. H. Gordon	6,277
Yorktown, Major General E. D. Keyes	6,555
Total	43,648

The garrison at Fort Monroe at that time consisted of the 3d New York, and that at Camp Hamilton of the 1st Battalion, 3d Pennsylvania Cavalry, and a troop of Pennsylvania cavalry. Fort Wool, as a dependency of Fort Monroe, was garrisoned by a detachment.

General Dix was ordered to New York on July 18, 1863, to succeed General Wool in command of the Department of the East. He was succeeded at Fort Monroe by Major General John G. Foster and the Departments of Virginia and North Carolina were consolidated into the Department of Virginia and North Carolina. Within the department, Fort Monroe was embraced in the District of Eastern Virginia, which included Fort Monroe, Yorktown, Williamsburg, Norfolk, Portsmouth, and the Eastern Shore, with headquarters at Norfolk. General Foster was relieved by General Butler in November.[31] At the time of Butler's arrival, the District of Virginia embraced the area controlled by garrisons at Gloucester Point, Yorktown, Portsmouth, Newport News, and Fort Monroe. There were nearly 21,000 troops in the district, of whom 1,300 were at Fort Monroe. The District of North Carolina, embracing Beaufort, New Bern, Plymouth, and Washington, had been reduced to slightly less than 9,000 troops. In December, the District of St. Mary's was added, with some 2,500 troops.[32] The garrison of Fort Monroe consisted of nine companies of the 3d Pennsylvania Heavy Artillery, to which were added by the end of December the 2d Battalion, U.S. Veterans' Reserve Corps, the 1st U.S. Colored Cavalry, some Army gunboats, and a Signal Corps detachment. Also, the post was for many months a point of exchange for prisoners of war, and General Butler was commissioner for the exchange of prisoners during the winter of 1863–1864.

During the two long years which followed the arrival of the Army of the Potomac on the Virginia Peninsula, that army fought many battles with the Army of Northern Virginia without material advantage to either. The plans for the campaign of 1864 contemplated the simultaneous movement of all available forces against the Confederate troops in the vicinity of Richmond. For close cooperation with the Army of the Potomac in its operations against Richmond, the Army of the James was organized from the troops in the Department of Virginia and North Carolina, reinforced by troops from North Carolina and points further south. This army was organized in two corps—the XVIII under Major General W. F. Smith and the X under Major General Q. A. Gilmore, the whole being commanded by General Butler. Petersburg was the immediate objective of the Army of the James.

Early in April, General U. S. Grant spent three days with General Butler at Fort Monroe to discuss with him the part the Army of the James was to take in the forthcoming campaign. Upon his departure Grant left with Butler a letter of instructions covering the conduct of his operations, and later in the month he sent Lieutenant Colonel Frederick T. Dent, his aide, to Fort Monroe with a second letter confirming the instructions contained in the first.[33]

On April 13, the troops of the X Corps left South Carolina for Fort Monroe, and by May 1 the whole force, amounting to about 36,000 men, was assembled in Virginia. With a view to keeping the plans for their employment in doubt, both corps were rendezvoused on the York River —the X Corps at Gloucester Point and the XVIII Corps in and around Yorktown.

On May 4 the campaign was opened by the Army of the Potomac on the Rapidan River north of Richmond. That same night the X and XVIII Corps were embarked on transports in the York River and moved to Hampton Roads, making a line of vesels stretching from Fort Monroe for some ten miles up the James River. At the head of this fleet lay the forces of Admiral Lee, consisting of five ironclad ships and many gunboats to serve as a convoy. At five o'clock on the morning of the fifth, General Butler started the movement by leading off with his steamer, the *Greyhound*; and by 6:00 a.m. the whole force was in motion. With the departure of Department Headquarters and of most of the troops in the vicinity, the war practically left Fort Monroe, for little more of a warlike nature happened there or nearby.

Despite the decrease in active operations, work continued throughout the war to modernize and strengthen Fort Monroe. On June 30, 1864, Major C. Seaforth Stewart, the engineer officer in charge of the works, reported fifty-two casemate guns and twenty-four 24-pounder flank howitzers in positions. There was also ninety-five guns and thirteen mortars mounted in barbettes. In addition to these, three platforms for 15-inch guns and twelve platforms which had been reinforced were ready and a number were in the process of reinforcement. At Fort Wool, there were no longer any guns mounted, but fifty-two casemates in the first tier were ready for their armament. Work continued on the fort, but appearance of cracks in some of the arches was a cause of concern.[34]

By June 30, 1864, the troops in the Department of Virginia and North

Carolina had been increased to about 90,000 men, of whom the greater part were in the X and XVIII Corps and Kautz's Cavalry Division with the army in the field. Within the District of Eastern Virginia were less than 7,000 troops remaining under Brigadier General George F. Shepley to garrison:[35]

Portsmouth (Brigadier General Israel Vogdes)
Norfolk (Captain Frederick Stewart)
Fort Monroe (Colonel Joseph Roberts)
  3d Pennsylvania Heavy Artillery (less detachments)
  2d Battalion, U.S. Veteran's Reserve Corps
Eastern Shore (Captain James A. Skelley)
Yorktown (Major Thomas J. Strong)

Seven months later the strength of the district had been reduced to around 5,000 men. There was at that time no garrison at Yorktown, but troops had been moved to Fort Magruder and to Newport News. Throughout the spring of 1865 the number of troops in the district remained at this figure until demobilization began.[36]

General Butler's attempt to capture Petersburg had ended with his army bottled up in Bermuda Hundred. The failure of his expedition against Fort Fisher near Wilmington, North Carolina, in December 1864, which had been outfitted at Fort Monroe, did not improve his standing in General Grant's eyes. He was therefore relieved from command of the Department of Virginia and North Carolina on January 7, 1865, and Major General E. O. C. Ord was assigned to the department and assumed command the following day.[37] Major General Alfred H. Terry's expedition which finally captured Fort Fisher sailed from Fort Monroe in January, as did Major General Godfrey Weitzel's expedition to Texas somewhat later. On February 6, the department again became the Department of Virginia, and General Terry succeeded to command on June 14, at which time headquarters were in Richmond.[38]

One final important act of the Civil War took place within sight of the walls of Fort Monroe. Francis P. Blair, a political advisor of President Lincoln, had received permission in December 1864 to visit President Davis in Richmond. As a result of this meeting, Davis on January 12 indicated his willingness to send representatives to a conference with Union authorities. President Davis appointed Vice President Alexander H. Stephens, Judge John A. Campbell, and Senator Robert M. T. Hunter as the Confederate commissioners. A meeting at army headquarters at City Point with Major Thomas T. Eckert, Lincoln's personal representative, almost brought about a collapse of negotiations. The Confederates managed to convince General Grant and Secretary Stanton that they were really trying to restore peace. Lincoln and Secretary of State William Seward therefore agreed to meet with the commissioners on February 3 in the cabin of the *River Queen* under the guns of Fort Monroe. The peace conference was a total failure. The Confederates wanted an armistice followed by the independence of the Confederacy. Lincoln remained firm that there would be no end to the fighting until the Confederates surrendered and the South rejoined the Union. With the failure of the conference the war dragged on to its tragic conclusion in the spring.[39]

Footnotes Chapter VI

[1] Maj. Gen. Geo. B. McClellan to Hon. Simon Cameron, Sept. 6, 1861, *OR*, Series I, Vol. V, pp. 586–587.

[2] Return of the Department of Virginia, Jan. 1862, and organization of the Department of Virginia, Jan. 31, 1862, *OR*, Series I, Vol. IX, p. 15.

[3] Return of the Department of the Peninusla, Jan. 1862, *ibid.*, p. 36.

[4] O'Brien, *op. cit.*, p. 72.

[5] Maj. Gen. Geo. B. McClellan to Maj. Gen. John E. Wool, Feb. 21, 1862; Edwin M. Stanton to Maj. Gen. John E. Wool, Feb. 22, 1862; *OR*, Series I, Vol. IX, pp. 15–16.

[6] Cowtan, *op. cit.*, pp. 66–69; O'Brien, *op. cit.*, pp. 63–64.

[7] Reports of the battle are in *OR*, Series I, Vol. IX, pp. 1–14, and *Official Records of the Union and Confederate Navies in the War of the Rebellion* (Washington: Government Printing office, 1894–1922), 26 vols., (hereafter cited as *NOR*), Series I, Vol. 7, pp. 3–87. H. Edgren, "Description of the Naval Battle of Hampton Roads," in Correll, *History of the Naval Brigade*.

[8] Cowtan, *op. cit.*, pp. 69–71. As an anticlimax to the battle, the gunboat *Whitehall*, which lay near one of the docks of Fort Monroe, caught fire during the night and was destroyed, her guns and ammunition exploding and scattering pieces of shell in all directions. One large piece fell within the fort.

[9] Edwin M. Stanton to Maj. Gen. John E. Wool, Mar. 18, 1862, *OR*, Series I, Vol. XI, Part III, p. 13.

[10] Beard, "The Castle of Rip Raps," p. 46.

[11] Maj. Gen. Geo. B. McClellan to Maj. Gen. John E. Wool, *OR*, Series I, Vol. IX, p. 23.

[12] Maj. Gen. Geo. B. McClellan to Capt. G. V. Fox, Mar. 12, 1862; G. V. Fox to Maj. Gen. George B. McClellan, Mar. 13, 1862; J. G. Barnard to G. V. Fox, Mar. 12, 1862; *NOR*, Series I, Vol. 7, pp. 99–100.

[13] Edwin M. Stanton to Gen. John E. Wool, Mar. 11, 1862; *OR*, Series I, Vol. IX, p. 26. 1st Lt. F. K. Baylor to Brig. Gen. J. W. Ripley, March 13, March 17, March 25, and April 2, 1862, Letters Sent by the Fort Monroe Arsenal, Records of the Office of the Chief of Ordnance, RG 156, NA. R. W. Daly, ed., *Aboard The USS Monitor: 1862* (Annapolis: United States Naval Institute, 1964), p. 84.

[14] Edwin M. Stanton to Maj. Gen. Wool, March 14, 1862, *OR*, Series I, Vol. IX, p. 31.

[15] Return of the Department of Virginia for March 1862, *OR*, Series I, Vol. XI, Part III, p. 54; Report of Maj. Gen. George B. McClellan, August 4, 1863, *OR*, Series I, Vol. XI, Part I, p. 7.

[16] Reports of the action are in *NOR*, Series I, Vol. 7, pp. 219–225.

[17] Reports of the engagement are in *OR*, Series I, Vol. XI, Part I, pp. 363–380, 406–408, 415–422. The engagement was variously called Lee's Mill, Dam No. 1, and Burnt Chimneys. For a detailed account of the Mulberry Island end of the Confederate line, see Emma-Jo L. Davis, "Mulberry Island and the Civil War, April 1861–May 1862" (Fort Eustis: Fort Eustis Historical and Archaeological Association, March 1967) in the U.S. Army Transportation Museum, Fort Eustis.

[18] Edwin M. Stanton to Maj. Gen. Wool, May 4, 1862; Maj. Gen. John E. Wool to Hon. E. M. Stanton, May 5, 1862; *OR*, Series I, Vol. XI, Part III, p. 138.

[19] Benjamin P. Thomas, *Abraham Lincoln* (New York: Alfred A, Knopf, 1952), p. 319. Reports of the action are in *NOR*, Series I, Vol. 7, pp. 328–338. *Battles and Leaders*, Vol. II, p. 151.

[20] Edwin M. Stanton to P. H. Watson, May 8, 1862, *OR*, Series I, Vol. XI, Part III, p. 153.

[21] Prentice G. Morgan, "The Forward Observer," *Military Affairs*, XXIII (Winter 1959–60), pp. 209–212.

[22] Report of Maj. Gen. John E. Wool, May 12, 1862; *OR*, Series I, Vol. XI, Part I, pp. 634–635.

[23] *Battles and Leaders*, Vol. II, p. 152.

[24] Naval Historical Foundation, *"The Virginia No Longer Exists"* (Washington: Naval Historical Foundation, n.d.).

[25] Inclosure to P. H. Watson to Maj. Gen. John E. Wool, May 16, 1862, *OR*, Series I, Vol. XI, Part I, p. 635.

[26] A. Lincoln to Maj. Gen. McClellan, June 1, 1862; General Orders No. 53, Department of Virginia, June 2, 1862; *ibid.*, pp. 205, 211.

[27] General Orders No. 84, War Department, July 22, 1862, *OR*, Series I, Vol. XI, Part III, p. 333.

[28] Dix, *op. cit.*, Vol. II, pp. 48–50.

[29] Richard P. Weinert, "Longstreet's Suffolk Campaign," *Civil War Times Illustrated*, VII (January 1969), pp. 31–39.

[30] Tri-monthly Return of the Department of Virginia (Seventh Army Corps), for May 31, 1863, *OR*, Series I, Vol. XVIII, p. 733.

[31] Dix, *op. cit.*, p. 76; General Orders No. 1, Fort Monroe, July 18, 1863, *OR*, Series I, Vol. XXVII, Part III, p. 723; General Orders No. 29, Department of Virginia and North Carolina, Nov. 11, 1863, Series I, Vol. XXIX, Part II, p. 447.

[32] General Orders No. 58, XVIII Corps, Dec. 22, 1863, *OR*, Series I, Vol. XXIX, Part II, p. 576.

[33] *New York Herald*, April 3, 1864, p. 1, and April 5, 1864, p. 5.

[34] Annual Report of the Progress Made in the Construction and Repairs of Fort Monroe, Old Point Comfort, Va. for the year ending June 30th, 1864; Annual Report of the Progress made in the Construction of Fort Wool, Hampton Roads, Va. for the year ending June 30th, 1864; RG 77, NA. Stewart had graduated first in the West Point class of 1846. He was brevetted lieutenant colonel in 1865 and retired as a colonel in 1886. *Heitman*, p. 924.

[35] Abstract of Return of the Department of Virginia and North Carolina for June 1864, and Organization of troops in the Department of Virginia and North Carolina, June 30, 1864, *OR*, Series I, Vol. XL, Part II, pp. 552–556.

[36] Abstract of Return of the Department of Virginia for January 1865, and Organization of the Troops in the Department of Virginia, January 31, 1865, *OR*, Series I, Vol. XLVI, Part II, pp. 333, 339–340.

[37] General Orders No. 1, Adjutant General's Office, Jan. 7, 1865; Special Orders No. 5, Armies of the United States; *OR*, Series I, Vol. XLVI, Part II, pp. 60, 61.

[38] General Orders No. 14, War Department, Feb. 6, 1865, *ibid.*, p. 421; Special Orders No. 72, Department of Virginia, June 14, 1865, *OR*, Series I, Vol. XLVI, Part III, p. 1278.

[39] Thomas, *op. cit.*, pp. 501–522; "Hampton Road's Conference," by Alexander H. Stephens in Lucian Lamar Knight, *Alexander H. Stephens, The Sage of Liberty Hall*, (1930), pp. 58–78; Justin G. Turner, "Hampton Roads Conference," *Civil War Times*, Vol. III, No. 9, (January 1962), pp. 12–16.

Chapter VII

Jefferson Davis at Fort Monroe

WITH THE COLLAPSE of the Southern cause, President Jefferson Davis of the Confederacy fled southward. He was captured near Irwinville, Georgia, on May 10, 1865, taken to Macon, and then sent to Savannah. From Savannah, the prisoner was taken by boat to Hilton Head, South Carolina, where he was placed on board the steamer *William P. Clyde* and convoyed by the sloop-of-war *Tuscarora* to Hampton Roads. Much of Davis's official family had left him, but enough had been captured to make an impressive party on the *Clyde*. Among the prisoners were Davis and his family; Clement C. Clay, former Confederate senator and commissioner to Canada, and his wife; Vice President Alexander H. Stephens; Postmaster General John H. Reagan; Lieutenant General Joseph Wheeler and his staff; Colonels William Preston Johnston and Francis R. Lubbock, aides to Davis; Burton N. Harrison, secretary to the President; and a number of subaltern officers.

The *Clyde* dropped anchor in Hampton Roads on May 19, and Lieutenant Colonel Benjamin D. Pritchard, 4th Michigan Cavalry, who had effected the capture of Davis, reported at once by wire to Washington. The captives were closely guarded on board the steamer and were permitted to hold no communication with the shore.[1] Nevertheless, the news spread rapidly and excitement grew intense as it was learned that the ship carried such a group of notable prisoners. Moreover, preparations under way within the fort indicated that some of the prisoners were to be placed in confinement at Fort Monroe. The arrival of Major General Henry W. Halleck from Richmond on May 20 and of Charles

A. Dana, Assistant Secretary of War, from Washington, to superintend operations only served to intensify the interest of the residents at Old Point Comfort.[2]

After several days spent on board the ship under the closest surveillance, the group of prisoners was broken up. Early on the morning of May 21, General Wheeler and his staff and Colonels Lubbock and Johnston were sent on the gunboat *Maumee* to Fort Delaware for safekeeping. A few hours later Stephens and Reagan boarded the *Tuscarora* to be carried to Fort Warren for confinement. The next day Harrison started on his way to Washington, where he was placed under guard in the Old Capitol Prison. Except for Davis and Clay, who remained on board the *Clyde,* the rest of the male prisoners were carried to Fort McHenry on the *Pawtuxent.* The women and children were sent south on the *Clyde* after Davis and Clay had been removed.

The Military District of Fort Monroe, to include the Peninsula as far west as Henrico and Hanover counties, exclusive, and also Mathews, Gloucester, Accomac, and Northumberland, was created on May 21, with Major General Nelson A. Miles commanding.[3] With demobilization completed, Old Point Comfort became the headquarters of the 5th Artillery, a status which it retained until November 13, 1867, when the Artillery School was again established.

On May 22, by special steamer from Baltimore, General Miles arrived to assume command of the fort and to become responsible for the security of Jefferson Davis and of Clement C. Clay. Almost immediately the debarkation of the two prisoners began. From the Engineer Wharf to the Water Battery and through the Water Battery postern into the fort, a line of sentinels marked the road over which the prisoners were to be taken to their places of confinement.

All being ready, General Miles, accompanied by a guard, proceeded by tug at precisely 1:00 p.m. to the *Clyde* to receive Davis. The procession formed at the Engineer Wharf with a detachment of the 4th Michigan Cavalry in the lead. Immediately behind came General Miles with Davis, arm in arm. Next in the column were a half dozen soldiers, followed by Clay and Colonel Pritchard, who was in charge of the guard. General Miles's detachment of enlisted men brought up the rear. Both Davis and Clay were dressed in plain suits of Confederate gray, with drab slouch hats, and Davis also wore a thin, dark overcoat. During the march to his cell, Davis bore himself erect, with composed features and firm step.

Davis was escorted into Casemate No. 2, on the first front, near the postern gate, and Clay was assigned to Casemate No. 4. Guards occupied Casemates Nos. 1, 3, and 5, on either side of and between the two prisoners. For several days blacksmiths, carpenters, and masons had been busily engaged in fitting up these casemates for use as cell and guard rooms. Each of the rooms intended for the prisoners was partitioned into two cells, that next to the embrasures to be occupied by the prisoners. The embrasures had been fitted with heavy iron bars and the archways between the casemates had been closed. The prisoners entered; and the clanging of the heavy doors behind them put a period to the final end of the rebellion.[4]

Of the next few months much of abuse and recrimination has been written. The treatment accorded Davis has been characterized as brutal and inhuman. Mrs. Davis was particularly bitter against General Miles, holding him responsible for all of her husband's suffering and ill health and overlooking the fact that practically all the restrictions imposed upon Davis were prescribed by higher authority. The conduct of General Miles in small things was annoying to the Confederate ex-President, but it should be noted that the severities of confinement were relaxed one by one upon General Miles's recommendation when they were specifically brought to his attention as adversely affecting Davis's health. Moreover, he, a young man of twenty-five, felt the responsibilities of his position keenly, and what he did was, he believed, required of him under his instructions.

Of all the factors affecting the conditions under which Davis was held, the most important is frequently overlooked. The late President of the Confederacy was not a political prisoner; he was an alleged criminal, charged with the basest of crimes, and he was a man of tremendous standing with his own people, who might attempt to rescue him. It was at that time generally believed throughout the North that Davis was implicated in the murder of President Lincoln. He was so charged in a proclamation by President Andrew Johnson, and the sum of $100,000 had been offered and had been paid for his capture under that charge. It is probable that President Johnson himself did not really believe the charge, for he had reason to know that Davis would have preferred to deal with Lincoln rather than with him, but the fact remains that Davis was initially charged with murder, and not with treason.

When the noted prisoner had been escorted into his inner cell by General Miles and the doors had been closed upon him, it is said that he first looked out through the embrasure, from which little could be seen. He then turned to one of the sentinels and inquired, "Which way does this embrasure face?" Receiving no reply, he repeated the question, thinking that the man had not heard him, but when his second query failed to elicit a response he asked the same question of the second sentinel. This man also remained silent, and Davis, throwing up his hands and breaking into a bitter laugh, remarked: "Well, I wish my men could have been taught your discipline."[5]

The arrangements for the two prisoners were the same. Each occupied the inner cell of his casemate, which was provided with an iron hospital cot, a chair, a table, and a movable stool closet. Upon the table was a Bible—the only reading matter. Before the doors leading to the outer room stood two sentinels. This door at the time was but a heavy wooden door fastened by iron bars from the outside, although it was contemplated that they should be grated as soon as possible. In the outer room two sentinels were stationed, and in this room was also an officer charged with the duty of seeing the prisoners every fifteen minutes. The outer door was locked, and without stood two more sentinels. Across the walk a line of sentinels paced before the casemates; a second line was stationed along the parapet overhead; and a third line was placed across the moat, on the glacis of the fort, opposite the casemates occupied by the prisoners. Admission to the interior of the fort was by pass only.[6]

The prisoners entered their cells on the afternoon of May 22. On the following morning Davis was shackled. More than any other one thing, this fact has rankled in the minds of his adherents and was the cause of most of the animus against General Miles. Undoubtedly, the action was unnecessary, but Dana had originally suggested that Davis be ironed. General Halleck had objected that it was scarcely necessary, whereupon Dana wrote instructions for General Miles in the name of the Secretary of War: "Brevet-Major-General Miles is hereby authorized and directed to place manacles and fetters upon the hands and feet of Jefferson Davis and Clement C. Clay, whenever he may deem it advisable in order to render their imprisonment more secure." Stanton, when notified, appears to have raised no objection, nor did Miles's report of May 24 to Dana announcing the shackling receive immediate official disapproval. "Yesterday I directed that irons be put on Davis's ankles, which he violently resisted, but became more quiet afterwards." In general, however, the Northern people failed to approve of the action.[7]

Davis felt himself terribly humiliated by the ironing, and he vigorously resisted while the chains were placed upon him. It fell to the lot of Captain Jerome E. Titlow, of the 3d Pennsylvania Heavy Artillery, as Officer of the Day, to place the anklets upon his notable prisoner. Entering the cell, followed by two blacksmiths, one of whom carried the heavy shackles, he found Davis resting upon his cot, weary after a sleepless night, with his food lying untouched on its tin plate near the bedside. Approaching the prisoner, he expressed his personal reluctance to perform the unpleasant duty to which he had been detailed. Davis, seeing the blacksmiths, understood and sprang to his feet to remonstrate. Upon his demand to see the commanding officer, Captain Titlow insisted that his orders were peremptory and would admit of no delay. It was evident that Davis would resist and Captain Titlow endeavored to dissuade him, the Officer of the Guard adding his own efforts to those of the Officer of the Day.

Jefferson Davis became dramatic. "Let your men shoot me at once," he cried; but Captain Titlow instructed the blacksmiths to do their duty. As the first stooped to put on the fetter, Davis, with a sudden access of energy, threw him violently off. Captain Titlow interposed and directed the Officer of the Guard to bring in four men. There was a short, violent struggle, but the end was inevitable. Flung prone upon his bed, with the four men holding him, the prisoner was securely shackled with fetters of heavy iron, some five-eighths of an inch in thickness and connected by a chain of similar weight. His object being effected, the Officer of the Day retired with his men, and the ex-President of a nation covered himself on his cot, bowed down by shame.[8]

At the time of his imprisonment, Davis was not in good health, and he naturally found his close confinement irksome. He was allowed no reading matter other than his Bible, and tobacco was not permitted. His food was furnished from the enlisted men's mess and was altogether too coarse to be suited to his condition. A lamp burned all night in his cell, throwing its beams into his already weakened eyes. Some of the mortar in the freshly bricked-up archways of the cell was still soft; and the odor of freshly applied whitewash was disagreeable to his sensitive nostrils. All these were bad enough, but to them was added broken sleep caused by the tramping of sentinels and clanging of doors and the loud voices attendant upon the change of reliefs throughout the night. With no recreation, with bodily discomfort, and with mental annoyance, it is not surprising that the prisoner's health failed.

Davis complained a great deal about the unhealthfulness of the casemate—a charge which was repeated later by Mrs. Davis. The attending physician reported that the ventilation was thorough, that the room was scrubbed clean, and that the whitewash acted as a disinfectant. The casemates had been occupied as quarters for fifty years without apparent evil effect, and they were used as quarters for officers and enlisted men well into the next century. Davis's ill health must therefore be charged in large part to a lack of exercise and to his mental condition, rather than to poisons within the walls or arising from the moat.

Little by little the more petty restrictions were removed. The surgeon, Brevet Lieutenant Colonel John J. Craven, was first called on the morning of May 24.[9] Accompanied by the Officer of the Day, he entered the cell and found the prisoner miserable, very much emaciated, and extremely nervous. Upon leaving Davis, he immediately submitted a recommendation that his patient be allowed tobacco and a prayer book. Miles telegraphed to Halleck for instructions and the request was granted during the day.[10] That evening Dr. Craven himself supplied Davis with tobacco and pipe. Two days later he was permitted to place the prisoner upon a more suitable diet and thereafter he furnished his patient from his own quarters with whatever he considered suitable.[11]

On Sunday, May 28, five days after they had been applied, the shackles were removed. This action seems to have been induced by a telegram from Secretary Stanton. Popular reports and public indignation caused the Secretary of War to telegraph on May 28: "Please report whether irons have or have not been placed on Jefferson Davis. If they have been, when it was done, and for what reason, and remove them." In reply, Miles wired: "I have the honor to state in reply to your despatch that when Jeff. Davis was first confined in the casemate, the inner doors were light wooden ones without locks. I directed anklets to be put upon his ankles, which would not interfere with his walking, but would prevent his running, should he endeavor to escape. In the meantime I have changed the wooden doors for grated ones with locks, and the anklets have been removed. Every care is taken to avoid any pretense for complaint, as well as to prevent the possibility of escape."[12]

Close confinement must have been torture to a mind as active as that of Davis. In his bare cell he had nothing with which to occupy himself except his Bible and his prayer book, and he found it difficult to keep his brain keyed up to the plane necessary for full appreciation of these works. In addition, his eyesight did not permit long-continued reading of fine print. Even his clothes were removed from his possession, General Miles taking charge and allowing a change of linen but once a week. His greatest enjoyment came from his talks with Dr. Craven and sometimes with the officer of the day, who always accompanied the doctor, but these conversations were limited in duration and in number—if not in scope. Chaplain Chevers secured admission once, but on June 8 General Miles was peremptorily ordered not again to admit the chaplain without first securing special permission.[13]

Dr. Craven did what he could for the prisoner but it was not enough to preserve health. When it became known that Davis was in a serious condition, General Miles required a daily written report from the doctor and he himself made periodic reports to Washington. On June 17, learning that the paceing of the two sentinels in his room at night disturbed Davis and prevented him from sleeping, General Miles ordered that the men should stand at ease during their two hours of guard, both day and night, instead of walking their post.

For a time in June it seemed that Davis was improving in health. On June 18, Dr. Craven noted that the prisoner appeared to be much stronger than he had been on his arrival, but he did not discontinue his efforts to secure amelioration of the conditions of confinement. On July 24, at his representation that the presence of the two men in the inner room counteracted every effort to quiet the nerves of the patient, the guards were ordered removed from the cell. On the same day, General Miles himself entered the cell and announced that thereafter Davis was to be permitted to walk for one hour each day upon the ramparts and to have such miscellaneous reading matter—books, papers, and magazines—as might be approved after perusal at headquarters. That afternoon Davis took his first walk—a short one, because of his weakened condition— accompanied by General Miles, the officer of the day, and four armed guards. Thereafter, he received books and newspapers freely, and weather and health permitting, went out every day for an hour's exercise. In the letter to General Miles authorizing these relaxations, it was suggested that the general visit Davis daily, it was directed that daily reports on the prisoner's health be submitted, and it was repeated that General Miles was to continue the utmost vigilance.[14]

Despite the efforts of his physician, Davis failed rapidly during July. He became alarmed about his failing eyesight; his nervous debility became extreme; and he grew more and more despondent. His appetite had failed and his weakness was becoming alarming to the doctor. Indications of erysipelas appeared on August 14 and two days later a carbuncle appeared upon his thigh. Dr. Craven felt that only a change of quarters would be sufficient to revive the prisoner's interest and to restore his health, and he so recommended, but without immediate result.

During this time one other slight concession was made. No knife or fork had been allowed at first and it had been necessary to cut up Davis's food before it was sent to him and to furnish a spoon with which it could be eaten. The knife and fork were authorized on August 25. In this connection, Dr. Craven suffered some loss. The meals were carried to the outer cell, passed in to the guards, and by them passed to the prisoner. American soldiers being then the same inveterate souvenir hunters that they are today, Dr. Craven seldom had his spoons returned to him. When Davis learned this he retained the spoon in his cell but, not to be outdone, the guards then began taking the napkins with which the tray was covered.[15]

By this time Davis had received permission for a limited correspondence with his family, the principal requirement being that his letters should pass through the Attorney General, although General Miles also exercised censorship. To prevent unauthorized correspondence, a specific request for writing materials had to be made each time the prisoner desired to write a letter and every sheet of paper had to be accounted for. Any paper not used was turned in with the letter. As a result, the letters were neither numerous nor entirely illuminating.

By the end of September, Dr. Craven's and General Miles's recommendations for a change of quarters began to bear fruit. Investigation indicating that improved conditions were vitally necessary to Davis's health, quarters were prepared for him in Carroll Hall, which stood in the bastion now occupied by Building 9. Miles had recommended the change on September 2 and reported the quarters ready ten days later, but authorization for the change was not received until September 28. The move was made on October 2, and Davis found his lot more comfortable.[16]

His room was in the southwest corner of the second story of Carroll Hall, a long, two-story brick building, 165 feet by 45 feet, extending almost due southwest-northeast across the bastion. The prison room, facing the interior of the fort, was 16 feet 6 inches by 15 feet by 12 feet in height. In the center of the southwest wall was a fireplace, on one side of which there was a recess with a shelf for books and pegs for clothes and on the other side of which was a closet. In the center of the southeast side of the room was a door (or French window), four feet wide, which looked out upon a piazza running the length of the building but which was closed by a fixed iron grating with glazed sash shutters outside. At the center of the northwest side of the room a door led into a hall dividing the building. This door was closed by an iron grating into which were inserted two panes of glass. At the center of the northeast side of the room, opposite the fireplace, a door opened upon another room, occupied by the officer of the guard, which furnished the sole entrance. This door was locked from the outside.

One sentinel walked along the passage, one along the piazza, and one in the room of the officer of the guard, each of them having a view of the interior of the room as he passed the door on his side of the room. Davis had his bed—an iron frame bed, equipped with two mattresses, sheets, blankets, and a cover, with two pillows and mosquito bar—in the southwest corner of the room, and in the opposite corner he had a water bucket, basin, and pitcher, with a stool to serve as a washstand. A small screen enabled him to wash unobserved. A chair and a small pine table completed the furnishings of the room. His clothes still remained in the possession of General Miles.[17]

His surroundings were so much improved that on October 11 he was led to write to his wife that the "dry air, good water, and a fire when requisite, have already improved my physical condition, and with increasing health all the disturbances due to a low vitality, it is to be expected will disappear as rapidly as has been usual with me, after becoming convalescent." Nevertheless, recovery was not rapid. The pacing sentries still disturbed his sleep, and he did not get as much exercise as he should. A short bridge and stairway had been built from the end of the piazza of the second floor of the building to the rampart on the west front so that he could take his walk without the necessity of descending to ground level and then climbing to the top of the parapet—no mean task for one in his weakened condition. Too, curious people who gathered to see the famous man during his walks disturbed him and hampered his recovery.

Clay and John Mitchel, another prisoner, were removed to Carroll Hall on about October 19. Mitchel was released before the end of the month and Clay secured his release on parole in April 1866.[18]

In November 1865, Dr. Craven took it upon himself to order for Davis an overcoat and some underwear suitable for the winter season at Fort Monroe. For this he was called upon for an explanation and directed to confine his conversation with the prisoner solely to matters pertaining to the health of the patient. Before long, he was relieved from the duty of attending Davis, whose care was transferred to Major George E. Cooper, Assistant Surgeon at the Post.[19]

By this time public opinion in the North had changed and the Northern papers began to criticize the treatment accorded the prisoners at Fort Monroe. In partial relief, the Adjutant General, on January 30, 1866, ordered thirty-six dollars a month to be furnished "from the rebel prison fund for furnishing the prisoners Davis and Clay with such food as they require and for payment of the laundresses who do their washing."[20]

Mrs. Davis, becoming alarmed over the reports of her husband's condition, telegraphed to President Johnson in April 1866, for permission to visit Davis. The Secretary of War directed that she be permitted to visit her husband under such restrictions as the commanding officer at Fort Monroe might consider consistent with the safety of the prisoner. She arrived at Old Point Comfort at four o'clock in the morning, May 3, 1866. At about half past ten she was escorted to one of the casemates, which had been assigned to her, and after some delay, during which she signed a parole, she was escorted to Carroll Hall.[21]

At first General Miles limited rather narrowly the hours which Mrs. Davis might spend with her husband, but later he permitted visits during the evenings. General Miles was authorized, if he considered it consistent with Davis's safekeeping, to give the prisoner the freedom of the fort by day on parole. This the general unhesitatingly did. Public opinion still continued to favor less rigorous treatment of Jefferson Davis, and after General Miles was relieved in September 1866, it was felt that surveillance could be materially reduced.[22]

Brevet Brigadier General Henry S. Burton, who succeeded General Miles, set off four rooms in the end of Carroll Hall for the use of Davis and his wife. Mrs. Davis was glad to leave the casemate which she had been occupying, and with a small kitchen at the back of the apartment she and her husband were as comfortable as people in their position could expect to be. She had established cordial relations with most of the women of the garrison, and it is probable that Mr. and Mrs. Davis, receiving courtesies from the garrison and having visitors from time to time from Baltimore, Richmond, and Washington, bringing with them necessities and delicacies, were not altogether unhappy, despite the fact that charges of treason still hung over the ex-President.

These charges had been making slow progress toward settlement. Following investigation of the original charges by Judge Advocate General Joseph Holt, it was the intention to try Jefferson Davis by a military commission for the alleged conspiracies. The Judiciary Committe of the House of Representatives, with the aid of Colonel Levi C. Turner, of the Bureau of Military Justice, took up the matter and examined the witnesses whose depositions had been obtained by the Judge Advocate General. The investigation quickly revealed that the conspiracy charge was based on forged evidence produced by a Sanford Conover. Conover had invented the entire conspiracy in order to obtain money by selling false information to the government.[23]

This seemed to settle the criminal charges but the possibility of conviction on a charge of treason remained. The first indictment for treason was at the May 1865 term of the United States Court at Norfolk, presided over by Judge John G. Underwood. This indictment was lost during the summer and was never again brought to light. Another indictment under the same charge was found against Davis in the District of Columbia, but no process, issued under it, was ever served and it also was abandoned.

In January 1866, the Secretary of War and the Attorney General recommended that Davis be tried in Virginia, with Chief Justice Chase presiding, but Chase declined to hold court in that State during the continuance of martial law. Finally, on May 10, 1866, Davis was indicted for treason in the circuit court of the United States for the District of Virginia, and his counsel—James T. Brady, of New York, William B. Read, of Philadelphia, and James Lyons and Robert Ould, of Richmond—appeared in court to inquire if the case was to be tried. Read demanded speedy trial, but on the following day the prosecution pointed out that the accused was not in the custody of the court, that the district attorney was too much engaged in official business to take up the case at the time, and that Davis himself was too ill to stand a long trial at that time of the year. Judge Underwood stated that the Chief Justice was to preside but could not be present before the October term of court, and the case was continued.

No court sat at Richmond for the October 1866 term, and it was not until the opening of the May 1867 term that Davis was brought before the court. He was still in very poor health, but his attorneys were unable to get the case brought up for final disposal. A soon as the May term opened, a writ of *habeas corpus* was, on application, issued and served on General Burton, who had been notified to comply with any writ issued by a Federal court in Virginia.[24]

General Burton took Davis to Richmond and appeared with him before the court on May 13. The defense announced itself ready for trial, but the Attorney General objected to trial at that term of the court and the objection was sustained. A motion to admit the accused to bail was then made and granted; and a bail bond, in the penalty of $100,000, was signed, among the signers being Horace Greeley, Gerrit Smith, and Cornelius Vanderbilt. Vanderbilt was not present, but he empowered his son-in-law, Horace F. Clark, to sign for him. The bond having been executed, the marshal having Davis in custody under the writ was directed to discharge the prisoner, which was done.

At the November term of the circuit court in Richmond, the Attorney General requested that the case be postponed until the following March to suit the convenience of the Chief Justice, who still failed to appear. Davis's counsel again announced themselves ready for the trial but agreed to the postponement in order to have Chase preside. The case continued to be postponed until December 3, 1868, when the final trial was begun. A motion to quash the indictment was argued at length. It was finally held that the general amnesty proclamation made by President Johnson before the trial began covered Davis's case; and on February 15, 1869, the indictments for treason were dismissed by an order declaring that "the District Attorney, by leave of the court, saith that he will not prosecute further on behalf of the United States against the above named parties upon separate indictments for treason." Shortly afterwards an order was entered reciting that inasmuch as the indictments had been dismissed Davis and his bondsmen were forever released.

His admission to bail closed Jefferson Davis's connection with Fort Monroe, but the bitterness caused by the conditions of his confinement were long in disappearing. Carroll Hall has long since disappeared, but the traditions of his two years at Fort Monroe will continue to live as long as the old fort stands, and just as long will Casemate No. 2 be pointed out as "the place where Jefferson Davis was confined after the Civil War."

Footnotes Chapter VII

[1] Lt. Col. B. D. Pritchard to The Adjutant General, May 19, 1865; Edwin M. Stanton to Lt. Col. Pritchard, May 19, 1865; *OR,* Series II, Vol. VIII, pp. 558–559.

[2] E. M. Stanton to Maj. Gen. Halleck, May 19, 1865; Maj. Gen. H. W. Halleck to Hon. E. M. Stanton, May 20, 1865; *ibid.,* pp. 559–560, 561.

[3] Special Orders No. 2, Military Division of the James, May 21, 1865; Special Orders No. —, Department of Virginia, May 21, 1865; *OR,* Series I, Vol. XLVI, Part III, pp. 1191–1192.

[4] Varina H. Davis, *Jefferson Davis, Ex-President of the Confederate States of America* (New York: Belford Co., 1890), Vol. II, pp. 646–652; C. A. Dana to Hon. E. M. Stanton, May 22, 1865; *OR,* Series II, Vol. VIII, pp. 563–564.

[5] Bvt. Lt. Col. John J. Craven, *Prison Life of Jefferson Davis* (New York: Carleton, 1866), p. 30.

[6] C. A. Dana to Hon. E. M. Stanton, May 22, 1865; *OR,* Series II, Vol. VIII, pp. 563–564.

[7] C. A. Dana to Bvt. Maj. Gen. Miles, May 22, 1865; Bvt. Maj. Gen. Nelson A. Miles to C. A. Dana; *ibid.,* pp. 565, 570–571.

[8] Craven, *op. cit.,* pp. 33–39; Chester D. Bradley, "Dr. Craven and the Prison Life of Jefferson Davis," *Virginia Magazine of History and Biography,* LXII (January 1954), pp. 72–76.

[9] Craven was born in New York in 1822. He was commissioned surgeon of the 1st New Jersey Infantry on April 30, 1861, and brevetted lieutenant colonel for faithful and meritorious service in 1865. Craven served as medical officer with the expeditions against Port Royal, S. C., and Fernandina, Fla., and distinguished himself in the siege of Fort Pulaski. He was chief medical officer in the operations against Charleston in 1863. In the spring of 1864, Dr. Craven was made Medical Director of the X Army Corps, and in January 1865 he became Chief Medical Officer of the Department of Virginia and North Carolina. He was mustered out of service on January 27, 1866, and died in 1893. Bradley, "Dr. Craven and the Prison Life of Jefferson Davis," pp. 79–94; *Heitman,* p. 336.

[10] Bvt. Maj. Gen. Nelson A. Miles to Maj. Gen. Halleck, May 24, 1865; Maj. Gen. H. W. Halleck to Maj. Gen. N. A. Miles, May 24, 1865; *OR,* Series II, Vol. VIII, p. 570.

[11] Craven, *op. cit.,* pp. 40–53.

[12] Edwin M. Stanton to Maj. Gen. Miles, May 28, 1865; Brig. Gen. N. A. Miles to Hon. Edwin M. Stanton, May 28, 1865; *OR,* Series II, Vol. VIII, p. 577.

[13] E. D. Townsend to Bvt. Maj. Gen. N. A. Miles, June 8, 1865, *ibid.,* p. 647.

[14] Craven, *op. cit.,* pp. 116, 119, 146–147, 151–152. Craven, curiously, gives the date Davis was allowed to leave his cell as June 24. Much of the *Prison Life* apparently was written by Charles G. Halpine and many portions of it are suspect. For a discussion of the book, see William Hanchett, "Reconstruction and the Rehabilitation of Jefferson Davis: Charles G. Halpine's Prison Life," *The Journal of American History,* LVI (September 1969), pp. 280–289; and Bradley, "Dr. Craven and the Prison Life of Jefferson Davis," pp. 50–94. Nelson A. Miles to Gen. E. D. Townsend, July 20, 1865; Edwin M. Stanton to Maj. Gen. Miles, July 22, 1865; Bvt. Maj. Gen. N. A. Miles to Brig. Gen. E. D. Townsend, July 23 and 24, 1865; *OR,* Series II, Volume VIII, pp. 710–711.

[15] Craven, *op. cit.,* pp. 183, 214–217, 219, 234–235.

[16] Bvt. Maj. Gen. Nelson A. Miles to Gen. E. D. Townsend, Sept. 2, 1865; E. D. Townsend to Maj. Gen. Miles, Sept. 4, 1865; Bvt. Lt. Col. L. H. Pelouze to Bvt. Maj. Gen. Nelson A. Miles, Sept. 28, 1865; Bvt. Maj. Gen. Nelson A. Miles to Gen. E. D. Townsend, Oct. 2, 1865; *OR,* Series II, Vol. VIII, pp. 740, 755, 761.

[17] Bvt. Lt. Col. L. H. Pelouze to Gen. E. D. Townsend, Sept. 29, 1865, *ibid.,* pp. 755–760. Craven, *op. cit.,* pp. 323–325.

[18] Maj. Gen. Nelson A. Miles to Col. Ed. W. Smith, Oct. 31, 1865; Maj. Gen. Nelson A. Miles to Gen. E. D. Townsend, Mar. 20, 1866; E. D. Townsend to Maj. Gen. N. A. Miles, Apr. 17, 1866; *OR,* Series II, Vol. VIII, pp. 782, 892, 899. William Dillon, *Life of John Mitchel* (London: Kegan Paul, Trench and Co., 1888), Vol. II, pp. 215–226.

[19] Craven, *op. cit.,* pp. 359–367. Cooper had been appointed an assistant surgeon in 1847 and promoted to major in 1861. He was brevetted lieutenant colonel and colonel during the war and was promoted lieutenant colonel in 1876. Cooper died in 1881. *Heitman,* p. 326.

[20] E. D. Townsend to Maj. Gen. N. A. Miles, Jan. 30, 1865, *OR,* Series II, Vol. VIII, p. 874.

[21] Varina Davis to President Johnson, Apr. 25, 1865; E. D. Townsend to Maj. Gen. N. A. Miles, Apr. 26, 1866; E. D. Townsend to Mrs. Varina Davis, Apr. 26, 1866; Maj. Gen. Nelson A. Miles to Gen. E. D. Townsend, May 3, 1866; *ibid.,* pp. 900, 901, 904–905. Varina Davis, *Jefferson Davis,* Vol. II, p. 757–759.

[22] E. D. Townsend to Maj. Gen. N. A. Miles, May 23, 1866; Maj. Gen. Nelson A. Miles to Gen. E. D. Townsend, May 25, 1866; *OR,* Series II, Vol. VIII, pp. 912–914; Varina Davis, *Jefferson Davis,* Vol. II, pp. 761, 772–773. Mrs. Davis states that the freedom of the fort was not granted until after Miles's departure.

[23] Report to Col. L. C. Turner, June 2, 1866, J. Holt to Hon. E. M. Stanton, July 3, 1866, L. C. Turner to Brig. Gen. J. Holt, Dec. 20, 1866; *OR,* Series II, Vol. VIII, pp. 921–923, 931–945, 978–980.

[24] Writ, May 1, 1867; E. D. Townsend to Bvt. Brig. Gen. H. S. Burton, May 8, 1867, *ibid.,* pp. 983–984, 985; J. G. Randall, *The Civil War and Reconstruction* (Boston: D. C. Heath and Company, 1953), pp. 807–808.

Chapter VIII

The Old Army
and Fort Monroe

FOLLOWING THE CLOSE of the Civil War, the entire Army entered a period of depression in which stagnation was so acute that the period has been—somewhat tritely—characterized as one of innocuous desuetude. In this respect, Fort Monroe suffered less, perhaps, than the rest of the Army, for at Fort Monroe was located the Artillery School. This post naturally showed the peculiar disorganization attendant upon the change from a wartime to a peacetime status. The reservation was cluttered with temporary buildings of wartime construction, which were forced to serve long beyond their period of serviceability; and all of the buildings and grounds bore the marks of that deterioration which results from the hard usage of a constantly changing wartime garrison. Repairs were few and replacement was entirely lacking, for Congress for many years was to be extremely frugal in its appropriations.

Immediately after the close of the Civil War the re-establishment of the Artillery School was determined upon, the first step being the creation of an Artillery Board to which questions might be referred for discussion and recommendation.[1] This board, which consisted of Lieutenant Colonel and Brevet Brigadier General Henry J. Hunt, Major and Brevet Colonel Albion P. Howe, Captain John Gibbon, and Captain and Brevet Lieutenant Colonel Samuel N. Benjamin, Secretary, was directed to "prepare and submit a project for an Artillery school to be established at Fort Monroe."[2] The results of the recommendations of the board were published on November 13, 1867, in General Orders No. 99, which announced the reopening of the school and gave in detail its organization.

The staff of the school consisted of three field officers of artillery (of whom the senior commanded the post and the school), the senior officer of ordnance stationed at the post, and the heads of the departments of instruction. The instruction batteries consisted of one battery from each of the five regiments of artillery, and the student personnel consisted of such officers and enlisted men as might be ordered to the school for instruction. Normally, brevet second lieutenants were sent to the school to take the course of instruction before joining their batteries. The adjutant of the post had also the duties of secretary to the staff of the school.

The instruction batteries were not relieved at any definite intervals, but the lieutenants assigned to the batteries were relieved by others each year. All lieutenants attending the school were assigned or attached to the batteries, and the routine of battery duty was expected of all alike. After the final examination at the end of the school year each officer was furnished with a certificate setting forth his standing and efficiency as an officer as determined by his record during the year. A failure to obtain a satisfactory certificate was to be a bar to promotion until, after further instruction, the officer passed the examination, but this regulation, although it stood for many years, was never strictly enforced.[3]

The captains of the batteries at Fort Monroe served, in addition to their duties as battery commander, as instructors in the various subjects taken up in the course of the school. These instructors participated in the meetings of the staff only when the results of examinations and the marks to be awarded in the subjects they taught were under consideration. The name of the school—The Artillery School of the United States Army—was adopted on December 26, 1867, at the first meeting of the staff at which all members were present.

A band, composed of one leader, one noncommissioned officer, and twenty privates, was attached to the school, the members of the band being enlisted for the school and distributed among the companies at the post. The extra pay of the band leader and all other expenses of the band were defrayed from the post fund, from which also were purchased the necessary text-books for the use of the school. Because of these extra expenses, the post fund was relieved from the usual obligation of remitting fifty percent of its net proceeds to the several regimental funds of the regiments represented by companies at the post.

The delays incident to the assembly of the instruction batteries and the preparation of the code of regulations and details of the course of instruction made it necessary to defer the opening of the school until April 1, 1868, on which date the first class began its practical work. On the preceding evening, Brevet Major General William F. Barry, detailed as commandant, had all the officers and noncommissioned officers assembled in the lecture room, where the general and special orders organizing the school and appointing the officers were read. This was followed by a lecture by General Barry on the course of instruction and the objectives in view.

The selection of Colonel and Brevet Major General William F. Barry for the task of reorganizing the Artillery School was particularly fortunate, for he brought to his new duties a vast enthusiasm, a distinguished career, and a wide experience.[4] Of him, Brigadier General William A. Kobbé wrote: "No outline of the school in those days should be without a tribute to General Barry. He was a devoted and enthusiastic artilleryman, infinitely and hopelessly, and perhaps unconsciously, hampered by a halt in the science that marked the beginning of transition from old to new. He took the greatest pride in the school, and the indifference of the War Department and of the artillery officers generally angered and depressed him; and he was tireless in urging its claims and begging for small sums of money from the Department or from Congress for school purposes. An unbending disciplinarian and extending his supervision to the dress and bearing of his officers on or off duty, he was also a kindly and most hospitable host and welcomed, with wife and daughters, all student officers at his quarters."

The practical work of the school occupied the first six months of the school year (April 1 to October 1) and comprised instruction in all the different kinds of guns, howitzers, and mortars used in the field, siege, and seacoast artillery service at that time; instruction in the nomenclature, construction, and uses of their different parts and of their carriages, and in the implements, weights of charges, projectiles, fuzes, etc.; instruction in the laying of platforms for siege guns, howitzers, and mortars, and for the heavy 10-inch and 13-inch seacoast mortars; and instruction in the transportation, mounting, and dismounting of the heavy carriages. The laboratory duties in so far as they concerned the artillery, target practice, and general instruction in practical gunnery, including the different methods of ascertaining initial velocities and ranges, were performed in as thorough a manner as circumstances would permit.

There was a daily parade, and the batteries drilled twice daily for an hour and a quarter. During the hours of drill, the band and the field musicians were required to practice. On Friday afternoon the instruction was in infantry drill exclusively, by company or by battalion as the commanding officer might designate. On Saturdays there were no military exercises except the mounting of the guard, the day being given up to police of the post and barracks. September was set apart for target practice with the different pieces and for laboratory work.

For thirty years, the garrison, except for the battery subalterns who were also student officers in the school, changed but slowly. Life at

Fort Monroe became routine; and routine became monotony. Once in a while troops were called away for short periods of detached service—a welcome break in garrison life—but such events were rare. An occasional funeral or an inauguration in Washington or a threatened disturbance elsewhere provided the excuse for short absences. Battery G, 1st Artillery, Battery A, 3d Artillery, and Battery C, 5th Artillery, were ordered to detached service in the South in October and November 1868 for temporary duty during elections. In September 1869, Battery G, 1st Artillery was sent to Washington to form a part of the funeral escort of the late Secretary of War, General John A. Rawlins.[5]

The examinations in the practical course of the school began on October 15, 1868, but they were interrupted and the opening of the theoretical course was delayed because of the three batteries on detached service. The student officers assigned to these batteries accompanied them, for all subalterns were required to do full company duty in addition to their school work. With the return of these organizations to the post, the theoretical part of the course was taken up, with instruction being given in mathematics, artillery, engineering, astronomy, law, mechanics, geography, military history, and tactics. The end of the course was somewhat delayed because of the interruption in October and November, but the examinations were finally completed on April 15, 1869, and the first class of the reorganized Artillery School was graduated on April 27, with General William T. Sherman presenting the diplomas.

During the year progress had been satisfactory. The members of the staff had been conscientious in their efforts to determine the most satisfactory methods of imparting instruction, and the experiences of the initial year induced them to carry the theoretical and practical courses together throughout the year (July and August excepted), with a single recitation of one and a half hours daily (Saturday and Sunday excepted) until September 1, after which date there were two recitations each day. Later it was decided to extend the theoretical course to include July and August.

The delay in the graduation of the Class of 1869 necessarily caused a delay in the opening of the new school year and it was not until May 17 that the incoming class, consisting of seventeen members, opened its course with the subject of algebra.

During the second year the staff continued to observe the original schedule and made practically no changes after the courses started. Toward the end of the school year, however, it was felt that the experience of the two years was sufficient to enable the staff to place the course upon a more practical working basis. Consequently, a committee was appointed to revise the whole course of theoretical instruction for officers and enlisted men with a view to fixing with more definiteness what the theoretical course should be. The committee recommended some changes in text-books, transferred astronomy to engineering, and discontinued mechanics, geography, and tactics, the course in tactics having been merely a course in Army regulations and artillery handbooks.

In July 1870, Battery G, 1st Artillery, Battery K, 2d Artillery, and Battery F, 4th Artillery, were ordered to Raleigh, North Carolina, partly because of the apprehension of an outbreak during the trial of certain members of the Ku Klux Klan, and partly because of the anticipation of disturbances during the local elections to be held in August. Leaving Fort Monroe on the twenty-sixth, the batteries arrived in Raleigh the same evening, where, together with Company D, 8th Infantry, they served as a battalion. The United States marshal for the district claimed that he was powerless to enforce his instructions, so occasional detachments guarded his office or accompanied deputy marshals making arrests. In general the troops were held in barracks—especially on election day— until September 30, when they returned to their proper stations.[6]

The course of the Artillery School as modified in 1870 continued without material change until 1875, although it was broken somewhat by the absence of the three batteries on detached service in North Carolina during the summer of 1870. The course of theoretical instruction embraced the subjects of mathematics, ordnance and gunnery, military engineering and surveying, military history, and military, constitutional, and international law. The method of pursuing these studies was very similar to that pursued at the Military Academy, that is, by recitations, questions, and demonstrations at a blackboard. In military history every officer was required, in addition to his regular recitations, to prepare and read before the class and staff of the school two essays or memoirs upon some battle or campaign or upon the military events of some epoch of special interest.

In the school for noncommissioned officers, every noncommissioned officer belonging to the five instruction batteries was required to attend the school for one full course of instruction; other enlisted men were also permitted to attend. This course was also both practical and theoretical. The practical course was very similar to that given the commissioned officers but it was not carried to the same extent, being restricted more to the duties of the noncommissioned officer and to the average capacity of the men receiving instruction. The theoretical course embraced mathematics, history of the United States, geography, reading, and writing. The subject of mathematics included the entire field of arithmetic, except for the more advanced men, who were carried as far as equations of the second degree in algebra.[7] By 1875 most of the lieutenants of artillery and a few officers from other branches of the service had received instruction at the Artillery School. As the courses became more fully developed it was recognized that one year was insufficient for the complete instruction of student officers when so much of their time was taken up in routine post duties and the course was therefore extended to two years by General Orders No. 89, War Department, 1875.

Interruptions came in 1876 and 1877. Exigencies of the public service demanded the withdrawal of Battery G, 1st Artillery, Battery A, 3d Artillery, Battery I, 4th Artillery, and Battery C, 5th Artillery, from November 1876 to February 1877 for duty in North Carolina. Again, in July 1877, the garrison was called upon for service elsewhere because of labor riots which kept the command away from Fort Monroe for about a month.[8]

The class which entered the Artillery School in the spring of 1876 was the first to take the two-year course, but the absence of the companies in North Carolina forced a suspension of school duties. An attempt was made to make the course as complete as possible, notwithstanding the lost time, but the practical instruction was interrupted in July 1877 when the absence of the major portion of the garrison caused another cessation of school duties.

One of the most distinguished officers ever to serve at Fort Monroe arrived on the post on March 28, 1877. Lieutenant Colonel Emory Upton, 4th Artillery, assumed the duties of Superintendent of Theoretical Instruction in the Artillery School. Upton had a brilliant combat record during the Civil War. Graduating from West Point in 1861, Upton became colonel of the 121st New York Infantry in 1862 and was promoted to brigadier general of volunteers in 1864. He received six brevets during the war, including that of major general for gallantry in the Battle of Winchester. Promoted to lieutenant colonel in the Regular Army in 1866, Upton launched a career as a brilliant military theoretician.

Upton was responsible for a new course on strategy and grand tactics at the Artillery School. He spent the next few months getting to know his fellow faculty members and preparing his new course. Upton had just returned from a world tour—arranged with the help of General Sherman—during which he studied the organization of several foreign armies. During his first few months at Fort Monroe, Upton finished the manuscript of *The Armies of Asia and Europe,* describing his trip, which was published in 1878. He then began work on a history of the military policy of the United States which was to have a profound impact on military thinking in America.

Upton was enthusiastic about his assignment to Fort Monroe. He believed that the United States had nothing to compare with the war colleges of Europe and hoped at the Artillery School to train a corps of officers who in any future war would be the chief reliance of the country.

By the end of his tour at Fort Monroe, Upton had completed his history of United States military policy through the campaigns of 1862. But by this time he was becoming bitter, disillusioned, and tired as a result of his failure to bring a fundamental change in American military organization. He exacted strict discipline from the troops, forced his officers and their wives to give religious instruction to the men, and required everyone to attend Sunday services. Keeping more and more to himself, Upton brooded on his future. He was relieved from duty at Fort Monroe on June 30, 1880, and promoted to colonel of the 4th Artillery. The following year, depressed over his seeming failure to influence the Army and gravely ill with the maddening pain of a brain tumor, Upton committed suicide. His *Military Policy of the United States* was resurrected by Secretary of War Elihu Root at the turn of the century and was published by the War Department in 1904.[9]

In 1878, Fort Wool briefly emerged from obscurity to become a center for scientific research. Johns Hopkins University had established an experimental laboratory to study marine zoology of the Chesapeake Bay and Professor W. K. Brooks visited the lower bay in April 1878 to select a site for the laboratory. Owing to the unhealthfulness of the shores of the bay near the Capes and the lack of suitable buildings, Professor Brooks selected Fort Wool as the best available site. He found the interior of the uncompleted fort still covered with building materials, but there were two large frame buildings which could be adapted for use as a laboratory. Brooks applied to Major General Quincy A. Gilmore, the superintending engineer of the fortifications, and on May 22 the Secretary of War granted permission for their use that summer.

Brooks, another professor from Johns Hopkins, and eight students arrived at Fort Wool on June 24 and continued their work until August 19. The laboratory was designed to furnish advanced students with opportunities for original research and to gather materials for winter work at the university. The opportunities for advanced work in the study of invertebrate embryology at Fort Wool were all that could be desired. A strong current runs close to the fort which carried with it at each turn of the tide an endless variety of free swimming animals and embryos and locomotive larvae. The summer spent at Fort Wool resulted in the publication of a collection of papers on the marine zoology of lower Chesapeake Bay.[10]

During the 'Seventies the Army began to show signs of reawakening; in the 'Eighties, with the assistance of Congress, progress became apparent; and by the late 'Nineties the revival and renovation and modernization of the Army was well under way. Professional progress may be said to date from about the middle of the 'Eighties; but professional matters were not the first to be taken up. Experiments had been conducted in ordnance design and manufacture and in Engineer construction; but the first real forward-looking step was the adoption of a housing program for the Army.

Practically all of the buildings standing at the posts garrisoned by the Army consisted of temporary and hasty wartime construction or of pre-war construction which had deteriorated materially from neglect and careless usage during the war. The first of the new construction followed an appropriation of $100,000 made by Congress during the fiscal year ending June 30, 1874, for the erection of buildings at San Antonio, Texas. Each year thereafter saw additional appropriations extending the amount of construction undertaken, the sums appropriated increasing, in general, with each year. By 1890, a total exceeding $4,100,000 had been appropriated for construction of barracks and quarters—a vastly greater sum, be it noted, than the same amount would be today.

Fort Monroe entered the building program by receiving $34,000 from the appropriations made during fiscal year 1880 and an additional $20,000 in the following year. With these amounts available, amelioration of housing conditions on the post was undertaken. Most of the older structures were demolished, and the greater part of the buildings now standing therefore date from 1880 or later years. For this reason, a description of the post as it existed prior to 1880 and of the living conditions at that time may be of greater interest than a detailed account of the minor events that occurred during the period.

Prior to the Civil War the wharf at which all shipping—government or private—landed was the Engineer Wharf (or Lighthouse Wharf). With the greatly increased traffic—both in freight and in passengers—which followed the transfer of military operations to the Virginia Peninsula in 1862, the old wharf became totally inadequate and a new one was decided upon. The approach to the fort from the old wharf by way of either the Main Gate or the East Gate was difficult because of the loose sand, and the new wharf was built in 1862 farther to the westward, at the foot of what is now Ingalls Road. To the new wharf was given the name Baltimore Wharf, principally because it was most used by boats from Baltimore.

Landing at the Baltimore Wharf, the first thing that struck the eye was the Hygeia Hotel, occupying much of the ground embraced in the present Continental Park on the water front. The Old Hygeia had been demolished in 1862. In 1863, Caleb C. Willard, one of the proprietors of the old hotel, was authorized to erect near the Baltimore Wharf, for the benefit of transient officers, a small one-story restaurant, or eating house, which became known as the Hygeia Dining Saloon. Ownership passed through several hands to Henry Clark, who applied for and, on June 25, 1868, received permission to "enlarge the said hotel."

On March 14, 1872, Clark formed a partnership with John E. Wilson, and the hotel was conducted under the firm name of Clark and Wilson until November 22, 1873, when it was assigned to Thomas Tabb, Harrison Phoebus, and G. S. Griffith, Jr., as trustees for the creditors, Clark and Wilson having failed. These trustees in 1874 sold the property under a court decree to Samuel M. Shoemaker. An act of Congress, approved February 19, 1875, authorized Shoemaker to enlarge the hotel, and reaffirmed the conditions of the joint resolution of June 25, 1868. At various other times and under other authority, Shoemaker enlarged and extended the hotel. These privileges were personal, yet Shoemaker, by deed dated July 10, 1876, sold his right to Harrison Phoebus without asking recognition or obtaining consent of the War Department to the transfer.

Phoebus, who was to be the dominant civilian figure in the area for some twenty years, had arrived at Fort Monroe in May 1866 as agent for the Adams Express Company. Through various business interests, he quickly acquired a respectable fortune. Under Phoebus, the Hygeia Hotel became one of the best known hotels in the country, attracting prominent people from all over the United States and even Europe. Phoebus repeatedly enlarged and improved the hotel until it eventually had accommodations for 1,000 guests. It grew into a palatial structure with each of its four stories girded by wide verandas. The hotel had the last word in the comforts of that day: hydraulic elevators, gas light, electric bells in every room, and bathrooms on every floor. To meet the competition of the inland spas, Phoebus provided Turkish, Russian thermo-electric, magnetic, mercurial, sulphur, vapor, and hot sea baths. There was a dancing pavilion of 7,000 square feet with the music provided by the Fort Monroe band.[11]

The gay social life at Fort Monroe during this period is reflected in an article which appeared in *Harper's Weekly* in 1888. The writer found:[12]

Every room of this big wooden labyrinth has its drowsing occupant, and, sleeping or waking, there are more beauties in the corridors of the Hygeia or along the shaded walks within the fort than one can meet in a decade of travel. . . . Perhaps the proximity of Fortress Monroe has not a little to do with the popularity of Old Point Comfort as a health resort. Day after day, in their dainty dresses, swarms of charming girls invade the fort, supervise the "mechanical maneuvers," criticize the battery drills, demoralize the "star gaugers" (a detachment of student-officers who are almost daily at work inpecting the bores of their barbette guns, and making impressions of familiar old cracks and flaws that every class has stumbled over for years past), and only appearing conquered by circumstances when they suddenly find themselves in attendance at target practice and compelled to stand the roar and concussion of the big black boomers. Even around the hotel the military air pervades. The Artillery Band comes in every day and plays in the *salon* adjoining the great dining room, and officers off duty dine with their friends, and point out the historic spots in the neighborhood. . . . And when sunset nears and the bugles blare the signal for parade, hundreds of gayly dressed visitors stream across the moat and through the resounding postern and out over the green carpet of the parade, where they make a picturesque group under the grove of oak-trees; and then the band strikes up, and the troops march out and form line of battle, and there is a brief quarter-hour of music and martial pomp, and then the officers march up to the front, briefly salute their commander, and are swallowed up in the throng of civilians; and then twilight comes, and an adjournment to the hotel, and an evening devoted to more music and dancing, and the artillery uniforms are evidently as much at home in the *salon* as on the ramparts.

The Hygeia Hotel occupied a patch of ground extending along the east side of the wharf and the main road leading therefrom to a point about 238 feet from low water mark and fronting the beach for about 190 feet, its southwest corner being a few yards inland from the present end of Ingalls Road. In 1881 it was greatly enlarged, being extended along the beach to a point east of the present band stand and thence away from the beach to the present line of officers' quarters. The hotel was razed in 1902 after the ownership had been acquired by the company operating the Chamberlin Hotel.

Beyond the Hygeia, to the east was the lighthouse, built in 1802; and almost immediately in front of the lighthouse were the abutments marking the ruins of the old Engineer Wharf. Immediately north of the hotel, east of the main road and at the corner south of the present post office, was Watkin's grocery and ship chandler's store, Watkins having succeeded to Bentley's jewelry and notion store. Between Building 138 and the present post office, was the book store of William Baulch, Post Trader. Back of Baulch's store stood the DeRussy house, erected in 1817 as a government stable, converted later into a barracks or prison for slaves and military prisoners employed upon the fortifications, and made into a dwelling house in about 1842.

Opposite the Hygeia, west of the road leading to the wharf, on the plot of ground now occupied by the Chamberlin Hotel, was the residence of the Quartermaster. Next to the north stood the office of the Adams Express Company, built in 1873, with a frontage of about thirty feet. Closely adjoining the Express Company's office on the north was the store of William H. Kimberly, built in 1868, with a frontage of about forty-eight feet.

On the grounds now occupied by the buildings of the Training and Doctrine Command was the Ordnance gun yard. This was a patch of ground about half an acre in extent, entirely surrounded by a fence made of old-time musket barrels with bayonets attached. These muskets had been ruined in a fire at the Washington Arsenal in 1866 and had been sent to Fort Monroe to be placed under the trip-hammer and reworked at the arsenal. This had never been done, and someone conceived the novel use to which the guns were put. Within the yard were many war relics, of which the most interesting were a number of 6- and 12-pounders surrendered by the British at Yorktown in 1781.

Extending east from the Baltimore wharf along the shore line back of the gun yard to somewhere near the present wharves was the Quartermaster wharf. This stood much closer in than the present shore line, which filled in extensively along that whole section of the beach after the construction of the wharf in about 1862. The washing of the tides between the pilings brought in the sand, which served to build up that part of the reservation.

Opposite the gun yard, north of Baulch's book store and about abreast the postern gate, was the Engineer Office. North of that stood the post office, which was called Old Point Comfort, the name it had long possessed. The name was changed to Fortress Monroe in about 1879. Some fifteen years later, the question of returning to the old name was brought up and the local military authorities mildly objected on the grounds that the name Old Point Comfort was dying out and was therefore no longer descriptive. The Secretary of War on February 25, 1885, pointed out that the name of the post was Fort Monroe, not Fortress Monroe, but the post office continued to be Fortress Monroe until November 15, 1941.

North of the post office was a bare stretch of ground which had formerly been occupied by the Old Hygeia Hotel. Baulch's Ice House and Billiard Parlor stood about on the ground now occupied by post headquarters and the fire house.

St. Mary's Church stood on its present site. Adjoining the church were two one-time stables, used in 1880 as quarters for employees of the post. Above these was a row of frame buildings erected by the Ordnance Department about 1838 for quarters for employees. Across the street was the Ordnance Machine Shop of the Fort Monroe Arsenal (now Building 27), which had been erected about 1860, and which, during the war, had employed between four and five hundred men in the manufacture of rifled cannon and other war materiel.

North of the machine shop, on the sites of Buildings 80 amd 100, were a number of frame buildings erected mainly in 1860 and 1861 as quarters for Ordnance employees. Across the road from these was the coal and wood yard, behind which the Quartermaster had a small wharf. The quarters of the Arsenal commander—Quarters 93, opposite Building 80—although built by the Ordnance Department, belong to the period of construction beginning in 1880. At the end of the causeway leading to Mill Creek bridge was a picket guard house, serving much the same purpose as the guard house there today.

The moat was bridged then, as now, by four principal entrances—the north, the east, and the west (or main) sallyports, and the postern gate. The Officers' Club was located in the flag bastion until 1959. A porch over the moat around the Fort Monroe Club was approved by the Secretary of War in 1894 and the first section was constructed soon thereafter. To provide for reaching the club rooms from the outside of the fort, a ferry was installed. This consisted of a small barge, or boat, familiarly known as the *Maid of the Moat*. The motive power was furnished by the would-be passenger. A rope ran from the boat through the pulleys on each side, and the passage was effected by boarding the boat and pulling on the rope. The club being then what it is now, patrons leaving the club were known to pull themselves off the boat instead of across the moat. A bridge replaced the boat just prior to World War I. Since the move of the club from the bastion to the former Beach Club, both the porch and the bridge have been removed.

Entering the fort by the Main Gate, one came first to the guard rooms —the rooms on either side of the archway of the sallyport. On one side was the room used for the confinement of prisoners, four cell rooms being connected with it. On the other side was the room used by the guard, a dark cell being connected with it for recalcitrant prisoners. Two other rooms accommodated the officer of the guard and the tools used by the prisoners.[13]

Just inside the entrance to the fort and slightly to the right was a two-story frame building used by the Artillery School. The first floor was an instruction room and the second floor a photograph gallery. Just beyond, toward the parade ground and facing the photograph gallery, was another frame structure used as a library for the school.

To the left, just within the main gate, was the hospital—a drab-colored brick structure, three stories high. The lower floor of the hospital comprised the dispensary and the storerooms, and the second and third floors were given over to four wards for the sick, each ward accommodating ten beds. A Surgeon and an Assistant Surgeon formed a part of the garrison to care for the sick. Behind the hospital a small brick building served as a kitchen and a mess room; and immediately north of the hospital a small frame building, erected during the war, was used as a matron's quarters.[14]

Just beyond the hospital was a small brick building now used as the post library. It contained the enlisted men's library and instruction rooms and housed a library of three or four thousand volumes. In the bastion in which Building 9 now stands was Carroll Hall, a three-story brick apartment house, containing offices on the first floor and eight sets of quarters for officers on the upper floors, each set consisting of three rooms.

The barracks stood on the northern side of the parade ground. They consisted of seven temporary frame buildings intended to house six companies and a band, each building being 120 feet long by 25 feet wide, one story high. These buildings rested on piles, the ground floor being some five feet above the level of the ground, and they stood some forty feet distant each from the other. Fifteen feet of the end of each building was set for the rooms of the first sergeant and the company office, the remainder of the building forming a single squad room. Twenty-five feet in the rear of each building was a detached frame kitchen. As is so likely to occur with temporary construction, these buildings had been built of green, unseasoned lumber, which, with the passing of time, shrank and opened the joints. In his report of 1870, the surgeon admitted that there was "more than a sufficiency of fresh air admitted." The bunks were made of iron frames with wooden slats and were provided two to every three men. They were covered with bed-sacks filled with straw, which was replaced by fresh straw once a month or oftener.

In the winter time it was found extremely difficult to keep the barracks sufficiently warm. Two 18-inch cylinder stoves were provided for each squad room and were kept burning at full capacity, day and night, by room orderlies. It was, however, impossible to keep the rooms at an equable temperature. As might be expected, the men near the stoves suffered from the heat given off by them and the men at a distance received no warmth at all. This formed grounds for periodic complaints; but the lack of accommodations for washing gave grounds for perpetual complaint.

The wash rooms were but twelve feet by five feet in dimension for each company and were built to the outside of the company kitchens. There were no tubs or other means of washing the whole body, except during the summer time when the men bathed in the bay at a point just about due east from the East Gate. During cold weather the only possible means of bathing was through the use of small hand wash basins in the barracks.[15]

In the rear of the barracks were the quarters of the married soldiers and laundresses. Those consisted of two two-story frame buildings, "badly built and worse arranged," with porches running the length of the south sides. Access to the second floor was gained by stairs running from the lower to the upper porch. Each building was occupied by fourteen families, seven on the first floor, and seven on the second. Each family had a suite of two rooms, one opening on the porch and connected to the other by a door.

The buildings had been constructed in part of green lumber and in part of old lumber taken from the laundresses' quarters which had been torn down in 1867. Here again shrinkage occurred, and the walls between rooms were opened to such an extent that the occupants of one room could not fail to see all that occurred in adjoining rooms. During the summer these buildings were very nearly uninhabitable. Imagine living in the month of August on the second floor of a frame building 87 feet long by 30 feet deep in which fourteen kitchen ranges were working at full blast doing the cooking for an equal number of families.[16]

Beyond the barracks, in the northeast bastion, were two Ordnance storehouses. Adjoining the barracks, to the east, was another two-story brick building, serving also as a Ordnance storehouse, on the site of which another barrack building has since been built. Next to the storehouse stood two sets of officers' quarters, known as Knox Row, built during the regime of General Barry.

Facing the East Gate was the residence of the commandant (No. 1), built about 1819. This was a handsome brick structure, approached by a broad flight of steps from both front and rear. The grounds surrounding the quarters were fenced off, and a fine garden and greenhouse were under charge of a soldier detailed to keep them up.

Near the quarters of the commandant, practically at the foot of the ramp leading to the top of the curtain of the fourth front, were the headquarters of the Artillery School, containing the printing plant and the offices of the adjutant and the sergeant major. Close by was a smaller building containing the office of the commandant. These both were ordinary frame structures, erected by General Butler during the war. West of the headquarters of the Artillery School stood a brick set of quarters belonging to the Ordnance Department, still in use (No. 50). This building was more or less isolated, being partially surrounded by parks containing guns and trophies.

In the southeast corner of the parade ground, to the left of the main walk (when facing headquarters) was the Siege Battery Park, containing siege guns and a siege howitzer. Across the walk, just about in front of Quarters 50, was the Light Battery Park, containing four 3-inch rifles and two brass 12-pounder Napoleon guns, with a battery of four 8-inch siege mortars in rear of these pieces—but in front of their caissons. Further to the west, just about on a line between the flagstaff bastion and the center of the barracks, was "Trophy Park," containing souvenirs of the surrender of Cornwallis at Yorktown in 1781. Three 10-inch siege mortars, each flanked by triangular piles of mortar shells, formed a triangle, in the center of which was a brass mortar, originally used to fire stones, which was surrounded by rows of 10-inch mortar shells, surmounted by a row of 8-inch rifle projectiles. The trophies consisted of three howitzers, which were surrendered at Yorktown, and a breech-loading Chinese gun, which was captured from the Koreans by the squadron under Rear Admiral John Rodgers in June 1871 and which bore in Chinese the following inscription: "19th Moon, of the Chinese Emperor, King Hi, A.D. 1681."

The post chapel—the Chapel of the Centurion—stood on its present site. Originally furnished with rough pine benches, and without chancel or chapel furniture, the chapel had gradually been improved, mainly through the efforts of Chaplain Osgood E. Herrick, and was in good condition.[17]

The Tuileries were also standing at this time. The origin of their name is unknown, but it probably lay in the fact that, except for No. 1, these were the most commodious and handsome buildings of the post at the time of their construction. Back of the Tuileries ran a small alley, known as "Ghost Alley," another name involved in mystery, but probably resulting from the intense darkness there at night, since no lights were provided until later.

The casemates of the first, second, and third fronts were used as quarters, officers occupying the first and second fronts and enlisted men occupying the third. At the end of the first front, in the casemates of the flagstaff bastion, was the officers' club. An officers' mess had been started in Carroll Hall in about 1852; and the Old Point Billiard Club was opened in 1869 in an Ordnance building near the commandant's quarters. This building burned to the ground on Christmas Eve, 1870, and in March 1871 the mess and the club combined and moved into the flagstaff bastion. The name "Fort Monroe Club" was adopted in 1875.

In the second front, the last two casemates were given over to the post bakery, which frunished bread to the garrison. Adjoining the ramp in the bastion separating the second and third fronts was the sutler's store, corresponding to the post exchange of today. Ammunition magazines were situated in the northwest bastion, near Carroll Hall, and in the northeast bastion.

The interior of the fort was as heavily wooded then as at present. The same live oaks were to be seen then as today; and the single large tree near the barracks is distinctly shown on the maps of 1880. Surgeon George E. Cooper, in a report of 1870, stated: "The live oak is found within the inclosure of the work, having been undisturbed when the clearing was made to build the fort." It is said that these live oaks, together with those near the present Fort Monroe Officers' Club north of the fort, are the northernmost live oaks to be found in the United States.[18]

The east sallyport led to the Water Battery, which has since been demolished. This battery extended from a point at the southern end of the southeast bastion (near the present enlisted men's swimming pool), opposite the east bastion. A covered way (a breast-high wall) led from the end of the Water Battery past a redan and a redoubt to the vicinity of the northwest bastion. From here around the eastern and southern sides of the fort to the southern end of the Water Battery there was only the gentle slope of the glacis of the fort, in part occupied by buildings.

Life at Fort Monroe would have been more pleasant had living conditions been better. There were, in 1870, only about a hundred and thirty rooms on the post available to the officers of the artillery garrison—all within the fort. There seem to have been four frame one-story buildings, of four, five, five, and eight rooms, respectively, one of these buildings being occupied by the Military Storekeeper. The brick buildings were the commandant's quarters (eight rooms), the two Tuileries (fourteen rooms each), and Carroll Hall (twenty-four rooms available for use as quarters and sixteen rooms used as offices, etc.). Quarters 3 was erected in 1875. The casemates of the first front acounted for twenty-four rooms (one of which was used to house a condenser of 5,000 gallons daily capacity), and the second front provided twenty-eight (two casemates being used for the bakery). Quarters 50 had not yet been turned over to the artillery and practically all of the quarters outside the fort were occupied by the Ordnance Department employees, there being something like a dozen buildings for them.

At that time the interior of the fort, not being provided with a drainage nor with a sewage system, was much damper than it is today. This perhaps accounts for the height to which the first floors of the Tuileries and of Quarters 1 were carried and for the lack of basements in buildings of the post-war period, which were, nevertheless, built at ground level. It was practically impossible to make use of basement floors, such as those of the Tuileries. To a considerable extent, the dampness in these lower rooms was caused by the cisterns with which the houses were provided and from which moisture seeped through the walls; but even where there were no cisterns the dampness was excessive. In the winter time it was possible to compensate for the moisture by keeping large fires burning in the basement. During the summer such fires were impracticable, and everything left in the basement was quickly covered with a greenish-white mold. The casemates were worse, because here the effect upon the health of long-continued dampness had to be considered, and if rheumatic and pulmonary diseases were to be avoided fires had to be kept going practically the year around.[19]

Inside the fort there were no sinks, in the general acceptance of the term. Officers living in the casemates made use of the officers' commode in the flagstaff bastion, which consisted of a series of six earth-closets. The families living in the casemates were obliged, if they had not furnished themselves with earth commodes, to make use of chamber utensils, which they emptied into the waters of the moat. The water closets of officers not residing in casemates were furnished with small boxes which were removed at variable periods, depending largely upon the temperature and season, and which were sprinkled with crude lime or with chloride of lime. The same arrangement cared for the hospital.

For the enlisted men, the sinks consisted of large copper tanks, mounted on wheels, which were run under the closets and which were changed every twenty-four hours, summer and winter. To save labor, orders provided that these should be used only at night, a main sink for day use being provided on the north side of the fort, outside the work, over a portion of Mill Creek beyond the low water mark. The night tanks were taken out of the fort and emptied into the waters of Hampton Roads northwest of the fort. The tides were depended upon to carry off the excrement, but at times, particularly during the summer, they were not sufficiently prompt, as all who passed became aware.[20]

On the whole, the police of the post was excellent, police details being sent out each morning to clean up the reservation. Carroll Hall was, upon occasion, reported as the sole exception to the general rule of satisfactory police. As this building was occupied by several families from among the officers of the garrison and was also used for library and museum purposes by the Artillery School, too many persons were responsible for its cleanliness and none actually kept clean its halls and stairs. From time to time it was necessary for the police detail or for a special fatigue detail to see that Carroll Hall kept up with the rest of the garrison in its appearance and its cleanliness.[21]

The water supply of the garrison was limited, there being scarcely enough for general use. In part, this had been cared for by the erection of large cisterns in connection with each house so that the rain water might be caught and kept. The later installation of a condenser of 5,000 gallons daily capacity in a casemate of the first front brought some relief, but the supply of water in adequate quantities remained—as it always had—a serious question which was not satisfactorily settled until 1898.[22]

As early as 1845 an effort had been made to sink a well to fresh water which, it was expected, would be found in sufficient quantity and with sufficient pressure to give an artesian well. In this first well, 225 feet of 8-inch pipe had first been sunk and then 283 feet of 5-inch pipe had been driven below the larger pipe before the attempt was given up. Work was suspended in 1851, but the results were not considered conclusive. Opinion still persisted that a well driven to a sufficient depth would find fresh water. A second well was therefore started by General Butler during the Civil War, his theory being that too small a pipe had been used in the first attempt. At the time of his relief a 12-inch pipe had been sunk to a depth of 340 feet, but with his departure operations were suspended, not to be resumed until 1867.

When operations were resumed, Colonel Henry Brewerton first withdrew 186 feet of 5-inch pipe and 120 feet of 8-inch pipe from the well of 1845, the 8-inch pipe to be driven inside the 12-inch pipe of the new well, which had been continued to a depth of 370 feet. At a depth of 517 feet, pipe of 4½ inches diameter, with screw ends, was inserted in the 8-inch pipe and driven to a depth of 570 feet, where a limited amount of saline water was found. Left undisturbed for twenty-four hours, this water rose to a height of four feet six inches above the level of the parade ground. Work continued on sinking the 4½-inch pipe until the well reached a depth of 906 feet below the ground level. At this depth, in August 1870, the work was suspended. In October 1871, operations were resumed by drilling, instead of boring, but little progress was made and work was again suspended in July 1872.

Nothing further was done until the subject was again brought up in 1890. In February 1891, Congress appropriated $6,000 for sinking a well at Fort Monroe but the amount was considered to be inadequate and the work was not at once undertaken. This sum would have permitted sinking a well to a depth of about a thousand feet, but the best available estimates indicated that water of a satisfactory quantity would not be found at a depth less than 1,200 to 1,500 feet. In February 1896, proposals were invited for sinking an artesian well under the available appropriation, but after an inquiry as to the character of water flowing from the well of the Chamberlin Hotel—which was decidedly saline— all bids were rejected, for there was no apparent prospect of obtaining a potable supply of water at a depth of less than a thousand feet.

In the meantime, it was decided not to await the results of well digging, and the post installed a supply system of its own. In 1885, after the erection of the brick barracks, the new system was completed. Water was brought across Mill Creek in pipes and delivered to tanks on the ramparts over the North Gate, whence it was distributed through the post. The water was drawn from surface wells on the north side of Mill Creek by means of a suction pump. The tank capacity was about 50,000 gallons, and the head of about sixty feet gave sufficient pressure for fire protection. This system continued to supply the garrison until 1898, when all quarters of the post were connected with the Newport News water system.

The post cemetery was situated to the west of a ridge of sand hills north of the fort—above the mortar batteries. It had been used for many years, and in the early part of the Civil War it was used to inter such as died at the Hygeia Hospital. In the years immediately following the war, many of the bodies were removed to the Hampton National Cemetery, and subsequently the remainder were removed and the cemetery abandoned, despite the fact that it had an estimated capacity of ten to fifteen thousand graves.[23]

For the enlisted men, the new barracks, built in 1879, materially improved conditions, as the new quarters did for the officers. The barrack building, in use today as an office building after modification, extended along the north side of the parade ground and was a fine, two-story brick structure of two wings, with a three-story center through which a sally-port was constructed. The building provided six sets of company quarters, forty-eight men to a company. A veranda ran the full length of the building on both floors. The offices, storerooms, wash rooms, kitchens, and dining rooms were on the first floor, and the squad rooms on the second. Steam heat was provided from a boiler house located immediately to the rear of the barrack building.

On one side of the sallyport at the center of the building was established a barber shop. On the other side, stairways ran to the second floor to a court martial room and to a "tank room" containing three large zinc tanks from which fresh water was supplied to the kitchens and bathrooms. The third floor of this section, under the clock tower, was the amusement room, in which were held dances, theatrical performances, and other amusements and gatherings until the floor was, about 1885, condemned and declared unsafe for dancing.

The interest of Captain James M. Ingalls in ballistics brought about the organization of the Department of Ballistics of the Artillery School in 1883, with him in charge. He at once prepared a text-book on ballistics, which was accepted and approved by the staff in May 1883, and was then published by the school. This is said to be the first work on exterior ballistics published in North America. Revised editions appeared in 1885 and 1886, and the work continued to be the standard treatise on exterior ballistics for a number of years.[24]

Beginning with the class of 1886, General Orders No. 108, Headquarters of the Army, 1885, changed from May 1 to September 1 of every alternate year the date for the relief of the graduating class. The primary object of this change was to adjust the time of leaving the Artillery School to that for the detail of lieutenants to the Military Academy, to light batteries, and to colleges, thereby avoiding for the government unnecessary expense and for the lieutenants the inconveniences of an additional move. Graduation exercises were thereafter held between June 20 and June 30 of the even-numbered years. In 1888 a limited course of instruction in submarine mining was introduced under the direction of Captain Ingalls.

During all the years preceding the outbreak of the Spanish-American War, the school progressed smoothly, without serious interruption of any sort and without much change in the personnel of the staff or faculty. The instruction companies were more or less permanent, as were the instructors, so that the change occurring in any one year was scarcely perceptible. General Barry had given way in 1877 to Colonel George W. Getty, who served as commandant until he was relieved by Colonel John C. Tidball in 1883.[25] This officer remained at the school until 1888, when Colonel Royal T. Frank succeeded to the command, which he retained until the war with Spain.[26]

Footnotes Chapter VIII

[1] General Orders No. 6, Adjutant General's Office, January 30, 1866.

[2] General Orders No. 16, Adjutant General's Office, March 12, 1866.

[3] General Order No. 3, Artillery School, February 25, 1868, NA, RG 393.

[4] Barry graduated from West Point in 1838 and served as a brigadier general of volunteers during the Civil War. He received four brevets during the war, including that of major general for gallant and meritorious service in the Atlanta Campaign. Barry became colonel of the 2d Artillery in 1865 and died in 1879. *Heitman*, p. 195.

[5] Fort Monroe Post Returns, October and November 1868 and September 1869, NA, RG 94.

[6] Fort Monroe Post Returns, July and September 1870, NA, RG 94.

[7] General Order No. 38, Artillery School, September 8, 1874, NA, RG 393.

[8] Fort Monroe Post Returns, November 1876, February and July 1877, NA, RG 94.

[9] Stephen E. Ambrose, *Upton and the Army* (Baton Rouge: Louisiana State University Press, 1964), pp. 96–97, 136–138, 145, 155. For a discussion of Upton's impact on the Army, see Russell F. Weigley, *History of the United States Army* (New York: The Macmillan Company, 1967), pp. 275–281, 336–340, 476, 497–498.

[10] *Chesapeake Zoological Laboratory* (Baltimore: Johns Hopkins University, 1878), pp. 1–4.

[11] Chester D. Bradley, *Harrison Phoebus: From Farm to Fortune* (Fort Monroe Casemate Museum, n.d.).

[12] Reprinted in "Fifty Years Ago at Fort Monroe," *Coast Artillery Journal*, 81 (March-April 1938), pp. 134–136.

[13] Circular No. 4, *A Report on Barracks and Hospitals with Descriptions of Military Posts* (Washington: War Department, Surgeon General's Office, 1870), p. 77.

[14] *Ibid.*

[15] *Ibid.*, pp. 74–75; Circular No. 8, *A Report on the Hygiene of the United States Army, with Descriptions of Military Posts* (Washington: War Department, Surgeon General's Office, May 1, 1875), p. 52.

[16] Circular No. 4, p. 75; Circular No. 8, pp. 52–53.

[17] Herrick served as post chaplain at Key West, Fla., from 1864 to 1867. He retired in 1890. *Heitman*, p. 526.

[18] Circular No. 4, p. 73.

[19] *Ibid.*, p. 74.

[20] *Ibid.*, p. 76.

[21] *Ibid.*, pp. 76–77.

[22] *Ibid.*, p. 78.

[23] *Ibid.*, p. 82.

[24] Ingalls had enlisted in the 16th Infantry in 1864 and was commissioned a second lieutenant in 1865. He transferred to the 1st Artillery in 1870, was promoted to captain in 1880, and retired as lieutenant colonel of the 5th Artillery in 1901. *Heitman*, p. 562.

[25] Getty graduated from West Point in 1840 and served during the Civil War as a brigadier general of volunteers. He became colonel of the 3d Artillery in 1870, transferred to the 4th Artillery in 1882, and retired in 1883. Getty was brevetted for gallantry once in the Mexican War and five times during the Civil War. He died in 1901. Tidball, who was born in Virginia, graduated from West Point in 1848. He served as colonel of the 4th New York Artillery during the Civil War, was colonel and aide-de-camp to General Sherman from 1881 to 1884, and became colonel of the 1st Artillery in 1885. Tidball was the author of the heavy artillery manual used for many years by the Artillery School. He received six brevets for gallantry during the Civil War. Tidball retired in 1889 and died in 1906. *Heitman*, pp. 452, 961; 1st Lt. Robert Arthur, "Historical Sketch of the Coast Artillery School," *Journal of the United States Artillery*, 44 (September-October 1915), pp. 198–200.

[26] Frank graduated from West Point in 1858 and served as a captain in the 8th Infantry during the Civil War. He was brevetted major and lieutenant colonel for gallantry during the war. He became lieutenant colonel of the 2d Artillery in 1889 and colonel of the 1st Artillery in 1894. During the Spanish-American War he served as a brigadier general of volunteers and in 1899 was promoted to brigadier general in the Regular Army and retired. He died in 1908. *Heitman*, p. 434; Arthur, "Historical Sketch of the Coast Artillery School," p. 200.

Chapter IX

The Modernization
of Fort Monroe

PRIOR TO THE CIVIL WAR the largest gun in service was the 10-inch
Rodman smoothbore, which discharged a projectile with an energy of
2,000 foot-tons. Under the stimulus of war necessity and experience, a
rapid development of ordnance began in which post-war guns rose rapidly
to around 6,865 foot-tons of energy. With this projectile development,
the old forts erected under the 1817 program were no longer adequate
for coast defense. Many of them retained some value as citadels, or keeps,
to secure the position against attack from the landward side and as flanking works for the protection of mine fields. With the introduction of
steam and armor in naval manufacture and with the development of
rifled guns and mortars, submarine mines, and elongated projectiles, it
was becoming apparent that the science of coast defense was entering a
new era. The new materiel had definitely destined our beautiful masonry
forts for the scrap heap and an entirely new system of coast fortification
had to be devised.

The extent to which the Army appreciated the fact that it was passing
through a period of transition was not, at this time, altogether apparent.
Under the influence of post-war lethargy—and of determined governmental economy—practically nothing of importance was accomplished
toward keeping our coast fortifications abreast of artillery and naval
developments in the twenty years which followed the war. From the
end of the Civil War to the Spanish-American War the Army had virtually
no guns other than the old smoothbores. New theories and new designs
followed individual research, but without appropriations the Army

could undertake no new construction and little experiment. The Artillery School struggled vainly to secure modern equipment and to teach modern methods, but no general revival of interest in military affairs became evident until about 1880.

In the meantime, the small sums that were appropriated by Congress were applied to the repair and upkeep of old fortifications. At Fort Monroe, nearly ready to celebrate its fiftieth anniversary, the work of upkeep was resumed in 1866. In that year operations were limited to the reinforcement of gun platforms, regrading the surfaces of the ramps, alteration of the Water Battery to adapt it to the 10-inch armament, erection of three front-pintle platforms[1] for 15-inch guns in the covered way, and some minor work.

Each year thereafter until 1886 saw additional work of this same general character. During 1867 gun platforms were relaid, the terreplain[2] and ramps were gravelled and repaired, and considerable repair work was effected in the Water Battery. In the following year work was limited mainly to the repair of floors, embrasures, terreplain, slopes, ramps, and roadways in the casemates, Water Battery, and redoubt. The most important work of the year was the construction of a breakwater on the beach opposite the second (southeast) front.

In 1869, in addition to the repairs that seemed always to be necessary, center-pintle platforms for 15-inch guns were laid in the fourth front and the parapet increased in thickness, and a similar gun platform was built in the covered way. In 1870 the principal work consisted of rebuilding the bridge leading to the Main Gate, the construction of two brick cisterns, and the remodeling of the prison and guard rooms on either side of the Main Gate. A breakwater, sheathed with planks, and backed by large stones, sand, etc., was built opposite fronts one and two during 1871, apparently replacing the breakwater of three years before.

No appropriations were made for the fiscal year 1872 and repairs were of a very minor character; but with the $42,500 available on July 1 for the next fiscal year, operations became somewhat more extensive. Projects prepared by the Board of Engineers for Fortifications for the modifications needed to adapt the fort for heavy guns of the largest size had been on hand for some time but, from want of appropriations, nothing had been accomplished beyond repairs and upkeep. The sum appropriated in 1872, reduced by $500 the following year, became $30,000 in 1874 and $20,000 in 1875. Nevertheless, in so far as these amounts permitted, the military authorities undertook to carry out the project of modification.

Six shot furnaces designed to heat shot to set wooden ships on fire were removed in 1873, and the masonry of the magazine and foundations for two guns were completed the next year. In 1874, also, a project was approved by the Secretary of War for a battery of ten heavy guns to be mounted outside the fronts one, two, and three, prepared by the Board of Engineers for Fortification. During the rest of the decade, however, operations were limited almost altogether to absolutely necessary repairs.

For Fort Monroe the approved plans for adapting the fort for efficient defense against naval vessels contemplated arming the channel front of the advanced redoubt with heavy barbette guns provided with suitable traverses and traverse magazines; mounting a similar armament in the re-entering place of arms,[3] located on the right of the redoubt in advance of front five; constructing a new open battery for barbette guns to the right of the old casemated Water Battery; and placing a few heavy guns in the salients of the main work and covered way. Little progress was ever made toward the completion of these plans, and in 1886 work on Forts Monroe and Wool was definitely suspended and all projects for modification of existing works were held in abeyance pending approval and publication of the findings of the Endicott Board.

This board, of which Secretary of War William C. Endicott was president, was convened as the "Board on Fortifications or Other Defenses" and was appointed by President Grover Cleveland under the provisions of an act of Congress approved March 3, 1885. Its duties included the selection of places along the coasts of the United States as sites for defensive works, the determination of the amount of armament required for each place, an estimate of costs, and a recommendation of priorities. The board was composed of Army, Navy, and civilian representatives. The report, which was voluminous and comprehensive, was published in 1886 and thereafter formed the basis of all sea-coast construction until changing conditions brought about a need for revision shortly after the Spanish-American War.

Nine-tenths of the armament recommended by the Endicott Board for our seacoast was to be mounted in detached batteries in rear of earthen parapets surmounting and protecting masonry magazines, bombproofs, and storerooms. The basic idea was fundamentally and completely opposed to the close grouping of guns which formed an essential part of the old system, and with the inauguration of the project the old stone and masonry forts, which had been erected at great cost and greater labor, were definitely relegated to the past. The fort at Old Point Comfort was left to stand an object of sentiment and beauty rather than one of utility. It had served its purpose, and now it gave way to a system of fortification which had, in principle, been in vogue a hundred years before.[4]

In the report of the Endicott Board, Hampton Roads was placed fifth in order of urgency, following New York, San Francisco, Boston, and the Great Lakes ports. The fortifications recommended for Fort Monroe included turrets, armored casemates, barbette batteries, mortar batteries, and submarine mines, with eighteen torpedo boats for service in

Hampton Roads and in Chesapeake Bay. The recommended armament consisted of four 16-inch 110-ton breech-loading rifles in two 2-gun turrets, ten 12-inch 50-ton breech-loading rifles in casemates, twenty 10-inch 27-ton breech-loading rifles on both disappearing and nondisappearing carriages, and sixteen 12-inch rifled mortars. Exclusive of the armament itself, the new construction would, it was estimated, cost $4,062,000. The armament and mountings were to cost $1,142,000. Four hundred submarine mines, together with the necessary mine equipment, added $208,000 to the estimate; and eighteen torpedo boats added $1,080,000. Fort Monroe, brought up to date, was thus to cost the nation some $7,492,000 from a total of $126,377,800 recommended for the entire coast.

During the fifteen years prior to 1890 no appropriations had been made for the construction of works for seacoast defense. In this period great advances had been made in the design and manufacture of ordnance, and it certainly appeared that the time had become propitious for the construction of coast fortifications. Many months were required in which to digest the recommendations of the Endicott Board and to prepare initial plans. With the appropriation of $1,221,000 in August 1890, and of $750,000 in February 1891, for the construction of defensive works at Boston, New York, San Francisco, Hampton Roads, and Washington, the Endicott project got under way. The initial allotment for Hampton Roads was $151,848, intended to provide a battery of two 10-inch guns.

New concepts of ordnance design had made possible the batteries proposed by the Endicott Board. The availability of steel and the ability to produce massive forgings permitted the development of the compound gun. The barrels of these guns were produced by the successive shrinking on of many separate concentric tube members rather than by machining it from a single casting. The development late in the century of machined breechblocks led to the adoption of breech-loading guns. New powders were also developed during this period greatly increasing muzzle velocities and led to the lengthening of gun barrels for more efficient operation.[5]

The modernization of Fort Monroe eventually resulted in the installation of 10-inch and 12-inch disappearing guns, 6-inch barbette guns, 3-inch barbette rapid fire guns, and 12-inch mortars. A few 8-inch barbette guns were also mounted, but these had disappeared by World War I. The 12-inch guns had a useful range of some 13,500 yards (seven to eight miles) with a 1,000-pound projectile. Although flat-trajectory guns with a firing angle limited to about fifteen degrees of elevation, these guns had a range to match or outshoot the battleships of that day. The disappearing guns were mounted on a carriage which utilized the energy of recoil to lower the gun within the emplacement, where it could be serviced and loaded, concealed and protected from the enemy until raised for the next shot.

The 12-inch mortars were grouped four to a pit. These stubby weapons were fired simultaneously to throw their 700-pound projectiles in high arcs to descend almost vertically on the lightly armored decks of ships. The two forward mortars of each pit were the least accessible and the most distant from the magazines and therefore took the longest to load. Since none of the mortars could be fired until the area was cleared, the rate of fire was held to the speed with which the front weapons could be loaded.

Both the disappearing guns and the mortars were mounted in massive emplacements. At Fort Monroe these emplacements had to be constructed on the beach and resembled at a distance small hills. Their concrete frontal walls were as much as twenty feet thick behind thirty or more additional feet of sand. The sand had a grass cover which both prevented erosion and helped camouflage the gun positions. The ammunition magazines for the disappearing guns were located immediately adjacent to the gun emplacements, but at a level several feet lower. They were protected by a roof of twelve or more feet of reinforced concrete. The projectiles were raised to the gun platform by a mechanical hoist and then moved to the guns by hand trucks.

The 3-inch and 6-inch guns used ammunition light enough to be handled manually. They were mounted behind steel shields on pedestal carriages, set in plain concrete emplacements with low surrounding parapets and adjacent protected magazines. The primary purpose of these guns was to protect the submarine mines which formed an important part of the harbor defenses.[6]

The rapid development in ordnance design, naval construction, and range finding and fire control which continued in the years immediately following the publication of the report of the Endicott Board led to numerous modifications in the original plan, even before it was undertaken, and its entire completion along the projected lines was probably never really contemplated. At the time at which work was first started, the approved project for Fort Monroe provided for five 12-inch guns on lifts, ten 10-inch guns on disappearing carriages, thirty-two 12-inch mortars, and submarine mines operated from two mining casemates. As will be seen, even this modified project received modification as the work progressed.[7]

Work began first on the redoubt north of the fort in October 1891. The redoubt had originally been built for small guns and infantry defense, but it had been changed in 1874 to a battery of six 15-inch guns. This conversion was left uncompleted in 1875 because of the lack of appropriations for fortifications. The massive stone platforms were arranged in sets of two, with the magazines in the intervals. The magazines with their sand covering also served as traverses. The work of removing the redoubt was difficult and it was March 1892 before mixing and laying of concrete for the new emplacement was begun.[8]

In December 1892 the construction of an emplacement for a third 10-inch gun on the beach north of the fort was authorized, but both of these emplacements were materially delayed pending a decision as to the particular type of carriage to be adopted.[9] Adoption of the Buffington-Crozier disappearing carriage enabled the work to be completed in the spring of 1896. The Buffington-Crozier carriage was designed by Col. Adelbert R. Buffington and Capt. William Crozier. The carriage consisted of a pair of massive lever arms to support the gun tube. When fired, the tube and the upper end of the arms were carried to the rear and downward by recoil energy, which at the same time raised a heavy lead counterweight attached to the opposite end of the arms. An advantage of this carriage was that regardless of the angle at which the gun was fired, it always recoiled to the same position with respect to the pavement behind the carriage. This made it possible to load the gun directly from the wheeled shot trucks on which the ammunition was brought from the magazines. It was possible with a well trained crew to fire two rounds per minute.[10]

The carriages and guns were mounted during 1897 and the batteries were turned over to the artillery at the close of the year. The total cost of Battery Bomford, the two-gun battery, was reported as $154,379.99. The single 10-inch gun emplacement, known at this time as Redoubt B, eventually formed part of Battery Church. The guns in Battery Bomford were two 10-inch Model 1888 M-II weapons. A Model 1888 M-I 10-inch disappearing gun was mounted in Redoubt B. These two models were similar in construction and power, the only difference being in the number of steel hoops used in their manufacture. They had a maximum range of 12,259 yards.[11]

The mortars were considered as coming next in point of urgency, and in March 1895 an allotment of $100,000 was made to provide for the construction of a mortar battery consisting of sixteen 12-inch mortars. Instead of the typical four-pit quadrangle, it was decided to place the four pits in a straight line, thereby reducing the cost of construction by something like $65,000. Trees were cleared, the railroad line from the wharf was extended to the proposed site of the battery just to the north of Redoubt B, and materials were collected during the year. Work on the battery itself was begun in August 1896, but with the possibility of war with Spain becoming greater every day efforts were made to rush the battery to completion. The carriages for the mortar battery arrived early in 1897 and were assembled that summer, but the mortars did not arrive until the following spring when war was certain and imminent. Hurried efforts succeeded in mounting the mortars during 1898 and the battery was completed by the summer of 1899. The Model 1890 M-I mortars were originally mounted on twelve Model 1896 and four Model 1891 carriages. The mortars had a range of between 2,210 yards and about 15,000 yards. The Model 1891 carriages were not altogether satisfactory and were changed in the fall of 1901 to conform to the rest of the battery. The four mortar pits were divided into two batteries, Battery Anderson consisting of the southern two pits and Battery Ruggles of the northern two.[12]

One other battery was started before the war with Spain. With funds appropriated under the act of March 3, 1897, it was proposed to construct an emplacement for one 10-inch gun mounted on an experimental disappearing carriage, model of 1894. The site chosen was in the small redan opposite the fifth front of the fort, and the work was undertaken in November 1897. This emplacement was eventually named Battery Humphreys.[13]

All through these first years of the project progress was slow, mainly because the available appropriations were limited and the places to be defended were numerous. The Spanish-American War brought greater liberality in appropriations with the National Defense Act and stimulated activity toward the completion of the project. At the outbreak of the war Fort Monroe had under way or completed the two-gun 10-inch battery in the redoubt, called Redoubt A, the one-gun 10-inch battery on the spit, called Redoubt B, the experimental 10-inch battery, and the sixteen-gun 12-inch mortar battery. During 1898, the following construction was undertaken:[14]

a. One 8-inch rifle mounted on A.R.F. barbette carriage, Model 1892. This gun had been mounted since 1895 on a platform at the northern end of the water battery for use in target practice. As this position was disadvantageous, the gun was moved to a platform behind cover of the mining casemate and was mounted in June. This battery was eventually designated Battery Barber. A 12-inch mortar on a Model 1891 carriage was also mounted north of the water battery for target practice in 1895.[15]

b. One 10-inch gun emplacement, begun in March, to be the right half of Redoubt B and to form, with the gun in that emplacement, a two-gun battery eventually named Battery Church. The gun was mounted in the fall of 1899 and was turned over to the artillery in January 1901.[16]

c. Two 10-inch gun emplacements, northeast of Redoubt A, begun in March to form a battery called Redoubt C. The guns were mounted in 1899 and the battery was turned over to the artillery in January 1901. The guns in this battery, eventually named Battery Eustis, were Model 1888 M-II disappearing rifles.[17]

d. Four 4.72-inch rapid-fire gun emplacements on the barbette tier of front 4 over the East Gate. Three emplacements were begun in April and completed during the summer, the fourth being added in 1899. These

British Armstrong rapid-fire guns, Model 1898, were the only quick firing modern armament at Fort Monroe during the Spanish-American War. The battery was subsequently designated Battery Gatewood, but the armament was removed soon after the turn of the century.[18]

e. Four 8-inch rifles temporarily mounted on the rampart of the fort, one on the site of a 15-inch Rodman gun in bastion No. 3 and the others in bastion No. 2 and on front 3. Two of these guns and their carriages were removed within the year and shipped elsewhere[19] and the others soon after.

f. Three 12-inch guns, begun in July, to form a single battery between Redoubts B and C. The guns and carriages were mounted in June 1901. This battery, which eventually was named Battery DeRussy, mounted three 12-inch disappearing rifles, Model 1895, on Model 1897 carriages. The guns had a maximum range of 11,636 yards.[20]

g. One 10-inch gun in the bastion near the East Gate, begun during the summer. The gun and carriage were received in 1900. This battery, which was never named, mounted an experimental 10-inch gun known as a depressing gun. The gun was removed soon after the turn of the century.[21]

While this modernization of the armament at Fort Monroe was being accomplished, there was an equal activity in the improvement of the post along other lines. Barracks and quarters had been built in the 'Eighties and were connected to a sewage system which had later been extended to include the entire post—non-military as well as military. Shortly after the housing program was undertaken, the Fort Monroe Arsenal transferred to the artillery all the buildings which it controlled inside the fort. Already the activities of the arsenal had been curtailed to such an extent as to presage the shutdown which occurred at the end of 1901, and ultimately all its buildings were transferred to the artillery.

One of the first improvements which had to be undertaken in preparation for the construction program was the enlargement of the wharfage facilities to accommodate the great quantities of heavy materials which would be used. The act of Congress making provision for the sundry civil expenses of the government for the fiscal year ending June 30, 1887, appropriated $100,000—to which $75,000 were subsequently added—for the construction of a wharf at Fort Monroe. The site which was selected for the new wharf included the Baltimore Wharf, so first the Engineer Wharf was repaired and enlarged and was then used as a landing place for all vessels stopping at Fort Monroe. Actual work on the main wharf was started early in August 1888, but progress was slow and the wharf was not completed and opened to the public until the latter part of September 1889. The storehouse on the wharf was finished in the summer of 1890. An iron pile bridge over Mill Creek, leading from the causeway to the town of Phoebus, was completed and opened to traffic during May 1890.

An important addition to post life during this period was made by the erection of the Chamberlin Hotel. The apparent prosperity of the Hygeia Hotel had indicated that another such hostelry could be supported on the reservation. Accordingly, a joint resolution of Congress, approved March 3, 1887, authorized John F. Chamberlin to construct a hotel, provided the consent of the State of Virginia should be obtained. Early in 1890 the Old Point Comfort Hotel Company was incorporated under the laws of Virginia to take over the right of Chamberlin. The company undertook the construction of the hotel but, because of an insufficiency of funds, was forced to discontinue work when the building was under roof but before it had been completed. Passing through the hands of a receiver, the property was taken over by the Hampton Roads Hotel Company and carried to completion. It was opened to the public on April 4, 1896, and continued for many years to be a popular resort hotel.[22]

The Chamberlin Hotel, which stood across the road leading to the main wharf from the Hygeia Hotel, became the social center of the post in the years before World War I. The hotel made every effort not only to attract the tourist trade, but also to become a gathering place for the officers of the garrison. After the full dress retreat parade held every afternoon on the parade ground, the young lieutenants could take their girls down to the Chamberlin for free tea and cookies. Many of the lieutenants formed a mess for a period at the hotel, being furnished with all the food they could eat for $42.50 a month. The hotel hostess introduced girls visiting the Chamberlin to the young officers. A favorite meeting place immediately before World War I was the "Padded Cell," a small room with a circular table and padded walls which provided a primitive sound proofing. The "Padded Cell" immediately adjoined the Chamberlin's ballroom where the afternoon tea dances were held. Although somewhat restricted by the war, the Chamberlin continued as the focus of the gay social life of Fort Monroe until the hotel burned to the ground early on the morning of March 7, 1920.[23]

In July 1894, the Artillery School moved its headquarters from the old buildings inside the fort into the new administration building (Building 77) just outside the main sallyport, now used for post headquarters. The Ordnance Machine Shop (Building 27) of the Fort Monroe Arsenal had already been turned over to the Artillery School and had been remodeled to serve as instruction rooms and laboratory for the school. Only the school library remained inside the fort.

Protection of the shore line also received attention during these years. The strip of beach south of the fort which is now referred to as the water front, had early received care, but the continuing erosion of the strip of sand to the northeast of the fort, leading to the cemetery, had passed comparatively unnoted until it was required to provide sites for the batteries to be constructed under the new project. It was then discovered that the tidal currents threatened soon to cut the strip entirely in two, and steps were immediately taken to preserve what still remained. In March 1891, the construction of four pile jetties, projecting into the water, was undertaken. The first of these was put in about nine hundred feet east of the Engineer Wharf, and the others were built at intervals of 500 to 1,000 feet.[24]

In a severe gale lasting four days in September 1894, the breakwater between the Hygeia Hotel tract and the Engineer Wharf was seriously damaged and the beach in the rear of jetty No. 1 was badly washed. This breakwater dated back to 1883, when 650 feet of sheet piling breakwater had been built and the space in the rear of the roadway had been filled and graded. It was decided, after the storm, to protect the beach with a sea wall of concrete placed four feet nine inches in front of the old pile breakwater. Work was started at the Engineer Wharf, and was completed by the end of August 1895. Three 12-foot spur jetties were built outward from the foot of the wall and steps of concrete were made and set in the wall for the convenience of the bathers. The area behind the wall was filled with sand. In August 1900, work was begun extending the sea wall to jetty No. 1, and by the end of June 1902, 508 feet of wall had been completed.

To assist in the movement of the large quantity of materials involved in the modernization of the post, rail connection with the outside world was highly desirable. The lines of the Chesapeake and Ohio Railway Company terminated at Phoebus, just about a mile from Fort Monroe. The question of extending the tracks to a point on the reservation had long been under discussion, and an act of Congress approved July 3, 1884, had authorized the extension under such restrictions as the Secretary of War might impose. The matter hung fire until 1890, principally because the interested parties could come to no agreement concerning the location of the station. Terms were finally agreed upon and a revocable license was granted in November 1895. This license restricted freight to that for residents of the post, definitely forbidding through shipments.

In the meantime, a street railway was added to the facilities of the post. Authority was conferred upon the Secretary of War by act of Congress approved March 3, 1891, to permit the Hampton and Old Point Electric Company "to construct, maintain, and operate a street railway over and upon the lands of the Government reservation at Fort Monroe, Va., upon such locations and upon such plans, dimensions, conditions, and requirements as may be prescribed and approved by the Secretary of War." Articles of agreement were signed in November, but were modified in March 1892, to permit extension of the tracks to the main wharf. This railway proved to be a great convenience to the inhabitants of the neighboring communities, and great quantities of fruit, vegetables, fish, oysters, crabs, etc., were shipped, via the electric road, from the wharf at Old Point Comfort.

On the evening of December 22, 1896, the three upper stories of the Sherwood Inn were burned, a fire having started on the upper story of the main building. The nucleus of this establishment consisted of a cottage erected by Dr. Robert Archer in 1843. Dr. Archer had originally been post surgeon but resigned to become post sutler and had built the cottage as a residence. At an early date the cottage became an eating-house. Its ownership passed through several hands to Mrs. S. F. Eaton in 1867. She continued in possession for twenty years, enlarging the property from time to time and operating it as a boarding house. By 1889 it had a capacity of 175 guests, and later it was called the New Sherwood. Ownership was acquired by the government during World War I, and the property served for a period as officers' quarters and mess until the completion of Randolph Hall in 1932, when the building was condemned and salvaged.

Fire control stations were required to accompany the installation of armament, and their construction was early undertaken. The first range finder tower was completed and transferred to the artillery in April 1896. Two observation stations and the second mining casemate were completed early in 1898. The tide station was finished in 1901.

For a good many years the Artillery School had been hampered by a lack of modern equipment, the student officers studying smoothbore guns long after rifled guns had been adopted throughout the world. This was all being remedied and much new equipment had been received when the war with Spain interrupted the operations of the school. The service of the student officers and of the instruction batteries were required elsewhere. The class was graduated on March 17, 1898, and the operations of the school were "temporarily suspended," the school board holding its last meeting on May 17.

This class of 1898 contained probably the most famous graduate of the Artillery School. First Lieutenant Peyton C. March, 5th Artillery, reported with the class and spent almost two years at Fort Monroe mastering the theoretical and practical instruction covering photography, engineering, chemistry, and electricity, besides artillery, mines, explosives, and ballistics. Clarence C. Williams later commented that, "Anything he had to do, he did well." March consistently ranked high, but Ernest Hinds led the class. March went on to become the Chief of Staff of the Army during World War I.[25]

The school had been in practically uninterrupted operation for thirty years, and had graduated nineteen classes, eight during the period of one-year courses and eleven during the period of two-year courses. Practically all of the lieutenants of artillery had taken the course at the school, many of them returning a second time. Not infrequently other branches of the service, and even the Navy or the Marine Corps, had been represented in the classes. The system of instruction had followed a slow but sure development to a higher plane. When the school was started in 1868, the course, for many reasons, was of only the most elementary character. This continued so until the change to the two-year course in 1876, when much of the elementary instruction was discontinued.[26] At about this time, and each year thereafter, Congress granted a small appropriation which provided the school with many machines, instruments, books, and other appliances essential to more advanced instruction. The school, springing from nothing, was, at the start, without experienced instructors. This gradually corrected itself, and once experienced instructors were secured they were retained at the school almost indefinitely.

The outbreak of the war with Spain closed the Artillery School, drew most of the garrison away, and made the post hospital into a general hospital. At the opening of the year 1898 there were stationed at Fort Monroe eight batteries. Battery G, 5th Artillery, had been there for more than twelve years, and only three of the eight batteries had been present for less than eight years. Four batteries joined between March and May, and Batteries I and K, 6th Artillery, were organized at the post late in March. Of these fourteen batteries, eight left the post before the end of June. The 1st Maryland Volunteers joined in May and July, but departed in September, reducing the garrison to six batteries, including the two new batteries of the 6th Artillery. Battery H, 4th Artillery, joined in September 1898, as did Battery G of the same regiment, in the following May. Batteries N and O, 4th Artillery, were organized at the post in April 1899. Seven of these batteries were ordered away during the spring, reducing the garrison to Batteries G, N, and O, 4th Artillery.[27]

An outbreak of yellow fever in the Soldiers' Home and in Hampton caused a quarantine of the post to be established on July 30, 1899. The entire garrison, except for a limited number of caretakers, was removed promptly to Plum Island to avoid the dread disease. The quarantine was lifted on August 15 but the troops remained away until after the end of the month, rejoining in September. Two batteries of the 1st Artillery joined in December, and four batteries left in the spring of 1900. Their place was taken by six batteries, the new garrison consisting of one battery from each of the seven regiments of artillery. These organizations were assembled for the purpose of constituting the instruction troops of the Artillery School whenever that institution should reopen its doors.[28]

The one local flurry of real excitement during the war came on April 22, 1898, when telegraphic instructions directed that the submarine mines be planted. A mine field of 105 mines was promptly set out, the number of mines on each line varying from six to fifteen. Regulations for the navigation of the mine field were promulgated on April 24 but their effectiveness may be questioned. Repairs to the mine field became a daily necessity, resulting partly from natural causes but mostly from the carelessness and indifference of masters of vessels passing through the field. Aside from the damage caused by shipping, the greatest trouble came from leaks and broken leads. The mine field was raised in August 1898.

The interruption caused by the war continued for three years before the authorities in Washington felt free to resume the courses at the Artillery School. It is probable that, had the war not occurred, there would nevertheless have been somewhat of a change in the system of conducting the school, for in 1897 the War Department had decided to effect its complete reorganization. Work along this line had been carried to the drafting of a code of regulations and its submission to the Adjutant General when the war necessitated a suspension of all school duty and the withdrawal of the greater part of the garrison.

Following the war the artillery was increased in strength, and the appointments incident to the increase, as well as those resulting from the war, brought into that branch a great many junior officers who had not yet had the opportunity to attend the Artillery School. The capacity of the school being definitely limited, the new regulations issued on April 28, 1900 provided for a return to a one-year course of instruction.[29]

The last of the school batteries arrived in June, and the detailed student officers reported shortly thereafter. The·personnel having joined, the Artillery School resumed operations on September 3, 1900, with Colonel Francis L. Guenther as commandant.[30]

Through all the movements of the garrison during and after the war, the Engineers continued actively their operations of constructing emplacements to receive new armament. The work begun in 1898 was hastened toward completion, for it constituted the major part of the program for Fort Monroe. Battery Irwin, an emplacement for a battery of four 15-pounder rapid-fire guns was undertaken in the early spring of 1900. The guns were mounted in 1902 and 1903, but were removed following World War I. This battery was on the main channel directly opposite Fort Wool.[31]

Immediately adjoining Battery Irwin, an emplacement for two 12-inch guns was begun in 1901. The construction of this battery necessitated the removal of the Water Battery in front of the East Gate of the fort. The two Model 1900 12-inch disappearing guns were mounted in 1905 and the battery was turned over to the artillery in the following year. The construction of Battery Parrott cost $211,500. This battery contained the most powerful weapons ever mounted at Fort Monroe and it became during the ensuing years a showpiece for the post and the Coast Artillery School. These guns each weighed fifty-nine tons and had a maximum range of about 17,000 yards. At 8,700 yards, shells from these guns could penetrate twelve inches of battleship armor, and even at the extreme range could still penetrate seven inches of armor.[32]

In the fall of 1901 work began on the last of the major batteries, an emplacement for two 6-inch guns. This battery, named Battery Montgomery, was completed in 1904 at a cost of approximately $24,000. The armament consisted of two 6-inch Model 1900 rifles on barbette carriages, protected by armor shields. The battery was located between Battery DeRussy and Battery Church. The guns had a range of 13,077 yards. This was the last of the batteries erected under the Endicott program to remain in service, the guns and carriages being removed in March 1948. The program was getting down to small calibers, and in the spring of 1902 platforms for two 2.4-inch Driggs-Schroeder rapid-fire guns were built on the barbette tier of the old fort for saluting purposes.[33]

Work also began soon after the turn of the century on the modernization of Fort Wool. Various plans had been proposed since the 1880's to modernize the uncompleted fort, but no work was actually undertaken until the program at Fort Monroe was nearly completed. Preparatory work for a battery of four 15-pounders began in December 1901 and actual construction commenced in June 1902. The battery, known as Battery Henry Lee, was finished during 1905 at a cost of approximately $40,000. In January 1903 work began on another 15-pounder battery of two guns. This battery, called Battery Jacob Hindman, was also completed in 1905 at a cost of approximately $14,800. During May 1903, an allotment of $1,000 was made to prepare drawings and investigate the sites for six 6-inch rifles on disappearing carriages. An appropriation of $165,000 was made in November 1903 for construction of these emplacements and the work was completed early in 1908. The 6-inch guns were divided into three two gun batteries called Batteries Ferdinand Claiborne, Alexander Dyer, and Horatio Gates. The completion of these batteries brought to an end the Endicott program in Hampton Roads. The 6-inch guns were similar to those at Battery Montgomery except that they were mounted on disappearing carriages. The two rapid fire batteries mounted 3-inch Model 1902 M1 guns on barbette carriages.[34]

As may be seen, in making provision for the later developments of war material, the details of the defense provided for Fort Monroe had departed materially from those recommended by the Endicott Board. Even so, the project had not remained entirely abreast of developments. The greater effective ranges possible with the later rifled cannon, increased efficiency in the design and operation of disappearing carriages, development of the 14-inch gun, improvements in range-finding and fire-control equipment, and changes in naval construction all pointed to a complete revision of the project recommended by the Endicott Board. The current project threatened to become obsolete even before it was completed.

Garrison review on parade ground of Fort Monroe about 1910.

Garrison drill and main barracks circa 1905

The fleet steaming past Fort Monroe about 1910.

Ruins of first Chamberlin Hotel following fire on March 7, 1920.

A 12-inch mortar pit prior to World War I.

Loading a 10-inch disappearing gun of Battery Church.

Loading a 12-inch disappearing gun in Battery Parrott while the gun in the background fires. World War I.

Firing one of the 12-inch disappearing guns.

3-inch rapid fire guns, M1898 - Battery Irwin ca. 1910; Chamberlin Hotel and Old Point Comfort Lighthouse in background.

Firing 12-inch disappearing gun of Battery DeRussy.

12-inch mortar of Battery Anderson firing.

69th Company, Coast Artillery Corps, poses on a 12-inch disappearing gun.

12-inch disappearing gun of Battery DeRussy in lowered position.

For this reason, the National Coast Defense Board, headed by Secretary of War William H. Taft, was convened in 1905 to resurvey the whole coast defense situation. The board went into considerable detail, added new places to the list of ports to be defended, recommended the exact number and calibers of guns and mortars to be emplaced at each port, and submitted careful estimates of the cost of emplacements, armament, sites, submarine mine equipment, power plants, searchlights, fire control equipment, and modernization of the older emplacements at each place. The major technical changes brought about by the Taft Board were in accessory harbor defense equipment.[35]

So far as the armament of Fort Monroe is concerned, modernization may therefore be considered to have ended with the completion of the work in hand in 1902. The changes which occurred after that date—whether in the nature of addition of new armament, equipment, and structures or of removal and demolition of some works erected under the earlier project—were until World War II all in the nature of modifications of a completed program. All of the old pieces were dismounted and removed, although a few of them still remain on the post as ornaments. The Lincoln Gun, the original 15-inch Rodman gun, is on the edge of the parade ground. Special mention might perhaps also be made of No. 40, now standing in the grassy triangle in front of post headquarters. No. 40 got it's name of "Lover's Gun" from its position in the Water Battery and its fame from the fact that it was the favorite trysting place for the youth of an earlier generation.[36]

Following the experiences of the Spanish-American War, a major reorganization of the Army took place. A significant aspect of this reorganization was the breaking up of the seven regiments of artillery in 1901 into separate companies of coast artillery and batteries of field artillery. All of these were placed in a single Artillery Corps, but in 1907 the two types of artillery were formally separated into the Field Artillery and the Coast Artillery Corps. As a result of the 1901 reorganization, the garrison at Fort Monroe was composed of the 6th, 13th, 35th, 41st, 58th, 69th, and 73d Companies, Coast Artillery Corps.

One other project remained before the modernization of Fort Monroe could be called complete. As a result of the reorganization there was a greatly increased number of officers demanding instruction at the Artillery School which seriously taxed the facilities of the institution and the housing capacity of the post. Nine officers had been graduated in 1901, thirteen in 1902, twenty in 1903, thirty-two in 1904, and forty-one in 1905, at which number the classes remained practically constant for a number of years. In addition to the regular school classes, all newly commissioned second lieutenants, whether from West Point or appointed directly from civil life, also were sent to Fort Monroe. These officers, known as "Incs" because they were members of the "incubator class," spent several months learning military fundamentals.

The personnel of the Artillery School consisted of the commandant, the adjutant, and the instructors and assistant instructors, in addition to the troops and the student personnel. The school board, consisting of the commandant as president and the heads of the various departments as members, met at least once a week during the course of instruction; and the commandant submitted quarterly reports to the Adjutant General. This latter requirement, however, was soon modified so as to require annual reports only.

The school for the enlisted men consisted at the start of only a "school for electrician sergeants." This school had been established at Fort Monroe on December 22, 1899, and was made a part of the Artillery School by General Orders No. 71, A.G.O., 1900. It did not long remain a part of the school, for in 1901, pursuant to General Orders No. 157, it was transferred to the School of Submarine Defense, at Fort Totten, New York.

Beginning with the regulations published in 1900 it was for seven or eight years customary to issue revised regulations for the Artillery School almost annually. In these regulations appears for the first time since the original organization of the school a provision exempting the student officers from all ordinary garrison duties, including courts martial, boards of survey, and such drills as were not included in the course of instruction. This provision was later extended to include the instructors and assistant instructors. During this second school year, attention was again turned to the instruction of the enlisted men, with the result that a class of gunnery specialists was formed to begin instruction on October 20, 1902.

To meet the expansion during these years, new school buildings and new barracks and quarters were required. These were provided in a program of construction which began in 1906 and continued until 1912, during which time all permanent barracks and quarters numbered higher than 100 were provided. The construction included two barrack buildings, a bachelor building, a post exchange, the school buildings and library, quartermaster and commissary buildings, and many quarters for officers and noncommissioned officers. Last to be provided under this program was the barrack building for the Coast Artillery School Detachment, which was completed in 1912. During the same period, practically all of the older buildings were completely overhauled or modified and brought up to date in the matter of conveniences.

Colonel Guenther had been replaced in command in March 1902 by Colonel John P. Story, who held the position until January 1904. Colonel Ramsay D. Potts succeeded to the command, in turn being replaced in October 1906 by Colonel Francis E. Harrison. Following the retirement of Colonel Harrison in early 1909, Lieutenant Colonel Clarence P. Townsley assumed command of Fort Monroe.[37]

With the completion of both the armament and housing programs, Fort Monroe became a strictly up-to-date and efficiently manned coast fort. By 1912, the Coast Artillery Corps had attained a higher degree of efficiency than it had ever before known. Its personnel was highly trained and fully competent to perform any task to which it might be detailed; its organizations were large enough to justify their existence and had few vacancies; and its morale was extraordinarily high. At Fort Monroe the officers and men were all comfortably housed and the post was provided with every facility required for its efficient operation. The Coast Artillery School, too, was in excellent condition, both physically and educationally, and was offering courses of instruction through which it deservedly attained high rank among military schools of the world.

With the separation of the Coast and Field Artilleries in 1907 came a reorganization of the Artillery School under the name of "The Coast Artillery School." In the spring of 1907, the War Department decided that the interests of the service in general and of the Coast Artillery in particular would be advanced by uniting the School of Submarine Defense, at Fort Totten, with the Coast Artillery School, at Fort Monroe, the combined school to be located at the latter place. The consolidation was duly effected, and the Officers' Division of the school, with its newly arranged course, opened on September 1, 1908, with ten officers in the advanced class and thirty in the regular class. The Enlisted Men's Division opened on October 1, with fifty-one men present for instruction in the three courses—artillery, electrical, and mechanical.

In 1909, new buildings for the Officers' Division and for the Enlisted Men's Division of the school and a new building for the library were completed and occupied. On July 1 of this same year was organized, under act of Congress approved March 3, 1909, a detachment of seventy-five enlisted men of various grades at the Coast Artillery School to give assistance and to perform the duties in connection with the school which had, prior to this time, been performed by men detailed from the Coast Artillery at large. In February, a secretary for the school was detailed, who relieved the adjutant of the Artillery District of Chesapeake Bay of all duties pertaining to the school, including disbursements and the command of the school detachment and of the detachment of casuals undergoing instruction.[38] With the changes made during the year, the School became a separate entity with its own personnel. This released it from much dependence on the garrison though it was still part of the post. The Commandant, being also the Commanding Officer of the Artillery District of Chesapeake Bay, had available the troops, batteries, and facilities of the post for such instruction and firings as required.

The most serious accident ever to take place at Fort Monroe occurred on the morning of July 21, 1910. The heavy coastal batteries were engaged in the largest battle practice held up to that time. Present at Fort Monroe were the Chief of Coast Artillery and the Chief of Ordnance as well as many other high ranking officers. As Gun No. 1 of Battery DeRussy fired, Lieutenant Colonel Townsley saw an object fly through the air and splash into Mill Creek. Knowing something was wrong, he ordered a cease fire and ran down the beach to the battery. Dead and wounded lay scattered about the gun pit. Smokeless powder burned everywhere, filling the air with acrid fumes. The breechblock of the 12-inch disappearing rifle was gone, blown off into Mill Creek. Townsley called for ambulances over a nearby telephone and then pitched in to fight the fires and care for the wounded.

Typical of the actions of the survivors was the bravery of Captain J. L. Prentice and Lieutenant G. P. Hawes. Both officers attacked the flames with their bare hands. Then, to prevent an explosion, they dove through the flames and carried unburned sacks of powder to a safe area away from the battery. Eight men had been killed by the blast. Three more died before morning. Funeral services were held on the parade ground attended by 2,000 people from nearby communities as well as the garrison of the fort.

The Chief of Ordnance later determined that the gun started to rise before the breechblock had been pushed home and rotated into place. The lanyard had to be hooked in place while the gun was in motion and the unfortunate artilleryman who had the task clung to the lanyard too long. The safety device failed to withstand the jerk and the gun went off. The presence of the 1,000 pound projectile in the tube prevented the blast from going out the muzzle with the result that the full force of the explosion went off in the gun pit.[39]

The only period of service away from the post for the garrison during this period came in 1911. The Mexican revolution which broke out in that year caused growing concern for the safety of the southwestern border area of the United States. As a precaution, and a show of strength, a large part of the Army was concentrated near the border. On the morning of March 11, 1911, the 6th, 35th, 41st, 69th, and 73d Companies, Coast Artillery Corps, boarded the transport *Kilpatrick* at Fort Monroe and sailed for Galveston, Texas. Upon arrival at Galveston, the companies became part of the 2d Provisional Regiment, Coast Artillery Corps, a unit which actually would have served as infantry in case of hostilities. The immediate crisis passed and the concentration of troops was dispersed. On July 10, the transport *Sumner* arrived at Fort Monroe carrying the 2d Provisional Regiment, which was disbanded at the post on the same day. The 4th Band and the 6th, 35th, 41st, 69th, and 73d Companies rejoined the garrison of Fort Monroe. Later that day, the 44th, 119th, and 143d Companies left for Fort Washington, Maryland, and the 21st Company for Fort Howard, Maryland.[40]

Colonel Townsley was succeeded in command by Colonel Frederick S. Strong on September 7, 1911, who in turn was succeded by Colonel Ira A. Haynes in February 1913. Haynes remained as commandant until August 1916.[41]

Fort Monroe witnessed another military first during this period. On August 5, 1915, Lieutenant Patrick N. Bellinger of the Navy conducted the first aerial spotting of artillery fire in a fixed wing airplane when he spotted firing by the Fort Monroe mortar batteries and signaled the ground by using Very pistol flares.[42]

The beginning of 1917 found the Coast Artillery School steadfastly pursuing its schedule in accordance with its program of the preceding years. Thirty-seven Regular officers, eight officers of the National Guard, and one officer of the Chilean Navy were taking the regular course for officers; fifty officers were receiving instruction in a preliminary, or basic, course for provisional second lieutenants; and 137 enlisted men were enrolled in the artillery, clerical, electrical, and radio courses of the Enlisted Men's Division. The object of these courses, as developed during the preceding fifty years, was the education of officers and enlisted men in the duties of the harbor defenses of the United States. The entry of this country into war, however, was soon to call for a complete readjustment in the training program.

Footnotes Chapter IX

[1] The pintle was an iron pin with key or nut at the top anchoring the front of the gun carriage chassis to a stone block. This permitted the carriage to swing 180° on traverse wheels that ran on an iron track also set on stone. The primary disadvantages of the front pintle carriage were limited traverse and lack of support under the center of the chassis when heavy guns were fired at high elevation. The center pintle carriage permitted 360° traverse and the strongest support was directly under the point of greatest strain. Ripley, *Artillery and Ammunition of the Civil War* (New York: Promontory Press, 1970), pp. 204, 207. Examples of platforms for both types of carriages may still be seen on the ramparts of Fort Monroe.

[2] The terreplain is that part of the rampart behind the parapet.

[3] The object of re-entering place of arms was to flank the branches of the covered way, and to contain the troops necessary for its defense. It was constructed with two faces forming a salient angle, in order to defend the approach to the glacis by a cross fire.

[4] Lewis, *Seacoast Fortifications*, p. 77.

[5] *Ibid.*, pp. 75–76.

[6] *Ibid.*, pp. 79–86.

[7] *Annual Report of the Chief of Engineers, 1892* (Washington, 1893), Part 1, p. 8.

[8] 1st Lt. George A. Zinn, "Demolition of Concrete Gun-Platforms and Magazines at Fort Monroe, Va.," *Journal of the United States Artillery*, 1 (October 1892), pp. 392–396.

[9] *Annual Report of the Chief of Engineers, 1894* (Washington, 1895), Part I, p. 10.

[10] Lt. Col. William H. Tschappot, *Text-Book of Ordnance and Gunnery* (New York: John Wiley & Sons, Inc., 1917), pp. 364–368; Lewis, *Seacoast Fortifications*, p. 80. Buffington had

graduated from West Point in 1861 and had been promoted to colonel of Ordnance in 1889. From 1881 to 1892 he was commanding officer of Springfield Armory. He was promoted to brigadier general and Chief of Ordnance in 1899, retired in 1901, and died in 1922. Crozier was an 1876 graduate of West Point. He served as a major of volunteers in the Spanish-American War and was ordnance officer of the China Relief Expedition. In 1901 he was jumped from captain to brigadier general and became Chief of Ordnance, serving in that position until 1918. In that year he was promoted to major general, retired in 1919, and died in 1942. *Heitman*, pp. 260, 342; *Assembly*, Vol. 2, No. 4 (January 1944).

[11] *Annual Reports of the Chief of Engineers, 1896*, Part I, p. 16, and *1897*, Part I, p. 16; Fort Monroe Fort Record Book in Casemate Museum; Frank T. Hines, *The Service of Coast Artillery* (New York: Goodenough & Woglom Co., 1910), p. 126. Battery Bomford was named by General Orders No. 78, Headquarters of the Army, May 25, 1903, in honor of Colonel George Bomford, Chief of Ordnance, under whose direction many valuable experiments were made on the best form of pieces for heavy ordnance. Bomford is generally credited for developing the Columbiad, which was the standard heavy gun before the introduction of the Rodman guns during the Civil War.

[12] *Annual Reports of the Chief of Engineers, 1896*, Part I, p. 16; *1897*, Part I, p. 16; and *1898*, Part 1, p. 23. Maj. John W. Ruckman, "Methods of Assembling Guns and Mortars and Their Carriages," *Journal of the United States Artillery*, 30 (1908), pp. 36–42. *Coast Artillery Journal*, 80 (May 1924), p. 387; Tschappot, *op. cit.*, pp. 372–375; Hines, *op. cit.*, pp. 119–120. Battery Anderson was named by General Orders No. 105, Headquarters of the Army, October 9, 1902, in honor of Brigadier General Robert Anderson, the defender of Fort Sumter. Battery Ruggles was named by General Orders No. 20, War Department, January 25, 1906, in honor of Brigadier General George D. Ruggles, Adjutant General of the Army, who served with distinction in the Civil War and the Spanish-American War.

[13] *Annual Report of the Chief of Engineers, 1897*, Part 1, p. 16. Battery Humphreys was named by General Orders No. 20, War Department, January 25, 1906, in honor of Lieutenant Colonel Charles Humphreys who served with distinction in the Civil War and the Spanish-American War.

[14] *Annual Report of the Chief of Engineers, 1898*, Part 1, p. 23.

[15] Ruckman, "Methods of Assembling Guns and Mortars and Their Carriages," p. 86. Battery Barber was named by General Orders No. 20, War Department, January 25, 1906, in honor of Brigadier General Thomas H. Barber, United States Volunteers.

[16] *Annual Reports of the Chief of Engineers, 1898*, Part 1, p. 23, and *1899*, Part 1, p. 25. Battery Church was named by General Orders No. 105, Headquarters of the Army, October 9, 1902, in honor of Albert E. Church, who served for many years as professor of mathematics at West Point.

[17] *Annual Reports of the Chief of Engineers, 1898*, Part 1, p. 23, and *1899*, Part 1, p. 25; Fort Monroe Fort Record Book. Battery Eustis was named by General Orders No. 105, Headquarters of the Army, October 9, 1902, for Colonel Abraham Eustis, first commandant of the Artillery School.

[18] *Annual Reports of the Chief of Engineers, 1898*, Part 1, p. 23, and *1899*, Part 1, p. 25; Fort Monroe Fort Record Book. The battery was named by General Orders No. 105, Headquarters of the Army, October 9, 1902, in honor of First Lieutenant Charles B. Gatewood, 6th Cavalry, who commanded the Indian Scouts in the expedition which captured Geronimo in 1886. Lieutenant Gatewood died at Fort Monroe in 1896. E. J. Sulzberger, Jr., "Brief Honor For an Indian Fighter," New Dominion Magazine Section, Newport News *Daily Press*, March 15, 1970, pp. 1, 4–6.

[19] *Annual Report of the Chief of Engineers, 1898*, Part 1, p. 23. One of these guns may still be seen in a photograph taken in about 1910.

[20] *Annual Reports of the Chief of Engineers, 1898*, Part 1, p. 23; *1899*, Part 1, p. 25; *1900*, Part 1, p. 23; Fort Monroe Fort Record Book; Hines, *op. cit.*, pp. 110–111. The battery was originally named by General Orders No. 105, Headquarters of the Army, October 9, 1902, in honor of Colonel Rene E. DeRussy, superintending engineer of the construction of Forts Monroe and Wool from 1838 to 1854. The name was changed by General Orders No. 15, War Department, January 28, 1909, which renamed it in honor of Brigadier General Gustavus A. DeRussy, who served with distinction during the Civil War. By the same order the name

Rene E. DeRussy was given to the military reservation at Waikiki, Hawaii.

[21] *Annual Report of the Chief of Engineers, 1900,* Part 1, p. 23; Fort Monroe Fort Record Book.

[22] *Norfolk Pilot,* April 5, 1896, p. 1.

[23] Interviews with Brig. Gen. R. L. Tilton, January 22 and April 1, 1972, and Colonel M. M. Kimmel, March 18, 1972; *Liaison,* Vol. III, No. 11 (March 13, 1920), p. 130, and No. 13 (March 27, 1920), pp. 152–153.

[24] Fort Monroe, Va., Plan showing location of Sea-Walls, completed, under construction and proposed. NA, RG 77.

[25] Edward M. Coffman, *The Hilt of the Sword* (Madison, Milwaukee, and London: The University of Wisconsin Press, 1966), p. 10. Williams was promoted to major general in 1918 and served from then until his retirement in 1930 as Chief of Ordnance. Hinds was also promoted to major general in 1918 and served as commandant of the Field Artillery School at Fort Sill from 1919 to 1923. He retired in 1928.

[26] Birkhimer, *op. cit.,* pp. 119–120.

[27] Fort Monroe Post Returns, March, May, June, July, and September 1898, and April and May 1899, NA, RG 94.

[28] *Ibid.,* September and December 1899, and January, February, and June 1900.

[29] General Orders No. 58, A.G.O., April 28, 1900.

[30] Guenther graduated from West Point in 1859. He was brevetted three times during the Civil War, including two for gallantry at Shiloh and Stones River. He was promoted to colonel of the 4th Artillery in 1896, served as brigadier general of volunteers during the Spanish-American War, and was promoted to brigadier general in the Regular Army just prior to his retirement in 1902. *Heitman,* pp. 492–493.

[31] *Annual Reports of the Chief of Engineers, 1900,* Part 1, p. 23, and *1902,* Part 1, pp. 23–24; Fort Monroe Fort Record Book; Hines, *op. cit.,* pp. 155–160. These guns had a range of 7,849 yards. The battery was named by General Orders No. 78, Headquarters of the Army, May 25, 1903, in honor of First Lieutenant Douglas S. Irwin, 3d Infantry, who was killed in action at the Battle of Monterrey in the Mexican War.

[32] *Annual Report of the Chief of Engineers, 1902,* Part 1, pp. 23–24; Fort Monroe Fort Record Book; Hines, *op. cit.,* p. 111; *Coast Artillery Journal,* 60 (May 1924), p. 387. The battery was named by General Orders No. 78, Headquarters of the Army, May 25, 1903, in honor of Captain Robert P. Parrott, Ordnance Department, the inventor of the Parrott guns and projectiles.

[33] Fort Monroe Fort Record Book; *Annual Report of the Chief of Engineers, 1902,* Part 1, pp. 23–24; Hines, *op. cit.,* pp. 142–143. Battery Montgomery was named by General Orders No. 78, Headquarters of the Army, May 25, 1903, in honor of Major Lemuel P. Montgomery, 39th Infantry, who was killed in action at the Battle of Horse Shoe Bend in 1814.

[34] Letters and Reports Sent by Superintendent James Ware Relating to Fort Wool, NA, RG 77; *Annual Report of the Chief of Engineers, 1902,* Part 1, pp. 23–24; Fort Monroe Fort Record Book; Hines, *op. cit.,* pp. 160–168. All of the batteries at Fort Wool were named by General Orders No. 194, War Department, December 27, 1904. Battery Lee was named for "Light Horse Harry" Lee, the father of Robert E. Lee. Hindman and Claiborne were both distinguished officers of the War of 1812. Dyer was a former Chief of Ordnance, and Gates received the thanks of Congress for his service in the Revolutionary War.

[35] Lewis, *Seacoast Fortifications,* pp. 89–94.

[36] Richard P. Weinert, Jr., *The Guns of Fort Monroe* (Fort Monroe: Fort Monroe Casemate Museum, 1974).

[37] Story graduated from West Point in 1865 and was commissioned in the infantry. He transferred to the artillery in 1870 and was promoted to colonel, Artillery Corps, in 1902. In 1904 he was promoted to brigadier general and Chief of Artillery, and in 1905 he became a major general. He retired in 1905 and died in 1915. Potts received a direct commission in the 3d Artillery in 1867 and became a lieutenant colonel, Artillery Corps, in 1903. He graduated from the Artillery School in 1870. He was promoted to colonel in 1905 and to brigadier general in 1908. Potts retired in 1914 and died in 1928. Harrison graduated from West Point in 1873 and from the Artillery School in 1882. He was promoted to lieutenant colonel, Artillery Corps, in 1906 and to colonel in 1907. Harrison retired on disability in January 1909 and died at Fort Monroe

in March 1909. Townsley graduated from West Point in 1881 and served in the Spanish-American War as a major of volunteers. He was promoted to lieutenant colonel, Coast Artillery Corps, in 1907 and to colonel in 1911, shortly before he left Fort Monroe. From 1912–1916, Colonel Townsley served as superintendent of the United States Military Academy. Townsley was promoted temporary major general in 1917, but retired and reverted to his permanent rank of brigadier general in 1918. He died in 1926. Arthur, "Historical Sketch of the Coast Artillery School," pp. 201–203; *Register of Graduates and Former Cadets of the United States Military Academy* (The West Point Alumni Association, 1970), pp. 260, 279.

[38] The Artillery District of Chesapeake Bay was established by General Orders No. 81, Headquarters of the Army, June 13, 1901. This was the tactical unit in command of the fortifications.

[39] Newport News *Daily Press,* July 22, 1910, pp. 1, 3. 2nd Lt. George L. Van Deusen, the only officer in the pit, had his legs badly broken when the explosion flung him across the gun pit. Van Deusen had graduated from West Point in 1909 and transferred to the Signal Corps following World War I. He rose to the rank of major general and was commandant of the Signal Corps School in World War II. He retired in 1948. The unit manning the gun was the 69th Company.

[40] Fort Monroe Post Returns, March and July 1911, NA, RG 94. Clarence G. Clendenen, *Blood on the Border* (London: The Macmillan Company, 1969), p. 146.

[41] Strong graduated from West Point in 1880 and from the Artillery School in 1884. He served as a major of volunteers in the Spanish-American War and was promoted to colonel in 1911. During World War I, Strong served as a major general and commander of the 40th Division. He retired in 1919 as a brigadier general and was promoted to major general in 1930. He died in 1935. Haynes graduated from West Point in 1883 and from the Artillery School in 1888. He was promoted to colonel in 1912. During World War I, he was promoted to brigadier general, National Army, and commanded the 64th Field Artillery Brigade. He returned to the rank of colonel in 1919 and was promoted to brigadier general and retired in 1923. Haynes died in 1955. Arthur, "Historical Sketch of the Coast Artillery School," pp. 202–203; *Register of Graduates,* pp. 278, 281.

[42] *Almanac of Naval Facts* (Annapolis: United States Naval Institute, 1964), p. 175. Bellinger, having risen to rear admiral, was in command of all Navy aviation in Hawaii at the time of Pearl Harbor.

Chapter X

The War to End Wars

TO UNDERSTAND EVENTS AT FORT MONROE during the first half of the Twentieth Century, it is necessary to fully appreciate the complex command relationships which existed. With the completion of the modern armament program, the previous relatively simple lines of command were altered to reflect the complexities of the new weaponry. At Fort Monroe the situation was made more confusing by the existence of the Coast Artillery School. Not only did the post have a primary tactical mission, but it was also the location of one of the major Army service schools. The two great wars of the century had a profound impact on the organization necessary to carry out these two distinct missions.

Prior to the outbreak of World War I, Fort Monroe had two separate but closely interlocked commands on one post with the usual services— the Quartermaster, Ordnance, Signal Corps, and Medical—under the Coast Defenses of Chesapeake Bay. Whereas for many years the school instruction had concentrated on harbor defense artillery and its allied subjects, the entrance of the country into war had created a demand for heavy mobile artillery. This added to the mission of the school the training of officers and enlisted specialists for duty with railway, tractor drawn, antiaircraft, and trench mortar artillery.

The Coast Defenses of Chesapeake Bay had the primary mission of the harbor defenses of the area, and, with it, the organization and training of many newly created units for both harbor defense and service with the army in the field.[1] While the Commandant of the Coast Artillery School was also Coast Defense commander there was an element of divided authority and responsibility requiring separate channels of communication with higher authority which required close coordination and judgment. Further, the size of each command required some decentralization relieving the commander of detail. This was eventually solved in July 1918 by the creation of a local higher headquarters, which became the Coast Artillery Training Center, though there always remained the separate line of communication to higher authority.

Before the war the system had operated harmoniously, and following the war it was, in a modified form, entirely satisfactory. In time of peace, duties become more or less routine in character and are performed by trained personnel operating under much less pressure than that resulting from war demands. In time of war, though, confusion can be avoided only when the system is so modified as to relieve the local commander of the details of direct command of two units. This was amply demonstrated during World War I, and the solution of the difficulty was found in the complete separation of the school and the coast defenses into two subordinate commands.

The first steps in the transformation of the post from a peace status into one of war were defensive in character. Before the war, pursuant to the current coast defense project, the government had acquired about 343 acres of land near Cape Henry for purposes of harbor defense. Elaborate permanent fortifications had been planned, and the station was garrisoned by the 5th and 2d Companies[2] from Fort Monroe in February 1917. The outbreak of war found the project for this station incomplete, and to serve for its immediate needs four 6-inch guns were mounted here in April.

Fisherman Island, a small island about a mile in length and strategically located near Cape Charles, was taken over from the Public Health Service and fortified and garrisoned for the emergency. One company from Fort Howard and one from Fort Monroe took station here in March, and four 5-inch guns were mounted in May for defensive purposes.

Fort Wool was garrisoned on April 24 by the 2d Company, Fort Washington, which was replaced in July by the 6th Company, Fort Monroe. This company was in turn replaced in September by the 8th Company, Virginia National Guard Coast Artillery. One antiaircraft gun was mounted at Fort Monroe, two at Newport News, and two at Hopewell, Virginia. Between Fort Monroe and Fort Wool a submarine net was laid in March, and a second net was laid in the vicinity of Thimble Shoals in August, where it remained in position until December 1918. The 4th and 7th Companies, Fort Monroe, were detached in May to Washington for service as guards at the Capitol.

With these defensive measures, the troops were prepared to man the necessary fixed and antiaircraft guns and searchlights, to maintain the submarine nets, to perfect the harbor mine work, and to train the personnel. There remained, however, the intensive measures of training officers and enlisted men for war service overseas, raising and training organizations, and providing enlisted specialists—electricians, radio operators, master gunners, clerks and sergeants major, and motor mechanics.

These duties involved a constant change in the personnel of the garrison through the arrival of incoming units or the creation of new units and through the receipt of great numbers of individuals and detachments. The first arrivals were one company from Fort Howard and one from Fort Washington, followed closely by two companies of the National Guard of Virginia. In May four companies of coast artillery troops were organized, and in August seven companies of the National Guard of Virginia joined. In the spring of 1918 five companies of coast artillery, two batteries of trench artillery, one balloon company, and one battery of heavy mobile artillery were organized, and two batteries of antiaircraft artillery and five more companies of the National Guard of Virginia joined at the post. In addition to these units, others were in the process of organization or of training at the time of the Armistice, and many temporary organizations were formed in connection with the training camps.

Our entry into the war created an immediate demand for officers. The need for the services of the officers undergoing instruction at the Coast Artillery School was so pressing that they could not be permitted to complete in their entirety the courses that were being pursued. Moreover, the character of the courses was, in general, unsuited to the probable assignments which the student officers would receive, so instruction was discontinued about June 1 and the students were detailed to other duties.

As it became evident that it would be necessary to train hundreds of officers for duty with heavy artillery in the field, the recently vacated buildings of the school naturally suggested that they be utilized and that Fort Monroe become the training center of the Coast Artillery Corps. That the plant was not equipped for instruction in the service of heavy mobile artillery, that its capacity was definitely limited, and that the available instructors were themselves uninstructed in matters of railway, tractor, trench, and antiaircraft artillery service were relatively unimportant. No other station was better prepared to undertake the creation of the new corps of heavy artillery.

For years the Coast Artillery School had been tending more and more to confine instruction to the problem of seacoast defense as distinguished from the general problem of artillery service. Garrison training had similarly been restricted to comparatively narrow limits. The possibility of the development of heavy mobile artillery for service in the field had occurred to but few officers prior to the advance of the Germans through Belgium, and none had been prepared for duty with such artillery. Now that it was upon them, a complete about-face in instructional methods was necessary and courses had to be prepared in an entirely new direction.[3]

World War I, unlike preceding wars, did not cause the Coast Artillery School to close its doors. Instead, it converted the school into a training center and brought about one of the most productive periods in the whole history of the institution. The tremendous increase in the size of the Army created a demand for officers and for enlisted specialists which could be filled only by quantity production. For the first time since the birth of the school quality was subordinated to quantity. The institution had to expand to meet the expansion in the Coast Artillery, and in its expansion its wartime objectives seemed to be:

(a) To train candidates for commissions, and to make sure that no man was commissioned in the Coast Artillery Corps without the proper fundamental education and training;

(b) To train commissioned officers in their duties as commanders of heavy artillery in the field;

(c) To amplify the military education of selected officers in order to prepare them for the more important positions with heavy artillery in the field and with the harbor defenses;

(d) To train selected enlisted men in the various specialist positions in the field and in the harbor defenses.

At the beginning the preparation of programs of instruction was particularly difficult because of a doubt as to the exact purposes of the program. Candidates for commissions in the Coast Artillery Corps were to be trained; but what were they to be called to do upon being commissioned? Twelve hundred of them reported at Fort Monroe in June, but at that time the decision to use coast artillery troops with the army in France had just been published. A definite statement of the policy to be followed was not announced until July 14, when the First Training Camp was more than half finished. The problem of organizing, arming, equipping, training, and dispatching units for service during the war was relatively simple when contrasted with this problem of providing and training officers to command them and all the other units raised for coast artillery service. This handling of officer candidates was a large part of the task allotted to Fort Monroe, and as a first preparatory step the regular garrison vacated their barracks, moving into tents on the beach. In so far as possible, the facilities of the post were organized to receive the influx of men which was to start in June.[4]

On May 14, 1917, at the opening throughout the United States of training camps for candidates for commissions, it was intended that all candidates should first receive a uniform basic course of training for a period of one month, after which they were to be distributed for further training in the duties of the branch of service for which they appeared to display the greatest aptitude. To receive such candidates for the second period in the Coast Artillery Corps, two training centers were established: One at Fort Monroe, to receive 1,100 or 1,200 candidates, and one at Fort Winfield Scott, California, to receive about 200.[5]

This general plan, although it brought the candidates to their branch camps with a basic training in infantry drill, visual signaling, bayonet drill, guard duty, marching, etc., developed such inconveniences that it was modified after the first camp and abandoned after the second camp. Candidates thereafter received all their training at the camp of the particular branch of service for which they had applied. The training center at Fort Winfield Scott also was discontinued with the close of the second camp, and after 1917 all coast artillery candidates received their training at Fort Monroe.

The first influx of officer candidates came in June, 1,200 being assembled from Plattsburg, Madison Barracks, Leon Springs, and Forts Myer, Niagara, Oglethorpe, McPherson, Benjamin Harrison, Sheridan, Snelling, Riley, and Logan H. Root, for the First Training Camp, which opened on June 18. Strictly speaking, this first camp did not come within the direct jurisdiction of the Coast Artillery School, nor yet was it a part of the Coast Defenses of Chesapeake Bay. War Department instructions had designated the coast defense commander as the commanding officer of the "Coast Artillery training camp . . . established at Fort Monroe," and he now had a third command added to the two which he already possessed.

The coast defense commander had, of course, an advantage in his authority to assign available personnel to the duties for which the individuals were most needed or were best qualified. Thus, officers carried on the rolls of the school might be called upon to conduct courses of instruction for the benefit of candidates for commissions, and officers assigned to the coast defenses might similarly be detailed to perform duties connected with the camp or with the school. It was, perhaps, just as well that one officer had at first direct and immediate command over all activities at the post. The commanding officers at Fort Monroe during World War I were Colonel Stephen M. Foote, Colonel John A. Lundeen, and Brigadier General Frank K. Fergusson.[6]

The facilities of the school were too limited to care for the large number of students. Its laboratories and classrooms were utilized to their capacity for teaching purposes, and the basement rooms of one of the barracks were used to add to the classroom space. Favorable weather, too, permitted considerable instruction out of doors, and the barracks inside the fort, in which the students were quartered, provided possibility of study under comparatively favorable conditions.

The instructors of this first camp were officers of the Regular Army, assisted by sergeants and noncommissioned staff officers, of whom a number remained on the post despite the acceptance of commissions by many in June. The heads of the instruction departments were attached to the school, but the other instructors, in general, came from the coast defenses.

The students were organized in eight training companies of 150 men each. Their instruction was based purely on coast artillery practice, it being assumed that the mechanical methods used in the Coast Artillery could, with little variation, be adapted to field use. The work of the camp was divided broadly into three periods of nine working days each, followed first by four days of lectures on a variety of subjects and then by a ten-day period of target practice. Division of the camp into sections enabled the instruction to be given by rotation until target practice was reached. One company was sent for part of its mechanical maneuvers to a 12-inch gun lying in a cradle of skids back of Battery Parrott. One after another, the section leaders were given a chance to show what they could do in moving that gun a few inches out of its cradle. After failing to make much progress, the instructor took charge, with some annoyance in his manner, and himself lined up the section, applying the rope according to his own ideas, and giving the command "Heave" with much authority. Unfortunately the rope promptly broke. The demonstration was tactfully changed into a general tug of war, and section pulled section till the period was over.

As there was no heavy artillery available, Colonel Foote announced that, "We proposed to use whatever guns we can get, big or little," and practice was held with 3-inch field pieces and with the fixed armament, using indirect methods and aerial observation to simulate as far as possible the methods used in land warfare.[7]

As might be expected, this large influx of men had its problems at first. The officer candidates found their first meal bad. The men hopefully announced that the cooks had not hit their stride yet and there would be a change. They were partly right, the meals got steadily worse. There was no fresh milk, no fresh vegetables, no fruit, poor meat, sand mixed with a little sugar, leaden bread, and no butter. After an especially bad meal, the men made a shambles of the mess room and then walked over to the Post Exchange for crackers and pop. This finally brought the situation to the attention of the senior officers, and after inspecting the mess changes were instituted which quickly brought an improvement in the quality of the food.

There were a few bits of excitement to liven up the training routine. One afternoon, following the last formation of the day there was a sudden bugle call to arms. The Regular garrison doubled to their guns and an orderly reported that a German submarine had been sighted coming past the Capes. Navy ships in Hampton Roads quickly put to sea. It was a distinct disappointment to the officer candidates gathered on the ramparts of the fort to watch the action when the recall was sounded and it was learned that the periscope was only a stray fish weir pole, kept upright on the incoming tide by the weight of barnacles on its lower end.

The enemy actually did visit Fort Monroe soon thereafter, but nobody knew it at the time. Under the aegis of the War Department, a Belgian showed up with an illustrated lecture on the war and the entire post turned out to hear him. Months later every garrison in the country received a message from Washington warning to be on the lookout for a German spy who gained access to military establishments by masquerading as a Belgian with an illustrated lecture on the war.[8]

The camp closed on August 15 and 766 candidates were commissioned, 137 as captains, 103 as first lieutenants, and 526 as second lieutenants. Two hundred of the second lieutenants were commissioned as provisional lieutenants in the Regular Army, the rest being commissioned in the Coast Artillery Reserve Corps.

While the first camp was under way it became apparent that a second series of training camps for civilian candidates for commissions would be necessary. These camps were opened in August. In the program for these camps, the uniform basic course for candidates in all branches of the service was abandoned in favor of separate courses for Infantry, Cavalry, and Field Artillery. Coast Artillery candidates were to receive the first four weeks of their instruction with the Infantry, although they were to be organized as Coast Artillery companies from the beginning.

In accordance with this program, the First and Second Companies, Fort Monroe Training Camp, were organized at Plattsburg, the Third at Fort Niagara, the Fourth at Fort Myer, the Fifth, Sixth, and Seventh at Fort Oglethorpe, the Eighth and Ninth at Fort Benjamin Harrison, the Tenth, Eleventh, and Twelfth at Fort Sheridan, and the Thirteenth at Fort Snelling. The First Company, Fort Winfield Scott Training Camp, was established at Leon Springs and the Second and Third at the Presidio of San Francisco. From these sixteen companies, 1,400 candidates were to be furnished to the two Coast Artillery camps.

To each of the companies destined to complete their training at Fort Monroe were sent a captain and two lieutenants, the latter being graduates of the first camp. About fifty other graduates of the first camp were selected as instructors for the second camp, and during the four weeks that the candidates were being trained elsewhere these instructors were given a rigorous special course at Fort Monroe to prepare them for their duties during the second camp. The policy throughout the war was to retain graduates from each camp to serve as instructors during the next succeeding camp, relieving the instructors held over from the last preceding camp. There was naturally many exceptions to the general policy, but on the whole officers were released for duty overseas at the earliest possible moment.[9]

The Second Training Camp was organized on September 22 with 1,277 candidates present. This number included about 126 provisional second lieutenants commissioned from civil life through examination and about fifty commissioned from the ranks. These students were instructed much according to the methods of the first camp, but the courses were amplified in some respects, although they had not yet become clearly defined. These courses were: Mortars, Major Caliber Guns, Mobile Artillery, Map Reading and Field Fortifications, Coast Artillery and Mobile Gunnery and Ammunition, Artillery Defense and Fire Control and Direction, Telephone and Signaling, and Administration.

One of the difficulties encountered was a lack of familiarity with mathematics on the part of many of the students, criticism that the officers being sent to France were unprepared in elementary mathematics having been received from General John J. Pershing, the Commanding General of the American Expeditionary Forces. Since the camp obviously could not take time to teach elementary mathematics in a crowded training period, authority was obtained to commission in the Infantry men who were otherwise qualified for a commission. Two first lieutenants and seventeen second lieutenants were commissioned in the Infantry at the end of the second camp, but in later camps men similarly situated were merely returned to their coast defenses.

The Second Training Camp came to a close on November 26, 1917, and 818 commissions were issued—147 as captains, 338 as first lieutenants, and 340 as second lieutenants in the National Army, and 126 as provisional second lieutenants in the Coast Artillery Corps. One hundred of these new officers were sent overseas at once, the rest going to coast defenses to train recruits and to organize overseas units. At the end of this camp some of the instructors were attached to the staff of the Coast Artillery School, but the whole teaching force was not given this status until the reorganization which preceded the fourth camp.[10]

These first camps were pioneer experiments and the instruction was based purely on coast artillery methods. The instruction was necessarily far from complete, for the staff of the school had many adjustments to make. Previously, the school had received from forty to fifty officers annually and had spent a year in imparting to them the instruction considered necessary in the training of a Coast Artillery Corps officer. Now it was being called upon to place 1,200 men, fresh from civil life, in the space formerly occupied by fifty, and to give them in three months a foundation which was to carry them successfully through their war service. That it was able to do so is, aside from all other considerations, sufficient justification for the maintenance of the school for the preceding fifty years.

With the approach of cold weather, the housing situation became acute. The increasing instructional staff demanded quarters, many of the outdoor activities needed to be placed under cover, the large garrison required additional barracks, and the Coast Artillery School—particularly the Enlisted Division—was feeling acutely a need for more space.

To meet these requirements in part, work was started about November 1 on a project which involved the construction of forty buildings of standard cantonment types. These buildings were erected as rapidly as possible and the local water, sewer, and lighting systems were enlarged to accommodate them. Contracts were so quickly executed that within three weeks the candidates were comfortably housed in these new buildings.

As this first project progressed it became apparent that a greatly expanded program would be necessary to meet the situation. Twenty-one successive authorizations in rapid succession called for the erection of about 250 buildings of about twenty different designs—section rooms, barracks, quarters, latrines, warehouses, gun sheds, etc. All over the post these mushroom growths sprang up—inside the fort, around the school, and along the beach north of the fort toward Buckroe. Before the year 1918 was far advanced the reservation had almost reached its maximum capacity—and the end was not yet in sight.[11]

With the creation of the National Army on November 1, 1917, and the enlargement of the Coast Artillery Corps to an authorized strength of 70,721 came a change in the method of selecting candidates for training camps. For the third and succeeding camps these came, for the most part, from among the enlisted men, who were sent direct to Fort Monroe from their organizations. Commissions in grades above that of second lieutenant were no longer authorized.

The Third Training Camp opened on January 5, 1918, with a total enrollment of 613 students. About 250 of these were provisional second lieutenants commissioned from civil life, who had been receiving infantry training at Fort Monroe during December. The remainder were enlisted men, the greater part of whom were recruits.

Instruction during this third camp was severely handicapped by the extraordinarily cold weather. Chesapeake Bay froze over. At the batteries, the command "remove—ice" had to be injected before the guns could be tripped. The course was greatly strengthened before the end of the camp by the arrival in February of Colonel Archibald H. Sunderland and Major Robert R. Welshimer from the Heavy Artillery School in France and of two officers of the French artillery.[12] In March there also arrived the 8-inch howitzers and 6-inch wheel mount guns to take the place of the fixed guns that had been used in the instruction. It now became possible to coordinate the instruction with that given in France and to teach field methods with field materiel. Instruction was centered in four departments—Administration, Gunnery, Materiel, and Topography—

and in other respects the course was improved. The Third Training Camp ended on March 26, when 447 commissions as second lieutenant were given out. Two hundred and forty-five of these new officers became provisional second lieutenants, and none of them received immediate assignment to duty overseas.[13]

Colonel Frank K. Fergusson, who had arrived from France, assumed the duties of commandant of the school on March 30, 1918, with Colonel Sunderland in immediate charge of the Training Camp and Officers School, and Major Welshimer as Director of Instruction. With the opening of the Fourth Training Camp on April 6, the camp became somewhat more clearly a part of the Coast Artillery School. Seven hundred and thirty enlisted men were admitted to this camp, but a general raising of standards and of requirements—especially in mathematics—increased the percentage of attrition above that of earlier camps. Only 467 candidates remained to receive commissions as second lieutenants at the close of camp on June 26. Of these, 100 received immediate oversea assigments.[14]

This output was disappointing because it was insufficient to meet the needs of the Coast Artillery Corps, but hopes of improvement were entertained when a stimulation of interest increased the number of candidates attending the Fifth Training Camp. This camp opened on July 6 with 981 enlisted men on its roles. Of these, many were college men, and it was felt that results would exceed those of the preceding camps.

The instruction was hampered by extremely hot weather, but the schedule was very similar to that of the fourth camp. Before the end of the course, the National Army, National Guard, Reserve Corps, and Regular organizations were merged in the single "United States Army," and all commissions became commissions in that Army rather than in the components thereof. Therefore, when the fifth camp closed on September 25, 696 graduates were commissioned second lieutenants, Coast Artillery, United States Army. One hundred were sent abroad at once.[15]

Almost from the date of their arrival, the French officers on duty with the Training Camp had urged the acquisition of a firing range where artillery practice might be held without the necessity of imagining that a visible target on the water was a target on land concealed from view by accidents of the terrain. Mulberry Island seemed most nearly to meet requirements and was therefore purchased, although it afforded only a 7,000-yard range. Camp Wallace was established on the James River, near Grove, to be used in connection with Mulberry Island, thereby providing for ranges of 20,000 yards. Camp Eustis proper was constructed on the mainland adjacent to Mulberry Island. Adjoining Camp Eustis on the James River the Air Service built a small camp to serve as a balloon school.

The first ground was broken for the erection of an office building in April 1918, and on May 3 Headquarters Company and Battery A, 2d Trench

Mortar Battalion, were sent from Fort Monroe to furnish military police and to dig target trenches. Actual building operations were started on the camp proper on April 28, and work was rushed with all possible speed. Batteries C and D, 61st Artillery, proceeded from Fort Monroe in the latter part of May to be the first troops to occupy the camp, and by the end of August the camp had accommodations for more than 19,000 men.

The development of Camp Eustis resulted in large part from the fact that the original system of organizing, equipping, training, and assembling regiments of heavy artillery in the coast defenses had not been entirely successful. A concentration of effort seemed necessary, and this was made possible by Camp Eustis. Hoboken, as a port of embarkation for heavy artillery troops, gave way to Newport News, and Camp Eustis became a concentration point and training center. Altogether about 20,000 men passed through the camp and about 13,000 more joined or were organized there and remained for demobilization. The 37th and 38th Brigades, the 4th Antiaircraft Battalion, the 13th, 14th, 15th and 16th Antiaircraft Companies, the 56th and 57th Ammunition Trains, and the 4th Trench Mortar Battalion were assembled and trained there; and six regiments of heavy artillery, three battalions of antiaircraft artillery, two ammunition trains, and a number of smaller units were demobilized there.[16]

The growth of Camp Eustis offered but little relief to the crowded conditions at Fort Monroe. Early in 1918, after the construction program was well under way, it became evident that there was actually not enough ground on the reservation to accommodate the buildings which would be necessary. The only solution was to make more.

Accordingly a fill was started along the shores of Mill Creek north and northwest of the fort to the vicinity of the railroad crossing. Temporary bulkheads were put up and sand was pumped in to build up the area now known as Randolph Park. On this land were erected the barracks units and study halls for the companies of the Sixth, or Continuous, Training Camp. Additional ground was similarly built by a fill between the railroad and street car trestles northwest of the Catholic chapel. Here buildings were erected for the use of the Department of Enlisted Specialists of the Coast Artillery School.[17]

The rate of production of officers having definitely fallen behind the demand and the physical capacity of Fort Monroe having been increased by about twenty-five acres, a reorganization was undertaken with a view to increasing the officer output. On July 30, 1918, the Coast Artillery Training Center was ordered established by the War Department, and its organization was completed and its operation begun on September 8. General Fergusson became commanding general of the Coast Artillery Training Center and Colonel Welshimer succeeded him as commandant of the Coast Artillery School. The Training Camp, the Coast Artillery

Board, the Library, and the Enlisted Division were definitely united in the Coast Artillery School, and the Training Center was made to consist of three subordinate commands: The Coast Artillery School, the Coast Defenses of Chesapeake Bay, and Camp Eustis.

After a period of uncertain status, the Training Camp had finally become a definite part of the school. Two hundred and seventy-five graduates of the fifth camp were retained as instructors in the enlarged program which was about to be undertaken. Under the Coast Artillery School, the Continuous Camp was devised whereby the Coast Artillery would be assured of a sufficient number of commissioned officers. Plans were completed early in September, and on the thirteenth the camp opened with the admission of the first unit—Company A, previously the 17th Company, Chesapeake Bay—with 200 candidates. Company B, with 217 members, began its work on September 23, and an additional company was organized each week thereafter until the formation of Company N.[18]

Fort Monroe had been speeded up until it was prepared for any contingency. With the Coast Artillery School to train officers, candidates, and enlisted specialists, with Fort Monroe and Camp Eustis to train enlisted men and to organize or receive units, and with the Coast Artillery Training Center to coordinate all activities, the Virginia Peninsula could undertake to meet any demand which might be made upon it.

The biggest task of the Coast Artillery School during the war was training officer candidates. Nevertheless, it was not found necessary to neglect the training of officers already commissioned, and for these a number of special and advanced courses were introduced. In a series of basic courses, each of six or eight weeks' duration, all the officers available between January and September 1918 were given instruction in gunnery, orientation, field fortification, materiel, gas, and target practice. In February, a series of five-week courses in antiaircraft artillery was started to prepare officers for admission to the American Antiaircraft School in France. In July, an eight-week advanced course in orientation was undertaken, each successive class consisting of twenty to forty officers.[19]

Not the least valuable of the special courses for officers was one undertaken in the summer of 1918 for Air Service officers. The purpose of this course was to give the student a consciousness of the artilleryman's problems, rather than a working knowledge of them. Candidates from Air Service ground schools arrived each week for a seven-week period of instruction, after which they were commissioned in the Air Service and sent to Langley Field, just up the Peninsula from Fort Monroe, to take a course of instruction for observers.[20]

In the Enlisted Men's Division the problem of readjustment was not so difficult of solution nor was the expansion so great as in the Officer's Division. By shortening the courses to twelve weeks and by starting new classes every three weeks, the division was enabled to attain a satisfactory rate of output in artillery, clerical, electrical, and radio specialists. The largest expansion came through the introduction of a course in motor transportation to meet the need for trained drivers of motorcycles, automobiles, trucks, and tractors. With the full development of this section of the school, the Enlisted Men's Division reached a productive capacity of fifty men from the artillery course, eighty from the clerical course, and 100 from the radio course every three weeks, and 190 from the motor transportation course every week.[21]

Within the school, three departments only were established: the Officers' Department, the Enlisted Men's Department, and the Tactical Department, each under a director. The director of the Tactical Department, under the supervision of the commandant, was charged with all details pertaining to infantry drill, physical exercise, quartering, messing, and supply of all enlisted men, and with general supervision of the officers' messes. In all other respects, the training came under the other two departments.

The Armistice brought all activity to an abrupt end and set in action a new line of activity. On November 11, there were present 2,870 candidates, of whom 2,174 were artillery candidates in the Officers' Department, 397 were aerial observers, and 299 were awaiting admission to the course. Before the inflow could be stopped the number grew to 2,933.

Armistice Day saw the nearest thing to actual conflict that the Virginia Peninsula witnessed during the war. A large number of heavy artillery units were at Camp Eustis and Camp Stuart, the holding station for the port of embarkation, ready to deploy to France when word came that the war was over. For many of the men, who had been training for over a year and eagerly awaiting a chance to see action, the news was a bitter blow. The troops were ordered to hold a victory parade in Newport News that afternoon. Glumly the troops trudged through the town, trying not to notice the jeers from some civilians who called then "tin soldiers" and "home guards."

Unfortunately, when the troops returned to camp they were all issued overnight passes. The men promptly returned to Newport News. Frustrated in their hopes to get to France, the men were bent on engaging in some sort of fight, and the actions of the parade spectators gave them the excuse they needed. In practically nothing flat, the main street of Newport News was a shambles. Both the city police and military police were powerless to stop the riot. Pawnbrokers' signs came down and were used as bowling balls along the sidewalks; barbers' poles were uprooted from their concrete bases and were used as battering rams against restaurant doors that did not open quickly. All trolleys were halted and volunteer signallers on their roofs dotted and dashed messages to each other by flashes of the trolley poles being swung against the overhead wires. Only one car was permitted to move, in order to give a tow to a sailor who was sitting proudly in an old bathtub he had tied to the rear coupling. A great bonfire was built, fed by anything inflammable that could be obtained. Although it was a riotous mob of soldiers, sailors, and marines, they remained good humored. Finally, the major who brought up a reserve battalion of military police circulated the rumor that a group of soldiers were being beaten up by some civilians at the far end of one of the bridges that separated the business and residential districts. At once the rioters swept across the bridge and the military police closed it behind them. Then having nowhere else to go, the men quickly returned to Camp Stuart. The Battle of Newport News was over.[22]

Demobilization preparations at Fort Monroe began as soon as the Armistice was announced. Units at Fort Monroe, other than organizations considered as belonging to the Regular Army, were mustered out in December. Instruction in the emergency courses in the Enlisted Men's Division was discontinued on November 30 and the men returned promptly to their organizations. In the Continuous Camp, candidates were given an opportunity of leaving the service at once, and many chose to receive their discharges. Others, however, desired to complete the course of instruction, and those who did so and were found qualified were graduated, commissioned in the Officers' Reserve Corps, and discharged at the termination of their course.

Officers returning from France flocked into Fort Monroe for many months, during which time the post gradually returned to a normal condition. That there should be a certain amount of disorganization incident to the sudden termination of activities and to the equally sudden change from mobilization to demobilization was inevitable. With the reduction of the garrison to that normally required for peace purposes, with the return of 3,000 candidates to their homes, and with the practical shut-down of the Coast Artillery School, the local organization became top-heavy. This condition gradually righted itself, although the Training Center continued to function until 1923. At that time Fort Monroe was provided with a normal garrison occupied in normal pursuits, and the Coast Artillery School had resumed the instruction interrupted in 1917. Fort Monroe was again on a peace status.

Footnotes Chapter X

[1] The Artillery District of Chesapeake Bay became the Coast Artillery Sub-District of Chesapeake Bay which in turn became the Coast Defenses of Chesapeake Bay in 1913.

[2] The 41st Company, Coast Artillery Corps, had been redesignated as the 2d Company, Fort Monroe, and the 118th Company, Coast Artillery Corps had been redesignated as the 5th Company, Fort Monroe, in 1916.

[3] 2d Lt. Geddes Smith, "Officers' Department," *Journal of the United States Artillery*, 50 (January-February 1919), pp. 1–2.

[4] *Ibid.*, pp. 8–9.

[5] *Ibid.*, pp. 4–6.

[6] Foote had graduated from West Point and became a colonel in 1911. He served as commandant of the Coast Artillery School from October 1, 1916, to August 23, 1917. He was a temporary brigadier general during World War I and commanded a field artillery brigade. After the war, he reverted to colonel and died in 1919. Lundeen had graduated from West Point in 1873 and retired in 1912 as a colonel. He was recalled to active duty in 1917 to act as President of the Coast Artillery Board and editor of the *Journal of the United States Artillery*. He served as commandant of the Coast Artillery School from August 23, 1917, to March 30, 1918, and then served as librarian of the school until relieved from active duty in 1919. He died in 1940. Fergusson graduated from West Point in 1896 and was a lieutenant colonel when the war started. He rose to brigadier general during the war and commanded the Coast Artillery Training Center from September 8, 1918, to January 31, 1919. Prior to assuming this position, he had been commandant of the school since March 30, 1918. Following the war, he reverted to his permanent rank and died in 1937 as a colonel. Smith, "Officers' Department," pp. 10–11; *Heitman*, pp. 428, 647, 417; *Cullum*, Vol. VIA, pp. 375, 180, 758–759.

[7] Smith, "Officers' Department," pp. 12–13.

[8] Lt. Colonel A. C. M. Azoy, "There Was No Place Like Home," *Coast Artillery Journal*, 81 (July-August 1938), pp. 263–269.

[9] Smith, "Officers' Department," pp. 18–20.

[10] *Ibid.*, pp. 20–24.

[11] *Ibid.*, pp. 81–82.

[12] Sunderland graduated from West Point in 1900 and was a distinguished graduate of the Coast Artillery School in 1912. He became a brigadier general in World War I and played a key role in the establishment of Camp Eustis. Following the war, Sunderland reverted to colonel and served as President of the Coast Artillery Board at Fort Monroe. In 1936 he was promoted to major general and Chief of Coast Artillery, which position he held until his retirement in 1940. General Sunderland died in 1963. Welshimer was a 1908 United States Naval Academy graduate, but was commissioned in the Coast Artillery Corps. He became a colonel in World War I and served as commandant of the Coast Artillery School from September 8, 1918, to January 29, 1919. He resigned his commission in 1919, but was re-appointed a major the following year. He changed the spelling of his last name to Welshmer in 1922 and transferred to the Infantry in 1935.

[13] Smith, "Officers' Department," pp. 24–26.

[14] *Ibid.*, pp. 30–34.

[15] *Ibid.*, pp. 34–41.

[16] Lt. Col. Fred M. Green, "The Coast Artillery Training Center and Camp Eustis," *Journal of the United States Artillery*, 50 (January-February 1919), pp. 118–126.

[17] Smith, "Officers' Department," p. 83.

[18] *Ibid.*, pp. 41–46.

[19] *Ibid.*, pp. 80–81.

[20] *Ibid.*, p. 79. The site of Langley Field on Back River had been selected by the War Department in 1916 and construction of the post was carried out under the direction of the Fort Monroe quartermaster. Originally intended as the U.S. Aviation and Experimental School, Langley Field was converted during World War I to training and tactical purposes. The post was named in honor of aviation pioneer Dr. Samuel P. Langley. Brigadier General William Mitchell carried out his famous experimental bombing of warships from Langley Field. Today the post is Langley Air Force Base and is also the site of a major National Aeronautics and Space Administration facility.

[21] Lt. Col. R. P. Hall, "Enlisted Men's Department," *Journal of the United States Artillery*, 50 (January-February 1919), pp. 85–117.

[22] Azoy, "There Was No Place Like Home," pp. 268–269.

Chapter XI

Between the World Wars

WITH THE CLOSE OF WORLD WAR I the various activities at Fort Monroe turned their attention to the resumption of peacetime operations. Demobilization, the necessary changes in personnel, and doubts as to the future strength of the Army and overall policies made readjustment difficult.

During 1919 and 1920, the Coast Artillery Training Center headquarters had become with the arrival of many senior officers from overseas top heavy with staff. At this time there were some grandiose ideas of retaining the Training Center as a super training headquarters. After General Fergusson left in January 1919, a bewildering number of officers occupied the positions of Training Center commander, Commandant of the Coast Artillery School, post commander of Fort Monroe, and commander of the Coast Defenses of Chesapeake Bay. Some of these officers held all four offices at the same time and some only one or two. The situation began to stabilize when Colonel Richmond P. Davis took command in November 1920 and became commandant and post commander in April 1921. Colonel Davis left in December 1922, being relieved by Brigadier General W. R. Smith in January 1923.[1]

The headquarters of the Third Coast Artillery District was established at Fort Monroe on May 15, 1923, and the Coast Artillery Training Center was discontinued.[2] The district commands were the new Coast Artillery commands corresponding to the seaward Corps Areas and were responsible for the command, supervision, and training of all Coast Artillery elements in their areas, including National Guard and

Organized Reserve activities and war planning. The Commanding General of the Third Coast Artillery District was also designated as Commandant of the Coast Artillery School and as post commander of Fort Monroe. The district commander for the first few years also commanded the coast defenses and Fort Eustis.

Except for Fort Eustis, which was closed in 1931, this district command structure remained the same until World War II. As commandant, the commanding general was responsible to the Chief of Coast Artillery and as district commander he was responsible to the Commanding General, Third Corps Area, for the harbor defenses and the post. In actual operation, the Coast Artillery School operated through the assistant commandant and the post and harbor defenses operated through the harbor defense commander, who was also the post executive.

For the Coast Artillery School, the added missions in heavy and antiaircraft artillery made extensive modifications in the pre-war schedules necessary. While the new program was being prepared, and while the process of demobilization kept students unavailable, the school utilized its well-equipped plant and its instructor personnel for a number of special courses. A basic course for reserve and temporary officers electing to remain in the service, a special course for the members of the class of 1920 of the Military Academy (graduated in 1918), a course for noncommissioned officers, a special course for enlisted men detailed to units of the Reserve Officers' Training Corps, and a vocational training school were established and successfully conducted during 1919.

The Enlisted Division, first to resume its normal schedule, reopened on April 7, 1919, with students in its artillery, clerical, electrical, and radio courses, as well as in a nautical course which was conducted until the need of providing personnel for the mine planter service had passed. The Officers' Division, not far behind, started its new program with a basic course for newly commissioned officers, which continued until 1921.

A course of instruction, corresponding to the courses which had been given since 1868, was begun in 1920 as a Battery Officers' Course, in which was taught primarily elementary tactics and the technique of seacoast, heavy, and antiaircraft artillery. At the same time, the creation of a Department of Tactics permitted the resumption of an advanced course, in which field grade officers and senior captains were taught the tactical employment of artillery in coastal and land warfare (with a special emphasis on the part played by the artillery as a member of the tactical team of the combined arms) and the tactical employment of the other arms up to brigade.

Short courses, introduced in 1920 and 1921, included special courses for officers and enlisted men of the Organized Reserves and the National Guard; special advanced courses in gunnery and in engineering, to which a very limited number of graduates from the battery officers' course were detailed; and refresher courses for the benefit of general officers desiring to learn something of coast artillery techniques and tactics and for senior officers of the Coast Artillery Corps whose duties kept them out of touch with developments within the corps.

A valuable addition to the school was the Department of Correspondence Courses, somewhat similar to the extension courses given by many universities and colleges. This department prepared, for instruction by correspondence, courses for Reserve and National Guard officers and, on occasion, Regular officers, using a series of courses and subcourses covering the tactics and the techniques of the several types of armament manned by the Coast Artillery Corps.

The personnel of the school consisted of the commandant, the assistant commandant, the secretary of the school, the librarian, the directors of the five departments, the instructors and assistant instructors, the student officers, the enlisted students, and the Coast Artillery School Detachment. The commandant, the assistant commandant, and the secretary formed the faculty board, which determined all matters relating to standing, rating or classification, and proficiency of students, and which acted in an advisory capacity on all matters which might be referred to it by the commandant. The students were detailed from the Coast Artillery at large to take the respective courses of instruction. Students successfully completing the regular, advanced, or special courses received appropriate diplomas or certificates setting forth the fact of their proficiency. The working force (clerks, storekeepers, assistants, orderlies, etc.) was provided by the Coast Artillery School Detachment, which consisted of 198 enlisted men of various grades under the command of the director of the Department of Enlisted Specialists.

The Coast Artillery School received some twenty-five officers in its advanced course for field grade officers, fifty in its course for battery officers, and a variable number—which might be placed at thirty to forty—in its special and refresher courses.

The school buildings had been designed and constructed for the school courses as contemplated in 1909 and these had been ample for the classes preceding World War I. Because of the increased number of courses, the increased number of students, and the consequent increased overhead, the school far outgrew its capacity following the war. Many of its activities were housed in temporary wooden structures which had been erected during the war to meet the temporary demands then being made on the school, and many of the students resided in similar structures. As had happened after the Civil War, and would happen after World War II, these buildings deteriorated rapidly but no replacements were immediately forthcoming.

On June 29, 1923, was held a centennial celebration of the occupation of Fort Monroe. In the course of the ceremonies the troops were reviewed and inspected, and addresses were delivered by Colonel James F. Howell, commanding the Coast Defenses of Chesapeake Bay, General Smith, Hon. Harry R. Houston, of Hampton, Congressmen S. O. Bland, of Virginia, and Major General John L. Hines, Deputy Chief of Staff of the Army.[3]

This was followed on May 24, 1924, by a centennial celebration of the opening of the Artillery School in 1824, which was attended by many military and civil officials, including General of the Armies John J. Pershing and the Governor of Virginia. After a review of the troops and a tour of the post, exercises were held in the Liberty Theater, where addresses were delivered by General Pershing, Hon. Harry R. Houston, member of the House of Delegates, and Governor E. Lee Trinkle.

That afternoon a battle command practice, under the direction of Colonel Howell, was held in honor of the distinguished guests. This practice was typical of the exercises conducted at Fort Monroe and Fort Story during this period. Five batteries participated in this practice, fire being directed upon two pyramidal targets towed by the mine planter *Schofield* at a range of about 9,000 yards and two pyramidal targets towed by the tug *Reno* at a range of about 7,000 yards. The *Schofield* targets, which simulated a battleship division, were fired upon by the two 12-inch disappearing guns of Battery Parrott; by Battery Anderson, which delivered pit salvos with two twelve inch mortars; by Battery Ashbridge, consisting of two 12-inch railway mortars brought to Fort Monroe by the 52d Artillery from Fort Eustis; and by Battery Taylor, a four-gun 155-mm. G.P.F. battery, brought to Fort Monroe by the 51st Artillery from Fort Eustis. The *Reno* targets, simulating a division of destroyers and mine sweepers, were engaged by the two 6-inch barbette guns of Battery Montgomery and by Battery Taylor. Following the gun firing, a target was towed across the mine field simulating a mine sweeper division. This attack on the mine field was met by the explosion of submarine mines, observation fire being used. Immediately afterward, an air attack on Fort Monroe was simulated by two planes from Langley Field towing sleeve targets, which were fired upon by the 3-inch guns of the 61st Artillery Battalion. The machine guns of the 61st Artillery Battalion then opened fire on low flying attack planes, represented by free balloons.[4]

During this first hundred years, the reservation had grown from 250 acres to approximately 300 acres. There had been some erosion along the eastern and southern shores. Before measures for the protection of the beaches were taken, the eastern shore ran 200 feet or more inland from its present line, and at the time Battery Parrott had been started the mean tide reached to the battery site. The construction of jetties and bulkheads carried the shore line out to about its present position.

On the water front the high tide line ran perhaps fifty or sixty feet inside the present seawall. Successive pilings and accompanying filling behind the pilings regained ground on this side of the post, and the seawall from the Engineer Wharf to the first bend in the wall, which marked the eastern limit of the Hygeia tract, was the approximate line of mean tide. Further west the water carried up well into Continental Park, under the southwestern corner of the Hygeia Hotel. Westward from the Baltimore Wharf the shore line ran diagonally across the site of the present Chamberlin Hotel, and the high tides reached into the grounds of the old gun yard, on which the buildings of the Training and Doctrine Command now stand. All this area, and much to the westward, has filled in since the Civil War.

Artificial additions made during World War I northwest of the Catholic chapel and north and east of Building No. 100 added some twenty-five acres to the reservation and provided space for many "shacks" standing in these two areas. The Liberty Theater and all buildings of a cantonment type north thereof stood on made ground, and much of the ground north of the railroad was also filled in.

Following the completion of the demobilization and reorganization at the end of the war, the garrison of Fort Monroe comprised the 6th, 35th, 41st, 58th, 69th, 140th, 168th, and 257th Companies, Coast Artillery Corps. In 1922, the 6th, 140th, 168th, and 257th Companies became the Headquarters Battery and Batteries A, B, and C of the 61st Artillery Battalion, an antiaircraft unit. Since 1901, the Coast Artillery Corps had never been organized into larger units than a company, except for the regiments which were organized during World War I, and such provisional battalions and regiments as were temporarily organized for specific purposes. These temporary organizations, when the purpose had been accomplished, were disbanded and their identity was lost. Thus, the *esprit,* which throughout the history of military organizations had always attached to regiments of whatever arm of the service and which was an important factor in building up morale, had been almost wholly lacking in the Coast Artillery Corps.

At the conclusion of World War I, the responsibility for the future development and operation of railway, antiaircraft, and heavy tractor artillery designed for use in coast fortifications, was assigned to the Coast Artillery Corps. Certain units which had served during the war with these various activities were continued in existence. As a result, the Coast Artillery developed into a corps consisting of a number of separate companies assigned to the duty of manning the armament of the harbor defenses, a regiment and three battalions of antiaircraft artillery, a regiment and a battalion of railway artillery, and three regiments of heavy tractor artillery. Such a mixture of organization was most undesirable. Furthermore, it was very noticeable that *esprit* was being developed in the battalions and regiments to a much higher degree than in the separate companies.

After long study of this problem, a plan was developed which standardized Coast Artillery organization. Sixteen regiments composed of American troops and two regiments of Filipino troops for duty in the harbor defenses and one additional antiaircraft regiment for duty in the Panama Canal Zone were organized in addition to the battalions and regiments already in existence. The designation of companies by number was abolished and they were called batteries. The existing battalions were expanded into regiments, the additional units so provided in each regiment remaining inactive. Each of the regiments formed for harbor defense was organized into a headquarters battery and either seven or ten lettered batteries.[5]

In pursuance of this policy, the 12th Coast Artillery was organized in the Harbor Defenses of Chesapeake Bay on July 1, 1924, with headquarters at Fort Monroe. The Headquarters Battery and Batteries A, B, and C were stationed at Fort Monroe while Batteries D and E were stationed in the Harbor Defenses of Baltimore. Batteries F and G remained inactive. Battery B was subsequently inactivated in 1930. The 61st Artillery Battalion was expanded into the 61st Coast Artillery (Antiaircraft), also on July 1, 1924. This regiment was to be composed of a headquarters and eight lettered batteries, but only Headquarters Battery and Batteries A, B, and E were active, all stationed at Fort Monroe.[6]

Fort Monroe now had two regimental organizations for the seaward and aerial defense of the locality and also assumed many duties in connection with the training of the Citizens' Military Training Camps, Reserve Officers' Training Corps Camps, National Guard camps, and Reserve Officers' training. The first ROTC camp, attended by about sixty cadets, was held in 1919. An increasing number of cadets attended the Fort Monroe camp during the next three years until the Coast Artillery ROTC was split in 1923 into four groups instead of the previous two. The ROTC camps were held annually at Fort Monroe through 1941, 370 cadets attending the final camp before World War II.[7]

During the period between the world wars, a large number of National Guard and Organized Reserve organizations spent their annual two weeks of active duty at Fort Monroe. Prior to World War II the Reserve units did not contain any enlisted men and consisted of cadres of officers. Many of these units during their active duty were used to run the Citizens' Military Training Camps. Another of the annual summer visitors to Fort Monroe during this period was the first class from West Point. The cadets spent a few days each summer receiving orientation to the guns and the Coast Artillery Corps. The stay of the cadets also usually marked the high point of the summer social season at the post.[8]

With its expansion and its greatly enlarged duties, Fort Monroe became a general officer's command again, and complete organizational separation of the school and harbor defenses was secured. All these changes of course necessitated a material increase in the administrative overhead and a considerable addition to the field grade officer personnel of the garrison.

Fort Monroe between the world wars was the headquarters or the station of the Third Coast Artillery District, the Coast Artillery School, the Harbor Defenses of Chesapeake Bay, and the Coast Artillery Board, all separate military activities. It was also a station for the Lighthouse Service and the U.S. Public Health Service, in addition to which it housed numerous civilian activities which called for a certain amount of thought and time on the part of the military authorities.

Although Fort Monroe had always been a place of experiment and test in artillery matters, an Artillery Board was not established until 1900. At various times throughout the history of the Army, boards had been convened to investigate and report upon questions of technical interest to the artillery, but no such boards had any degree of permanence before the Civil War. Early in 1866 a "permanent Artillery board" was organized in Washington to which matters affecting the artillery arm of the service were to be referred for discussion and recommendation.[9] The board functioned less than a year and then discontinued operations, although it appears to have been neither discharged nor replaced.

In 1900, pursuant to General Orders No. 58, A.G.O., a "Board of Artillery," consisting of the heads of departments, was organized at the Artillery School. In 1905 the organization was changed so that the board no longer consisted necessarily of the heads of departments, although they were still subject to individual detail to the board, the remaining members coming from battery and fire commanders at the post. Except for a change of name to the "Coast Artillery Board" in 1907, no other change of importance in the status or composition of the board was made until World War I.[10]

In 1918 the Coast Artillery Board became a part of the Coast Artillery Training Center. In April 1919, the duties of the board were taken over by the Development Division of the Training Section and the Board, as such, ceased temporarily to exist, but in December of the same year it was revived as a unit separate from the Training Section. Early in 1920 the board resumed its pre-war status, and in February 1922 it was reorganized. Its principal duty was to act in an advisory capacity to the Chief of Coast Artillery. It investigated and submitted recommendations on all subjects pertaining to the Coast Artillery which might be referred to it or which it might initiate, and practically every technical question requiring consideration by the Chief of Coast Artillery was submitted to the board. The board had always been closely allied with the school and in 1923 became a separate element of the school under the commandant, who forwarded all its reports to the Chief of Coast Artillery.[11]

With the Coast Artillery School and the Coast Artillery Board, Fort Monroe was the hub of the Coast Artillery Corps—the center of coast artillery activity. Possessed of a salubrious climate and easily accessible from all parts of the country by boat, rail, or motor, this beautiful post was the natural home for the Coast Artillerymen, for it was the one station to which, sooner or later, all Coast Artillerymen came, many of them returning one or more times.

For two decades after 1920, the Coast Artillery School continued to improve its military education training. Courses were changed or supplanted, new techniques were incorporated into instruction, and there were many innovations made. One important development during the period was the increased cooperation between the Coast Artillery and both the Navy and the Air Corps. Many opportunities were offered Coast Artillery School instructors and students to witness Navy materiel and gunnery methods. Each year a series of five or six lectures was given at the school by selected officers from the Fifth Naval District. For several years the Navy and the Coast Artillery held joint battle practices off the Virginia Capes, and several student officers were invited to Guantanamo, Cuba, to observe the Navy battle practice there.[12]

Brigadier General Robert E. Callan followed General Smith in command from December 1924 to June 1929. Major General Henry D. Todd served as the commanding general from June 1929 to September 1930.[13]

With each successive year of this period, more emphasis was placed upon courses in antiaircraft artillery at the expense of older courses. In 1926, and each fall for the next three years, the 61st Coast Artillery journeyed to Aberdeen Proving Ground, Maryland, to conduct tests of antiaircraft equipment for a War Department Board. The regiment made the trip to Maryland partly by road and partly by water, thus gaining some experience in field operations. When Brigadier General Stanley D. Embick became commandant in September 1930, he voiced his views at the opening session of the school on the importance of antiaircraft in the defense of harbors. As a result of this emphasis the instruction in antiaircraft artillery was increased until it was upon a par with seacoast artillery. The Coast Artillery School began training students to act as instructors at stations where antiaircraft artillery was new or as exchange instructors at flying schools of the Air Corps. By this latter arrangement, Coast Artillery instructors conducted a course in materiel and methods at the Air Corps Tactical School at Maxwell Field, Alabama, and in return, instructors from the Air Corps gave a course for advanced students at Fort Monroe. To coordinate instruction, officers from Fort Monroe visited the Air Corps Tactical School and the Command and General Staff School at Fort Leavenworth, Kansas, and participated in antiaircraft and Air Corps exercises at Fort Knox, Kentucky. In April 1931, upon recommendation by the Coast Artillery School, three planes and five officers from Langley Field were specifically assigned to Fort Monroe for antiaircraft artillery target practice missions.[14]

Financial restraints stemming from the Great Depression resulted in significant changes in the elaborate organization of Coast Artillery devised in 1924. These changes resulted in a significant shift in the garrison at Fort Monroe. Fort Eustis was abandoned in the spring of 1931 and the units stationed there were distributed to other posts. The regimental headquarters and one battalion of the 52d Coast Artillery (Railway) moved to Fort Hancock, New Jersey. The 3d Battalion, 52d Coast Artillery, and the 1st Battalion, 51st Coast Artillery (155-mm. Towed), took up garrison at Fort Monroe in May 1931. At the same time that the railway and tractor regiments were arriving, the 61st Coast Artillery (Antiaircraft) was leaving Fort Monroe. The 61st Coast Artillery made an epic truck road march to its new station—Fort Sheridan, Illinois—by way of Fort Knox. Reductions in the total number of active regiments led the following year to another change at Fort Monroe. One harbor defense regiment —the 2d Coast Artillery—was inactivated in Panama. Since the 12th Coast Artillery at Fort Monroe did not have a very long history, it was decided to replace it with the 2d Coast Artillery, the lineage of which extended back to 1821. On May 1, 1932, the 12th Coast Artillery was inactivated and Batteries H, C, and D were redesignated as Batteries A, C, and E of the 2d Coast Artillery. Various changes in battery designations took place in the following years, but the 2d Coast Artillery remained at Fort Monroe until 1944.[15]

The policy of emphasizing antiaircraft artillery instruction resulted in an equal distribution of both theoretical and practical training in antiaircraft and seacoast artillery. The broadening of the course of instruction affected each branch of the school. The Advanced Course students received more instruction in the tactics and technique of antiaircraft artillery, the Battery Officers' Course studied materiel, gunnery, and adjustment of antiaircraft fire. Instructors in the Advanced Engineering Course concentrated on antiaircraft position-finding equipment, data transmission systems, searchlights, sound locators, and comparators. In order that a nucleus of officers might be formed who would be highly qualified for engineering work in the development of antiaircraft artillery materiel, courses were extended one month. The Master Gunners' Course was revised to include work in meteorology and in the use of the Jackson antiaircraft camera.

After the introduction of the single-conductor submarine mine cable in 1928, many officers were found lacking in knowledge of this improvement in submarine mining and the Battery Officers' Course was lengthened to include this instruction. In 1930, the Submarine Mine Depot moved from Fort Totten, New York, to Fort Monroe, thus completing the transfer begun in 1908 when the Submarine Mine School had moved to Fort Monroe. In 1932 the course in submarine mining was completely revised to include special instruction for prospective ship commanders in the technique and tactical use of the submarine mines. [16]

In 1929, a Special Refresher Course had been started at the school for senior officers who had been detached from the Coast Artillery Corps for a considerable time. Its purpose was to inform these officers of all new developments in materiel and firing methods. Although there was no prescribed time limit to the course, it usually lasted about three months. In 1931, however, it was reduced to eight weeks and remained at that length until 1934, when it was discontinued. [17]

The Battery Officers' Course for National Guard and Organized Reserve officers was held each year, with increasing emphasis upon antiaircraft, in keeping with the policy of the school. Each spring, at the conclusion of the course, the officers divided into two groups, one proceeding to Aberdeen Proving Grounds for antiaircraft and machinegun practices, the other to Fort Eustis to man 8 and 12-inch railway artillery. The original six weeks course was increased to eight weeks, and finally to twelve weeks in 1937. [18]

The Great Depression of 1929 was slow in being felt by the Coast Artillery School. The Economy Bill of 1933 cut deeply into the budget of the school and cast an ominous cloud over Fort Monroe. The first disruption came in June 1933 when the annual battle practice at Fort Story was cancelled after a part of the troops had already moved from Fort Monroe. The battle practice was cancelled by the War Department because the school year was terminated approximately three weeks earlier than planned. The student officers and many of the instructors were required to report on short notice for duty with the Civilian Conservation Corps. The school lost 60 percent of its staff and faculty to this duty, most of the officers being sent to camps in California and the Rocky Mountain states. In addition to the officers from the school, thirty-six officers and 165 enlisted men of the garrison also went into the field with the Civilian Conservation Corps.

The quota of student officers and faculty of the school was reduced 51 percent and 33⅓ percent, respectively. As a direct result, one of the major courses at the school, the Battery Officers' Course, was merged with the Advanced Technical Course in 1934. The new course was called the Regular Course, and lasted ten months instead of the usual nine months of the former courses. There had always been a great demand

for the Battery Officers' Course, and every Coast Artillery officer above
the rank of first lieutenant was given the privilege of taking it. Because
of the curtailment, however, many officers had to wait before they could
be accepted.[19]

Just before the impact of the Great Depression was felt at Fort Monroe,
the first extensive permanent construction since World War I was undertaken. The owners of the Chamberlin Hotel had intended to build a new
hotel to replace the one destroyed in 1920, but for years financial problems delayed the project. To be quite honest, the Fort Monroe headquarters did not want a new civilian hotel on the reservation because
of the administrative and jurisdictional problems which it would present.
Despite this local lack of enthusiasm, the War Department on April 30,
1926, gave the Old Point Hotel Corporation a license for a new hotel, but
stipulated work would have to start within six months. A further six month
extension was granted when the corporation still encountered problems.
On the morning of April 30, 1927, General Callan and Colonel Russell P.
Reeder, the Third Coast Artillery District executive, were waiting with
the intention of immediately notifying the War Department of the failure
of the lessee to comply with the terms. At 10:45 a.m., however, ground
was broken and the work got slowly underway. The new hotel, at that
time called the Chamberlin-Vanderbilt Hotel, opened to the public on
April 7, 1928. The hotel, now called simply the Chamberlin Hotel, is
still in operation. Following colonial lines of architecture, it is a modern
fire-proof structure of brick and concrete. It rises to a height of eight
stories, with the addition of a roof garden, from which a commanding
view of the surrounding bay and country can be obtained.[20]

In December 1930, the recreational facilities for officers of the post
were greatly improved with the dedication of the new Beach Club and
a golf course. The Beach Club was located just south of Battery Anderson on Chesapeake Bay and the golf course extended along the sand spit
and the pine woods between the mortar batteries and Mill Creek. Brigadier
General Stanley D. Embick, the commandant of the Coast Artillery
School, originated the project in 1930 to fill a long recognized need for a
recreation center for officers during the hot and humid summer at Fort
Monroe. The club was built of logs cut on the Fort Eustis Reservation
with soldier labor and some help fom club funds and post utilities. The
building included a stone chimney which still stands.

Late in 1931 the north wing of the new bachelor officers' quarters, Randolph Hall, was completed. Located on the east side of Ingalls Road
on the fill just south of the Mill Creek bridge and guard house, it contained thirty-four rooms. South of Randolph Hall, in the area near the
Liberty Theater, a complex of apartments for the student officers of the
Coast Artillery School was erected at about the same time.[21]

Even while these additions were being made to the post, Fort Monroe almost lost one of its most historic buildings. On April 23, 1933, First Sergeant Thomas E. Austin of Battery F, 52d Coast Artillery, had died. Austin had been a hard bitten, but much respected, old soldier of long service. The post chaplain had once visited the first sergeants in one of his frequent efforts to get the men to come to chapel. When he reached Sergeant Austin he was told in no uncertain terms that, "If I went to Church the Chapel would burn up."

The funeral of the sergeant was set for April 24. Funerals were not infrequent at Fort Monroe. There was an old caisson at the post with two old cavalry horses who, according to the men, were so experienced that if harnessed to the caisson they would walk to the chapel and back up to the front door. The deceased was placed in the chapel before the ceremony and at the appointed time the band and escort took position facing the chapel door.

The band had played appropriate music outside and the chaplain was well underway with the service when someone cried "Fire!" At the peak of the roof of the chapel nave, immediately above the sanctuary arch, fire had broken through the ceiling. The fire call was sounded and the reveille gun was fired, as was then the custom on fire call. The band and escort rushed to the sacristy to render assistance. Some of the soldiers carried the casket out of the chapel and placed it on the porch of the quarters next to the chapel. The fire department arrived and the fire was soon under control, but not until it had done considerable damage to the chapel roof and end of the nave over the sanctuary arch. Fortunately, none of the stained glass windows in the sanctuary were damaged. An investigation disclosed that post painters had been burning and scraping old paint off the eaves and cornices and somehow had set fire to the cornice. The fire worked its way up inside the roof and came out the top. The fire was put out quickly enough so that it appeared that the main damage was to the pipe organ which had been installed in 1929. The chapel was repaired in a few months and a new organ was acquired, but over thirty years later serious structural damage as a result of the fire was discovered.[22]

Another disaster struck Fort Monroe during 1933 which was to be of much greater impact and more far reaching effect on the post. On the evening of August 22, 1933, a large hurricane approached Hampton Roads. A torrential rain, accompanied by strong winds off the bay, struck the post at high tide. By daylight on the morning of August 23, the water had risen over the first floors of the buildings in Camp 2, just to the north of the fort. At 5 a.m. the post adjutant was awakened from a peaceful sleep by a telephone call from the commander of the 246th Coast Artillery, the Virginia National Guard unit which was billeted in the camp during its summer training. The colonel asked the adjutant how long the storm would last. "I had just awakened from a sound sleep and did not, at first, catch the importance of what he was trying to tell me. I told him that it would blow itself out shortly." The colonel answered that was good news as the wooden barracks were afloat and smashing into each other. He had already ordered his men to move with all their property to the second floors. Realizing finally the danger of the situation, the adjutant told him to evacuate the temporary barracks and move his men to the permanent barracks inside the fort. The National Guardsmen and some Reservists who were also in the camp completed the evacuation by 6:30.

Daylight revealed the full extent of the disaster. At 10:30 a.m. high tide reached a level of 9.4 feet compared with the normal high of 3 feet. Waves washed across the post and the officer of the day reported to post headquarters in a row boat. The uniform of the day for officers call was bathing suits. The antiaircraft gun park north of the mortar batteries, known as Wilson Park, was demolished and the guns damaged. All the noncommissioned officers' quarters along the bay were damaged and many were swept off their foundations. Besides the extensive damage to the World War I temporary camps, the tractor, truck, and mobile searchlight buildings near the mortar batteries were damaged beyond repair. The magazines were flooded and the railway between the fort and Phoebus was swept off its trestle and the Mill Creek bridge was badly damaged. The main wharf was battered and about one third of its planking was washed away. The post water supply was interrupted and electric current was cut off. Trees were uprooted, roads blocked, and the entire reservation filled with litter from trees, debris, and rubbish washed ashore by the storm. Miraculously, no one was killed or seriously injured on the post.

The work of cleaning up began immediately, only to be interrupted on September 16 by another major hurricane. This time there was some advance warning and luckily the wind was blowing against the tide. The tide rose to 7.2 feet, but only Fenwick Road was flooded. The moat, which had been eighteen inches over its bank during the first hurricane, did not overflow. Power was again knocked out for about a day, but no additional serious damage to the post was done. It was the opinion of the board of officers which surveyed the result of the storm that the relatively light damage resulted from everything which could be damaged having already been smashed by the earlier storm.

A survey conducted immediately after the first storm revealed that the damage was much greater than estimated at first. The sand spit had been cut in the Wilson Park area and Fort Monroe was temporarily an island. The new beach club and golf course had been destroyed. In order to rehabilitate the post, restoring it to the condition that it was in prior to the storm, nearly $650,000 was requested to replace vital installations damaged or destroyed. In addition to this sum, it was obvious that if Fort Monroe was to be retained as a post a large seawall would have to be built along Chesapeake Bay. A low seawall had been constructed on the Hampton Roads side of the post around the turn of the century, but the bay side was open beach.[23]

The hurricanes of 1933 were a great disaster for the post, but happily they occurred at a time when the government was beginning its massive spending program to counteract the Great Depression. As a result, the post received financial support which would have been unheard of during the previous decade. From this time until the beginning of World War II, Fort Monroe undertook a massive construction and rehabilitation program which resulted in the post as it appears today.

An immediate allocation of $1,646,246 became available for Fort Monroe. Of this sum, $1,000,000 was for a concrete seawall, thirteen feet high above mean low water, extending from the area north of the mortar batteries to the old seawall on Hampton Roads. Other major projects were a new central garage opposite the North Gate of the fort, five duplex sets of noncommissioned officers' quarters, and a noncommissioned officers' club. The remainder of the money was used for rebuilding the main pier, the Engineer Wharf, the Quartermaster Wharf, and the Fort Wool Wharf, and for repairs to buildings, roads, walks, phone communications, observation stations, parapets, and power plants. A small office building for the Coast Artillery Board was constructed across the street from the Chamberlin Hotel. Additional funds were also received for six sets of duplex noncommissioned officers' quarters, the completion of Randolph Hall, and various shops and magazines.[24]

In addition to these major projects, several others were undertaken which were to be of long lasting benefit to the post. The Mill Creek shore line to the north of the fort was filled in to provide for a new quartermaster utilities area and for a sewage disposal plant. Land acquired for this project brought the reservation to its present area of 583.55 acres. Until the completion of the sewage disposal plant in the fall of 1937, the sewage of Fort Monroe had been emptied into Chesapeake Bay, often causing pollution problems during the summer months. A new Beach Club was built, this time raised to the level of the top of the new seawall. A significant addition to the club facilities was a large swimming pool, which opened on July 22, 1934, and is still in use. The band stand, which had been the former bathing pavilion of the Hygeia Hotel, was destroyed in the hurricane. It was replaced with a new band stand in what is now Continental Park, which witnessed its first concert on April 8, 1934. An attempt was made to replace the trees and other vegetation destroyed by the hurricane, but this effort met with little success and today the only large trees on the upper end of the reservation are some live oaks near the Officers Club. No trace remains of the pine forest which once covered this area.[25]

Fort Monroe played an important part in Civilian Conservation Corps activities during the depression. Besides providing numerous officers for CCC duty throughout the country, more than 5,000 enrollees for the CCC camps were processed at Fort Monroe in 1933. This was a severe test for the post's training facilities and imposed a heavy burden on the greatly depleted officer personnel. The following year, another 6,300 CCC replacements were processed at Fort Monroe and sent out to camps in the field.[26]

While CCC activities and the construction program added a new feature to life at Fort Monroe things began to return to normal in 1934. The normal summer camps were conducted for the National Guard, ROTC, CMTC, Organized Reserves, and the West Point cadets. The garrison was again able to conduct its own target practices, with, however, only half the usual annual allowance of ammunition.

An added attraction during the 1934 training season was the arrival of the 1st Battalion, 10th Marines, in late September. The battalion consisted of nine officers and 240 enlisted men, formed into a 155-mm. GPF battery and a .50-caliber antiaircraft machine gun battery. In typical Marine fashion, they arrived with four airplanes attached from the Fleet Marine Force. The battalion made the trip from Quantico to Norfolk by Navy transport, and then to Fort Monroe by barge. They landed at Fort Monroe after dark, and demonstrating their naval training, had only one man fall overboard during the unloading. The firing position of the GPF battery was placed on the beach near Buckroe so as not to interfere with the work on the seawall. The 51st Coast Artillery helped by donating some fire control equipment. After nearly a month of training and two target practices, the battalion returned to Quantico.[27]

Brigadier General Joseph P. Tracy, who served as commander of Fort Monroe during this period of turbulence and significant construction, was transferred in November 1936. His replacement was one of the most distinguished officers in the Coast Artillery Corps—Brigadier General John W. Gulick. General Gulick had served as Chief of Coast Artillery from 1930 to 1934 and remained as commandant of the Coast Artillery School and commanding general of the Third Coast Artillery District until his retirement in November 1938.[28]

There was a final flurry of construction on the post toward the end of the decade. The sewage disposal plant, after many delays, was finally completed near the end of 1937. At the same time, work began on a new post theater to replace the old Liberty Theater which had been built in 1920. The theater faces Tidball Road, immediately behind the officers' quarters on the west side of Ingalls Road. Funds for the construction were supplied by the WPA and the Army Motion Picture Service. It seats about 900 and was one of the first buildings on the post to be air conditioned. Work began in late 1937 and the new theater opened in November of 1938.

A new Quartermaster Detachment barracks was completed early in 1939. Very extensive alterations to the old barracks facing the parade ground were also undertaken at this time. The rear wing of the hospital was razed and a new wing constructed. An addition was added to the Coast Artillery School Detachment mess and barracks, and a new addition to the Enlisted Specialists' School was also built.[29]

A major reorganization of the garrison took place, effective November 1, 1938. Headquarters Battery and Battery D of the 3d Battalion, 52d Coast Artillery, were inactivated and the personnel used to form Batteries B and D of the 2d Coast Artillery. Battery B manned the antiaircraft searchlights, Battery D the antiaircraft machine guns, while Battery C continued to man the 3-inch antiaircraft guns. Battery A was in charge of the submarine mines and Battery E served as the caretaker detachment at Fort Story. Battery F, 52d Coast Artillery, remained to man the railway guns and mortars and the Headquarters Battery and Batteries A and B of the 51st Coast Artillery were in charge of the 155-mm. GPF's.[30]

The United States Army in the late 1930's began to emerge from one of its most trying periods. Reduced in 1927 to an authorized strength of only a little more than 118,000 men, the Army was equipped with obsolete and worn out equipment. Adequate funds had not been available to buy new equipment, conduct proper research and development, or to enable the few troops available to take part in field exercises. The obviously deteriorating international situation finally resulted in the late 1930's in the first steps being taken to again make the Army a real fighting unit.

Besides the badly needed construction, the first indications of this change in military policy to be apparent at Fort Monroe were the revival of field exercises in the late 1930's. A provisional antiaircraft battalion of the 2d Coast Artillery spent two months in 1938 at Fort Bragg, North Carolina, participating in a joint antiaircraft-Air Corps exercise. In the summer of 1939, Fort Monroe furnished thirteen officers and 338 men to the III Corps Special Troops during the First Army maneuvers held in the vicinity of Manassas, Virginia.[31]

While Fort Monroe began to emerge from the lethargy of the peaceful 1930's, war again drew nearer to the post. The officers of the garrison did not know how close war actually was in the summer of 1939 when they staged a reception for the officers of H.M.S. *Exeter* at the Beach Club. The arrival of the British heavy cruiser in Hampton Roads marked the social highlight of the summer season. The hospitality was reciprocated by a party on the *Exeter*. The cruiser soon sailed and on December 13,

1939, in company with H.M.S. *Ajax* and H.M.N.Z.S. *Achilles,* brought the dreaded German raider *Graf Spee* to bay and so badly damaged her that she was soon scuttled in Montevideo harbor, Uruguay.[32]

Growing concern for the security of American outlying possessions soon had a direct impact on Fort Monroe. The War Department established the Puerto Rican Department on July 1, 1939, and decided to send immediate reinforcements to the island. Toward the end of August, Brigadier General Edmund L. Daley, the department commander, was notified that if war broke out in Europe he would be sent one antiaircraft battalion, one 155-mm. GPF coast artillery battalion, and a company of engineers. The German invasion of Poland on September 1, 1939, resulted in the quick sending of these promised reinforcements.

Battery D, 69th Coast Artillery (Antiaircraft), was the first to arrive in Puerto Rico on September 25. The U.S. Army Transport *St. Mihiel* sailed from New York on October 15 with the major portion of the troops bound for the Caribbean. The following day, the *St. Mihiel* dropped anchor in Hampton Roads. The 1st Battalion, 51st Coast Artillery, stationed at Fort Monroe since 1931, had been selected as the 155-mm. GPF battalion. The battalion had sent a motor convoy to New York to load its equipment on the transport. The Casemate Club opened the season on a sad note with a farewell party for the officers of the battalion. Now the men, carrying full field gear, were loaded on a lighter which was towed out to the waiting transport.

The void left by the departure of the 51st Coast Artillery was quickly filled. Existing Coast Artillery regiments were being filled up to strength and many new units were being formed. At Fort Monroe, the 70th Coast Artillery (Antiaircraft) was organized in late 1939 and began building from scratch. There was considerable turbulence in the personnel of the garrison as officers and men were transferred to the 70th Coast Artillery or to other posts to fill vacancies in the expanding Army.[33]

Footnotes Chapter XI

[1] Davis had graduated from West Point in 1887 and had been promoted to colonel in 1914. He served during World War I as a brigadier general and commanded the 162d and 151st Field Artillery Brigades. Davis was promoted to permanent brigadier general when he left Fort Monroe. He retired in 1929 and died in 1937. Smith had graduated from West Point in 1892 and was promoted to colonel in 1917. At the beginning of the war he was on the staff of the Coast Artillery School and emplaced the mine net in Hampton Roads. He rose to major general and commanded the 36th Division. Following his departure from Fort Monroe, Smith was promoted to permanent major general and served as superintendent of the United States Military Academy from 1928 to 1932. He retired in 1932 and died in 1941. *Heitman,* pp. 360, 905; *Cullum,* Vol. VIA, pp. 454, 620–621, Vol. VII, pp. 251, 337–338.

[2] Ltr A.G. 323.43—3rd C.A., April 25, 1923 (File No. 300.1/19464).

[3] "Centennial Celebration at Fort Monroe," *Coast Artillery Journal,* 59 (July 1923), pp. 87–88; Newport News *Daily Press,* June 30, 1923, pp. 1, 2.

⁴ "The Coast Artillery School Centennial Exercises," *Coast Artillery Journal*, 60, (June 1924), pp. 443–451; Newport News *Daily Press*, May 24, 1924, pp. 1, 6, 9.

⁵ Lt. Col. H. C. Barnes, "A Regimental Organization for the Coast Artillery Corps," *Coast Artillery Journal*, 60 (April 1924), pp. 293–299.

⁶ "The Twelfth Coast Artillery (HD)," *Coast Artillery Journal*, 66 (March 1927), pp. 253–254; "Sixty-first Coast Artillery (Antiaircraft)," 67 (September 1927), pp. 245–247.

⁷ "C.M.T. Camp, Fort Monroe, Virginia," *Coast Artillery Journal*, 67 (October 1927), p. 366; Lt. Col. Hartman L. Butler, "Fort Monroe, Virginia, R.O.T.C. Coast Artillery Camp 1923," 59 (November 1923), pp. 403–404; Maj. Richard F. Beirne, "The Fort Monroe Reserve Officers' Camp, 1923," 59 (September 1923), pp. 279–280; "Target Practice of the Virginia National Guard, 1923" (November 1923), pp. 441–443; Maj. Franklin W. Reese, "Third Coast Artillery District," 84 (July-August 1941), p. 382.

⁸ "The Coast Artillery School," *Coast Artillery Journal*, 72 (March 1930), pp. 246–249; "Organized Reserve Camps, 1930," and "List of National Guard Camps for Field Training, 1930," 73 (July 1930), pp. 59–60; "The 246th Coast Artillery (HD) at Fort Monroe," 76 (November-December 1933), p. 470.

⁹ General Orders No. 6, Headquarters of the Army, January 30, 1866; Birkhimer, *op. cit.*, pp. 186–187, 378.

¹⁰ Col. H. J. Hatch, "A History of the Coast Artillery Board and Its Work," *Coast Artillery Journal*, 60 (June 1924), pp. 453–469.

¹¹ *Ibid.*; Col. A. H. Sunderland, "The Coast Artillery Board," *Coast Artillery Journal*, 76 (July-August 1933), pp. 261–264.

¹² "Coast Artillery School Moves to San Francisco," *Coast Artillery Journal*, 89 (May-June 1946), p. 38.

¹³ Callan had graduated from West Point in 1896 and served in command of a field artillery brigade as a temporary brigadier general during World War I. He was promoted to permanent brigadier general in 1921, and after serving at Fort Monroe from 1924 to 1929 he was promoted to major general in 1931 and served as Assistant Chief of Staff G-4 of the War Department. He retired and died in 1936. Brig. Gen. Charles D. Roberts, the commanding general at Fort Eustis, served briefly in 1929 as commander of the Third Coast Artillery District before the arrival of General Todd. Todd had graduated from West Point in 1890 and also commanded a field artillery brigade as brigadier general during World War I. He was promoted to brigadier general in 1920 and major general in 1927. He served at Fort Monroe from August 28, 1929, until his retirement on August 31, 1930. General Todd died in 1964. *Heitman*, pp. 274–275, 964; *Cullum*, Vol. VII, pp. 408–409; "Maj. Gen. Harry D. Todd, Jr., Retires," *Coast Artillery Journal*, 73 (September 1930), pp. 259–262.

¹⁴ "Coast Artillery School Moves to San Francisco," pp. 38–39; "The Coast Artillery School" *Coast Artillery Journal*, 71 (November 1929), pp. 418–419; 72 (February 1930), pp. 157–158; (March 1930), p. 246; (June 1930), p. 530; "The 61st Coast Artillery (AA), Fort Monroe," *Coast Artillery Journal*, 71 (October 1929), p. 31. Embick graduated from West Point in 1899 and was an honor graduate of the Artillery School in 1903. During World War I, while serving as a colonel in the Signal Corps, he was awarded the Distinguished Service Medal for his service with the Supreme War Council. He was promoted to brigadier general in 1930 and served as commandant of the Coast Artillery School from September 1, 1930, to April 25, 1932. He was promoted to major general in 1936 and in 1935 and 1936 served as Assistant Chief of Staff, War Plans Division, and was Deputy Chief of Staff from 1936 to 1938. Promoted to lieutenant general, he retired in 1941, but was immediately recalled to active duty. During World War II he served as a member of the Permanent Joint Board of Defense of the United States and Canada, the Inter-American Defense Board, and the Joint Strategic Survey Committee. He was relieved from active duty in 1946 and died in 1957. *Heitman*, p. 404; *Cullum*, Vol. VIII, p. 120; Maurice Matloff, *Strategic Planning for Coalition Warfare, 1943–1944* (Washington: Department of the Army, 1959), p. 108; Forrest C. Pogue, *George C. Marshall: Ordeal and Hope, 1939–1942* (New York: The Viking Press, 1966), p. 132.

¹⁵ "The Coast Artillery School," *Coast Artillery Journal*, 72 (June 1930), pp. 532–534; Maj. J. H. Cunningham, "The March of the 61st Coast Artillery (AA)," *Coast Artillery Journal*, 74 (January 1931), pp. 9–17; "Fort Monroe," *Coast Artillery Journal*, 75 (May-June

1932), p. 224. The 12th Coast Artillery was first activated in 1924 and the oldest battery serving at Fort Monroe was Battery A, which had been organized in 1899 as Battery N, 5th Artillery. Battery H, 2d Coast Artillery, had been organized in 1798 and Battery C in 1810. Battery E was activated and stationed at Fort Story. "The Twelfth Coast Artillery (HD)," *Coast Artillery Journal,* 66 (March 1927), pp. 253–254.

[16] "Coast Artillery School Moves to San Francisco," p. 39; "The Coast Artillery School," *Coast Artillery Journal,* 71 (September 1929), pp. 237–238.

[17] "The Coast Artillery School," *Coast Artillery Journal,* 71 (November 1929), p. 411.

[18] "The Coast Artillery School," *Coast Artillery Journal,* 72 (January 1930), p. 76.

[19] "Notes from Fort Monroe," *Coast Artillery Journal,* 76 (July-August 1933), p. 304.

[20] Diary of Maj. Harrington W. Cochran, November 4, 1935, in Casemate Museum. Reeder had served in the Ohio volunteers during the Spanish-American War and had been commissioned in the Regular Army in 1899. He was promoted to colonel in 1924. His last tour of duty before retirement in 1936 was as commanding officer of the Harbor Defenses of Chesapeake Bay. *Heitman,* p. 821.

[21] "Dedication of the Fort Monroe Golf Course and Beach Club," *Coast Artillery Journal,* 74 (February 1931), pp. 143–144; "The Coast Artillery School," *Coast Artillery Journal,* 75 (January-February 1932), pp. 67–68; Brig. Gen. Rollin L. Tilton, "Notes on Fort Monroe, 1930 to 1946," pp. 1–2, in Casemate Museum.

[22] "Notes from Fort Monroe," *Coast Artillery Journal,* 76 (May-June 1933), p. 216; Diary of Maj. Harrington W. Cochran, Diary 5, April 24 and 25, 1933; Tilton, Notes on Fort Monroe, pp. 2–4.

[23] "Fort Monroe Damaged by Hurricane," *Coast Artillery Journal,* 76 (November-December 1933), pp. 440–441; Report on the Rehabilitation, Preservation and Expansion of Fort Monroe, Virginia, 1933; Cochran Diary, Diary 4, August 23, 24, 25, and September 16, 1933; "The 246th Coast Artillery (HD) at Fort Monroe," *Coast Artillery Journal,* 76 (November-December 1933), p. 470. A marker on the steps of Building 138 shows the height the water reached on August 23.

[24] "The Coast Artillery School," *Coast Artillery Journal,* 76 (November-December 1933), pp. 441–444.

[25] Maj. J. D. Powers, "Fort Monroe, Notes," *Coast Artillery Journal,* 77 (January-February 1934), pp. 51–53; Maj. J. D. Powers, "Fort Monroe News Letter," *Coast Artillery Journal,* 77 (May-June and November-December 1934), pp. 215–216, 456–458; 2d Lt. H. Bennett Whipple, "Fort Monroe," *Coast Artillery Journal,* 80 (November-December 1937), p. 510; Cochran Diary, Diary 4, April 8, 1934, and July 22, 1934.

[26] "Notes from Fort Monroe," *Coast Artillery Journal,* 75 (July-August 1933), p. 304; Maj. Joshua D. Powers, "Fort Monroe News Letter," *Coast Artillery Journal,* 77 (May-June 1934 and November-December 1934), pp. 216, 456.

[27] Maj. J. D. Powers, "Fort Monroe News Letter," *Coast Artillery Journal,* 77 (November-December 1934), pp. 456–457.

[28] Tracy had graduated from West Point in 1896 and was promoted to brigadier general in 1931. He retired in 1938 and died in 1950. Gulick had entered the Army as a lieutenant in the 1st North Carolina Infantry during the Spanish-American War and had served as a captain in the 47th United States Volunteer Infantry during the Philippine Insurrection. Appointed a first lieutenant in the Artillery Corps in 1901 he served at Fort Monroe from 1904 to 1911 and at various times from 1915 to 1917. During World War I he served as chief of staff of Army Artillery of the First Army in France. He was appointed major general and Chief of Coast Artillery in 1930, and upon his relief from that position in 1934 he was promoted to permanent brigadier general. General Gulick died in 1939. *Heitman,* pp. 483, 968; "Major General John W. Gulick," *Coast Artillery Journal,* 72 (May 1930), pp. 382–384.

[29] "Fort Monroe," *Coast Artillery Journal,* 80 (November-December 1937), p. 510; 82 (March-April 1939), p. 168, and (May-June 1939), p. 267.

[30] Maj. L. W. Goeppert, "Fort Monroe," *Coast Artillery Journal,* 81 (November-December 1938), p. 491.

[31] "Fort Monroe," *Coast Artillery Journal,* 81 (November-December 1938), p. 491, and 82 (July-August 1939), p. 369; Jean R. Moenk, *A History of Large-Scale Army Maneuvers in the United States, 1935–1964* (Ft Monroe: HQ USCONARC, 1969), pp. 23–26.

[32] Maj. L. W. Goeppert and Lt. J. DuV. Stevens, "Fort Monroe," *Coast Artillery Journal,* 82 (July-August 1939), p. 369.

[33] "Fort Monroe," *Coast Artillery Journal,* 82 (November-December 1939), pp. 584–585; Newport News *Daily Press,* October 15, 1939, pp. 1D, 5D, and October 17, 1939, p. 9; Stetson Conn, Rose E. Engelman, and Byron Fairchild, *Guarding the United States and Its Outposts* (Washington: Department of the Army, 1964), pp. 324–325.

Chapter XII

Fort Monroe During World War II

FEW OF THE HARBOR DEFENSES of the United States were able effectively to carry out their missions with the armament which existed prior to World War II. The situation was particularly serious in Chesapeake Bay. Up until World War I, the twelve mile wide entrance to the bay had made effective defense impossible. It was not until 1920–1922 that the construction at Fort Story of Batteries Pennington and Walke, four 16-inch howitzers, had made a start on the outer defenses. Consequently, in the Harbor Defenses of Chesapeake Bay most of the armament was situated at Fort Monroe, far back from the entrance to the bay. Except for the 6-inch guns of Battery Montgomery, the armament of Fort Monroe consisted of outmoded mortars and the slow and hardly more useful disappearing carriage guns. To accomplish the mission of the harbor defense required that enemy ships be prevented from closing within 35,000 yards of Capes Henry and Charles. The two batteries sited at Cape Henry had a range of 24,540 yards and were not able to do this, nor did they have support.[1]

Although Fort Monroe's guns no longer played a major part in the defense of Chesapeake Bay, they did have responsibility for the protection of Hampton Roads, the inner mine field, the antisubmarine net and gate, and the control of shipping. Fort Monroe was also the headquarters of the Chesapeake Bay Sector, vital to the seaward defense of the area, and with its responsibility for the Coast Artillery School, the Coast Artillery Board, and the Submarine Mine Depot, as well as its many service command logistical responsibilities, it played a role equaled only during the Civil War.

Fort Monroe's participation in World War II started with the partial mobilization of the Army in the fall of 1940. Major General Frederic H. Smith at that time commanded the Third Coast Artillery District, including the Harbor Defenses of Chesapeake Bay, and the post of Fort Monroe, all under the Third Corps Area. As Commandant of the Coast Artillery School, he was also responsible to the Chief of Coast Artillery for the school, Coast Artillery Board, and Submarine Mine Depot. When the mobilization took place, the Third Coast Artillery District passed to the command of First Army and the Northeast Defense Command, commanded by Lieutenant General Hugh A. Drum. The Third Corps Area retained responsibility for service, supply, and certain administrative matters as well as civil protection. The Coast Artillery School, with the Coast Artillery Board and Submarine Mine Depot, became a separate command on October 10, 1940, under the command of Brigadier General Frank S. Clark. General Clark remained responsible to the Chief of Coast Artillery.[2]

General Smith remained with the Third Coast Artillery District until January 4, 1941, when he left to assume command of the VII Army Corps. Brigadier General Rollin L. Tilton had assumed command of the Harbor Defenses of Chesapeake Bay on November 9, 1940, and succeeded General Smith in command of the district. General Tilton had been assigned by General Smith to the command of the post upon his arrival, which was confirmed by War Department orders on December 19.[3]

During the spring of 1940, the units at Fort Monroe conducted extensive practice firing. Battery A, 2d Coast Artillery, fired the 6-inch guns at Battery Montgomery; Battery D, 2d Coast Artillery, fired a target practice with the 12-inch disappearing guns of Battery DeRussy; Battery F, 2d Coast Artillery, conducted a target practice with the 8-inch railway guns and school instruction with 75-mm. field guns; and Batteries C and E, 70th Coast Artillery, fired 3-inch antiaircraft guns and automatic weapons at Fort Story for the National Guard class of the Coast Artillery School.[4]

In the early 1930's, the Army had adopted the 16-inch barbette carriage gun as the standard harbor defense weapon against capital ships, but little work had been done to actually improve the harbor defenses. Until the fall of France in June 1940 the possibility of any naval attack on the American coast line had appeared remote. From that time until the fate of the British and French fleets became known, the United States faced the real possibility of serious naval inferiority in the Atlantic. This brought about a complete reassessment of harbor defenses. The Harbor Defense Board report of July 27, 1940, recommended the general adoption of the 16-inch gun as the primary weapon and the 6-inch gun as the secondary weapon in all fixed harbor defenses. The 16-inch gun had a maximum range of about twenty-five miles, and, at least theoretically, could keep any hostile ship at a safe distance from the harbor areas. The board also proposed the construction of new 6-inch two-gun barbette carriage batteries, which would provide long-range fire (about fifteen miles maximum) against cruisers and other lighter ships. These would greatly reinforce the earlier 6-inch and 3-inch semi-modern barbette carriage guns that were to be retained. The plans called for the abandonment of the obsolete and obsolescent seacoast batteries as soon as the new batteries were installed. Thereafter the harbor defenses could be manned with substantially fewer troops. Formal approval of the modernization program was given by the Secretary of War in September 1940. This program included two 16-inch batteries each at Fort Story and Fort Winslow, one 16-inch battery at Fort Monroe, two 6-inch batteries each at Fort Story and Fort Winslow, and one 6-inch battery at Fort Wool.[5]

Work on construction of the new batteries took a long time under the best of circumstances. From the beginning the modernization program had to compete with the general and rapid expansion of the whole Army, and the program was also slowed by the continuously expanding naval construction program. The War Department in the late summer of 1941 decided to limit active work to those batteries that could be completed by June 30, 1944. In November 1942, nine low priority 16-inch batteries on which work had not yet started, including the battery at Fort Monroe and one battery at Fort John Custis, were eliminated from the projects by the War Department. In August 1943, thirteen 6-inch batteries, most of which were near completion, were suspended from further construction because of an expansion in the more pressing field artillery program which had caused a shortage of gun tubes. Included in this reduction were batteries at Fort Wool and Fort John Custis.[6]

In addition to Fort Monroe, the Harbor Defenses of Chesapeake Bay included Fort Story at Cape Henry. This post had been started in 1917 and its armament was greatly augmented by the 1940 modernization program. To complete the coverage of the mouth of Chesapeake Bay, Fort Winslow, located near Kiptopeke on Cape Charles and Fisherman Island, was added in September 1940. In February 1942, this post was redesignated Fort Custis because of local sentiment and in October 1942 it was redesignated Fort John Custis to avoid confusion with Fort Eustis. Land for the Little Creek Mine Base was acquired from the Pennsylvania Railroad in December 1941. Approximately 10,000 square feet was taken over and construction started, including storage space, barracks, and other buildings. The site was adjacent to the Pennsylvania Railroad ferry landing in Princess Anne County, on Little Creek. Mine planters assigned to the Harbor Defenses of Chesapeake Bay and the mine batteries used this as their base for mine field operations, although the mine facilities for the inner mine field were retained at Fort Monroe.[7]

The expansion of the garrison of the Harbor Defenses of Chesapeake Bay was both spectacular and rapid. On June 1, 1940, the 1st Battalion, 57th Coast Artillery, was activated at Fort Monroe and the 2nd Battalion, 69th Coast Artillery, was activated at Fort Story. The 69th Coast Artillery moved to Fort Monroe at the end of June. On July 1, the 504th Coast Artillery (Antiaircraft) was redesignated as the 74th Coast Artillery and was activated at Fort Monroe using the personnel of the 69th Coast Artillery. The 2d Battalion, 69th Coast Artillery, was then transferred, less personnel, to Fort Crockett, Texas. The 70th Coast Artillery was also transferred from Fort Monroe at the end of June to Fort Screven and Fort Moultrie. On July 1, the 503d Coast Artillery was redesignated as the 71st Coast Artillery (Antiaircraft) and activated at Fort Monroe. A tent camp was established on the parade ground inside the fort, and soon recruits who had been quartered with the 2d Coast Artillery began taking their places in the tent city. The regiment was transferred to Fort Story on July 31, making the trip on the mine planter *Schofield.*[8]

Fort Monroe once again played host to a President of the United States when Franklin D. Roosevelt visited the post on July 29. A twenty-one gun salute was fired as the President's yacht, the *Potomac,* approached the main wharf, and honors were sounded by the band of the 2d Coast Artillery. The President, accompanied by General Smith, proceeded to Wilson Park along a route lined with troops of the various units of the garrison. At Wilson Park, Battery C, 2d Coast Artillery, fired a 3-inch antiaircraft gun demonstration course. Battery D, 2d Coast Artillery, fired two demonstration courses with the 37-mm. antiaircraft battery, and Battery B, 2d Coast Artillery, and Battery D, 74th Coast Artillery, displayed antiaircraft searchlights and .50-caliber machine guns. After the demonstration, the President's party proceeded back through the old fort and then on to Langley Field. After visiting Langley Field and Newport News, the President's party returned to Fort Monroe to board the *Potomac.*[9]

The changes in the garrison up to this time had involved units of the Regular Army. In September, the National Guard was mobilized and another influx of new units into the Harbor Defenses of Chesapeake Bay took place. The 246th Coast Artillery (Harbor Defense) of the Virginia National Guard settled in tents at Fort Monroe and Fort Story, while the 213th Coast Artillery of the Pennsylvania National Guard and the 244th Coast Artillery of the New York National Guard occupied Camp Pendleton. Camp Pendleton, the Virginia State Rifle Range located just south of Virginia Beach, had been taken over by the Army in August as a training camp for mobile coast artillery units. It was used throughout the war as a Coast Artillery Training Center for units assigned to the sector and for many coast artillery and other smaller units designated for overseas bases and attached for organization and training. As soon as facilities at Camp Pendleton were available, the two mobile units at Fort Monroe, the 57th and 74th Coast Artillery, were moved there. The 57th Coast Artillery made the move in February 1941, making a welcome change from tents to barracks. At the same time, the 213th Coast Artillery was transferred from Camp Pendleton to Camp Stewart, Georgia. The 74th Coast Artillery was transferred from Fort Monroe to Camp Pendleton during June and July. Fort Monroe was totally unsuited for any mobile unit training as well as being overloaded with its own garrison and the Coast Artillery School troops.[10]

The 2d Coast Artillery was also undergoing major changes during this period. Battery F, 52d Coast Artillery, had been inactivated early in 1940 and responsibility for the railway artillery was assumed by the newly activated Battery F, 2d Coast Artillery. Battery G, a harbor defense searchlight unit, was organized in January 1941. The regiment had now grown large enough to be organized into two battalions. Batteries H and I were activated at the end of April 1942. During the early days of 1941, the regiment's main mission was cadre training for the Coast Artillery Training Center at Fort Eustis. During World War II, Fort Eustis did not form part of the Chesapeake Bay Sector and was entirely independent of Fort Monroe.[11]

In 1939, funds had been appropriated for the construction of a new building especially designed to meet the needs of the Submarine Mine Depot. Work began in March 1940 and was completed in October. The new brick and concrete fire-proof building was located east of the site formerly occupied by the old Liberty Theater. It was designed, in collaboration with personnel on duty at the depot, by the Corps of Engineers and was erected under the supervision of the local District Engineer. The Submarine Mine Depot, commanded throughout the war by Colonel Delmar S. Lenzner, originally had 12 officers, 1 warrant officer, 32 enlisted men, and 10 civilians assigned. During the war this increased to 12 officers and warrant officers, 120 enlisted men, and many civilians. The Submarine Mine Depot was charged with the development, procurement, and supply of all the coast artillery submarine mine equipment, cable, and floating equipment and manufactured much of the electrical and allied equipment. The building—Building 28—now houses post engineer operations.[12]

General Drum visited Fort Monroe and made an inspection of the harbor defense on January 9 and 10, 1941. He returned on May 19 to witness the first command post exercise conducted by the Third Coast Artillery District. This command post exercise was one of a series which he held for all the districts. The one at Fort Monroe was conducted by the staff of the Second Coast Artillery District and the Third Coast Artillery

District conducted a similar one on September 9 to 11 for the First Coast Artillery District in New England. While at Fort Monroe, General Drum brought up the question of a protected command post for the district and approved the plan to convert the third front of the fort for this purpose. Command post exercises became a regular part of the training in the following months.[13]

On June 10, 1941, the 16-inch howitzers at Fort Story fired their first regular service practice since 1928. Over 500 spectators, including officials, newspapermen, news photographers, and newsreel representatives, watched Battery A, 246th Coast Artillery, fire the big guns. In addition to the 16-inch howitzers, the units of the Harbor Defenses of Chesapeake Bay also fired during this period 3-inch antiaircraft guns, 3-inch seacoast guns, .30- and .50-caliber machine guns, 37-mm. guns, 75-mm. guns, 155-mm. guns, and the 8-inch railway guns.[14]

The old Third Coast Artillery District headquarters had been in the post headquarters building at Fort Monroe. This proved to be totally inadequate to the needs of the Chespeake Bay Sector. The new mine casemate for the Hampton Roads mine groups was installed in the East Gate end of the third front casemates. It was decided to renovate and modernize the entire third front and the Hampton Roads Groupment (the Fort Monroe tactical command) and the Chesapeake Bay Sector headquarters moved in during June 1942. At the same time, work was undertaken on the new signal station on the parapet near the East Gate and this was completed and the surveillance radar for the Hampton Roads Groupment was installed in November.

The hospital at Fort Monroe was also expanded and renovated. Occupancy of the Fort Monroe 90-unit housing project near Phoebus, known as College Court, on August 15, 1941, had done much to alleviate the quarters problem for noncommissioned officers. Work got underway in the latter part of August 1941 on a large fill of part of Mill Creek to provide more land area for training. At Fort Story and Camp Pendleton temporary buildings sufficient to house two regiments at each post were constructed. In addition, a 200 bed hospital was constructed at Fort Story. At Fort Eustis, buildings were constructed to house 14,000 troops at the Coast Artillery Replacement Center.

Since the early 1930's, there had been concern that the only main road out of Fort Monroe was old Route 60, through Phoebus and Hampton, thence to Newport News and up the Peninsula or to the James River Bridge. This was at best a two lane road through the business districts of Phoebus, Hampton, and part of Newport News. It crossed the narrow Queen Street Bridge in Hampton, was congested, circuitous, and totally inadequate for military purposes. Langley Field had a similar problem in that travelers had to come through Hampton to get to Fort Monroe or to go up the Peninsula.

General Tilton and Colonel E. A. Lohman, the commanding officer of Langley Field, therefore recommended in 1941 the construction of a new military road. Going over a new bridge from Fort Monroe, through the residential section of Phoebus, north of Hampton, and direct to the James River Bridge, the road bypassed all congested and built-up areas and saved several miles. It picked up the Langley Field road about half way between downtown Hampton and Langley Field, crossed Yorktown road, and made direct connecion with Routes 60 and 168 in Warwick.

The new road met strong opposition from business interests and property owners in Phoebus and Hampton. The road was certified as essential by the War and Navy Departments and was undertaken by the Public Roads Administration and the State Highway Department. Moving without public notice, the route was surveyed, plans prepared, rights-of-way secured, and construction started in early 1942. The contracts amounted to about $1,500,000 for approximately nine and one half miles of road and the new bridge into Fort Monroe. The railroad trestle into the post from the Mill Creek Guard House, abandoned after the 1933 hurricane, and still in existence was taken as the route into the post and was used for the initial fill. By entering the post in the dock area, all hotel and main dock traffic bypassed the main post. At the same time, the ferry slip of the Old Point-Willoughby Spit Ferry was moved from its location adjacent to the hotel garage to a point north on the new road, thus clearing the Mine Dock area for new construction. The entire project was completed in February 1943. The old Mill Creek Bridge into Phoebus was retained for local use and for the desirability of two bridges.[15]

The 71st Coast Artillery joined the 44th Division in war games on the A. P. Hill Military Reservation during July 1941. In September, most of the mobile units in the district went to the First Army maneuvers in North Carolina. These maneuvers well illustrated the Army's problems in rounding out its tactical organizations. While the 244th Coast Artillery and the 71st Coast Artillery went as complete units with the II Army Corps, the 57th Coast Artillery sent two battalions as infantry and one as service troops while the 74th Coast Artillery sent two batteries as truck units. The 244th Coast Artillery's 155-mm. guns were sent to the maneuver area on flat cars and then moved throughout the maneuvers by tractor. The regiment participated in different problems every week, gaining valuable experience in blackout convoys, infantry, rapid emplacement and removal of guns, camouflage, communications by radio and telephone, and supply in the field. All of the mobile units benefited from the training. There was some confusion when on November 6 the War Department ordered the 2d Battalion, 57th Coast Artillery, deployed to the Pacific. The battalion was supposed to be in San Francisco by November 27 and it was necessary to ask First Army to release it, return it to Camp Pendleton, and get it properly equipped. The battalion finally moved out in December.[16]

The Third Coast Artillery District was the peacetime command of the Third Corps Area charged with the training of the National Guard and Organized Reserve units assigned to the Harbor Defenses of Chesapeake Bay, its only regular unit. In time of war it became the Chesapeake Bay Sector, a part of the Eastern Defense Command, operating with the Fifth Naval District and with coterminous boundaries. The sector operating area included the coastal zone from the Delaware-Maryland border to the southern boundary of Onslow County, North Carolina, about twenty-five miles north of Wilmington.

Little had been done in the construction of the new batteries for the Harbor Defenses of Chesapeake Bay by the end of 1941. The harbor defense was augmented by the employment of the mobile armament then on hand for Coast Artillery School training. At Fort Story, one 2-gun battery of 8-inch railway guns and a 4-gun battery of 155-mm. guns were emplaced. The 8-inch railway battery and the 155-mm. batteries at Fort Monroe were earmarked for Fort Winslow on Cape Charles. The War Department took a dim view of moving this armament in 1941, but during the summer the firing spurs and trackage for the railway battery were constructed and the firing positions for the 155-mm. battery at Fisherman Island were laid out. Battery Montgomery at Fort Monroe at this time was equipped with one of the first experimental seacoast radar sets.[17]

General Drum had issued instructions on May 22, 1941, establishing a permanent harbor defense alert. The fort signal stations and groupment command posts at Fort Story and Fort Monroe operated on a twenty-four hour schedule and in close liaison with the Navy. The armament was in service and manned on a training status. At Fort Story the 155-mm. battery and the antiaircraft battery and at Fort Monroe Battery Montgomery and an antiaircraft battery were manned on a twenty-four hour basis. The Fifth Naval District had at the same time established the Inshore Patrol, with its command post at Fort Story. The Navy had also laid hydrophones to seaward for the surveillance of the bay entrance at night or in conditions of poor visibility. The submarine net at the entrance to Hampton Roads, less the gate, had also been completed. The station at Fort Story became the first Harbor Entrance Control Post and the joint command post of the Harbor Defenses of Chesapeake Bay and the Inshore Patrol.

As the international situation deteriorated, there was a gradual increase of the alert, the Army mission being to support the Navy within the defensive coastal area. On November 4, 1941, secret orders were issued all commanders to attack and destroy any German or Italian forces within the area. By December 4, 1941, all troops had returned from maneuvers and the Harbor Defenses of Chesapeake Bay was fully manned and on partial alert. The alert batteries had their fire control and one gun crew in the emplacements at all times and the remainder of the battery within call. The strength at Fort Monroe was as follows:

Headquarters & Headquarters Battery, 3d CA District & HD	39
1319th Service Unit and Casuals	600
96th Ordnance Company (MM)	82
2d Coast Artillery	1,071
246th Coast Artillery	427
USAMP *Schofield*	65
Coast Artillery School and Board, Mine Depot	2,708
Total	4,992

In addition to the troops at Fort Monroe, there were 3,867 men at Fort Story and 5,112 at Camp Pendleton.[18]

The first reports of the attack on Pearl Harbor reached Fort Monroe about 3:15 p.m. on December 7. At 5:55 p.m. the Chief of Staff of First Army called General Tilton and directed him to alert the harbor defense and to cooperate with the Navy. Orders were immediately issued placing the harbor defense on full alert and directing the other elements of the command to take all precautions. Shortly thereafter Major General Henry C. Platt, the Third Corps Area commander, ordered General Tilton to take measures to protect important utilities in the area, especially the James River Bridge. A platoon of the 74th Coast Artillery was sent that night to guard the bridge, a detachment from Fort Monroe to guard the Hampton Power Plant, and a detachment from the Antiaircraft Training Center at Fort Eustis to guard the Newport News Waterworks. The following day a battery of the 244th Coast Artillery was placed in the railroad yards at Portsmouth to have troops in that area in case of emergency. At that time there was a great deal of fear of sabotage and the troops were deployed mainly to reassure the public. The coast artillery troops were gradually returned to their proper duties and the last of them was relieved on December 23 when a battalion of the 116th Infantry arrived in Norfolk and took over all civil protection under Third Corps Area control.

The Third Coast Artillery District officially became the Chesapeake Bay Sector of the Eastern Defense Command on December 12. The harbor defenses had initiated the underwater defense of the bay on December 8. The first line of controlled mines, in the main channel off the Capes, was laid by December 16 and in operation. The 8-inch railway battery at Fort Winslow was sent from Fort Monroe by way of Baltimore on December 19 and, after some delay in getting its battle allowances of ammunition, was ready for action on December 29.

The antiaircraft defense of the area was also initiated on December 8. The 71st Coast Artillery and the 74th Coast Artillery occupied positions covering the Naval Operating Base, Norfolk, and the Navy Yard in Ports-mouth. The 34th Antiaircraft Brigade, comprising the 70th, 94th, and 212th Coast Artillery, was ordered into the sector and occupied positions at Langley Field, Baltimore, and Washington, with brigade headquarters in Norfolk. Prior to the completion of all these movements, First Army on December 14 organized the First Army Antiaircraft Command. This command took over all antiaircraft defense and functioned operationally under First Air Force. The sector was relieved of antiaircraft defense responsibilities, although the Norfolk command remained under the sector for joint operations and for many logistical matters.[19]

General Tilton had made a reconnaissance of Beaufort Inlet, North Carolina, in November and had decided to protect the harbor with a bat-talion of 155-mm. guns. Beaufort Inlet was a good small harbor with dock facilities and a small Navy Section Base at Morehead City. At the west side of the entrance to the harbor stood Fort Macon, a brick fort erected at about the same time as Fort Monroe and long abandoned by the Army. The Governor of North Carolina turned the park which included the fort over to the Army, and additional land was leased. The 1st Battalion, 244th Coast Artillery, left Camp Pendleton on December 18 and went into posi-tion at Fort Macon. Headquarters of the Temporary Harbor Defenses of Beaufort Inlet and a Harbor Entrance Control Post were established in Fort Macon.

Of the troops at Camp Pendleton, the 2d Battalion, 57th Coast Artillery, left on December 10 for San Francisco and the 2d Battalion, 244th Coast Artillery, deployed to Alaska on December 23. The 3d Battalion, 244th Coast Artillery, had been depleted to fill the deploying units, but it was rebuilt and departed on January 17, 1942, for San Francisco. The regi-mental headquarters of the 244th Coast Artillery eventually joined the 1st Battalion of the regiment at Beaufort Inlet and served as harbor defense headquarters.

On December 19, the 116th Infantry, and the 1st Battalion, 111th Field Artillery, of the 29th Division began moving into the sector to act as a mobile force. The mission of the mobile force was to observe and patrol the coastline, repel enemy raids or landing attempts, be prepared to pro-tect the interior of the sector against attack by airborne troops, and to support the harbor defenses in local defense. The Cape Charles Defense Force, consisting of the 1st Battalion, 116th Infantry, plus Battery A, 111th Field Artillery, was stationed at Westover, Maryland, with outposts at Ocean City, Maryland, Chincoteague, and Exmore, Virginia. The Cape Henry Defense Force, consisting of the 116th Infantry and 1st Battalion, 111th Field Artillery (less detachments), covered the sensitive Cape Henry area and the coast as far south as Oregon Inlet, North Carolina. This force was based at Camp Pendleton with an outpost at Manteo,

North Carolina. Another defense force, consisting of the 3d Battalion, 116th Infantry, and Battery C, 111th Field Artillery, was based at New Bern, North Carolina.[20]

The Hotel Chamberlin was taken over by the Navy on January 1, 1942. Known as the U.S. Hotel Chamberlin, the building was purchased by the government to be operated jointly for commissioned officers of all branches of the service. The hotel helped to alleviate the shortage of housing which confronted the Fifth Naval District and the Chespeake Bay Sector. The hotel was operated by its former managers under the direction of the Navy.[21]

The greatest activity in the area during the war took place in 1942. This was the height of the German submarine campaign and the threat of possible attack on coastal cities existed. Hampton Roads became, with New York, the major Atlantic base for overseas operations. The establishment of the Amphibious Force Atlantic Fleet at Little Creek and the naval training operations in the protected waters of Chesapeake Bay, made Hampton Roads a major training area. On June 18, 1942, the Hampton Roads Port of Embarkation was established at Newport News, with Camp Patrick Henry as its major staging area.

Joint operations of the Chesapeake Bay Sector and Fifth Naval District were conducted through a Joint Operations Center, the Harbor Entrance Control Posts, and the Coast Defense Warning Service. The sector headquarters was at Fort Monroe with a liaison officer at Fifth Naval District. The Joint Operations Center was established at the headquarters of the Fifth Naval District at the Naval Operating Base, Norfolk.

The Harbor Entrance Control Posts were the joint command posts of the Inshore Patrol and the harbor defense command. Their mission was to collect and disseminate information of activities in the defensive area, to control shipping entering or leaving port, and to take prompt and decisive action in case of hostilities. The Signal Station at Fort Monroe became Harbor Entrance Control Post No. 2. This post controlled the entrance into Hampton Roads with the gate vessel on the anti-submarine gate off Thimble Shoals.

The Defense Warning Service was the sector intelligence agency for the observation and security of the coastline. It was based on the coast artillery observation posts (fire control stations), the Coast Guard Life Saving Stations, reports from the Inshore Patrol, and the outposts and patrols of the mobile force. Information funneled in through warning centers at Westover, Fort Story, Fort Monroe, and New Bern to the Joint Operations Center.

The underwater defense project provided an outer defense of twenty-two groups (nineteen mines each) of controlled mines in two fields of two lines each in the main channel northeast of Cape Henry, controlled

from Fort Story, and an inner defense of six groups in two lines in Chesapeake Bay near Thimble Shoals Light, controlled from Fort Monroe.
Also included in this project was a Navy mine field of 365 contact mines
laid on January 17, 1942, between the tip of Cape Charles and the north
edge of the main channel, linking up with the controlled Army mine field.
The controlled field was kept at "safe" normally and when shipping was
entering or leaving but was put on "contact" whenever the harbor defense
commander decided that the tactical situation required it, at night, or
under conditions of poor visibility. There was an opening in the field for
ships, but there was a great deal of trouble with ships getting off course
and striking the mines. The situation was finally corrected by using small
buoys to show the opening. On March 16, the only mineplanter in the
command, the *Schofield,* was ordered to Delaware Bay for a month to
put down a mine field there. This seriously reduced the efficiency of the
field at the Virginia Capes and delayed the planting of the inner field.

An anti-motor torpedo boat net southwest of Thimble Shoals was emplaced from Fort Monroe on the north to Willoughby Spit on the south,
with a gate in the main channel. This net was in operation by March 1 and
another net was placed across the entrance to the York River soon thereafter. The gate to the net and the inner mine field were controlled from
Harbor Entrance Control Post No. 2 at Fort Monroe. They were normally
left open for shipping except on instructions from the Joint Operations
Center.[22]

During the submarine campaign of 1942, which began with the sinking
of an American tanker on January 17, the Harbor Defenses of Chesapeake
Bay operated jointly and in close support of the Approach and Entrance
Force. Joint operations, the control of shipping entering and leaving port,
the firing of warning shots, and the control of the mine fields settled into
an established routine. A new protected command post for the Harbor
Defenses of Chesapeake Bay was established in July at Fort Story. The
installation of surveillance radar permitted observation over all water
areas regardless of weather conditions. Unidentified shipping or signals
were quickly run down by patrol craft under radar control from the Harbor
Entrance Control Post.

During the submarine operations the Navy had much difficulty keeping
in touch with small patrol craft and fishing vessels. In June someone suggested trying pigeons, and the Chesapeake Bay Sector obtained a loft from
Fort Monmouth which was placed at Fort Story. After the necessary training for the pigeons, they were given to designated patrol and fishing vessels
for the transmission of intelligence or emergency messages. These pigeons
brought back considerable information concerning the sighting of submarines.[23]

On the night of February 16, the American tanker *E. H. Blum* approached the Capes in a thick fog. The ship was known to be friendly but failed to answer radio calls. Tracked by radar, she approached the Army mine field where she struck and sank. The Coast Guard cutter *Woodbury* picked up all of her crew and the vessel was later salvaged. The incident is interesting as it was the first case where the harbor defense radar picked up and tracked, in the fog, a ship. The fire control sections not only predicted where she would touch the Army mine field, but also where she would strike the Navy contact mine field. Had the ship used her radio she could have been brought in safely.

On April 14, the U.S.S. *Roper* engaged a submarine which she spotted through the aid of radar about fifteen miles off Oregon Inlet. On closer approach and illumination by the destroyer's searchlights, the submarine crew ran toward their guns but were machine gunned by the destroyer. The *Roper* then opened fire and made a hit on the conning tower. The submarine then either submerged or sank and the *Roper* laid a pattern of depth charges. At daylight, aided by the 65th Observation Group from Langley Field, the destroyer began picking up bodies. Twenty-nine bodies were recovered and brought to the Naval Operating Base in Norfolk. An examination of papers found on the men showed that the submarine was the *U-85*. This was the first German submarine sunk by an American destroyer in World War II. In accordance with a joint agreement the Chesapeake Bay Sector arranged for the burial of the Germans in the National Cemetery in Hampton. The enemy sailors were buried with full military honors. It was given out locally that the burial was that of merchant seamen killed in recent sinkings and picked up on the beaches or out at sea.

Lookout Bight, a natural harbor seven miles east of Beaufort Inlet, is formed by Cape Lookout and protected by an old breakwater. During the anti-submarine campaign it formed an ideal refuge, being established as a patrolled anchorage by the Eastern Sea Frontier on April 10, 1942. Cape Lookout was a dreary, wind swept sand spit, reached only by water and, except near the Coast Guard station, offering few gun positions in the sand dunes.

Occupation of this site materially extended the harbor defense mission. With deep water on either side, a seacoast battery with almost all around fire was required. At the urgent request of Admiral Manly H. Simons, the Commandant, Fifth Naval District, General Tilton on April 10 sent Battery A, 193d Field Artillery Battalion, from the Beaufort Inlet Mobile Force to Cape Lookout to give some protection pending the move of a platoon of two 155-mm. guns from the 244th Coast Artillery. The 244th completed this move in May. Meanwhile, Admiral Simons had made available two 5-inch barbette guns and two 6-inch barbette guns from Norfolk for Beaufort. After some delay, funds for the construction of emplacements for these guns were approved and the 5-inch battery at Cape Lookout was completed in September and the 6-inch battery at Fort Macon in November. These two batteries gave ample protection to the harbor and anchorage.

The Sector's problems in Beaufort Inlet were not yet over, however, for the 244th Coast Artillery was destined for overseas service. This had been foreseen and on July 18 Battery H, 2d Coast Artillery, had been sent to Beaufort. Battery K, 2d Coast Artillery, which was mobilized at Charleston, arrived on August 31. Finally, a small harbor defense headquarters battery was authorized and Beaufort Inlet was secure. The 1st Battalion, 244th Coast Artillery, left for overseas on August 15.

Early in June 1942, three or four submarines were believed to be operating in Fifth Naval District waters. At 5:00 p.m. on June 15, a northbound convoy of thirteen ships was standing into Chesapeake Bay following the swept channel. Five minutes later, just as the convoy was turning, an observer at one of the harbor defense stations reported that one ship had exploded and caught fire. The harbor defense alerted all batteries, notified the Joint Operations Center, and called for a plane to search the area. Less than half an hour later, a second tanker was struck. Neither the plane, the harbor defense stations, nor the convoy could find evidence of any submarine. The harbor defense remained on the alert, but the plane was released. At 8:13 p.m., the British corvette *Kingston Ceylonite,* which had been part of the convoy escort, exploded and sank just to the west of the other incidents. The corvette went down with all hands. One of the tankers remained afloat and was eventually salvaged. The harbor defense remained on the alert until 11:40 p.m., when alert was reduced to one battery and the mine fields at "contact," when there was no shipping in the channel, while the searchlights were used to search for survivors. Two days later an American collier was sunk in the same area. Sweeping operations in the channel had been conducted regularly by the Navy. The morning after the incident a special sweep was made and five mines exploded. Eight more mines were found in later sweeps. The incident occurred within range of the armament, but there had been no reports on submarine contacts in the vicinity and it was concluded that a submarine had come in under cover of darkness or poor visibility and had laid the mines some time before.

The three sinkings caused considerable excitement among the summer crowds at Virginia Beach, made worse by the arrival of sightseers from Norfolk when the news spread. Troops from the Cape Henry Defense Force were finally put into Virginia Beach to keep the main roads open and straighten things out.[24]

On June 19, all Fort Story elements were again alerted in the early morning on a report of a submarine in the vicinity of the outer mine fields. That evening all elements at Fort Monroe went on alert and the gate was closed on the report of a submarine in the bay. The mine fields were maintained on "contact" and the gate kept closed all night. The report proved erroneous and no submarine actually entered Chesapeake Bay during the war.

Again on September 21, on the report of an unidentified contact on the hydrophone loops and an explosion in the Navy mine field, all elements were alerted and continued on alert through September 24. The mines were placed on "contact" and "Closed Port" procedures were employed intermittently. There was much valuable shipping, many combat elements, and a large part of the North African invasion force assembling in the bay at this time. The senior officer present afloat ordered two destroyers to stations just inside the entrance to the bay to operate in support of the harbor defense. Another destroyer was placed at the Lynnhaven anchorage, one at York Spit, and one in Hampton Roads to assist in protecting shipping against motor torpedo boat raids. The North African expedition had conducted its landing training at Little Creek. After completing training, the troops assembled on their transports up the bay. Security was tight and little about the expedition was known locally. On October 22, the sector was informed that the expedition would move out in two units on October 23 and 24. The movement took about four hours each morning and passed without incident.

Various changes in the armament were made as operations indicated their necessity. The armament at Fort Story did not adequately cover the Examination Anchorage in Lynnhaven Roads, just inside Cape Henry, which was used for the examination of questionable ships and as an anchorage for coastal convoys. A battery of two 3-inch guns was installed inside Cape Henry to cover the anchorage and give some anti-motor torpedo boat defense to the Cape Henry side of the bay entrance. A second battery of two 3-inch guns was installed at Fisherman Island to cover the north flank of the Navy mine field and for anti-motor torpedo boat defense on the Cape Charles side. In August, the 1st Battalion, 52d Coast Artillery (Railway) arrived at Fort Custis and took over the positions of the old 8-inch railway batteries with modern armament.[25]

Throughout the submarine campaign Sector Mobile Forces had been employed in direct support of the Coast Guard stations, on the beaches, and in patrolling the coastal areas. On January 21, 1942, the 111th Infantry, the 1st Battalion, 109th Field Artillery, an Engineer battalion, a Quartermaster truck company, and a Medical collecting company, totaling nearly 6,000 troops, were assigned as a permanent Sector Mobile Force. With the organization of the permanent force, the headquarters section of the 111th Infantry was established at Fort Monroe as a tactical and administrative unit of the Chesapeake Bay Sector. One battalion combat team remained on the Eastern Shore, one in the New Bern-Beaufort Inlet area, and the regimental team, less detachments, and with a provisional tank company, remained in the Cape Henry area. Due to the dispersion of the Mobile Force training was almost impossible. The 111th Infantry, after the First Army maneuvers, had been broken up into small units on guard duty in various cities. By rotating units on outpost and intensifying training in the base camps, an effort was made to improve training and discipline and to bring equipment up to standard. Except for the field artillery units which were rotated to a firing center at Beaufort Inlet, training was not good during 1942.

When the Mobile Force first came to the Chesapeake Bay Sector they had camped where they could in armories, fire stations, schools, and other available buildings as well as tents. As the situation stabilized, temporary camps were built for the battalion combat teams at Westover and New Bern, with various small outpost camps. In early 1943 the Cape Henry Defense Force moved from Camp Pendleton to Camp Ashby, about half way between Virginia Beach and Norfolk.[26]

Throughout the war intensive training activities were conducted at Fort Monroe and all the posts of the Harbor Defenses of Chesapeake Bay. In the summer of 1942, a simulated bombing attack, assisted by the Chemical Warfare Section of the Chesapeake Bay Sector, was conducted at Fort Monroe. After the attack, a critique was held to discuss the multiple phases of defense, damage control, and associated subjects in an effort to uncover defects. On September 17, 1942, the most spectacular exercise of the war took place at Fort Monroe. A provisional infantry rifle company, reinforced by one section of 60-mm. mortars, launched a surprise attack on the fort. The defenders were a provisional rifle platoon, reinforced by one section of .30-caliber machine guns. Shielded by a mortar barrage simulated by dynamite charges, the aggressor force forded the moat of the fort, and employing nets, scaled the fort's inner parapet, overcoming fierce resistance. The attack was covered by a smokescreen. Planes from Langley Field assisted the attackers by dropping flour sacks simulating bombs, making strafing runs, and then dropping cloth dummies to simulate a parachute assault. The radio station and signal station were captured, but the aggressors were stopped within 100 yards of the sector headquarters. In November, a night attack under blackout conditions took place on the fort. The small amphibious force had the mission of destroying the garrison's fire control station, represented by the band stand. It took the defenders just twenty-seven minutes to repel the attack; so little time, in fact, that newspaper photographers arrived too late to cover the operation.

Toward the end of 1942, limited service men began to replace the troops in the coast artillery units. Drawn mainly from the midwest and northeast,

450 of these soldiers were assigned to man the batteries of the Harbor Defenses of Chesapeake Bay, replacing men who were then shipped overseas. On October 27, Fort Story witnessed a demonstration of a new type of amphibious landing barge. While high ranking officers of the British and American navies watched, 200 of these limited service recruits from Fort Monroe disembarked from the barges. Carrying full packs and rifles, the recruits waded ashore through chest-high surf.

During this same period, the scrap drive began which was to strip Fort Monroe of most of its historic armament. During 1942, Fort Monroe alone contributed more than 2,000,000 pounds of scrap metal to the campaign. Sources of this huge scrap pile were old cannon, spools of steel cable, and tons of discarded mines. The first of the armament to go were the 12-inch mortars of Batteries Anderson and Ruggles, followed early in 1943 by the 12-inch rifles of Battery Parrott. The 12-inch rifles of Battery DeRussy remained in service until the middle of 1944, when they also went to the scrap heap. In addition to the armament of the post, German guns captured in World War I which had stood for twenty years in front of post headquarters and in Theater Circle were also scrapped. A few weapons managed to escape the scrap drive. By request of President Roosevelt, the Department of the Interior acquired from the Coast Artillery School several bronze cannon from the Revolutionary War to be added to the display at Saratoga National Historical Park. These trophies were all part of the materiel surrendered by General Burgoyne on October 17, 1777. By the end of the war, only four muzzle-loading Rodman guns remained of the original heavy armament of Fort Monroe.[27]

The strength of the Chesapeake Bay Sector fluctuated, particularly as regiments moved out from the Provisional Coast Artillery Brigade at Camp Pendleton, and new units were formed. The strength at Fort Monroe in February 1943 was typical.

Headquarters & Headquarters Co, Chesapeake Bay Sector	158
Headquarters & Units, Mobile Force	164
1319th Service Command	892
2d Coast Artillery	1,936
Coast Artillery School and allied units	2,866
96th Ordnance Company	91
Total	5,107

In addition to the troops at Fort Monroe, there were 3,312 at Fort Story, 776 at Fort John Custis, 579 at the Little Creek Mine Base, 3,162 in the Cape Henry Defense Force, 1,008 in the Cape Charles Defense Force at Westover, 1,013 in the Beaufort Inlet Defense Force, 527 in the Temporary Harbor Defenses of Beaufort Inlet, and 1,413 at Camp Pendleton.[28]

Some idea of the magnitude of the operations of the Harbor Defenses of Chesapeake Bay may be gained from the fact that during 1943 a total of 31,944 ships of one kind or another passed in or out of the Virginia Capes and were examined, entered, or cleared by the Harbor Entrance Control Posts. That was an average of 87 ships a day. By the end of the year, some 100 ships a day were entering or leaving. This included one overseas convoy of 60 to 70 ships every ten days which assembled in Lynnhaven Roads under harbor defenses protection and then passed out to sea under escort.

Studies in late 1940 had convinced the Army that it had no adequate weapons to deal with motor torpedo boats. Coast Artillery School tests in 1941 indicated that the best weapon would be the new 90-mm. antiaircraft gun. Because of the shortage of such guns, existing 3-inch fixed guns had to serve as makeshift anti-motor torpedo boat weapons until late 1942. The convoys in Lynnhaven Roads, the naval vessels in Hampton Roads, and the many vessels in Chesapeake Bay presented an attractive target for torpedo boat attacks. The problem was further complicated by the wide entrance to the bay—some 20,000 yards—which was all navigable by light draught motor torpedo boats. The problem had been partially met by the installation of 3-inch rapid fire batteries at Fort Story and Fisherman Island. These guns were replaced in 1943 by the installation of four new 90-mm. radar controlled batteries. One battery was mounted in Battery Parrott and replaced the old 12-inch disappearing guns, two were erected at Fort Story, and one went to Fisherman Island. A weakness in the center at the extreme range of the guns was met by attaching a destroyer to the Approach and Entrance Force.[29]

The controlled mine fields caused much trouble, since the mines available at the beginning of the war were of a buoyant type that rested only fifteen feet below the water's surface, and passing ships frequently fouled the connecting cables. Late in 1942 a new type of Army ground mine became available and a revision of the harbor defense underwater defense project was undertaken. The Navy contact mine field had been down almost a year and the mines had "walked" or broken adrift. Few were found when the field was finally swept up. The wide entrance to the bay made observation impossible at night and in conditions of low visibility, and a full mine defense was required. The planting of the new controlled mines was started in February 1943 and was completed in August. The new mines proved to be most reliable and efficient. By joint agreement with the Navy, the northerly part of the field, controlled from Fisherman Island, was maintained on "contact fire" and the fields in the main channel and Hampton Roads on "surveillance" under normal conditions. Planted and maintained from Little Creek and Fort Monroe, the mine field required three mine planters, many small boats, and three batteries of coast artillery troops totalling 25 officers, 25 warrant officers, and 600 enlisted men.[30]

The beach patrol had been a serious drain on the Mobile Force and had so dissipated its strength that the combat value of the force as a unit was small and combat training was next to impossible. By a joint agreement in November 1942 and an increase in Coast Guard strength, the Coast Guard gradually took over the beach patrol and permitted the concentration of the Defense Forces in the base camps, except for certain outposts at vital beaches. Intensive training was undertaken and the combat efficiency of the force rapidly improved during the first half of 1943. During July the entire Mobile Force was concentrated in the Croatan National Forest south of New Bern for combined maneuvers. During the exercise, the Defense Forces on the Eastern Shore and at Cape Henry were replaced by the 46th Coast Artillery, acting as infantry, from Camp Pendleton.

In September, warning orders were received for all mobile units to be prepared for overseas movement. The 101st Cavalry (Mechanized), was ordered to replace the 111th Infantry and arrived on October 17. The 111th Infantry then concentrated at Camp Pendleton and departed on October 28 for San Francisco and the Pacific. The 176th Field Artillery, which had earlier replaced the 109th Field Artillery, passed to Army Ground Forces control at Camp A. P. Hill on October 19. The service elements of the Mobile Force remained assigned to the Chesapeake Bay Sector.

The 101st Cavalry, less detachments, became the Cape Henry Defense Force with station at Camp Ashby. One squadron headquarters, one reconnaissance troop, and service elements were assigned to the Cape Charles Defense Force at Westover, and a similar squadron was assigned to the Beaufort Inlet Defense Force and stationed at Morehead City. The Coast Guard took over all beach patrol, except at Virginia Beach, and the cavalry confined themselves to heavy motorized patrols of periodic sweeps through their areas.

On November 1, 1943, the War Department reduced the category of defense of the Eastern Defense Command to a coastal frontier probably free from attack, but which must provide nominal defense for political reasons to repel raids by submarines, surface vessels, or isolated raids by aircraft. The strength of the Eastern Defense Command was drastically reduced in December and it reorganized into two large sectors. The Chesapeake Bay Sector was absorbed into the Southeastern Sector, which included the coast from New York to Key West.

The Harbor Defenses of Chesapeake Bay absorbed all of the Chesapeake Bay Sector obligations in the Hampton Roads area. General Tilton again became commanding general of the Harbor Defenses of Chesapeake Bay. The Temporary Harbor Defenses of Beaufort Inlet and the Sector Mobile Force passed to the control of the Southeastern Sector, which had its headquarters at Raleigh. The surplus coast artillery units were concentrated at Fort Monroe and Fort

Story and then transferred to the Army Ground Forces as replacements.

The change in the status of the Harbor Defenses of Chesapeake Bay resulted in major changes in the garrison of Fort Monroe. In early March 1944, the headquarters and headquarters batteries of the 1st, 2d, and 3d Battalions of the 2d Coast Artillery along with Battery N, less the seacoast searchlight platoon, were transferred to Camp Rucker, Alabama. In September, the remaining elements of the 2d Coast Artillery were reorganized into the 2d Coast Artillery Battalion and the 175th Coast Artillery Battalion. Of these units, Headquarters and Headquarters Detachment, 2d Coast Artillery Battalion, and Batteries A and D, along with Battery A, 175th Coast Artillery Battalion, were stationed at Fort Monroe. The headquarters of the 175th Coast Artillery Battalion was established at Fort Story. Fort John Custis was garrisoned by Battery F, 2d Coast Artillery Battalion, and Battery B, 175th Coast Artillery Battalion. A further reduction and reorganization took place in March 1945. Headquarters and Headquarters Battery and Batteries A and F, Harbor Defenses of Chesapeake Bay, were stationed at Fort Monroe, Batteries C, D, and E at Fort Story, and Battery B at Fort John Custis. Batteries B and C, 2d Coast Artillery Battalion, the only elements remaining of the battalion, and the 6th Coast Artillery Mine Planter Battery were stationed at Little Creek.[31]

Despite the drastic reductions in the garrison and status of alert during the last year of the war, training activities continued in the Harbor Defenses of Chesapeake Bay. In the fall of 1943, a light tank unit was assigned to Fort Monroe. The tanks were the first ever used on the post and the crews soon completed a special course in their operation. The first members of the Women's Army Corps were assigned to Fort Monroe late in the year, three second lieutenants being placed on duty with the post and two with the Coast Artillery School.

At Fort John Custis the batteries began a new training program in December with the allotment of funds permitting the railway guns to leave the post for a land firing maneuver. Several successful marches involving shuttle movements, entrucking, and detrucking were carried out. During one of these exercises, the railway batteries moved out at dawn of the first day and laid out spur tracks on which a simulated practice was conducted with field artillery methods. Rain and snow made the exercise more realistic, with the troops bivouacked in a wooded area adjacent to the firing point.

On July 15, 1944, the Officer's Beach Club was destroyed by an early morning fire. A new brick Beach Club was completed by the following May 30 and included a large dining room and an outside patio area extending to the seawall. The swimming pool was not damaged by the fire and a large tent was used for club activities during the summer of 1944. During the summer of 1944, workmen began removing a large number of temporary wooden barracks near the Officer Candidates School, and the area was cleaned up and restored to its prewar appearance. This work was helped along by another major hurricane on September 14. Considerable damage to temporary buildings in all installations of the command resulted, but no lives were lost and practically all barracks, dayrooms, and other structures were soon restored.

After the harbor defense headquarters was again established at Fort Monroe, the joint command post remained at Fort Story. Both Harbor Entrance Control Posts continued operation, and the mine command was retained intact. The alert armament was reduced to one 6-inch battery and one anti-motor torpedo boat battery at Fort Story, the same at Fisherman Island, and the anti-motor torpedo boat battery in Battery Parrott at Fort Monroe. The remaining armament was placed on full maintenance status with reduced personnel. Submarine contacts continued in the area and the last attack occurred on April 23, 1945.

With the general improvement in the situation in 1945, defense measures were gradually reduced and in March orders were received to start taking up the mine field. This was a major operation, made more difficult by the fact that the War Department in December 1944 had turned over the two large mine planters—the *Knox* and the *Murray*—to the Navy for use in the Pacific. As a consequence, only the old mine planter *Schofield* and what others that could be borrowed were available for the work. By August, all but some fifteen groups had been brought up and there was 125,000 pounds of TNT on hand for which the harbor defense could not get disposition. Orders were finally received to dispose of the TNT and it was dumped about 100 miles at sea. The remaining mines were deliberately blown up where they rested. The work was finally completed late in October, except for a few mines which were disposed of later.[32]

Early in 1945, Fort Monroe, due to its central location and facilities, was designated by the commanding general of the Southeastern Sector as the distributing agency for replacements in the various harbor defenses of the sector. Former coast artillery and antiaircraft personnel returning from overseas were sent to Fort Monroe from several redistribution centers for reassignment. After a furlough, these troops received a complete indoctrination in coast artillery. Approximately 125 men were processed every three weeks and assigned to the various harbor defenses within the sector.

The Southeastern Sector had never been more than a sort of overall administrative headquarters and with the removal of the small mobile forces remaining it was discontinued on May 1, 1945. The Harbor Defenses of Chesapeake Bay passed to the direct control of the Eastern Defense Command. After the German surrender on May 8, the alert status was

Battery Eustis in action.

8-inch railway gun of Battery F, 52d Coast Artillery, in the 1930's.

One of the 3-inch A.A. guns of Battery No. 2, 1942.

Battery Montgomery - left gun; 6-inch Barbette Mount M1900, June 1938 (Col. A.A. Currie)

12-inch disappearing gun of Battery DeRussy in action.

Fort Wool shortly after World War II. The new Battery Gates is to the right.

Fort Monroe as seen from the air about 1950.

Chapel of the Centurion, built in 1858, as it appeared early in the Twentieth Century.

Quarters 17, "The Tuileries," Where Robert E. Lee lived.

Quarters of the commanding general at Fort Monroe.

Brig. Gen. Rollin L. Tilton, commander of Fort Monroe and the Chesapeake Bay Sector during World War II.

General Jacob L. Devers

Main sally port of Fort Monroe as it appears today.

asemated 16-inch barbette gun of Battery Ketcham, Fort Story, during
'orld War II.

General Donn A.
Starry, CG
TRADOC

General William E. DePuy,
first commander of
TRADOC

further reduced and finally ended with the Japanese surrender on August 14. The Harbor Defenses of Chesapeake Bay then returned to a peacetime basis.[33]

While the Harbor Defenses of Chesapeake Bay had been occupied with the defense of the area, the Coast Artillery School continued to function throughout the war. Early in 1940, a gradual change was noticeable in the school. Work in both the Officers' and Enlisted Men's Divisions was tapered off, and the standard courses were brought to an orderly, if abbreviated, termination. Students graduated at odd times and left at once to join old organizations that were being expanded or new ones being formed.

On July 1, 1940, the school emergency program began with a series of six refresher courses of a month's duration. The groups ranged in size from 16 officers in the first course to 89 in the fifth and averaged 60 for the series. The refresher course was made necessary by the expansion of the Coast Artillery Corps and by the greatly increased stress on antiaircraft. By September 14, when the last class graduated each officer had received instruction in antiaircraft artillery, automatic weapons, searchlights, and antiaircraft materiel. The course culminated in a week of firing the 3-inch antiaircraft gun, the 37-mm. antiaircraft gun, and the .30- and .50-caliber machine guns.

The rapid expansion of the Coast Artillery School planned for the fall of 1940 required greatly enlarged facilities. The area bounded by Camp 3, Battery Eustis, and the seawall was filled in order to raise the surface about three feet. On this fill twelve temporary barracks were built as well as additional buildings for classrooms, mess halls, and the necessary supply establishments. The buildings in the old stable area were razed to make way for the increase in the enlisted specialist classes. In the vicinity of the tractor shed four barracks, a mess hall, a day room, and a store room were constructed for the enlisted course. This new construction provided facilities for 480 student officers and 400 enlisted specialists.

The expansion of the Coast Artillery School classes was directly geared to the completion of the new construction. The constructing quartermaster, however, was not directly under the control of either General Clark, the school commandant, or General Tilton, the post commander. The constructing quartermaster worked under tremendous difficulties due to delays in the shipment of lumber and other construction materials, inadequacy of trained men in the local civilian labor force, and difficulties imposed by jurisdictional disputes by labor unions. In addition to the work at Fort Monroe, he was also in charge of various other construction projects for the War Department in the Tidewater area. Despite the lack of official authority, General Clark closely supervised the construction activities for the school and managed to have each new weekly set of buildings ready for the entering group of students. Several times this was accomplished by the narrowest margin, with workmen hammering the finishing touches as the student officers moved in.[34]

Beginning September 15, 1940, the courses had been extended in length to ten weeks, but the same organization that governed the four week course was retained. The course of instruction from September to February, which included National Guard and Reserve officers in each group, was for antiaircraft artillery only. In order to provide sufficient instructors, the faculty of the Coast Artillery School was augmented, mainly by Reserve officers on extended active duty. By September 1941, the faculty had increased approximately six-fold.

Intervening in the series of refresher courses were three replacement center courses, timed and devised to fit the needs of the replacement centers which were being organized to receive the influx of selective servicemen. Two of these courses were in antiaircraft and one in seacoast artillery. The Department of Enlisted Specialists also initiated refresher courses for noncommissioned staff officers in electricity, motor transportation, and radio.

One of the most important contributions of the Coast Artillery School during this period was the establishment of an Officer Candidate School. The original plan was to include four consecutive courses of instruction, each of three months' duration. The Officer Candidate School, as first conceived, was for selected enlisted men of the Regular Army and the National Guard, each class to be made up of 125 students. The first group that arrived, however, consisted of 200 men. The class was organized in July 1941 in the new quarters in Camp 3. The candidates were selected on the basis of demonstrated leadership ability. Educational requirements were waived; education of members of the first class ranged from one year of high school to that required for the degree of doctor of laws. The second group of candidates began their studies in October. This course was shortened to twelve weeks, a length established for all future courses until October 1943, when the course was lengthened to seventeen weeks. By January 1, 1942, new construction at Camp 3 and Battery Bomford permitted doubling the output of officers. Beginning on that date, 100 officer candidates were admitted every two weeks. From 1942 until the Officer Candidate School was discontinued in April 1944, it had produced a total of 2,066 new officers.[35]

Inadequate facilities to take care of the contemplated increase in the number of officer candidates to be trained during 1942 necessitated moving the school to Camp Davis, near Wilmington, North Carolina, in February 1942. Early in 1942 the Antiaircraft Artillery Command was activated and the commanding general was directed to establish an Antiaircraft Artillery School at Camp Davis. In order to carry out this directive separating antiaircraft from the other coast artillery functions, it was necessary to transfer the seacoast Officer Candidate School back to Fort Monroe and to separate antiaircraft instructor and student personnel and equipment from the Coast Artillery School for the movement to Camp Davis. The move of the relevant divisions of the Coast Artillery School was made during April 1942. On March 1, 1942, the 514th Coast Artillery (Antiaircraft) had been activated at Camp Davis for the specific purpose of acting as a demonstration unit for the Coast Artillery Officer Candidate School. One battery of this regiment had been sent to Fort Monroe for use in connection with training officers and enlisted students at the school, but this battery was returned to Camp Davis in the latter part of March 1942.

The directive which created the Antiaircraft Artillery Command also established the Antiaircraft Artillery Board. The board was activated March 9, 1942, with temporary station at Fort Monroe, where it functioned until its move to Camp Davis in late May. A tentative split in personnel and operations of the Coast Artillery Board was made immediately after March 9, although both sections continued to operate at Fort Monroe. Eight officers and one warrant officer were formally transferred from the Coast Artillery Board to the new board in April.[36]

General Clark was relieved on 15 January 1942 as commandant by Brigadier General Lawrence B. Weeks.[37] As a result of the reorganization of the War Department in March 1942, the Coast Artillery Corps became a part of the Army Ground Forces and the Coast Artillery School was placed under the Replacement and School Command.

In November 1941, a Field Officers' Course was organized to train field officers in the tactics of their branch and in command and staff duties. This course was of four weeks duration and had as its main purpose the instruction of new field officers in the tactics and training of antiaircraft and seacoast artillery. Courses alternated in the ratio of two antiaircraft and one seacoast, but with the removal of antiaircraft instruction to Camp Davis, the course at Fort Monroe was limited to seacoast artillery. From 1942 to 1945, there were a total of 2,332 officers and 4,848 enlisted men graduated from the seacoast courses at the Coast Artillery School.

There were a few diversions during the war years. One of the miniature airplane targets fell into Mill Creek and, carried by the tide, was caught under the Mill Creek Bridge. The lieutenant in charge of the targets was climbing down the side of the bridge searching for the small-scale plane, when an elderly lady passing by, startled to see a well-dressed officer clinging to the bridge supports, exclaimed, "Young man, what in the world are you doing?" Without thinking he answered, "Madam, I am looking for an airplane!" The woman put her nose in the air and stomped off muttering to herself.

On a somewhat more serious note, Signal Corps camera crews spent the summer and fall of 1943 at Fort Monroe filming the planting and firing of controlled submarine mines. Scenarios for the training films were prepared by the Department of Training Publications of the Coast Artillery School, which also arranged for the personnel and equipment appearing in the film.[38]

Due to the gradual enlargement during the period of temporary emergency, the Coast Artillery School was much better prepared for the war than it had been during World War I. Despite the fact that most instructors retained from the early classes had little or no military training, and that all courses had to be thoroughly condensed, the school was able to provide the Coast Artillery Corps and other arms with fully trained officers and men where and when they were needed.

Footnotes Chapter XII

[1] Tilton, "Notes on Fort Monroe," p. 15; 1st Lt. William M. Bronk, A History of the Eastern Defense Command, p. 21.

[2] Lt. Col. Lloyd W. Goeppert and Capt. Walter F. Ellis, "Fort Monroe," *Coast Artillery Journal*, 83 (November-December 1940), p. 566. General Smith graduated from West Point in 1903. During World War I, he served with the field artillery in France as a colonel. In the late 1930's he was promoted to brigadier general and commanded the Pacific Sector of the Panama Canal Department. General Smith became commandant of the Coast Artillery School and commanding general of the Third Coast Artillery District on November 22, 1938, and remained in command of the district until December 31, 1940. He was promoted to major general and commanded the Antiaircraft Training Center at Camp Davis prior to his retirement in 1943. General Smith died in 1961 at Fort Monroe. *Assembly,* XX (Spring 1961), pp. 79–80. General Clark had been appointed a second lieutenant in 1909 and served as a lieutenant colonel in World War I. From 1919 to 1924 he was at Fort Monroe as librarian of the Coast Artillery School and editor of the *Journal of the United States Artillery*. He returned in 1935 to command the 1st Battalion, 2d Coast Artillery, and was assistant commandant of the school in 1937 and 1938. During the 1930's he had two tours of duty in the War Plans Division of the General Staff and was one of the main authors of the famous RAINBOW war plans. He was promoted to brigadier general on October 1, 1940, and commanded an antiaircraft artillery brigade in Australia and the Harbor Defenses of Boston later in World War II. General Clark retired in 1945. Brig. Gen. Frank S. Clark, *The Chronicle of Aunt Lena* (Charlotte: Heritage Printers, Inc., 1962), pp. 362–364.

[3] Tilton, "Notes on Fort Monroe," pp. 10–11; Maj. Franklin W. Reese and Lt. George H. Burgess, "Fort Monroe," *Coast Artillery Journal*, 84 (January-February 1941), p. 72; Clark, *op. cit.,* p. 367; Special Orders No. 298, War Department, December 19, 1940. General Tilton was appointed a second lieutenant in 1909 and served at Fort Monroe until 1910. He served as a lieutenant colonel during World War I and returned to Fort Monroe as an instructor at the Coast Artillery School in 1919. He graduated from the Advanced Course of the Coast Artillery School in 1929 and served as secretary of the school until 1933. He was commanding the 6th Coast Artillery in San Francisco when he was promoted to brigadier general on October 1, 1940. Following the war, General Tilton served as Inspector General of Army Ground Forces and headed the War Department Seacoast Defense Armament Board. He retired in 1948.

[4] "Fort Monroe," *Coast Artillery Journal*, 83 (March-April 1940), p. 182 and (May-June 1940), p. 285.

[5] Conn, Engelman, and Fairchild, *op. cit.,* pp. 47–49; History of the Eastern Defense Command, pp. 22, 23.

⁶ Conn, Engelman, and Fairchild, *op. cit.*, p. 53; History of the Eastern Defense Command, p. 24.

⁷ History of the Harbor Defenses of Chesapeake Bay, pp. 2–3; Tilton, "Notes on Fort Monroe," p. 16.

⁸ "Fort Monroe," *Coast Artillery Journal,* 83 (September-October 1940), pp. 470–472.

⁹ *Ibid.*

¹⁰ Lt. Col. Goeppert and Capt. Ellis, "Fort Monroe," *Coast Artillery Journal* 83 (November-December 1940), p. 566; Tilton, "Notes on Fort Monroe," pp. 11–12; Maj. Reese, "Fort Monroe," *Coast Artillery Journal,* 84 (March-April 1941), p. 172. Colonel Manning Kimmel, commander of the 57th Coast Artillery, stated that General Smith shifted the mobile regiments because the training on the tractors of the regiments was tearing up Fort Monroe. Interview, March 18, 1972.

¹¹ Maj. Reese and Lt. Burgess, "Fort Monroe," *Coast Artillery Journal,* 84 (January-February 1941), pp. 72–75.

¹² Col. Delmar S. Lenzner, "The New Submarine Mine Depot," *Coast Artillery Journal,* 83 (November-December 1940), pp. 537–538. Colonel Lenzner was commissioned a second lieutenant in 1910 and served as a lieutenant colonel during World War I. He retired in 1948.

¹³ Maj. Reese, "Third Coast Artillery District," *Coast Artillery Journal,* 84 (July-August 1941), pp. 381–382.

¹⁴ Maj. Reese, "Third Coast Artillery District," *Coast Artillery Journal,* 84 (May-June 1941), pp. 284–285, and (July-August), pp. 381–382.

¹⁵ "Fort Monroe," *Coast Artillery Journal,* 84 (January-February 1941), p. 72; Tilton, "Notes on Fort Monroe," pp. 4–5; Lt. Alonza F. Colonna, "Chesapeake Bay Sector," *Coast Artillery Journal,* 86 (September-October 1943), p. 74.

¹⁶ "Third Coast Artillery District," *Coast Artillery Journal,* 84 (September-October 1941), p. 494, and (November-December 1941), p. 630; Maj. Reese, "Fort Monroe," *Coast Artillery Journal,* 85 (January-February 1942), pp. 82–84.

¹⁷ Tilton, "Notes on Fort Monroe," pp. 13–14, 16.

¹⁸ *Ibid.,* pp. 19–21.

¹⁹ Maj. Reese, "Fort Monroe," *Coast Artillery Journal,* 85 (January-February 1942), p. 82; Tilton, "Notes on Fort Monroe," pp.21–23; General Order No. 2, Chesapeake Bay Sector, December 19, 1941; Clark, *op. cit.,* p. 392.

²⁰ Maj. Reese, "Chesapeake Bay Sector," *Coast Artillery Journal,* 85 (March-April 1942), pp. 76–77.

²¹ Maj. Reese, "U.S. Hotel Chamberlin," *Coast Artillery Journal,* 85 (March-April 1942), pp. 52–54.

²² Tilton, "Notes on Fort Monroe," pp. 26–29.

²³ *Ibid.,* pp. 40–41.

²⁴ *Ibid.,* pp. 37–39.

²⁵ *Ibid.,* pp. 41–43.

²⁶ *Ibid.,* pp. 43, 45–46; Letter, Brig. Gen. W. G. Skelton to the author, June 4, 1971. General Skelton commanded the Mobile Force from January 1943 until the deployment of the 111th Infantry.

²⁷ Lt. Col. James B. Anderson, "Chesapeake Bay Sector," *Coast Artillery Journal,* 85 (September-October 1942), p. 101; Capt. Alfred C. Andrews, "Chesapeake Bay Sector," *Coast Artillery Journal,* 85 (November-December 1942), pp. 88–89, and 86 (January-February 1943), p. 89; "The Coast Artillery School," *Coast Artillery Journal,* 86 (March-April 1943), p. 90.

²⁸ Tilton, "Notes on Fort Monroe," pp. 46–47.

²⁹ *Ibid.,* pp. 50–51.

³⁰ Conn, Engelman, and Fairchild, *op. cit.,* p. 50; Tilton "Notes on Fort Monroe," pp. 51–52.

³¹ Letter AG 370.5/2, HQ Southeastern Sector to Distribution, 2 March 1944, subject: Movement Orders; General Orders No. 13, Southeastern Sector, 19 September 1944; General Orders No. 17, Harbor Defenses of Chesapeake Bay, September 29, 1944; General Orders No. 3, Southeastern Sector, March 29, 1945; Station List No. 4, Southeastern Sector, April 1, 1945; Tilton, "Notes on Fort Monroe," pp. 52–55.

³² Lt. Alonza F. Colonna, "Chesapeake Bay Sector," *Coast Artillery Journal*, 86 (November-December 1943), p. 69 and 87 (January-February 1944), p. 73, (March-April 1944), p. 83; "Southeastern Sector," *Coast Artillery Journal*, 87 (July-August 1944), p. 74, and (November-December 1944), p. 81; Capt. Colonna, "Harbor Defenses of Chesapeake Bay," *Coast Artillery Journal*, 88 (July-August 1945), p. 85; Tilton, "Notes on Fort Monroe," pp. 57–58.

³³ "Southeastern Sector," *Coast Artillery Journal*, 88 (March-April 1945), pp. 80–81; Tilton, "Notes on Fort Monroe," p. 58.

³⁴ "Coast Artillery School Moves to San Francisco," p. 40; Brig. Gen. F. H. Smith, "The Coast Artillery School in the Emergency," *Coast Artillery Journal*, 83 (September-October 1940), pp. 402–409; Clark, *op. cit.*, p. 372.

³⁵ "Coast Artillery School Moves to San Francisco," pp. 40–41; Col. Clifford D. Windle, "The Coast Artillery School Keeps Pace," *Coast Artillery Journal*, 85 (January-February 1942), pp. 25–27; *The Replacement and School Command*, Army Ground Forces Study No. 33, 1946, pp. 207, 219; "The Coast Artillery School," *Coast Artillery Journal*, 86 (September-October 1943), pp. 60–61; Clark, *op. cit.*, p. 395.

³⁶ "Coast Artillery School Moves to San Francisco," p. 41; Lt. Col. Alvin M. Cibula, *The Antiaircraft Command and Center*, Army Ground Forces Study No. 26, 1946, pp. 116, 118.

³⁷ Clark, *op. cit.*, p. 395. General Weeks graduated from West Point in 1913 and served as a major in the Signal Corps during World War I. He was adjutant of the Harbor Defenses of Chesapeake Bay in 1927 and 1928 and had been on the Coast Artillery School staff since 1939 when he was promoted to brigadier general and named commandant on January 10, 1942. He reverted to colonel when he was relieved as commandant on November 11, 1945, but retired as a brigadier general in 1948. General Weeks died in 1959. *Assembly*, XIX (Fall 1960), pp. 87–88; *Register of Graduates*, p. 334.

³⁸ "Coast Artillery School Moves to San Francisco," p. 41; *The Replacement and School Command*, p. 207; "The Coast Artillery School," *Coast Artillery Journal*, 86 (March-April 1943), p. 88, and (November-December 1943), pp. 40–41, 66.

Chapter XIII

The Changing Mission

FOR THE FIRST FEW MONTHS following the end of the war, there was uncertainty as to the future mission of the post, the future of the harbor defenses and the coast artillery as a whole, as well as the complications of demobilization and reduced and changing personnel. The modernization of the harbor defenses had been practically completed, making the Harbor Defenses of Chesapeake Bay the most powerful on the east coast. Fort Monroe retained its mission of the defense of the inner mine field and of Hampton Roads. The Coast Artillery School, the Coast Artillery Board, and the Submarine Mine Depot continued their normal operations. Major General Robert T. Frederick succeeded General Weeks as commandant of the school on November 11, 1945.[1] But even as Fort Monroe appeared to be returning to normal, plans were being made for the post-war Army that would dramatically change the mission of the old post.

In August 1945, the Army Ground Forces recommended to the War Department that a comprehensive study be made of the entire subject of fixed harbor installations for the continental United States. Among its recommendations was that antiaircraft gun defenses of harbor installations be provided by fixed antiaircraft armament as an integral part of the harbor defenses. A survey lasting many months was then made of the fixed seacoast defenses. There was a common desire to evaluate the installations in the light of modern times and not to be guided by historical precedents in holding on to outmoded fortifications.[2]

Even while the eventual fate of the coast artillery was under study in the War Department, the troops at Fort Monroe remained busy. Full advantage was taken of the good weather during the summer of 1945 to complete target practices with the 6-inch, 90-mm., and 40-mm. guns. The men of the garrison also completed their small arms qualifications. Late in the year, Fort Monroe was designated as a replacement center for the Eastern Defense Command. Regular Army enlistees and veterans with too few points for early discharge were sent to the post for basic training, retraining, or simple processing. The men included recruits, those from other arms who were transferred to the Coast Artillery Corps, and experienced Coast Artillerymen who had reenlisted. The men were taught everything from the rudiments of infantry drill to the service of the 6-inch guns. Over 1,000 men were eventually trained at Fort Monroe. After a delay caused by weather conditions, the new 16-inch rifles of Battery Ketcham at Fort Story fired their first practice on November 27. Battery D, Harbor Defenses of Chesapeake Bay, conducted the practice in conjunction with the Seacoast Test Section of Army Ground Forces Board No. 1, the former Coast Artillery Board. A total of twenty rounds, six trial and fourteen for record, were fired with one broadside and one bow-on hit being recorded.[3] Battery Winslow, the 16-inch emplacement at Fort John Custis, had also been completed and proof fired.

Early in 1946 the Army in the continental United States was reorganized. Effective March 1, the Harbor Defenses of Chesapeake Bay was released from assignment to the Eastern Defense Command and was assigned to the Replacement and School Command of Army Ground Forces. The Replacement and School Command was charged with the responsibility of preparing plans for the defense of the Chesapeake Bay region, and with coordinating with the Fifth Naval District, First Army, interested local commanders, and the Army Air Forces. The Commandant of the Coast Artillery School was assigned on that date as commanding general of the Harbor Defenses of Chesapeake Bay and also acted as agent of the Replacement and School Command. When General Frederick assumed command of the harbor defenses, General Tilton beame the harbor defense executive while still retaining command of Fort Monroe. At this time, only Batteries A and F, Harbor Defenses of Chesapeake Bay, were assigned to Fort Monroe. Battery A was on temporary duty at the Little Creek Mine Base and never actually returned to the post.[4]

During March, plans were formulated which were to dramatically change the mission of Fort Monroe. Headquarters of Army Ground Forces had been located for most of the war at the Army War College —the present Fort Lesley J. McNair—in Washington, D. C. Following the war, the Chief of Staff of the Army desired that Army Ground Forces and the Tactical Air Command, which supplied close support to ground troops, should be located in close proximity in an area convenient to Washington. Various sites were surveyed and Army Ground Forces recommended the Fort Monroe-Langley Field area as the most suitable. In making his recommedation, General Jacob L. Devers, the commanding general of Army Ground Forces, stated that the facilities in this area were generally considered adequate for the headquarters, but indicated certain exceptions:[5]

a. The number of quarters available for married officers and noncommissioned officers is inadequate. Estimates indicate that approximately 404 married officers and 419 married warrant and noncommissioned officers will have to locate their families off the Post. While little if any off-the-post housing is now available in this area, it is believed that the next six months will see considerable alleviation of this condition as shipyards in the area reduce their personnel and vacancies occur in Federal housing projects in the vicinity.

b. The two Headquarters will require a total of 146,000 square feet of office space. Buildings now occupied by the Coast Artillery School and Harbor Defense Headquarters will furnish 69,200 square feet while buildings at Langley Field now occupied by the Army Airways Communication System will provide 56,890—a total of 126,090 square feet. This leaves a deficiency of 20,510 square feet.

c. Present facilities at Fort Monroe do not provide a central mess, suitable accommodations for visitors or an adequate cafeteria service for the officers, noncommissioned officers, and civilians who will work in the Headquarters but live off the Post and must, consequently, obtain one or more meals on the Post. As previously indicated there will be a considerable number in this category.

At this time General Devers strongly recommended that the Chamberlin Hotel be acquired by the Army since the two top floors could be utilized for office space, other floors could provide quarters for assigned personnel and official transients, and messing and cafeteria facilities would be available on the lower floors. The hotel was scheduled to revert to the Reconstruction Finance Corporation on March 1 for sale as surplus to the highest bidder. General Devers' recommendations had no effect as the Secretary of War declared on March 19 that the War Department had no desire to acquire the Chamberlin Hotel. Army Ground Forces then tried to effect a compromise wherein the War Department would lease the land on which the hotel was located to the operator. Such an arrangement would permit the establishment of minimum rates to be charged to service personnel, secure the reservation of accommodations for transient service personnel, sanction the sanitary inspection of the hotel and its employees by the post commander, and in the case of illegal or unlawful operations by or with the knowledge of the management, secure the revocation of the lease. These substitute proposals met with no better success and in July the War Department replied: "This recommendation (dated 1 July 1946) has been referred to the Secretary of War, and it is his decision that the Chamberlin Hotel is not to be retained as property in which the War Department has interest." The hotel had been operated for officers of the armed services under Navy supervision until March 6, 1946. On February 25, 1947, it was announced that the hotel was sold to Mr. L. U. Noland, the operator of a chain of hotels in Richmond, and at the same time it was announced that the policy regarding service personnel was to continue. The sale was made under the terms of the lease of April 26, 1926, which gave the commanding general certain inspection rights. On June 22, 1966, the lease on the hotel site was extended for another fifty years.[6]

The War Department had announced on April 1, 1946, that Army Ground Forces would move to Fort Monroe, and it was contemplated that the transfer would take place between August 15 and 30. There were many factors in this change in locations. It was necessary to find a new location for the Coast Artillery School and the units attached to it. Despite the opposition of the Norfolk Chamber of Commerce, which tried to have the Coast Artillery School relocated at Fort Story, it was the recommendation of Army Ground Forces that the school be transferred to Fort Winfield Scott, California. Seacoast artillery installations in the Harbor Defenses of San Francisco were considered to be equal, if not superior, to those in the Harbor Defenses of Chesapeake Bay. Army Ground Forces estimated that the transfer of the Coast Artillery School would cost approximately $616,380 to move the necessary equipment and personnel to the West Coast and to convert the buildings there to the school's use. The Transportation Corps Board, which had moved to the post in 1945, was transferred to Fort Eustis. For the time being, the Submarine Mine Depot remained at Fort Monroe.[7]

Preparations for these major changes began immediately. Colonel Logan C. Berry, the headquarters commandant of Army Ground Forces, arrived in April to survey the facilities of the post. Colonel Berry was assigned as the deputy post commander upon his arrival and after Army Ground Forces moved he was in actual command of the post. Effective May 25, the Harbor Defenses of Chesapeake Bay was relieved from assignment to the Replacement and School Command and placed under Second Army. General Tilton replaced General Frederick as the harbor defense commander at this time. The headquarters was moved from Fort Monroe to Fort Story.[8]

General Frederick left on May 28 and the transport for the school arrived and loaded on May 30. The Coast Artillery School formally departed Fort Monroe for Fort Winfield Scott on June 1, leaving Battery F as the last Coast Artillery Corps unit at the post. Virtually the entire post was cleared to allow for the renovation of the buildings to office facilities for Army Ground Forces. In August and September the new garrison began to move in with the activation of the 14th Transportation Company (Car) and the transfer of the 89th Military Police Company from Washington.

On August 1, Fort Monroe was withdrawn from the Harbor Defenses of Chesapeake Bay, except that the harbor defense installations on the post remained the responsibility of the harbor defense commander.[9]

General Tilton was relieved of command of the Harbor Defenses of Chesapeake Bay on June 14. Colonel Kenneth McCatty assumed command of the harbor defenses at Fort Story. The following day General Tilton turned command of Fort Monroe over to Colonel Berry, for General Devers, and reported to Washington as Acting Inspector General of Army Ground Forces. He was subsequently appointed to head a board of officers known as the War Department Seacoast Defense Armament Board. The board was directed to examine all seacoast defense armament and to determine which defenses could be eliminated, what obsolete equipment removed, what equipment could be stored, and what other appropriate action should be taken. At this time it was the policy of the War Department that seacoast armament would continue to exist, but that its role would be reduced to a training or standby condition that was the most economical in terms of money and men. In accordance with directions, the Tilton Board while examining the seacoast installations encouraged local commanders to initiate appropriate action to effect personnel savings with the least practical delay.[10]

Army Ground Forces in May 1947 informed the commanders of First, Second, Fourth, and Sixth Armies that it was planned that all harbor defense installations and facilities in their areas would be processed for surplus except mine fields and submarine mine facilities, modern 6-inch guns covering the mine fields, modern 16-inch guns, base and control stations, and minimum buildings to support the retained facilities. This action was followed in August 1947 by a recommendation of General Devers to the War Department that a re-examination of the matter of seacoast artillery was deemed appropriate at that time. Beginning in November, the Department of the Army began reducing the remaining seacoast armament. It had originally been intended that Fort Monroe would retain its mission of protecting Hampton Roads. Battery Montgomery had been listed as obsolete and recommended for removal by the board. The new Battery Gates of 6-inch long range guns at Fort Wool, which was incomplete, had been recommended for retention, but was subsequently eliminated. With the further reduction of the harbor defenses starting in November 1947, the armament in Battery Parrott was removed and with the elimination of the mine field Fort Monroe ceased to be a harbor defense post.[11]

Army Ground Forces officially had begun operations at Fort Monroe on October 1, 1946. General Devers proceeded from his quarters to the command building escorted by Troop B, 3d Cavalry Reconnaissance Squadron, and the Army Ground Forces Band, both of which had arrived from Fort George G. Meade, Maryland, for the ceremony. A seventeen gun salute by Battery Irwin marked General Devers' assumption of command. Two 3-inch guns which had been located at Battery Lee on Fort Wool were transferred to Battery Irwin on May 31 to serve as a saluting battery. These guns are now the last remaining coast artillery armament at Fort Monroe.[12]

The physical setup at Fort Monroe was compact and made for efficient staff cooperation. The personnel of Headquarters, Army Ground Forces, were not subject to the frequent interruptions to current work that the close proximity to the War Department General and Special Staff Sections in Washington had caused, but contact with the next higher echelon of command was a matter of hours when necessary. Command of the armies in the continental United States was placed under the commanding general of Army Ground Forces, who was made responsible for operations and training in the army areas. Each army in turn was made responsible for operation, training, and administrative functions in its area. The armies were so organized that in the event of the outbreak of hostilities the tactical and administrative sections could be separated. The administrative elements would then assume the duties and functions formerly handled by the old service commands while the tactical groups would be free to constitute a mobile tactical headquarters.[13]

This organization remained in effect until March 1948, when it was decided to relieve Army Ground Forces of its administrative responsibilities for the armies so that greater effort could be concentrated on training. Army Ground Forces was redesignated as the Office, Chief of Army Field Forces, and command of the armies passed to the Department of the Army.

On February 1, 1955, in order to provide more economical and effective direction of the armies of the United States, the Office, Chief of Army Field Forces, was redesignated as Headquarters, Continental Army Command—commonly called CONARC. CONARC retained its primary mission of training and again assumed direct command of the continental armies. General John E. Dahlquist, the Chief of Army Field Forces, remained as commander of CONARC. General Dahlquist had also been the post commander of Fort Monroe, the actual operation of the post being handled by a deputy post commander. On March 1, 1955, the post was separated from CONARC and placed under Second Army. Colonel Malcolm D. Jones assumed command of Fort Monroe.

Inasmuch as the primary mission of the post station complement and the Second Army units stationed at Fort Monroe was to support CONARC, General Willard G. Wyman, the commanding general of CONARC, in April 1956 requested that direct lines of authority be established to insure the commanding officer of Fort Monroe would be responsive to the requirements of CONARC. Second Army was advised that with the exception of antiaircraft artillery personnel, all troops stationed at Fort Monroe would wear the CONARC shoulder patch rather than the Second Army patch. Second Army would communicate with Fort Monroe agencies on a lateral basis and not as though Fort Monroe was a subordinate unit in the Second Army chain of command. In addition, the Fort Monroe commander was advised that he would report directly to the Chief of Staff of CONARC on all policy matters requiring local determination, without reference to Second Army; on operational and policy matters requiring submission of recommendations to, or remedial action by, Second Army; and for resolution of all actions directed by Second Army, compliance with which would impair, or affect adversely, the capability to support CONARC.[14]

On January 1, 1957, the headquarters was redesignated as the United States Continental Army Command. The reorganization of the Army in 1962, while not affecting the basic mission of CONARC, added important operational responsibilities to the command at Fort Monroe. In addition to its role as a theater army type command for the tactical Army establishment within the continental United States, CONARC commanded the continental armies, the Army Reserve, and the Army training base, and provided the commander and staff for the Army component of the United States Strike Command. CONARC was responsible for achieving combat readiness of Army units in the United States, for the training of individual officers and enlisted men, and for operating and managing those Army installations and resources which supported the active Army and Reserve Component units.[15]

Although not directly involved, Fort Monroe played an important part in most of the major military operations since World War II. Direction of all training, the mobilization of reserve units, and the preparation of units and individual replacements for deployment during the Korean War, the Berlin Crisis of 1961, the Cuban Crisis of 1962, the intervention in the Dominican Republic in 1965, and the Vietnam War came from Fort Monroe. The command at Fort Monroe also took a significant part in the use of Army troops in civil disturbances during this period.

While CONARC and its predecessors occupied a key position in the Army as a whole, several changes to the post itself occurred. The last vestiges of the coast artillery era disappeared by 1950. The 6-inch guns of Battery Montgomery were scrapped in March 1948 and the battery itself was demolished in the early 1950's to make room for the Wherry family housing units. The 90-mm. guns on Battery Parrott had been designated as the saluting battery in 1948, but these also were removed in December 1950. The two 3-inch guns at Battery Irwin remained, but there no longer was ammunition available for use as a saluting battery. Eventually, a battery of four 105-mm. howitzers was furnished for a saluting battery. The emplacements of Battery Bomford and Battery Barber were removed in March 1951 by Company A, 981st Engineer Battalion (Construction). Battery Eustis was also removed in March 1959 by Company A, 19th Engineer Battalion, to provide room in the housing area. Battery Humphreys and the original redan disappeared shortly thereafter. The Harbor Defenses of Chesapeake Bay were inactivated on January 1, 1950, and the Submarine Mine Depot was discontinued on May 4, 1950.[16]

When Army Ground Forces moved to Fort Monroe in 1946, one of the major problems was a severe shortage of family housing on the post. This was remedied in part with the completion in October 1953 of the Wherry housing project, consisting of 206 units in 53 buildings. The Wherry housing stretches along Chesapeake Bay from just north of the old fort to the Fort Monroe Officers' Club. The housing area surrounds Batteries De Russy and Church and was the cause of the demolition of Batteries Eustis and Montgomery.

The last artillery unit to serve at Fort Monroe was an antiaircraft artillery battalion. The 56th Antiaircraft Artillery Battalion was transferred from Camp Stewart, Georgia, to Fort Monroe on January 6, 1953. The battalion headquarters was located at Fort Monroe while the batteries were scattered about the lower Peninsula. Originally a 90-mm. gun unit, the battalion was converted in 1955 to a missile unit. The battalion was inactivated on September 1, 1958, and replaced by the 4th Battalion, 51st Artillery, which remained at Fort Monroe until its inactivation on July 26, 1960.

The officers' club had been located in the flag bastion of the old fort since March 1871. This club, and its location, was probably the best known of any officers' club in the army. Difficulties in maintenance, however, began to cause serious problems. Water seeping through the stone and brick work of the ramparts posed a threat of serious damage to the valuable possessions of the club. The sharp increase in the officer population of the post following World War II also resulted in considerable overcrowding of the limited facilities of the old club. In 1959, General Herbert B. Powell, at that time commanding CONARC, ordered that the club be moved to the Officers' Beach Club. The last party in the old club was held on May 18. The Beach Club was remodeled, the outdoor dance floor being enclosed to serve as the main dining room of the club, and additions were added to both ends of the building. As a temporary expedient the Beach Club was adequate, but there were problems here too. The floor of the dining room originally having been outside, it sloped at an angle to allow rain to run off. Eating in the dining room was often an experience as peas rolled slowly across the plate. In 1967, the situation was finally remedied when the club was completely rebuilt and the floor finally leveled.

The only remaining portion of the Beach Club built in 1934 is the fireplace and chimney in the Casemate Room which still proudly displays a Coast Artillery Corps inscription. As a result of the reconstruction, the post had a fully modern officers' club

An historic era came to an end when the Army relinquished control of the main wharf in December 1959. The wharf had been recommended to be disposed of as excess to Army needs in 1954, but the proposal ran into legal obstacles and adverse public opinion. Finally, approval was obtained to turn the wharf over to the District Engineer for disposal, thus terminating the activities of the Baltimore Steamship Packet Company which had operated ships to Old Point Comfort since 1894. The wharf was demolished in 1961.[17]

In the fort itself, the casemates of the second front were remodeled in 1959 to serve as a Chapel Center. The Chapel of the Centurion itself underwent a major restoration in 1969. It was discovered that the damage of the 1933 fire had not completely repaired. The entire chapel was raised and placed on a solid foundation for the first time, the fire damage was completely repaired, and the interior was renovated to restore it as nearly as possible to the original design.

In December 1949, Colonel Paul R. Goode, the deputy post commander of Fort Monroe, had invited Dr. Chester D. Bradley to confer with him on the establishment of a museum. An active museum committee of interested citizens of the Tidewater area was formed to draw up plans for a museum. Their findings were submitted to General Mark W. Clark, the Chief of Army Field Forces and post commander of Fort Monroe, in June 1950. General Clark approved the idea the following month and accepted the honorary chairmanship of the first museum committee. The Fort Monroe Casemate Museum opened on June 1, 1951, in the casemate which had been occupied by Jefferson Davis. Two more casemates were added to the museum during the next three years. The museum eventually was absorbed into the Army museum system in 1968 and additional casemates were subsequently added. All of the casemates were extensively remodeled to bring them as close to their original condition as possible. The entire fort was designated as a National Historic Landmark on December 19, 1960, and certified as such on May 9, 1961, with a suitable marker placed by the main sallyport.

A significant change in the role of Fort Monroe took place during 1973. In an effort to streamline command arrangements and to save funds, the Department of the Army underwent another major reorganization. The United States Continental Army Command was phased out by the end of 1973 and was replaced at Fort Monroe by the United States Army Training and Doctrine Command (TRADOC). CONARC's functions relating to the Strategic Army Force, the Reserve Components, and unit training were transferred to a new United States Army Forces Command at Fort McPherson, Georgia. TRADOC's mission was individual training, education, and combat developments. It commanded the training centers, service schools, combat development functional centers, and training oriented installations and managed the Reserve Officer Training Corps program. Despite the major shuffle of functions and personnel, the number of troops and civilians assigned to Fort Monroe increased slightly.[18]

When Fort Monroe was established over 150 years ago, the primary purpose of the post was the improvement of the service of artillery—the development of uniformity in doctrine, method, and the technique of its branch of the service. Today its energies are still mainly devoted to the training of the Army, but now all branches of the service are encompassed in its responsibility. Fort Monroe has accomplished its mission in the past, and, whatever may arise, it is prepared to accomplish its mission in the future.

Footnotes Chapter XIII

[1] General Frederick was one of the most outstanding young generals of World War II. Graduating from West Point in 1928 and the Coast Artillery School in 1938, he was a captain at the time the Army expansion began. By 1942 he had risen to colonel and commander of the 1st Special Service Force, the forerunner of today's Special Forces. He was promoted to brigadier general and major general in 1944, leading the 45th Infantry Division during the last year of the war. General Frederick retired in 1952 and died in 1970. He was awarded two Distinguished Service Crosses, two Distinguished Service Medals, the Silver Star, two Legions of Merit, two Bronze Star Medals, the Air Medal, and eight Purple Hearts. *Cullum,* Vol. VII, pp. 2108–2109; Vol. VIII, p. 753; Vol. IX, p. 575.

[2] Dr. Sina K. Spiker, Col. William G. Weaver, and Lt. Col. Joseph Rockis, Planning Activities of Army Ground Forces During the Demobilization Period, 1 September 1945–10 March 1948, AGF Demobilization Study No. 14, pp. 61–63.

[3] Capt. Alonza F. Colonna, "Harbor Defenses of Chesapeake Bay," *Coast Artillery Journal,* 88 (September-October 1945), p. 84, and 89 (January-February 1946), p. 88.

[4] Letter 381/s(C)(23 Feb 46)GNGCT-3, Army Ground Forces to Distribution, 23 February 1946, subject: Defense of Continental United States; Station List No. 2, Eastern Defense Command, 1 February 1946. Battery A was the former Battery A, 2d Coast Artillery, and is now the 5th Battalion, 2d Air Defense Artillery. This battalion, an antiaircraft unit, served in Vietnam.

[5] Lt. Col. Wilson B. Powell, Headquarters, Army Ground Forces During the Demobilization Period, AGF Demobilization Study No. 4, pp. 156–157.

[6] *Ibid.,* pp. 158–160; Master Planning Construction Program, Permanent Installation Planning Board, Fort Monroe, 1949, p. 10; Letter, Norfolk District Engineer to Chief of Engineers, 31 August 1966, subject: Report of Termination of Investment.

[7] Headquarters, Army Ground Forces During the Demobilization Period, p. 160; "2 New Army GHQ Move to Area Soon," Newport News *Daily Press,* April 13, 1946, pp. 1, 5.

[8] Special Order No. 94, Harbor Defenses of Chesapeake Bay, 11 May 1946; "HDCB, Now at Story, Put Under 2d Army," Newport News *Daily Press,* May 26, 1946, p. 14.

[9] General Orders No. 90, War Department, 15 August 1946; "MP's Observe Fifth Year of Organization," Newport News *Daily Press,* September 26, 1946, p. 9; "Coast Artillery School Moves to San Francisco," p. 41.

¹⁰ Letter, AGPA-G-334, AGO, July 11, 1946, subject: War Department Seacoast Defense Armament Board.

¹¹ Planning Activities of Army Ground Forces During the Demobilization Period, pp. 63–71.

¹² "AGF To Start Moving to Fort Monroe Next Tuesday, Finish Oct. 1," Newport News *Daily Press,* September 20, 1946, p. 8; "Military Ceremony to Mark Opening of AGF at Fort Monroe," *ibid.,* October 1, 1946, p. 11; "Gen. Devers And AGF Take Over at Monroe," *ibid.,* October 2, 1946, p. 1.

¹³ Headquarters, Army Ground Forces During the Demobilization Period, p. 161.

¹⁴ USCONARC Summary of Major Events and Problems, Fiscal Year 1956, Section I, Part I, Tab. B.

¹⁵ The Story of Fort Monroe, Information Office, Fort Monroe, 1971; U.S. Army— Progress '63, Office of the Chief of Information.

¹⁶ Letter AICTG 472, Col. K. McCatty to Second Army, January 30, 1948, subject: Use of Tactical Armament for Salute Firing; Letter AIAOR-S 472.1, Commanding General, Second Army, to Commanding General, Fort Monroe, June 8, 1948, subject: Saluting Guns; Letter AICTG 660.2, Harbor Defenses of Chesapeake Bay to Second Army, May 24, 1949, subject: Harbor Defense Installations; Newport News *Daily Press,* "It's Only Enemy—Anti-quation," p. 3-A; General Orders No. 1, Department of the Army, January 3, 1950; General Orders No. 19, Department of the Army, June 14, 1950.

¹⁷ Summary of Major Events and Problems, Fiscal Year 1957, USCONARC G-4 Section; Summary of Major Events and Problems, Fiscal Year 1960, Vol. V, USCONARC G-4 Section, pp. 7–8.

¹⁸ Command Information Fact Sheet #1-73, HQ CONARC, January 1973, CONUS Re-organization 1973.

Bibliography

The official records of Fort Monroe, upon which much of this volume is based, consist of approximately 113 cubic feet of material now in the National Archives. These post records, however, form only a portion of the War Department records relating to the post. A small amount of material relating to the Coast Defenses of Chesapeake Bay is found in Record Group 392, United States Army Coast Artillery Districts and Defenses, 1901–42. A large portion of the records of the Coast Artillery School, as well as other material, is in the records of the Office of the Chief of Coast Artillery, Record Group 177. The records of the Office of the Chief of Ordnance, Record Group 156, contain much information about the armament of Fort Monroe and the records of the Fort Monroe Arsenal. There is a large body of material relating to the construction of the fort in the records of the Office of the Chief of Engineers, Record Group 77. In addition to these major collections of material pertaining to Fort Monroe, much additional information may be found scattered in the records of The Adjutant General's Office, Record Group 94, the records of the Department of Virginia and the First Military District, Record Group 98, and the Office of the Quartermaster General, Record Group 92. Besides these records which have been retired to the National Archives, some material remains at Fort Monroe and Fort Eustis. The Fort Record Book of Fort Story, which contains extensive material relating to the Harbor Defenses of Chesapeake Bay and the Chesapeake Bay Sector, is in the Transportation Corps Museum at Fort Eustis. The Fort Record Book of Fort Monroe and the diaries of Major Harrington W. Cochran, the post adjutant, from 1933 to 1936, are in the Casemate Museum at Fort Monroe. Also at Fort Monroe are the letters received by the post commander from 1824 to 1827 and copies of orders received from 1829 to 1835.

In addition to these sources, Brigadier General Rollin L. Tilton made available his manuscript *Notes on Fort Monroe, 1930 to 1946,* a copy of which is in the Casemate Museum, and the official *History of the Chesapeake Bay Sector.* He provided various other documents and participated in extensive taped interviews. The Casemate Museum also has the daily journals maintained by General Tilton from the time he assumed command of Fort Monroe in 1940 to his retirement as Inspector General, Army Ground Forces, in 1948. Brigadier General Frank S. Clark has furnished a bound set of *Liaison,* a weekly newspaper published at Fort Monroe from 1918 to 1920, and rosters of officers serving at the post in the 1930's. Colonel Manning M. Kimmel, Jr., made a taped interview which provided much interesting information on life at the post prior to World War I and at the beginning of World War II.

The following bibliography contains the major books and articles used in the preparation of this book. Not included in the bibliography are numerous articles from the *Journal of the United States Artillery,* the *Coast Artillery Journal, Assembly,* the alumni magazine of the United States Military Academy, the *Casemate Chronicle,* the monthly newspaper of Fort Monroe, and the Newport News *Daily Press.* Citations to the articles used from these sources will be found in the footnotes. Two popular series of pamphlets, *Tales of Old Fort Monroe,* prepared by the Casemate Museum, and the *Syms-Eaton Museum Horn Book Series,* prepared by the Syms-Eaton Museum of Hampton, both contain much interesting information.

Adler, Herbert F., "Jefferson Davis At Fort Monroe," *Military Review,* Vol. XLVII, May 1967, pp. 71–76.

Ambrose, Stephen E., *Upton and the Army.* Baton Rouge: Louisiana State University Press, 1964.

American State Papers: Military Affairs, 7 vols., Washington: 1834–1860.

Ammen, Daniel, *The Atlantic Coast.* New York: The Blue & Gray Press, n.d.

Arber, Edward, *Travels and Works of Captain John Smith.* Edinburgh: John Grant, 1910.

Arthur, Robert, *The Coast Artillery School, 1824–1927.* Fort Monroe: The Coast Artillery School, 1928.

Avery, Elroy M., *A History of the United States and Its People.* Cleveland, 1904–1909.

B(—), R(—), *The History and Present State of Virginia, in Four Parts.* London: 1705.

Barnard, John G., *Notes on Sea-Coast Defence: Consisting of Sea-Coast Fortification, The Fifteen-Inch Gun, and Casemate Embrasures.* New York: D. Van Nostrand, 1861.

Beverly, Robert, *The History of Virginia.* Richmond: 1855.

Birkhimer, William E., *Historical Sketch of the Organization, Administration, Materiel and Tactics of the Artillery, United States Army.* New York: Greenwood Press, 1968.

Bradley, Chester D., and Bradley, Miriam D., "The Cradle of the American Nation—The Virginia Peninsula," *Virginia Medical Monthly,* Vol. 76, September 1949, pp. 436–443.

Bradley, Chester D., "Dr. Craven and the Captivity of Jefferson Davis at Fort Monroe," *Virginia Medical Monthly,* Vol. 83, May 1956, pp. 197–199.

Bradley, Chester D., "Dr. Craven and the Imprisonment of Jefferson Davis," *The Iron Worker,* Vol. XXXVIII, No. 3, Summer 1974, pp. 2–13.

Bradley, Chester D., "Dr. Craven and the Prison Life of Jefferson Davis." *Virginia Magazine of History and Biography,* Vol. LXII, January 1954, pp. 72–76.

Bradley, Chester D., *Harrison Phoebus: From Farm to Fortune,* Fort Monroe, Casemate Museum, n.d.

Bradley, Chester D., "Jefferson Davis in Prison," *Manuscripts,* Spring 1958.

Bradley, Chester D., "President Lincoln's Campaign Against the *Merrimac,*"

Journal of the Illinois Historical Society, Vol. LI, Spring 1958, pp. 59–85.

Brief History of the Eleventh United States Infantry, A. Fort Benjamin Harrison: 1926.

Brown, Alexander, *English Politics in Early Virginia History.* Cambridge: 1901.

Brown, Alexander, *The First Republic in America.* Boston: 1898.

Brown, Alexander, *Genesis of the United States.* Boston, 1890.

Brownell, Charles de W., *The Indian Races of North and South America.* Hartford, 1873.

Bruce, Philip A., *Economic History of Virginia in the Seventeenth Century.* 2 vols., New York: 1896.

Bruce, Phillip A., *Institutional History of Virginia in the Seventeenth Century.* New York: 1910.

Burk, John, *The History of Virginia.* 4 vols., Petersburg: 1816.

Butler, Benjamin F., *Butler's Book.* Boston: 1892.

Campbell, Charles, *History of the Colony and Ancient Dominion of Virginia.* Philadelphia: J. B. Lippincott and Co., 1860.

Campbell, J. W., *A History of Virginia.* Philadelphia: 1813.

Carter, Maj. Gen. William H., "Bvt. Maj. Gen. Simon Bernard," *Journal of the Military Service Institution,* Vol. LI, pp. 147–155.

Chandler, J. B., and Thames, R. B., *Colonial Virginia.* Richmond: 1907.

Chesapeake Zoological Laboratory. Baltimore: Johns Hopkins University, 1878.

Clendenen, Clarence G., *Blood on the Border.* London: The Macmillan Company, 1969.

Coast Artillery School, *Catalogue of the Coast Artillery School, 1918–19.* Fort Monroe: 1918.

Coast Artillery Training Center, *Report of the Commanding General for the Period January 1, 1917, to August 31, 1919.* Fort Monroe: 1919.

Coffman, Edward M., *The Hilt of the Sword.* Madison, Milwaukee, and London: The University of Wisconsin Press, 1966.

Corell, Philip, *History of the Naval Brigade, 99th N.Y. Volunteers, Union Coast Guard.* New York: Regimental Veteran Association, 1905.

Cowtan, Charles W., *Services of the Tenth New York Volunteers (National Zouaves) in the War of the Rebellion.* New York: Charles H. Ludwig, 1882.

Craven, Bvt. Lt. Col. John J., *Prison Life of Jefferson Davis.* New York: Carleton, 1866.

Cullum, George W., *Biographical Register of the Officers and Graduates of the U.S. Military Academy.* Boston and New York: Houghton, Mifflin and Co., 1891.

Daly, R. W. (ed.), *Aboard the USS Monitor: 1862.* Annapolis: United States Naval Institute, 1964.

Davenport, Alfred, *Camp and Field Life of the Fifth New York Volunteer Infantry (Duryea Zouaves),* New York: Dick and Fitzgerald, 1879.

Davis, George W., *Military and Civil Occupation of Old Point Comfort, Virginia.* Washington: 1893.

Davis, Varina H., *Jefferson Davis, Ex-President of the Confederate States of America.* New York: Belford Co., 1890.

Dillon, William, *Life of John Mitchel.* London: Kegan Paul, Trence & Co., 1888.

Dix, Morgan, *Memoirs of John Adams Dix*. 2 vols., New York: Harper & Co., 1883.

Dodd, William E., *Jefferson Davis*. Philadelphia: 1907.

Dyer, Frederick, *A Compendium of the War of the Rebellion*. New York and London: Thomas Yoseloff, 1959.

Emmerson, John C., Jr., *Steam Navigation in Virginia and North Carolina*. Portsmouth, Va.: 1949.

Endicott, William C., *Report of the Board on Fortifications or Other Defenses Appointed by the President of the United States Under Provisions of the Act of Congress Approved March 3, 1885*. Washington: 1886.

Executive Journals of the Council of Colonial Virginia. Richmond: Virginia State Library, 1925.

Fiske, John, *Old Virginia and Her Neighbours*. 2 vols., Boston: 1897.

Fitzpatrick, John G. (ed.), *The Diaries of George Washington, 1748–1799*. Boston: 1925.

Fort Monroe Mess, *Officers, Constitution, By-laws, and Members*. Fort Monroe: 1915.

Freeman, Douglas Southall, *R. E. Lee*. 3 vols., New York and London: Charles Scribner's Sons, 1934.

Fulgham, Matthew T., "Historic Fort Monroe," *The Iron Worker*, Vol. XVI, Spring 1952, pp. 1–12.

Gordon, Armistead C., *Jefferson Davis*. New York: 1918.

Gray, Frederic W., and Bradley, Chester D., "The Medical History of Jefferson Davis," *Virginia Medical Monthly*, Vol. 94, January 1967, pp. 19–23.

Hakluyt, Richard, *The Trve Pictvres and Fashions of the People in that Parte of America novv called Virginia . . . Translated out of Latin into English by Richard Hacklvit*. Franckfort [De Bryl]: 1590.

Hakluyt, Richard, *Virginia richly valued, By the description of the maine land of Florida, her next neighbor: . . . . Written by a Portugall gentlemen of Eluas, emploied in all the action, and tranlated out of Portuguese by Richard Haklvyt*. London: 1609.

Hammond, John M., *Quaint and Historic Forts of North America*. Philadelphia: 1915.

Hamor, Ralph, *A True Discourse of the Present Estate of Virginia, and the successe of the affaires there till 18 of Iume, 1614*. London: 1615.

Hanchett, William, "Reconstruction and the Rehabilitation of Jefferson Davis: Charles G. Halpine's Prison Life," *The Journal of American History*, Vol. LVI, September 1969, pp. 280–289.

Hariot, Thomas, *A briefe and true report of the new found land of Virginia: of the commodities there found and to be raysed, as well marchantable, as others for victuall, building and other necessarie uses for those that are shalbe the planters there; and of the nature and manners of the natural inhabitants: . . .* London: 1588.

Haskin, William L., *The History of the First Regiment of Artillery From Its Organization in 1821, to January 1st, 1876*. Portland: 1879.

Haydon, F. Stansbury, *Aeronautics in the Union and Confederate Armies*. Baltimore: The Johns Hopkins Press, 1941.

Heitman, Francis B., *Historical Register and Dictionary of the United States Army*. Washington: Government Printing Office, 1903.

Hines, Frank T., *The Service of Coast Artillery*. New York: Goodenough & Woglon Co., 1910.

History of the US Army Air Defense School, Fort Bliss, Tex., n.d.

Hitsman, J. Mackay and Sorby, Alice, "Independent Foreigners or Canadian Chasseurs, *Military Affairs*, Vol. XXV, Spring 1961, pp. 11–17.

Howe, Henry W., *Passages from the Life of Henry Warren Howe, consisting of Diary and Letters Written During the Civil War, 1861–1865*. Lowell, Mass.: Courier-Citizen Co., 1899.

Jackson, Donald (ed.), *Black Hawk: An Autobiography*. Urbana: University of Illinois Press, 1955.

James, Marquis, *The Life of Andrew Jackson*. Garden City: Garden City Publishing Co., 1940.

Johnson, Charles F., *The Long Roll*. East Aurora, N.Y.: The Roycrofters, 1911.

[Johnson, Robert], *Nova Britannia, Offering Most Excellent fruites by Planting in Virginia*. London: 1609.

Jones, Robert R., (ed.), "The Mexican War Diary of James Lawson Kemper," *The Virginia Magazine of History and Biography*, Vol. 74, October 1966.

Journals of the House of Burgesses of Virginia, 1659/60–1776. 12 vols., Richmond: 1905–1914.

Keith, Sir William, *The History of the British Plantations in America*. London: 1738.

Kimball, William J., "The Little Battle of Big Bethel," *Civil War Times Illustrated*, Vol. VI, June 1967, pp. 28–32.

Kingsbury, Susan M. (ed.), *The Records of the Virginia Company of London, 1619–1624*. 2 vols., Washington: 1906.

Kirchner, Lt. David, "American Harbor Defense Forts," *U.S. Naval Institute Proceedings*, Vol. 84, August 1958, pp. 92–101.

Kirchner, David P., and Lewis, E. R., "American Harbor Defenses: The Final Era," *U.S. Naval Institute Proceedings*, Vol. 94, January 1968, pp. 84–98.

Knight, Lucian Lamar, *Alexander H. Stephens, The Sage of Liberty Hall*. Athens, Ga.: 1930.

Lee, Henry, *Memoirs of the War in the Southern Department of the United States*. New York: 1870.

Lewis, Emanuel Raymond, *Seacoast Fortifications of the United States: An Introductory History*. Washington: Smithsonian Institution Press, 1970.

Lossing, Benson J., *The Pictorial Field Book of the Revolution*. 2 vols., New York: 1850–1852.

Lossing, Benson J., *Pictorial History of the Civil War in the United States of America*. 3 vols., Hartford: 1868–1870.

Marshall, John, *Life of George Washington*, . . . Philadelphia: 1833.

McClellan, George B., *McClellan's Own Story*. New York: Chas. L. Webster & Co., 1887.

McIlvane, H. R., *Legislative Journals of the Council of Colonial Virginia*. 3 vols., Richmond: 1918–1919.

Military Historical Society of Massachusetts, *Operations on the Atlantic Coast, 1861–1865, Virginia, 1862, Vicksburg*. Boston: 1912.

Morgan, Prentice G., "The Forward Observer," *Military Affairs*, Vol. XXIII, Winter 1959–60, pp. 209–212.

Naval Historical Foundation, *"The Virginia No Longer Exists."* Washington: Naval Historical Foundation, n.d.

Navy Department, *Official Records of the Union and Confederate Navies in the War of the Rebellion*. Washington: Government Printing Office, 1894–1922.

O'Brien, John Emmet, *Telegraphing in Battle*. Scranton, 1910.

Palmer, William P., *Calendar of Virginia State Papers and Other Manuscripts, 1652–1789*. 4 vols., Richmond: 1876–1884.

Patterson, H. K. W., *War Memories of Fort Monroe and Vicinity*. Fort Monroe: 1885.

Peters, Lylas B., "Fort Monroe In Historic Tidewater Virginia," *U.S. Lady*, Vol. 2, October 1957, pp. 21–26.

Prucha, Francis Paul, *Guide to the Military Posts of the United States*. Madison: The State Historical Society of Wisconsin, 1964.

Rachal, William M. E., "Walled Fortress and Resort Hotels," *Virginia Cavalcade*, Vol. II, Summer 1952, pp. 20–27.

Ripley, Warren, *Artillery and Ammunition of the Civil War*. New York: Promontory Press, 1970.

Rouse, Parke, Jr., "Low Tide at Hampton Roads," *U.S. Naval Institute Proceedings*, Vol. 95, July 1969, pp. 77–86.

Seager, Robert, II, *and Tyler too, a Biography of John & Julia Gardner Tyler*. New York, Toronto, and London: McGraw-Hill Book Co., Inc., 1963.

Six, Georges, *Dictionnaire Biographique des Generaux & Amiraux Francais de la Revolution et de l'Empire (1792–1814)*. Paris: Georges Saffroy, 1934.

Smith, John, *The Generall Historie of Virginia, New-England, and the Summer Isles: with the names of the Adventurers, Planters, and Governours from their beginning Ano: 1583, to this present 1624*. London: 1624.

Smith, John, *A trve Relation of such occurrences and accidents of noate as hath hapned in Virginia since the planting of that collony, which is resident in the South part thereof, till the last returne from thence*. London: 1608.

Smith, John, *The True Travels, Adventures, and Observations of Captaine John Smith, in Europe, Asia, Africa, and America, from Anno Domini 1593 to 1629*. London: 1630.

Stanton, Edwin M., *Letter of the Secretary of War, Transmitting Report on the Organization of the Army of the Potomac, and of Its Campaign in Virginia and Maryland, Under the Command of Maj. Gen. George B. McClellan, from July 26, 1861, to November 7, 1862*. Washington: 1864.

Stedman, Charles, *The History of the Origin, Progress, and Termination of the American War*. 2 vols., London: 1794.

Stick, David, *The Outer Banks of North Carolina*. Chapel Hill: The University of North Carolina Press, 1958.

Stith, William, *History of the Discovery and Settlement of Virginia*. Williamsburg: 1747.

Strode, Hudson, *Jefferson Davis, American Patriot*. 3 vols., New York: Harcourt, Brace and Company, 1955.

Taft, William H., *Report of the National Coast-Defense Board Appointed by the President of the United States by Executive Order, January 31, 1905*. Washington: 1906.

Thomas, Benjamin P., *Abraham Lincoln*. New York: Alfred A. Knopf, 1952.

Tidball, John J., *Manual of Heavy Artillery Service for the use of the Army and Militia of the United States*. Washington: James J. Chapman, 1891.

Tschappot, Lt. Col. William H., *Text-Book of Ordnance and Gunnery*. New York: John Wiley & Sons, Inc., 1917.

Tunstall, Nannie W., *"No. 40," A Romance of Fortress Monroe and the Hygeia*. Richmond: 1890.

Tyler, Lyon G., *The Cradle of the Republic*. Richmond: 1906.

Tyler, Lyon G., *History of Hampton and Elizabeth City County, Virginia*. Hampton: 1922.

Tyler, Lyon G. (ed.), *Narratives of Early Virginia, 1606–1625*. Barnes and Noble, Inc., 1966.

U.S. Army Recruiting News, March 15, 1923.

Upton, Emory, *The Military Policy of the United States*. Washington: Office of the Chief of Staff, 1912.

Virginia Board of Immigration, *Virginia: a Geographical and Political Summary*. Richmond: 1876.

Virginia Historical Society, *The Virginia Historical Collections*. 11 vols., Richmond: 1882–1892.

Wallace, Lee A., Jr., "The First Regiment of Virginia Volunteers, 1846–1848," *The Virginia Magazine of History and Biography*, Vol. 77, January 1969, pp. 54–57.

War Department, *General Regulations for the Army; or, Military Institutes*. Washington: 1825.

War Department, *Outline Description of the U.S. Military Posts and Stations in the Year 1871*. Washington: Quartermaster General's Office, 1872.

War Department, *A Report on Barracks and Hospitals with Descriptions of Military Posts*. Surgeon General's Office Circular No. 4; Washington, 1870.

War Department, *A Report on the Hygiene of the United States Army, with Descriptions of Military Posts*. Surgeon General's Office Circular No. 8; Washington, 1875.

War Department, *United States Military Reservations, National Cemeteries, and Military Parks*. Washington: 1916.

War Department, *War of the Rebellion: A Compilation of the Official Records of the Union and Confederate Armies*. 130 vols., Washington: Government Printing Office, 1880–1901.

Warner, Ezra J., *Generals in Blue*. Baton Rouge: Louisiana State University Press, 1964.

Warner, Ezra J., *Generals in Gray*. Baton Rouge: Louisiana State University Press, 1959.

Webb, Alexander S., *The Peninsula—McClellan's Campaign of 1862*. New York: 1902.

Weigley, Russell F., *History of the United States Army*. New York: The Macmillan Company, 1967.

Weinert, Richard P., *The Guns of Fort Monroe*. Fort Monroe Casemate Museum, 1974.

Weinert, Richard P., "Longstreet's Suffolk Campaign," *Civil War Times Illustrated*, Vol. VII, January 1969, pp. 31–39.

Werner, Herbert A., *Iron Coffins*. New York, Chicago, and San Francisco: Holt Rinehart and Winston, 1969.

Wertenbaker, Thomas J., *Virginia Under the Stuarts, 1607–1688*. Princeton: 1914.

Winwar, Frances, *The Haunted Palace: A Life of Edgar Allan Poe*. New York: Harper & Brothers, 1959.

Appendix A

COMMANDING OFFICERS AT FORT MONROE
I. POST OF FORT MONROE

Capt. Mann P. Lomax, 3d Artillery	Jul 1823 to Feb 1824
Bvt. Maj. Benjamin K. Pierce, 4th Artillery	Feb 1824 to 31 Mar 1824
*Bvt. Col. Abraham Eustis, 4th Artillery	31 Mar 1824 to 31 Jan 1825
*Bvt. Brig. Gen. John R. Fenwick, 4th Artillery	31 Jan 1825 to 1 Aug 1825
*Bvt. Col. Abraham Eustis, 4th Artillery	1 Aug 1825 to 13 Nov 1828
*Col. James House, 1st Artillery	13 Nov 1828 to 12 Oct 1829
*Bvt. Col. John de B. Walbach, 1st Artillery	12 Oct 1829 to 12 Dec 1830
*Col. James House, 1st Artillery	12 Dec 1830 to 21 Sep 1831
Bvt. Maj. Raymond M. Kirby, 1st Artillery	21 Sep 1831 to 1 Oct 1831
Bvt. Lt. Col. William J. Worth, 1st Artillery	1 Oct 1831 to 12 Oct 1831
*Bvt. Col. Abraham Eustis, 4th Artillery	12 Oct 1831 to 22 Jun 1834
Bvt. Lt. Col. Alexander C. W. Fanning, 4th Artillery	22 Jun 1834 to Aug 1834
Bvt. Brig. Gen. Walker K. Armistead, 3d Artillery	Aug 1834 to 10 Nov 1836
Capt. Charles Mellon, 2d Artillery	10 Nov 1836 to 7 Jan 1837
Bvt. Capt. Timothy Green, 1st Artillery	7 Jan 1837 to 8 May 1837
Lt. Col. James Bankhead, 4th Artillery	8 May 1837 to 17 Jul 1837
Bvt. Maj. John L. Gardner, 4th Artillery	17 Jul 1837 to 5 Sep 1837
Bvt. Brig. Gen. Abraham Eustis, 1st Artillery	5 Sep 1837 to 21 Oct 1837
Bvt. Maj. John Erving, 4th Artillery	21 Oct 1837 to 21 Nov 1838
Lt. Col. Rene E. DeRussy, Corps of Engineers	21 Nov 1838 to 2 Sep 1841
Bvt. Col. Alexander C. W. Fanning, 2d Artillery	2 Sep 1841 to 23 Dec 1841
Capt. Samuel Mackenzie, 2d Artillery	23 Dec 1841 to 12 Jul 1842
Lt. Col. Ichabod Crane, 4th Artillery	12 Jul 1842 to 1 Aug 1842
Bvt. Brig. Gen. John de B. Walbach, 4th Artillery	1 Aug 1842 to 19 Oct 1848
Bvt. Brig. Gen. James Bankhead, 2d Artillery	19 Oct 1848 to 9 Nov 1853
Col. Ichabod Crane, 1st Artillery	14 Nov 1853 to 2 Jun 1855
Lt. Col. Silas Casey, 9th Infantry	2 Jun 1855 to 3 Jul 1855
Col. George Wright, 9th Infantry	3 Jul 1855 to 15 Dec 1855
Bvt. Lt. Col. Francis Taylor, 1st Artillery	15 Dec 1855 to 20 May 1856
Bvt. Col. John L. Gardner, 1st Artillery	20 May 1856 to 8 Dec 1856
Capt. Albion P. Howe, 4th Artillery	8 Dec 1856 to 15 Jan 1857
Capt. James Totten, 2d Artillery	15 Jan 1857 to 5 Feb 1857
Capt. John F. Reynolds, 3d Artillery	5 Feb 1857 to 3 Mar 1857
Capt. Albion P. Howe, 4th Artillery	3 Mar 1857 to 18 Apr 1857
Bvt. Lt. Col. Martin Burke, 2d Artillery	18 Apr 1857 to 31 May 1857
*Bvt. Col. Harvey Brown, 2d Artillery	31 May 1857 to 26 Nov 1859
*Bvt. Col. Justin Dimick, 2d Artillery	26 Nov 1859 to 19 Oct 1861
Maj. Joseph Roberts, 4th Artillery	19 Oct 1861 to 15 Sep 1862
Col. Samuel M. Alford, 3d New York Infantry	15 Sep 1862 to 10 Jun 1863
Bvt. Maj. Gen. Joseph Roberts, 3d Pennsylania Artillery	10 Jun 1863 to 1 Nov 1865
Bvt. Lt. Col. Henry A. DuPont, 5th Artillery	1 Nov 1865 to 5 Dec 1865
Bvt. Brig. Gen. Henry S. Burton, 5th Artillery	5 Dec 1865 to 11 Jun 1867
Bvt. Lt. Col. Henry A. DuPont, 5th Artillery	11 Jun 1867 to 15 Jul 1867

Bvt. Brig. Gen. William Hays, 5th Artillery	15 Jul 1867 to 28 Nov 1867
*Bvt. Maj. Gen. William F. Barry, 2d Artillery	28 Nov 1867 to 1 Mar 1877
*Bvt. Maj. Gen. George W. Getty, 3d Artillery	1 Mar 1877 to 9 Jul 1883
Bvt. Col. Richard Lodor, 3d Artillery	9 Jul 1883 to 12 Aug 1883
Bvt. Lt. Col. LaRhett L. Livingston, 4th Artillery	12 Aug 1883 to 5 Nov 1883
*Bvt. Maj. Gen. John C. Tidball, 1st Artillery	5 Nov 1883 to 5 Nov 1888
*Col. Royal T. Frank, 1st Artillery	5 Nov 1888 to 19 May 1898
Lt. Col. Henry C. Hasbrouck, 4th Artillery	19 May 1898 to 27 Jun 1898
Col. William P. Lane, 1st Maryland Infantry	27 Jun 1898 to 7 Sep 1898
Maj. John L. Tiernon, 1st Artillery	8 Sep 1898 to 31 Mar 1899
Maj. Samuel M. Mills, 6th Artillery	31 Mar 1899 to 4 Apr 1899
Capt. William F. Stewart, 4th Artillery	4 Apr. 1899 to 6 May 1899
*Col. Francis L. Guenther, 4th Artillery	6 May 1899 to 22 Feb 1902
Maj. Clement L. Best, Jr., Artillery Corps	22 Feb 1902 to 10 Mar 1902
*Col. John P. Story, Artillery Corps	10 Mar 1902 to 24 Jan 1904
Maj. Albert S. Cummins, Artillery Corps	24 Jan 1904 to 21 Feb 1904
*Col. Ramsay D. Potts, Artillery Corps	21 Feb 1904 to 11 Aug 1906
Maj. Frederick S. Strong, Artillery Corps	11 Aug 1906 to 22 Oct 1906
*Col. George F. E. Harrison, Coast Artillery Corps	22 Oct 1906 to 14 Jan 1909
Maj. Isaac N. Lewis, Coast Artillery Corps	14 Jan 1909 to 5 Feb 1909
*Lt. Col. Clarence P. Townsley, Coast Artillery Corps	5 Feb 1909 to 7 Sep 1911
*Col. Frederick S. Strong, Coast Artillery Corps	7 Sep 1911 to 27 Feb 1913
*Col. Ira A. Haynes, Coast Artillery Corps	27 Feb 1913 to 15 Aug 1916
Lt. Col. Henry D. Todd, Jr., Coast Artillery Corps	15 Aug 1916 to 1 Oct 1916
*Col. Stephen M. Foote, Coast Artillery Corps	1 Oct 1916 to 23 Aug 1917
*Col. John A. Lundeen, Retired	23 Aug 1917 to 30 Mar 1918
*Brig. Gen. Frank K. Fergusson	30 Mar 1918 to 31 Jan 1919
**Col. Robert R. Welshimer, Coast Artillery Corps	8 Sep 1918 to 29 Jan 1919
**Col. Eugene Reybold, Coast Artillery Corps	29 Jan 1919 to 19 Jan 1920
Brig. Gen. William Chamberlaine	31 Jan 1919 to 9 Sep 1919
Brig. Gen. Johnson Hagood	9 Sep 1919 to 30 Sep 1919
Brig. Gen. Adelbert Cronkhite	30 Sep 1919 to 1 Sep 1920
**Col. Jacob C. Johnson, Coast Artillery Corps	19 Jan 1920 to 3 Nov 1920
Brig. Gen. Johnson Hagood	1 Sep 1920 to 8 Sep 1920
Col. William E. Cole, Coast Artillery Corps	8 Sep 1920 to 3 Nov 1920
Col. John C. Gilmore, Jr., Coast Artillery Corps	3 Nov 1920 to 28 Apr 1921
*Col. Richmond P. Davis, Coast Artillery Corps	28 Apr 1921 to 28 Dec 1922
Col. Jacob C. Johnson, Coast Artillery Corps	28 Dec 1922 to 11 Jan 1923
*Brig. Gen. William R. Smith	11 Jan 1923 to 20 Dec 1924
*Brig. Gen. Robert E. Callan	20 Dec 1924 to 3 Jun 1929
Col. George A. Nugent, Coast Artillery Corps	3 Jun 1929 to 27 Aug 1929
*Maj. Gen. Henry D. Todd, Jr.	28 Aug 1929 to 31 Aug 1930
*Brig. Gen. Stanley D. Embick	1 Sep 1930 to 26 Apr 1932
Col. Harold E. Cloke, Coast Artillery Corps	26 Apr 1932 to 1 Aug 1932
*Brig. Gen. Joseph P. Tracy	1 Aug 1932 to 16 Dec 1936
*Brig. Gen. John W. Gulick	17 Dec 1936 to 30 Nov 1938
*Maj. Gen. Frederic H. Smith	1 Dec 1938 to 9 Nov 1940
**Brig. Gen. Frank S. Clark	10 Oct 1940 to 10 Jan 1942
Brig. Gen. Rollin L. Tilton	9 Nov 1940 to 15 Jun 1946
**Brig. Gen. Lawrence B. Weeks	10 Jan. 1942 to 11 Nov 1945

**Maj. Gen. Robert T. Frederick	11 Nov 1945 to 28 May 1946
Col. Logan C. Berry, Cavalry	15 Jun 1946 to 1 Oct 1946
Gen. Jacob L. Devers	1 Oct 1946 to 29 Jul 1949
Gen. Mark W. Clark	16 Sep 1949 to 13 Jun 1952
Gen. John R. Hodge	26 Jun 1952 to 30 Jun 1953
Gen. John E. Dahlquist	1 Sep 1953 to 21 Feb 1956
Col. Malcolm D. Jones	21 Feb 1956 to 30 Jun 1956
Col. Charles Wesner, Field Artillery	1 Jul 1956 to 31 Jul 1957
Col. Paul R. Jeffrey, Infantry	1 Aug 1957 to 1961
Col. Roy F. Zinser, Infantry	1961 to 30 Sep 1964
Col. Robert B. Pridgen, Infantry	1 Oct 1964 to 31 Dec 1966
Col. Henry L. Gordner, Infantry	1 Jan 1967 to 1 Sep 1970
Col. Joseph J. Jackson, Infantry	2 Sep 1970 to 31 Dec 1972
Col. Bernard Big, Infantry	1 Jan 1973 to 22 Jan 1976
Col. Barton M. Hayward, Field Artillery	23 Jan 1976 to

---

*Also commandant of the Coast Artillery School or its predecessors.
**Served only as commandant of the Coast Artillery School.

II. HIGHER HEADQUARTERS AT FORT MONROE
Military Department No. 4
Bvt. Brig. Gen. Abraham Eustis   5 Sep 1837 to 21 Oct 1837
Military Department No. 7
Bvt. Brig. Gen. John De B. Walbach   1 Aug 1842 to 19 Oct 1848
Military Department No. 4
Bvt. Brig. Gen. James Bankhead   19 Oct 1848 to   9 Nov 1853
Department of Virginia
Maj. Gen. Benjamin F. Butler, U.S. Volunteers   22 May 1861 to 17 Aug 1861
Bvt. Maj. Gen. John E. Wool   17 Aug 1861 to   2 Jun 1862
Department of Fort Monroe
Maj. Gen. John A. Dix, U.S. Volunteers   2 Jun 1862 to 15 Jun 1862
VII Army Corps
Maj. Gen. John A. Dix, U.S. Volunteers   15 Jun 1862 to 27 Sep 1862
Department of Virginia
Maj. Gen. John A. Dix, U.S. Volunteers   27 Sep 1862 to 15 Jul 1863
Department of Virginia and North Carolina
Maj. Gen. Benjamin F. Butler, U.S. Volunteers   11 Nov 1863 to   5 May 1864
Military District of Fort Monroe
Maj. Gen. Nelson A. Miles, U.S. Volunteers   22 May 1865 to   1 Sep 1866
Coast Artillery Training Center

Brig. Gen. Frank K. Fergusson	8 Sep 1918 to 31 Jan 1919
Brig. Gen. William Chamberlaine	31 Jan 1919 to 9 Sep 1919
Brig. Gen. Johnson Hagood	9 Sep 1919 to 30 Sep 1919
Brig. Gen. Adelbert Cronkhite	30 Sep 1919 to 1 Sep 1920
Brig. Gen. Johnson Hagood	1 Sep 1920 to 8 Sep 1920
Col. William E. Cole	8 Sep 1920 to 3 Nov 1920
Col. Richmond P. Davis	3 Nov 1920 to 28 Dec 1922
Col. Jacob C. Johnson	28 Dec 1922 to 11 Jan 1923
Brig. Gen. William R. Smith	11 Jan 1923 to 15 May 1923

Third Coast Artillery District

Brig. Gen. William R. Smith	15 May 1923 to 30 Dec 1924
Brig. Gen. Robert E. Callan	20 Dec 1924 to 3 Jun 1929
Col. George A. Nugent	3 Jun 1929 to 4 Jun 1929
Brig. Gen. Charles D. Roberts	4 Jun 1929 to 27 Aug 1929
Maj. Gen. Henry D. Todd, Jr.	28 Aug 1929 to 30 Aug 1930
Brig. Gen. Stanley D. Embick	1 Sep 1930 to 25 Apr 1932
Brig. Gen. Joseph P. Tracy	2 Aug 1932 to 24 Nov 1936
Brig. Gen. John W. Gulick	3 Jan 1937 to 12 Oct 1938
Maj. Gen. Frederic H. Smith	22 Nov 1938 to 4 Jan 1941
Brig. Gen. Rollin L. Tilton	4 Jan 1940 to 11 Dec 1941

Chesapeake Bay Sector

Brig. Gen. Rollin L. Tilton	12 Dec 1941 to 29 Feb 1944

Army Ground Forces

Gen. Jacob L. Devers	1 Oct 1946 to 9 Mar 1948

Army Field Forces

Gen. Jacob L. Devers	10 Mar 1948 to 30 Sep 1949
Gen. Mark W. Clark	1 Oct 1949 to 5 May 1952
Gen. John R. Hodge	8 May 1952 to 30 Jun 1953
Gen. John E. Dahlquist	24 Aug 1953 to 31 Jan 1955

United States Continental Army Command

Gen. John E. Dahlquist	1 Feb 1955 to 28 Feb 1956
Gen. Willard G. Wyman	1 Mar 1956 to 31 Jul 1958
Gen. Bruce C. Clarke	1 Aug 1958 to 30 Sep 1960
Gen. Herbert B. Powell	1 Oct 1960 to 31 Jan 1963
Gen. John K. Waters	1 Feb 1963 to 29 Feb 1964
Gen. Hugh P. Harris	1 Mar 1964 to 28 Feb 1965
Gen. Paul L. Freeman	2 Apr 1965 to 30 Jun 1967
Gen. James K. Woolnough	1 Jul 1967 to 31 Oct 1970
Gen. Ralph E. Haines	1 Nov 1970 to 31 Jan 1973
Gen. Walter T. Kerwin, Jr.	1 Feb 1973 to 30 Jun 1973

United States Army Training & Doctrine Command

Gen. William E. DePuy	1 Jul 1973 to 30 Jun 1977
Gen. Donn A. Starry	1 Jul 1977 to

Appendix B

TROOPS STATIONED AT FORT MONROE

Organization	From	To	Remarks
Co. G, 3d Art.	25 Jul 1823	14 Mar 1826	
Co. C, 4th Art.	— Feb 1824	15 Nov 1826	
Co. D, 4th Art.	— Feb 1824	27 Mar 1826	
Co. I, 4th Art.	— Feb 1824	27 Mar 1826	
Co. G, 2d Art.	— Mar 1824	22 Mar 1826	
Co. F, 3d Art.	— Apr 1824	12 May 1826	
Co. F, 1st Art.	28 Apr 1824	25 Mar 1826	
Co. D, 2d Art.	28 Apr 1824	25 Oct 1826	
Co. H, 2d Art.	28 Apr 1824	19 Mar 1826	
Co. D, 3d Art.	29 Apr 1824	27 Mar 1826	
Co. E, 1st Art.	19 May 1824	21 Oct 1826	
Co. I, 2d Art.	— Mar 1826	23 Mar 1828	
Co. I, 3d Art.	— Mar 1826	8 Apr 1828	
Co. D, 1st Art.	— Apr 1826	23 Mar 1828	
Co. E, 2d Art.	— Apr 1826	23 Mar 1828	
Co. H, 3d Art.	— Apr 1826	8 Apr 1828	
Co. A, 4th Art.	— Apr 1826	25 Mar 1828	
Co. B, 1st Art.	— May 1826	21 Mar 1828	
Co. H, 4th Art.	31 May 1826	30 Mar 1828	
Co. F, 2d Art.	31 Oct 1826	9 Nov 1828	To Charleston, S.C.
Co. A, 1st Art.	13 Nov 1826	19 Dec 1830	To Wilmington, N.C.
Co. B, 4th Art.	16 Jan 1827	6 Nov 1828	To Fort McHenry, Md.
Co. I, 1st Art.	1 Apr 1828	10 Sep 1831	To New Bern, N.C.
Co. G, 4th Art.	8 Apr 1828	14 Nov 1828	To Fort Columbus, N.Y.
Co. A, 2d Art.	14 Apr 1828	25 Nov 1828	To Charleston, S,C.
Co. B, 2d Art.	14 Apr 1828	25 Nov 1828	To Charleston, S.C.
Co. E, 4th Art.	14 Apr 1828	9 Nov 1828	To Baltimore, Md.
Co. G, 1st Art.	19 Apr 1828	19 Dec 1830	To Wilmington, N.C.
Co. B, 3d Art.	8 May 1828	18 May 1829	To Fort Independence, Mass.
Co. E, 3d Art.	8 May 1828	22 May 1829	To New London, Conn.
Co. E, 1st Art.	13 Nov 1828	30 May 1832	To Castle Pinckney, S.C.
Co. B, 1st Art.	15 Dec 1828	31 Oct 1832	To Fort McHenry, Md.
Co. H, 1st Art.	15 Dec 1828	16 Dec 1831	To New Bern, N.C.
Co. A, 1st Art.	14 May 1831	30 May 1832	To Fort Moultrie, S.C.
Co. G, 1st Art.	14 May 1831	19 Jun 1832	To Chicago, Ill.
Co. C, 4th Art.	7 Oct 1831	19 Jun 1832	To Chicago, Ill.
Co. G, 4th Art.	7 Oct 1831	19 Jun 1832	To Chicago, Ill.
Co. B, 3d Art.	21 Oct 1831	19 Jun 1832	To Chicago, Ill.
Co. H, 3d Art.	21 Oct 1831	22 Jun 1832	To Chicago, Ill.
Co. E, 3d Art.	29 Oct 1831	19 Jun 1832	To Chicago, Ill.
Co. C, 1st Art.	31 Dec 1831	18 Nov 1832	To Fort Moultrie, S.C.
Co. B, 4th Art.	3 Nov 1832	18 Nov 1832	To Fort Moultrie, S.C.
Co. G, 1st Art.	7 Nov 1832	23 Dec 1832	To Charleston, S.C.
Co. B, 3d Art.	7 Nov 1832	23 Dec 1832	To Fort Moultrie, S.C.
Co. E, 3d Art.	7 Nov 1832	23 Dec 1832	To Fort Moultrie, S.C.
Co. H, 3d Art.	7 Nov 1832	29 Nov 1833	To Fort Mitchell, Ala.

Organization	From	To	Remarks
Co. C, 4th Art.	7 Nov 1832	23 Dec 1832	To Fort Moultrie, S.C.
Co. G, 4th Art.	7 Nov 1832	23 Dec 1832	To Fort Moultrie, S.C.
Co. A, 4th Art.	16 Apr 1833	29 Nov 1833	To Fort Mitchell, Ala.
Co. G, 1st Art.	1 May 1833	31 May 1833	To Beaufort, N.C.
Co. B, 3d Art.	1 May 1833	29 Nov 1833	To Fort Mitchell, Ala.
Co. E, 3d Art.	1 May 1833	26 May 1836	To Fort Mitchell, Ala.
Co. C, 4th Art.	1 May 1833	29 Nov 1833	To Fort Mitchell, Ala.
Co. A, 1st Art.	6 May 1833	29 Nov 1833	To Fort Mitchell, Ala.
Co. B, 4th Art.	6 May 1833	29 Nov 1833	To Fort Mitchell, Ala.
Co. H, 1st Art.	13 Jun 1833	29 Nov 1833	To Fort Mitchell, Ala.
Co. I, 1st Art.	27 Nov 1833	29 Nov 1833	To Fort Mitchell, Ala.
Co. C, 3d Art.	13 Dec 1833	1 Mar 1835	To Fort King, Fla.
Co. I, 3d Art.	15 Dec 1833	1 Mar 1835	To Fort King, Fla.
Co. C, 1st Art.	18 Apr 1834	27 Feb 1835	To Fort King, Fla.
Co. I, 1st Art.	18 Apr 1834	26 May 1836	To Fort Mitchell, Ala.
Co. F, 2d Art.	18 Apr 1834	27 Feb 1835	To Fort King, Fla.
Co. A, 4th Art.	18 Apr 1834	9 Oct 1835	To Fort Washington, Md.
Co. B, 4th Art.	19 Apr 1834	26 May 1836	To Fort Mitchell, Ala.
Co. C, 4th Art.	19 Apr 1834	14 Nov 1835	To Fort Hamilton, N.Y.
Co. A, 4th Art.	2 Dec 1835	30 Jun 1836	To Garey's Ferry, Fla.
Co. I, 4th Art.	21 May 1836	26 May 1836	To Fort Mitchell, Ala.
Detachments	30 Jun 1836	4 Oct 1836	Field and Staff.
Co. C, 2d Art.	4 Oct 1836	7 Jan 1837	To Charleston, S.C.
Co. A, 2d Drag.	— Dec 1836	7 Jan 1837	To Charleston, S.C.
Co. I, 2d Drag.	— Dec 1836	7 Jan 1837	To Charleston, S.C.
Detachments	7 Jan 1837	15 Jul 1842	Recruits and Invalids
1 Co., D.C. Vols.	21 Oct 1837	21 Oct 1837	To Garey's Ferry, Fla.
Co. K, 3d Art.	— Jul 1838	19 Nov 1838	To Florida
Co. C, 2d Art.	2 Sep 1841	15 Jul 1842	
Co. H, 2d Art.	2 Sep 1841	30 Apr 1842	To Fort Columbus, N.Y.
Co. K, 2d Art.	2 Sep 1841	30 Apr 1842	To Fort Columbus, N.Y.
Co. G, 4th Art.	10 Jul 1842	30 Aug 1845	To Aransas, Tex.
Co. H, 4th Art.	10 Jul 1842	8 Jun 1846	To Point Isabel, Tex.
Co. C, 4th Art.	11 Jul 1842	29 May 1846	To recruiting
Co. D, 4th Art.	11 Jul 1842	1 Sep 1845	To Aransas, Tex.
Co. K, 4th Art.	11 Jul 1842	15 Nov 1842	To Fort McHenry, Md.
Co. E, 4th Art.	12 Jul 1842	1 Sep 1845	To Aransas, Tex.
Co. F, 4th Art.	12 Jul 1842	23 Jun 1846	To Point Isabel, Tex.
Co. I, 4th Art.	12 Jul 1842	30 Aug 1845	To Aransas, Tex.
Co. A, 4th Art.	4 Sep 1845	29 May 1846	To recruiting
Co. K, 4th Art.	29 May 1846	14 Oct 1846	To Point Isabel, Tex.
Co. A, 4th Art.	9 Aug 1846	14 Oct 1846	To Point Isabel, Tex.
Co. C, 4th Art.	9 Aug 1846	2 Nov 1846	To recruiting.
Detachments	2 Nov 1846	13 Jul 1848	Recruits.
5 Cos., 1st Va.	3 Jan 1847	25 Jan 1847	
1 Co., 1st Va.	8 Jan 1847	26 Jan 1847	
Co. C, 4th Art.	30 Mar 1847	28 May 1847	To Vera Cruz, Mex.
Co. B, 13th Inf.	*— Apr 1847	10 Jun 1847	To Point Isabel, Tex.
Co. A, 11th Inf.	*— May 1847	24 Jul 1847	To Mexico.
1 Co., Voltigeurs	*— Jun 1847	29 Jun 1847	To Vera Cruz, Mex.

Organization	From	To	Remarks
Co. M, 4th Art.	*31 Jul 1847	20 Oct. 1847	To Mexico.
1 Co., Va. Vols.	4 Sep 1847	11 Dec 1847	To Mexico.
1 Co., Va. Vols.	4 Oct 1847	25 Nov 1847	Merged with Talbot's Co.
Co. M, 3d Art.	13 Jul 1848	24 Sep 1848	To Newport, R.I.
Co. A, N.C. Vols.	22 Jul 1848	28 Jul 1848	Mustered out.
Co. B, N.C. Vols.	22 Jul 1848	28 Jul 1848	Mustered out.
Co. E, N.C. Vols.	22 Jul 1848	28 Jul 1848	Mustered out.
Co. G, N.C. Vols.	22 Jul 1848	28 Jul 1848	Mustered out.
Co. D, 3d Art.	25 Jul 1848	21 Sep 1848	To Newport, R.I.
Co. K, 1st Va.	28 Jul 1848	28 Jul 1848	Mustered out.
1st Va. (less Co. K)	28 Jul 1848	— Aug 1848	Mustered out.
Co. B, 3d Art.	29 Jul 1848	21 Sep 1848	To Newport, R.I.
Co. M, 4th Art.	29 Jul 1848	21 Oct 1848	To Fort Morgan, Ala.
Co. A, 3d Art.	8 Aug 1848	21 Sep 1848	To Newport, R.I.
Co. G, 3d Art.	8 Aug 1848	18 Sep 1848	To Boston Harbor, Mass.
Co. I, 3d Art.	8 Aug 1848	24 Sep 1848	To California.
Co. A, 4th Art.	13 Aug 1848	6 Nov 1848	To Pensacola, Fla.
Co. C, 4th Art.	13 Aug 1848	22 Oct 1848	To New Orleans, La.
Co. D, 4th Art.	13 Aug 1848	13 Oct 1848	To Tampa, Fla.
Co. E, 4th Art.	13 Aug. 1848	13 Oct 1848	To Tampa, Fla.
Co. H, 4th Art.	13 Aug 1848	6 Nov 1848	To Pensacola, Fla.
Co. F, 4th Art.	14 Aug 1848	22 Oct 1848	To New Orleans, La.
Co. L, 4th Art.	14 Aug 1848	22 Oct 1848	To New Orleans, La.
Co. G, 4th Art.	15 Aug 1848	6 Nov 1848	To Pensacola, Fla.
Co. K, 3d Art.	16 Aug 1848	18 Sep 1848	To Boston Harbor, Mass.
Co. L, 3d Art.	16 Aug 1848	18 Sep 1848	To Boston Harbor, Mass.
Co. H, 3d Art.	17 Aug 1848	18 Sep 1848	To Boston Harbor, Mass.
Co. I, 4th Art.	2 Sep 1848	21 Oct 1848	To Fort Morgan, Ala.
Co. C, 2d Art.	9 Oct 1848	11 Nov 1853	To Fort Meade, Fla.
Co. G, 2d Art.	11 Oct 1848	11 Nov 1853	To Fort Meade, Fla.
Co. A, 2d Inf.	22 Nov 1848	26 Dec 1848	To California.
Co. F, 2d Inf.	22 Nov 1848	26 Dec 1848	To California.
Co. A, 2d Art.	16 Apr 1851	9 Nov 1852	To Fort McHenry, Md.
Detachments	11 Nov 1853	17 Dec 1853	Field and staff.
Co. B, 1st Art.	17 Dec 1853	25 Oct 1856	To Fort Dallas, Tex.
Co. E, 1st Art.	17 Dec 1853	25 Oct 1856	To Fort Dallas, Tex.
Co. M, 1st Art.	30 Jan 1854	12 Dec 1854	To Key Biscayne, Fla.
Co. L, 1st Art.	24 Feb 1854	12 Dec 1854	To Key Biscayne, Fla.
Co. D, 3d Art.	23 Apr 1854	6 May 1854	To California.
Co. G, 3d Art.	23 Apr 1854	6 May 1854	To California.
Co. I, 3d Art.	23 Apr 1854	6 May 1854	To California.
Co. K, 3d Art.	23 Apr 1854	6 May 1854	To California.
Co. A, 9th Inf.	*26 Mar 1855	15 Dec 1855	To California.
Co. F, 9th Inf.	*22 May 1855	15 Dec 1855	To California.
Co. G, 9th Inf.	*22 May 1855	15 Dec 1855	To California.
Co. B, 9th Inf.	*26 Mar 1855	15 Dec 1855	To California.
Co. H, 9th Inf.	*— Jun 1855	15 Dec 1855	To California.
Co. I, 9th Inf.	*— Jun 1855	15 Dec 1855	To California.
Co. D, 9th Inf.	*17 Mar 1855	15 Dec 1855	To California.
Co. K, 9th Inf.	*— Aug 1855	15 Dec 1855	To California.

Organization	From	To	Remarks
Co. E, 9th Inf.	*17 Mar 1855	15 Dec 1855	To California.
Co. C, 9th Inf.	*26 Mar 1855	15 Dec 1855	To California.
Detachments	25 Oct 1856	7 Dec 1856	
Co. G, 4th Art.	7 Dec 1856	1 May 1860	To Fort Randall, N.T.
Co. F, 2d Art.	14 Dec 1856	4 Sep 1857	To Fort Leavenworth, Kan.
Co. M, 2d Art.	28 Jan 1857	4 Sep 1857	To Fort Leavenworth, Kan.
Co. C, 3d Art.	28 Jan 1857	16 Apr 1858	To Fort Leavenworth, Kan.
Co. I, 2d Art.	25 Apr 1857	1 May 1860	To Fort Ridgley, Minn.
Co. B, 2d Art.	23 Nov 1857	14 Sep 1861	To Washington, D.C.
Co. A, 1st Art.	13 Jun 1858	24 Jan 1861	To Fort Pickens, Fla.
Co. D, 1st Art.	13 Jun 1858	2 Apr 1860	To Baton Rouge Barracks, La.
Co. K, 3d Art.	16 Jan 1859	14 Sep 1861	To Washington, D.C.
Co. D, 4th Art.	14 Aug 1859	10 May 1862	To Norfolk, Va.
Co. F, 3d Art.	28 Sep 1859	14 Sep 1861	To Washington, D.C.
Co. L, 2d Art.	10 Apr 1860	14 Sep 1861	To Washington, D.C.
Co. C, 1st Art.	19 Apr 1860	10 Sep 1861	To Cape Hatteras.
Co. L, 4th Art.	26 May 1860	24 Feb 1862	To Newport News, Va.
3rd Mass.	20 Apr 1861	5 Aug 1861	To Camp Hamilton, Va.
4th Mass.	20 Apr 1861	27 May 1861	
Co. G, 6th Mass. Art.	25 May 1861	17 Jun 1862	To Newport News, Va.
10th N.Y.	1 Jul 1861	30 Apr 1862	To Camp Hamilton, Va.
Co. A, 1st N.Y. Mtd. Rifles	29 Aug 1861	19 Jan 1862	To Camp Hamilton, Va.
Co. B, 1st N.Y. Mtd. Rifles	29 Aug 1861	19 Jan 1862	To Camp Hamilton, Va.
Co. H, 99th N.Y.	15 Sep 1861	12 Sep 1862	To Norfolk, Va.
Bat. 2, Wis. Lt. Art.	28 Jan 1862	12 Sep 1862	To Camp Hamilton, Va.
Bat. 4, Wis. Lt. Art.	28 Jan 1862	12 Sep 1862	To Camp Hamilton, Va.
Co. D, 99th N.Y.	12 Mar 1862	12 Sep 1862	To Norfolk, Va.
Co. A, 99th N.Y.	1 Sep 1862	12 Sep 1862	To Norfolk, Va.
3d N.Y.	13 Sep 1862	10 Jun 1863	To Suffolk, Va.
Co. A, 3d Pa. Art.	10 Jun 1863	3 Feb 1864	To Graham's Naval Brigade
Co. D, 3d Pa. Art.	10 Jun 1863	22 Aug 1864	To Graham's Naval Brigade
Co. C, 3d Pa. Art.	10 Jan 1863	31 Oct 1865	Mustered out.
Co. E, 3d Pa. Art.	10 Jun 1863	22 Aug 1864	To Graham's Naval Brigade
Co. F, 3d Pa. Art.	10 Jun 1863	29 Aug 1863	To Portsmouth, Va.
Co. G, 3d Pa. Art.	10 Jun 1863	29 Aug 1863	To Portsmouth, Va.
Co. I, 3d Pa. Art.	10 Jun 1863	31 Oct 1865	Mustered out.
Co. K, 3d Pa. Art.	10 Jun 1863	31 Oct 1865	Mustered out.
Co. B, 3d Pa. Art.	25 Aug 1863	7 Oct 1863	
Co. M, 3d Pa. Art.	1 Oct 1863	31 Oct 1865	Mustered out.
Co. F, 3d Pa. Art.	4 Oct 1863	17 Nov 1863	
Co. G, 3d Pa. Art.	4 Oct 1863	31 Oct 1865	Mustered out.
Co. F, 3d Pa. Art.	4 Feb 1864	9 Mar 1864	To Camp Hamilton, Va.
Bat. A, 5th Art.	1 Nov 1865	20 Mar 1868	To Richmond, Va.
Bat. B, 5th Art.	1 Nov 1865	10 Jun 1867	To 2nd Mil. District.
Bat. C, 5th Art.	1 Nov 1865	18 Nov 1876	To North Carolina.
Bat. H, 5th Art.	1 Nov 1865	10 Jun 1867	To 2nd Mil. District.
Co. G, 8th Me.	29 Nov 1865	6 Jan 1866	Mustered out.
Co. A, 12th Inf.	7 Jan. 1866	14 Mar 1866	
Co. E, 12th Inf.	7 Jan 1866	3 Feb 1866	To Camp Hamilton, Va.
Co. G, 12th Inf.	7 Jan 1866	24 Aug 1866	To Washington, D.C.

Organization	From	To	Remarks
Co. C, 12th Inf.	3 Feb 1866	13 Aug 1866	To Yorktown, Va.
Co. B, 12th Inf.	14 Mar 1866	31 Mar 1866	
Co. H, 12th Inf.	31 Mar 1866	24 Aug 1866	To Washington, D.C.
Co. D, 12th Inf.	13 Aug 1866	24 Aug 1866	To Washington, D.C.
Co. F, 21st Inf.	5 Oct 1866	1 Jun 1867	To Camp Hamilton, Va.
Co. G, 29th Inf.	5 Nov 1866	5 May 1867	To Camp Hamilton, Va.
Co. B, 29th Inf.	3 Jun 1867	9 Jun 1867	
Co. A, 21st Inf.	13 Jun 1867	1 Nov 1867	To Yorktown, Va.
Co. E, 21st Inf.	19 Oct 1867	29 Nov 1867	To Petersburg, Va.
Co. F, 21st Inf.	13 Nov 1867	4 Dec 1867	To Camp Hamilton, Va.
Bat. F, 4th Art.	26 Nov 1867	15 Jan 1871	To Fort Foote, Md.
Bat. A, 3d Art.	3 Dec 1867	18 Nov 1876	To North Carolina.
Bat. G, 1st Art.	18 Dec 1867	18 Nov 1876	To North Carolina.
Bat. K, 2d Art.	7 Jan 1868	7 Dec 1887	To Jackson Barracks, La.
Bat. A, 4th Art.	30 Sep 1870	24 Oct 1870	To Graham, N.C.
Bat. I, 4th Art.	9 Jan 1871	18 Nov 1876	To North Carolina.
Bat. G, 1st Art.	5 Feb 1877	18 May 1898	
Bat. A, 3d Art.	5 Feb 1877	1 Jun 1885	To Washington Barracks, D.C.
Bat. I, 4th Art.	5 Feb 1877	3 Apr 1898	
Bat. C, 5th Art.	5 Feb 1877	4 Jun 1885	To Fort Columbus, N.Y.
Bat. M, 3d Art.	1 Jun 1885	15 Oct 1896	To Fort Canby, Wash.
Bat. G, 5th Art.	4 Jun 1885	21 Jun 1898	To Tampa, Fla.
Bat. I, 2d Art.	5 Dec 1887	17 Mar 1898	To Fort Caswell, N.C.
Bat. H, 4th Art.	6 Apr 1888	19 May 1898	To Tampa, Fla.
Bat. F, 1st Art.	2 Jun 1888	17 Mar 1898	To Tybee Island, Ga.
Bat. B, 3d Art.	2 May 1889	8 Jun 1899	To San Francisco, Cal.
Bat. E, 4th Art.	5 Jun 1893	26 Jun 1899	To North Point, Md.
Bat. K, 4th Art.	5 Jun 1893	18 Mar 1898	To Sheridan's Point, Va.
Bat. I, 1st Art.	17 Oct 1896	17 Mar 1898	To Fort Morgan, Ala.
Bat. F, 4th Art.	20 Mar 1898	19 Apr 1898	To Chickamuga Park, Ga.
Bat. I, 6th Art.	*29 Mar 1898	4 Apr 1899	To Honolulu, H.I.
Bat. K, 6th Art.	*29 Mar 1898	4 Apr 1899	To Honolulu, H.I.
Bat. F, 6th Art.	31 Mar 1898	12 Apr 1899	To Philippine Islands.
Bat. H, 6th Art.	31 Mar 1898	12 Apr 1899	To Philippine Islands.
Bat. E, 6th Art.	20 May 1898	21 Jun 1898	To Tampa, Fla.
1st Bn., 1st Md.	26 May 1898	7 Sep 1898	To Camp Meade, Pa.
2d Bn., 1st Md.	26 May 1898	7 Sep 1898	To Camp Meade, Pa.
3d Bn., 1st Md.	6 Jul 1898	7 Sep 1898	To Camp Meade, Pa.
Bat. H, 4th Art.	25 Sep 1898	27 Jun 1899	To Fort Mott, N.J.
Bat. N, 4th Art.	*13 Apr 1899	5 Aug 1899	To Plum Island, N.Y.
Bat. O, 4th Art.	*13 Apr 1899	5 Aug 1899	To Plum Island, N.Y.
Bat. G, 4th Art.	6 May 1899	5 Aug 1899	To Plum Island, N.Y.
Detachments	5 Aug 1899	13 Sep 1899	
Bat. G, 4th Art.	13 Sep 1899	2 Feb 1901	Became 41st Co., C.A.C.
Bat. N, 4th Art.	13 Sep 1899	24 Jun 1900	To Fort Hunt, Va.
Bat. O, 4th Art.	13 Sep 1899	24 Jun 1900	To Fort Hancock, N.J.
Bat. B, 1st Art.	5 Dec 1899	18 Jan 1900	To Key West Barracks, Fla.
Bat. N, 1st Art.	5 Dec 1899	18 Jan 1900	To Key West Barracks, Fla.
Bat. B, 2d Art.	1 Feb 1900	2 Feb 1901	Became 13th Co., C.A.C.
Bat. E, 2d Art.	1 Feb 1900	31 May 1900	To Fort Fremont, S.C.

Organization	From	To	Remarks
Bat. N, 3d Art.	1 Feb 1900	2 Feb 1901	Became 35th Co., C.A.C.
Bat. M, 6th Art.	25 Jun 1900	2 Feb 1901	Became 69th Co., C.A.C.
Bat. G, 1st Art.	26 Jun 1900	2 Feb 1901	Became 6th Co., C.A.C.
Bat. N, 5th Art.	26 Jun 1900	2 Feb 1901	Became 58th Co., C.A.C.
Bat. B, 7th Art.	27 Jun 1900	2 Feb 1901	Became 73rd Co., C.A.C.
6th Co., C.A.C.	2 Feb 1901	24 Jul 1916	Became 6th Co., Fort Monroe.
13th Co., C.A.C.	2 Feb 1901	27 Feb 1910	To Philippine Islands.
35th Co., C.A.C.	2 Feb 1901	29 Mar 1908	To Philippine Islands.
41st Co., C.A.C.	2 Feb 1901	19 Apr 1916	To Fort Oglethorpe, Ga.
58th Co., C.A.C.	2 Feb 1901	24 Jul 1916	Became 3rd Co., Ft Monroe.
69th Co., C.A.C.	2 Feb 1901	19 Apr 1916	To Fort Oglethorpe, Ga.
73rd Co., C.A.C.	2 Feb 1901	11 Apr 1916	To Canal Zone.
118th Co., C.A.C.	*14 Oct 1901	24 Jul 1916	Became 5th Co., Ft Monroe.
45th Co., C.A.C.	22 May 1907	7 Dec 1907	To Fort Caswell, N.C.
79th Co., C.A.C.	22 May 1907	2 Dec 1907	To Fort DuPont, Del.
165th Co., C.A.C.	*20 Nov 1907	30 Apr 1908	To Fort Totten, N.Y.
166th Co., C.A.C	*20 Nov 1907	19 Apr 1916	To Fort Oglethorpe, Ga.
167th Co., C.A.C.	*20 Nov 1907	30 Jul 1908	To Fort Totten, N.Y.
168th Co., C.A.C.	*20 Nov 1907	19 Apr 1916	To Fort Oglethorpe, Ga.
169th Co., C.A.C.	*20 Nov 1907	24 Jul 1916	Became 9th Co., Ft Monroe.
C.A. School Det.	*1 Jul 1909	28 May 1946	To Fort Winfield Scott, Cal.
35th Co., C.A.C.	18 May 1910	24 Jul 1916	Became 1st Co., Ft Monroe.
1st Co., Ft. Monroe	24 Jul 1916	31 Aug 1917	Became 1st Co., Ches. Bay.
3d Co., Ft. Monroe	24 Jul 1916	31 Aug 1917	Became 3rd Co., Ches. Bay.
5th Co., Ft. Monroe	24 Jul 1916	26 Feb 1917	To Fort Story, Va.
6th Co., Ft. Monroe	24 Jul 1916	6 Jul 1917	To Fort Wool, Va.
9th Co., Ft. Monroe	24 Jul 1916	31 Aug 1917	Became 9th Co., Ches. Bay.
2d Co., Ft. Monroe[1]	6 Sep 1916	26 Feb 1917	To Fort Story, Va.
4th Co., Ft. Monroe[2]	6 Sep 1916	8 May 1917	To Washington, D.C.
7th Co., Ft. Monroe[3]	14 Sep 1916	8 May 1917	To Washington, D.C.
8th Co., Ft. Monroe[4]	14 Sep 1916	6 Apr 1917	To Fort Wool, Va.
2d Co., Ft. Washington	27 Feb 1917	18 Apr 1917	To Fort Wool, Va.
4th Co., Ft. Howard	27 Feb 1917	30 Mar 1917	To Fisherman's Island, Va.
1st Co., Va. CANG	9 Apr 1917	26 Aug 1917	To 117th Tn. & M.P.
2d Co., Va. CANG	9 Apr 1917	26 Aug 1917	To 117th Tn. & M.P.
2d Co., Ft. Washington	23 Apr 1917	24 Apr 1917	To Fort Wool, Va.
8th Co., Fort Monroe	24 Apr 1917	20 Jul 1917	To Fisherman's Island, Va.
10th Co., Fort Monroe	*18 May 1917	20 Jul 1917	To 8th Prov. C.A.
11th Co., Fort Monroe	*18 May 1917	20 Jul 1917	To 8th Prov. C.A.
12th Co., Ft. Monroe	*1 Jun 1917	20 Jul 1917	To 8th Prov. C.A.
13th Co., Ft. Monroe	*1 Jun 1917	31 Aug 1917	Became 5th Co., Ches. Bay.
Hq. Co., 8th Prov. C.A.[5]	— Jul 1917	20 Jul 1917	To Fort Adams, R.I.
8th Co., Va. CANG	16 Aug 1917	15 Sep 1917	To Fort Wool, Va.
5th Co., Va. CANG	17 Aug 1917	23 Dec 1917	Became Bat. B, 60th Art.
4th Co., Va. CANG	22 Aug 1917	14 Sep 1917	To Fisherman's Island, Va.
6th Co., Va. CANG	27 Aug 1917	1 Feb 1918	Became 6th Co., Ches. Bay.
7th Co., Va. CANG	27 Aug 1917	1 Feb 1918	Became 11th Co., Ches. Bay.
3d Co., Va. CANG	29 Aug 1917	15 Sep 1917	To Fort Story, Va.

Organization	From	To	Remarks
9th Co., Va. CANG	30 Aug 1917	23 Dec 1917	Became Bat. F, 60th Art.
1st Co., Ches. Bay	31 Aug 1917	1 Jun 1922	Became 35th Co., C.A.C.
3d Co., Ches. Bay	31 Aug 1917	1 Jun 1922	Became 58th Co., C.A.C.
9th Co., Ches. Bay	31 Aug 1917	31 Aug 1919	Merged with 3rd Co., C.B.
5th Co., Ches. Bay	31 Aug 1917	1 Jul 1921	Became Gun Bat., 1st AA Bn.
S.C. Balloon Det.	— Sep 1917	1 Feb 1918	Became 24th Balloon Co.
8th Co., Ches. Bay[6]	14 Sep 1917	23 Dec 1917	Became Hq. Co., 60th Art.
6th Co., Ches. Bay[7]	15 Sep 1917	23 Dec 1917	Became Bat. E, 60th Art.
Hq. Co., 60th Art.	23 Dec 1917	3 Apr 1918	To Camp Stuart, Va.
Bat. B, 60th Art.	23 Dec 1917	3 Apr 1918	To Camp Stuart, Va.
Bat. E, 60th Art.	23 Dec 1917	3 Apr 1918	To Camp Stuart, Va.
Bat. F, 60th Art.	23 Dec 1917	3 Apr 1918	To Camp Stuart, Va.
6th Co., Ches. Bay[8]	1 Feb 1918	1 Jul 1921	Became S.L. Bat., 1st AA Bn.
11th Co., Ches. Bay	1 Feb 1918	31 Aug 1919	Merged with 4th Co., C.B.
13th Co., Ches. Bay	*1 Feb 1918	31 Aug 1919	Merged with 4th Co., C.B.
24th Balloon Co.	1 Feb 1918	23 Mar 1918	To Morrison, Va.
Hq. Co., 2nd T.M. Bn.	*4 Feb 1918	3 May 1918	To Mulberry Island, Va.
Bat. A, 2nd T.M. Bn.	*4 Feb 1918	3 May 1918	To Mulberry Island, Va.
29th Balloon Co.	*23 Mar 1918	7 Aug 1919	To Fort Story, Va.
14th Co., Ches. Bay	*23 Mar 1918	6 Dec 1918	Mustered out.
15th Co., Ches. Bay	*4 Apr 1918	6 Dec 1918	Mustered out.
16th Co., Ches. Bay	*8 Apr 1918	6 Dec 1918	Mustered out.
Bat. C, 61st Art.	3 May 1918	19 May 1918	To Camp Eustis, Va.
Bat. D, 61st Art.	3 May 1918	26 May 1918	To Camp Eustis, Va.
12th Co., Va. CANG	10 May 1918	20 Jun 1918	To Chester, Pa.
13th Co., Va. CANG	10 May 1918	25 Jun 1918	To Sparrows Point, Md.
14th Co., Va. CANG	10 May 1918	19 Jun 1918	To Curtis Bay, Md.
10th Co., Va. CANG	12 May 1918	19 Jun 1918	To Curtis Bay, Md.
11th Co., Va. CANG	12 May 1918	20 Jun 1918	To Chester, Pa.
Bat. F, 74th Art.	*24 Jun 1918	10 Sep 1918	
17th Co., Ches. Bay	*8 Jul 1918	6 Dec 1918	Mustered out.
1st A.A. Bat.	*— Jul 1918	— Dec 1918	Mustered out.
2d A.A. Bat.	*— Jul 1918	— Dec 1918	Mustered out.
Hq. Co., 3d Bn., 74th Art.	*— Aug 1918	10 Sep 1918	
41st Art.	*1 Oct 1918	22 Dec 1918	Mustered out.
Hq. Co., C.A.T.C.	*12 Oct 1918		Disbanded.
Det. 17th Art.	*8 Nov 1918	1 Jan 1919	Mustered out.
Hq. 44th Art. Brig.	8 Nov 1918	22 Dec 1918	Mustered out.
36th Art.	3 Dec 1918	19 Dec 1918	Mustered out.
4th Co., Ches. Bay[9]	— Nov 1918	1 Jun 1922	Became 69th Co., C.A.C.
7th Co., Ches. Bay[10]	— Nov 1918	14 Sep 1921	To inactive.
Hq. 32d Art. Brig.	— Jan 1919	14 Jan 1919	Mustered out.
3d A.A. Sector	11 Jan 1919	21 Jan 1919	Mustered out.
7th T.M. Bn.	11 Jan 1919	1 Mar 1919	Mustered out.
6th T.M. Bn.	14 Jan 1919	26 Jan 1919	Mustered out.
7th A.A. Sector	20 Jan 1919	30 Jan 1919	Mustered out.
8th Co., Ches. Bay[11]	— Mar 1919	1 Jul 1921	Became M.G. Bat., 1st AA Bn.
Bat. C, 52d Art.	20 Apr 1919	22 Aug 1919	To Camp Eustis, Va.

Organization	From	To	Remarks
Bat. D, 52d Art.	20 Apr 1919	23 Sep 1919	To Camp Eustis, Va.
M.T. Co. No. 79	*8 Jan 1920	28 Nov 1928	To Camp Eustis, Va.
1st Co., Baltimore[12]	21 Nov 1920	21 Nov 1920	Became 9th Co., Ches. Bay.
2d Co., Baltimore[13]	21 Nov 1920	21 Nov 1920	Became 10th Co., Ches. Bay.
9th Co., Ches. Bay	21 Nov 1920	1 Jul 1921	Became Hq. Det., 1st AA Bn.
10th Co., Ches. Bay	21 Nov 1920	14 Sep 1921	To inactive.
Hq. Det. & C. Tn.,			
1st AA Bn.	1 Jul 1921	1 Jun 1922	Became 140th Co., C.A.C.
S.L. Bat., 1st AA Bn.	1 Jul 1921	1 Jun 1922	Became 6th Co., C.A.C.
Gun Bat., 1st AA Bn.	1 Jul 1921	1 Jun 1922	Became 257th Co., C.A.C.
M.G. Bat.,			
1st AA Bn.	1 Jul 1921	1 Jun 1922	Became 168th Co., C.A.C.
2d Co., Ches. Bay	31 Aug 1921	1 Jun 1922	Became 41st Co., C.A.C.
6th Co., C.A.C.	1 Jun 1922	1 Jun 1922	Became Bat. A, 61st Art. Bn.
35th Co., C.A.C.	1 Jun 1922	30 Jun 1924	To C.D. of the Columbia.
41st Co., C.A.C.	1 Jun 1922	30 Jun 1924	To Canal Zone.
58th Co., C.A.C.	1 Jun 1922	1 Jul 1924	Became Bat. A, 12th C.A.
69th Co., C.A.C.	1 Jun 1922	30 Jun 1924	To San Francisco, Cal.
140th Co., C.A.C.	1 Jun 1922	1 Jun 1922	Became Hq. Bat., 61st Art. Bn.
168th Co., C.A.C.	1 Jun 1922	1 Jun 1922	Became Bat. C, 61st Art. Bn.
257th Co., C.A.C.	1 Jun 1922	1 Jun 1922	Became Bat. B, 61st Art. Bn.
Hq. Bat.,			
61st Art. Bn.	1 Jun 1922	30 Jun 1924	Became Hq. Bat., 61st C.A.
Bat. A, 61st Art. Bn.	1 Jun 1922	30 Jun 1924	Became Bat. A, 61st C.A.
Bat. B, 61st Art. Bn.	1 Jun 1922	30 Jun 1924	Became Bat. B, 61st C.A.
Bat. C, 61st Art. Bn.	1 Jun 1922	30 Jun 1924	Became Bat. E, 61st C.A.
Hq. Bat., 12th C.A.	1 Jul 1924	29 Apr 1932	Inactivated.
Band, 12th C.A.	1 Jul 1924	29 Apr 1932	Inactivated.
Battery A, 12th C.A.	1 Jul 1924	29 Apr 1932	Inactivated.
Battery B, 12th C.A.	1 Jul 1924	14 Mar 1930	Inactivated.
Battery C, 12th C.A.	1 Jul 1924	29 Apr 1932	Inactivated.
Hq. Bat., 61st C.A.	1 Jul 1924	14 May 1931	To Ft. Sheridan, Ill.
Battery A, 61st C.A.	1 Jul 1924	14 May 1931	To Ft. Sheridan, Ill.
Battery B, 61st C.A.	1 Jul 1924	14 May 1931	To Ft. Sheridan, Ill.
Battery E, 61st C.A.	1 Jul 1924	14 May 1931	To Ft. Sheridan, Ill.
Battery A, 51st C.A.	8 May 1931	16 Oct 1939	To Camp Buchanan, Puerto Rico.
Battery B, 51st C.A.	8 May 1931	16 Oct 1939	To Camp Buchanan, Puerto Rico.
Hq. Bat., 1st Bn.,			To Camp Buchanan,
51st C.A.	14 May 1931	16 Oct 1939	Puerto Rico.
Hq. Bat., 3d Bn.,			
52d C.A.	15 May 1931	31 Oct 1938	Inactivated.
Battery D, 52d C.A.	15 May 1931	31 Oct 1938	Inactivated.
Battery F, 52d C.A.	15 May 1931	1 Feb 1940	Inactivated.
Hq. Bat., 2d C.A.	30 Apr 1932	1 Oct 1944	Became Hq. Bat., 2d C.A. Bn.

Organization	From	To	Remarks
Band, 2d C.A.	30 Apr 1932	12 May 1944	Became 69th Army Ground Forces Band.
Battery C, 2d C.A.	30 Apr 1932	25 Jan 1944	To Fort John Custis, Va.
Battery H, 2d C.A.	30 Apr 1932	1 Sep 1935	Inactivated.
Battery A, 2d C.A.	1 Sep 1935	1 Oct 1944	Became Battery A, 2d C.A. Bn.
Battery B, 2d C.A.	1 Nov 1938	1 Oct 1944	Became Battery B, 2d C.A. Bn.
Battery D, 2d C.A.	1 Nov 1938	1 Oct 1944	Became Battery A, 175th C.A. Bn.
70th Coast Art. (AA)	4 Nov 1939	26 Jun 1940	To Fort Screven, Ga.
Battery F, 2d C.A.	1 Feb 1940	1 Oct 1944	To Fort Story, Va.
2d Bn., 69th C.A.	28 Jun 1940	1 Jul 1940	To Fort Crockett, Tex.
Hq. Bat., 1st Bn., 57th C.A.	1 Jun 1940	20 Feb 1941	To Camp Pendleton, Va.
Battery A, 57th C.A.	1 Jun 1940	20 Feb 1941	To Camp Pendleton, Va.
Battery B, 57th C.A.	27 Jun 1940	20 Feb 1941	To Camp Pendleton, Va.
Hq. Bat. 1st Bn., 2d C.A.	1 Aug 1940	2 Mar 1944	To Camp Rucker, Ala.
96th Ordnance Co.	?	17 Feb 1944	To Fort Bragg, N.C.
6th C.A. Mine Planter Battery	?	Jun 1946	USAMP *Schofield.*
Hq. Bat., 2d Bn., 2d C.A.	1 Aug 1940	2 Mar 1944	To Camp Rucker, Ala.
Hq. Bat., 2d Bn., 246th C.A.	16 Sep 1940	2 Feb 1942	To Ft. Story, Va.
Battery D, 246th C.A.	16 Sep 1940	19 Dec 1941	To Ft. John Custis, Va.
Battery F, 246th C.A.	16 Sep 1940	30 Apr 1942	To Ft. John Custis, Va.
Battery H, 246th C.A.	16 Sep 1940	8 Feb 1943	To Ft. Story, Va.
1st Bn., 74th C.A.	14 Nov 1940	18 Jul 1941	To Camp Pendleton, Va.
Hq. Bat., 57th C.A.	3 Jan 1941	20 Feb 1941	To Camp Pendleton, Va.
2d Bn., 57th C.A.	3 Jan 1941	20 Feb 1941	To Camp Pendleton, Va.
Hq. Bat., 74th C.A.	3 Jan 1941	18 Jul 1941	To Camp Pendleton, Va.
2d Bn., 74th C.A.	3 Jan 1941	18 Jul 1941	To Camp Pendleton, Va.
Battery G, 2d C.A.	3 Jan 1941	6 Sep 1941	Inactivated.
Battery K, 2d C.A.	6 Sep 1941	30 Apr 1942	Inactivated.
1319th Service Cmd. Unit	11 Feb 1941	Jun 1946	Became 2124th A.S.U.
Battery G, 2d C.A.	13 Jan 1942	1 Oct 1944	Became Battery D, 2d C.A. Bn.
Hq. and Hq. Company, C.B.S.	1 Mar 1942	17 Mar 1944	To Camp Hood, Tex.
Hq. Company, 111th Infantry	28 Apr. 1942	28 Oct 1943	To Camp Stoneman, Calif.
Hq. Bat., 3d Bn., 2d C.A.	30 Apr 1942	2 Mar 1944	To Camp Rucker, Ala.
Battery H, 2d C.A.	30 Apr 1942	18 Jul 1942	To Ft. Story, Va.
Battery I, 2d C.A.	30 Apr 1942	14 May 1942	To Little Creek Mine Base, Va.
Battery N, 2d C.A.	30 Apr 1942	2 Mar 1944	To Camp Rucker, Ala.
18th C.A. Mine Planter Battery	1 Dec 1942	5 Dec 1942	USAMP *Ringgold;* to Point Pleasant, W.Va.

Organization	From	To	Remarks
21st C.A. Mine			USAMP *Spurgin;* to
Planter Battery	1 Jan 1943	25 Jan 1943	Point Pleasant, W.Va.
22d C.A. Mine			
Planter Battery	20 May 1943	21 Oct 1943	USAMP *Bundy*
Hq. and Hq. Bat.,			
H.D.C.B.	29 Feb 1944	25 May 1946	To Ft. Story, Va.
69th Army Ground			
Forces Band	12 May 1944	28 May 1946	To Ft. Winfield Scott, Calif.
Hq.Bat., 2d C.A.Bn.	1 Oct 1944	1 Apr 1945	Inactivated.
Bat. A, 2d C.A. Bn.	1 Oct 1944	1 Apr 1945	Became Battery A, H.D.C.B.
Bat. D, 2d C.A. Bn.	1 Oct 1944	1 Apr 1945	Inactivated.
Battery A,			
175th C.A. Bn.	1 Oct 1944	1 Apr 1945	Became Battery F, H.D.C.B.
Battery A, H.D.C.B.	1 Apr 1945	?	To Little Creek Mine Base, Va.
Battery F, H.D.C.B.	1 Apr 1945	20 Jul 1946	Inactivated.
9381st T.S.U.			
Ord. Det.	?	4 May 1950	Inactivated.
14th Transportation			
Co. (Car)	12 Aug 1946	15 June 1970	Inactivated.
89th Military			
Police Co.	Sep 1946	16 Feb 1949	Inactivated.
WAC Detachment,			
AGF[14]	1 Oct 1946	15 Dec 1959	Became WAC Co., CONARC
2124th Army Service			Became U.S. Army
Unit	25 Oct 1946	31 Dec 1956	Garrison, Ft. Monroe
50th Army Band	14 Nov 1946	24 Jun 1972	Became Continental Army Band
Co. C, 503d M.P. Bn.	16 Feb 1949	15 Oct 1950	To Ft. Bragg, N.C.
559th Military			
Police Co.	14 Oct 1950	29 Mar 1973	Inactivated.
56th Antiaircraft			
Art. Bn.	6 Jan 1953	1 Sep 1958	Inactivated.
584th Ordnance Det			
(IFCR)	1 Jul 1953	2 May 1955	Inactivated.
180th Military			
Intel. Det.	29 Dec 1953	1 Jul 1962	To Fort Hood, Tex.
125th Military			
Police Det.	14 Feb 1955	1 Aug 1957	To Ft. Bragg, N.C.
7100th Area Service			
Unit	15 Aug 1955	1 Jan 1957	Disbanded.
U.S. Army Garrison			Became Hq. TRADOC &
Ft. Monroe	1 Jan 1957	30 Jun 1975	U.S. Army Garrison
553d Ordnance Det.			
(EOD)	22 Jan 1957	Aug 1965	To South Vietnam.
4th Bn., 51st Artillery	1 Sep 1958	26 Jul 1960	Inactivated.
WAC Co.,			
USCONARC[15]	15 Dec 1959	29 Aug 1974	Inactivated.
8th A.G. Data Proc.			
Unit	22 Jun 1962	22 Jun 1964	Inactivated.

Organization	From	To	Remarks
100th Aviation Co. (Prov)	27 Oct 1962	2 Dec 1962	Inactivated.
501st Transportation Det.	21 Mar 1966	15 May 1970	Inactivated.
38th Public Info. Det.	10 Feb 1967	20 Sep 1968	Inactivated.
6th Military History Det.	30 Oct 1967	15 Jun 1973	Inactivated.
27th Public Info. Det.	1 Nov 1968	28 Aug 1975	Inactivated.
Continental Army Band[16]	24 Jun 1972		
498th Medical Det (Fld Amb)	26 Jun 1972	19 Aug 1973	Inactivated.
228th Medical Dispensary	26 Jun 1972	19 Aug 1973	Inactivated.
560th Military Police Co.[16]	29 Mar 1973		
Hq Co TRADOC & US Army Garrison[16]	1 Jul 1975		
72d Tactical Control Flight[16]	14 Jan 1976		USAF
74th Tactical Control Flight	Oct 1976	Dec 1976	USAF: to Pope Air Force Base, N.C.

---

*Organized at Fort Monroe.

[1]Formerly 41st Co., C.A.C.
[2]Formerly 69th Co., C.A.C.
[3]Formerly 166th Co., C.A.C.
[4]Formerly 168th Co., C.A.C.
[5]Formerly 118th Co., C.A.C.
[6]Formerly 8th Co., Fort Monroe.
[7]Formerly 6th Co., Fort Monroe.
[8]Formerly 6th Co., Va. CANG.
[9]Formerly 4th Co., Fort Monroe.
[10]Formerly 7th Co., Fort Monroe.
[11]Formerly 4th Co., Va. CANG.
[12]Formerly 140th Co., C.A.C.
[13]Formerly 103d Co., C.A.C.
[14]Became WAC Detachment, OCAFF, 15 Mar 1948; WAC Detachment, Hq Continental Army Command, 1 Feb 1955; and WAC Detachment, United States Continental Army Command, 1 Jan 1957.
[15]Became WAC Company, USATRADOC, 1 Jul 1973.
[16]Present garrison.

Index